Studies in Modern Childhood

Studies in Modern Childhood

Society, Agency, Culture

Edited by

Jens Qvortrup

First published 2005 by
PALGRAVE MACMILLAN
Houndmills, Basingstoke, Hampshire RG21 6XS and
175 Fifth Avenue, New York, N.Y. 10010
Companies and representatives throughout the world

PALGRAVE MACMILLAN is the global academic imprint of the Palgrave
Macmillan division of St. Martin's Press, LLC and of Palgrave Macmillan Ltd.
Macmillan® is a registered trademark in the United States, United Kingdom and
other countries. Palgrave is a registered trademark in the European Union and
other countries.

ISBN-13: 978–1–4039–3933–3 hardback
ISBN-10: 1–4039–3933–0 hardback

This book is printed on paper suitable for recycling and made from fully
managed and sustained forest sources.

A catalogue record for this book is available from the British Library.

Library of Congress Cataloging-in-Publication Data

Studies in modern childhood : society, agency, culture / edited by Jens Qvortrup.
    p. cm.
  Includes bibliographical references and index.
  ISBN 1–4039–3933–0 (cloth)
  1. Children.   2. Children – Social conditions.   3. Child development.
4. Postmodernism.   I. Qvortrup, Jens.

  HQ767.9.S83   2005
  305.23 – dc22

                                                             2005043359

10   9   8   7. 6   5   4   3   2   1
14 13 12 11 10 09 08 07 06 05

Printed and bound in Great Britain by
Antony Rowe Ltd, Chippenham and Eastbourne

Contents

Figures and Tables

Figures

Tables

Acknowledgements

The chapters in this volume were first given as lectures at a series of doctoral seminars at the Norwegian Centre for Child Research (NOSEB). These well-attended seminars, with participants from all the Nordic countries, convened in 2002 and 2003 at the Norwegian University of Science and Technology, Trondheim, and at the University of Oslo. All the papers have subsequently been revised or rewritten and now appear as original contributions to social studies of childhood. The authors are all well-known scholars within this field. They were, of course, given a free hand in formulating and presenting their contributions, although it was expected that they remained within their research specialization. The doctoral students who attended the seminar series have benefited very much from this opportunity to hear scholars from many countries and to discuss their ideas.

I am pleased now to have the opportunity to present the lectures as book chapters for a much wider audience. It goes without saying that the chapters cannot cover the full scope of what has come to be known as the social studies of childhood; it can be said, however, that the authors all convey to the readers the most recent state of their research within their particular fields of expertise.

I am, first, delighted that the lecturers/authors have given their time and insight. I am grateful to all the doctoral students who attended the seminars and shared their theses with the invited lecturers and to the latter also for taking part in this exchange of ideas. I am indebted to the invited discussants of the lectures for their valuable comments and for initiating the discussions: Petter Bae Brandtzæg, Eva Gulløv, Leo B. Hendry, Anne Trine Kjørholt, Charlotte Koren, Birgit Hertzberg Kaare, Håkon Leiulfsrud, Per Miljeteig, Kari Moxnes, Randi Dyblie Nilsen, Axel West Pedersen, Barbara Rogers, Einar Øverbye.

I want to thank NOSEB (of which I was the director when the series of seminars took off) for organizing the seminars, my successor Dr Anne Trine Kjørholt for supporting the undertaking and not least Karin Ekberg, NOSEB's senior executive officer, for her tireless cooperation and competent backing of the whole project. Finally, thanks are due to the Research Council of Norway for not only supporting this project through its Programme on Welfare Research, but for taking a generous interest in the new strands within childhood research.

JENS QVORTRUP
Trondheim, November 2004

Notes on Contributors

Hilde Bojer has been Associate Professor of Economics at the University of Oslo, Norway, since 1972. Her research interest is distributional justice with particular stress on the position of children and women. Her book, *Distributional Justice: Theory and Measurement*, was published in 2003. At present she is working on a project concerning the theoretical justification of the welfare state.

Sara Bragg works as a Lecturer in Media Studies at the University of Sussex, UK, and as a consultant at the Centre for the Study of Children, Youth and Media at the Institute of Education, University of London, UK. She is co-author (with David Buckingham) of *Young People, Sex and the Media: the Facts of Life?* (2004) and (with Michael Fielding) of 'Students as Researchers: Making a Difference?' (2003).

David Buckingham is Professor of Education at the Institute of Education, London University, UK, where he directs the Centre for the Study of Children, Youth and Media (www.ccsonline.org.uk/mediacentre). He is the author, co-author or editor of eighteen books, including *Children Talking Television* (1993), *Moving Images* (1996), *The Making of Citizens* (2000), *After the Death of Childhood* (2000) and *Media Education* (2003).

William A. Corsaro is the Robert H. Shaffer Class of 1967 Endowed Professor of Sociology at Indiana University, Bloomington, USA, where he teaches courses on the sociology of childhood and ethnographic research methods. Corsaro is the author of several books, among them *Friendship and Peer Culture in the Early Years* (1985), *We're Friends, Right: Inside Kids' Culture* (2004), *The Sociology of Childhood* (2nd edn, 2004) and the forthcoming monograph (with Luisa Molinari), *I Compagni: Italian Children's Transition from Preschool to Elementary School*.

Kirsten Drotner is Professor at the Department of Literature, Culture and Media Studies, University of Southern Denmark. Her research areas include media history, audience studies, methodology and youthful media culture, and she has written widely in Danish. In English, she has co-authored *English Children and their Magazines, 1751–1945* (1988) and *Researching Audiences* (2003). She has also contributed to a number of anthologies and scholarly journals.

Judith Ennew, Senior Research Associate in the Centre for Family Research, University of Cambridge, UK, has been an activist and researcher in children's rights since 1979. She has worked in Latin America, Africa, South and South-East Asia and Eastern Europe on children's rights issues including, recently, the UN Secretary General's Global Study on Violence against Children, and is currently based in Bangkok. She is author of many books, reports and articles.

Ivar Frønes is Professor of Sociology, University of Oslo, Norway. His scientific works cover a variety of fields, with emphasis on culture, childhood and youth. He was the founding editor of the journal *Childhood*. His publications cover a variety of themes related to childhood, including *Among Peers* (1995) and a number of books in Norwegian.

Heinz Hengst is Professor of Social and Cultural Sciences at the Hochschule Bremen and a member of the Institut für Popularkultur und Kinderkultur at the University of Bremen, Germany. His main research interests are childhood, children's culture and generational relations. His most recent co-edited publications are *Kinder, Körper, Identitäten* [Children, bodies and identities] (2003) and *Per una sociologia dell'infanzia* [Towards a sociology of childhood] (2004).

Allison James is Professor of Sociology at the University of Sheffield, UK. Since the late 1970s she has helped pioneer contemporary research with children. Her work focuses on children as social actors and most recently on aspects of law and social policy as it relates to children's experiences. She is co-author and co-editor of numerous articles and books on childhood including *Constructing and Reconstructing Childhood* (1990/1997), *Theorizing Childhood* (1998), *Research with Children* (2000) and *Constructing Childhood: Theory, Policy and Social Practice* (2004).

Chris Jenks is Professor of Sociology and Pro-Vice-Chancellor at Brunel University, UK. He is also a co-editor of the journal *Childhood*. Among his books related to childhood are pioneering volumes such as *The Sociology of Childhood* (1982), *Childhood* (1996) and the co-authored (with James and Prout) *Theorizing Childhood* (1998). His interests cover a wide range, for instance within the cultural fields, with numerous publications including volumes on *Culture: Critical Concepts in Sociology* (2002) and *Aspects of Urban Culture* (2001).

Cindi Katz is Professor of Geography at the City University of New York, USA. Her work concerns children and the environment, and the consequences of global economic restructuring for everyday life. She has published widely in edited collections and in journals, and her most recent books are *Growing Up Global: Economic Restructuring and Children's Everyday Lives* (2004) and the co-edited *Life's Work: Geographies of Social Reproduction* (2004). She is currently working on a project focused on late twentieth-century American childhood and another on the social wage.

Stephen Kline is a Professor at Simon Fraser University, Canada. He has taught courses in, among other things, video game culture, audience research methods, children's media cultures and media education (http://www.sfu.ca/media-lab/). His scholarly writing includes numerous scientific articles, research reports and books, including *Out of the Garden* (1993), and he is co-author of *Digital Play* (2003) and *Researching Audiences* (2003). His current research focuses on the media-saturated lifestyles of contemporary families, online gaming and on the development of media education strategies.

Michael Lavalette is a Senior Lecturer in Social Policy at the University of Liverpool, UK. He has written widely on child labour and childhood, including *Child Employment in the Capitalist Labour Market* (1994), *A Thing of the Past* (1999) and the co-authored (with McKechnie) *Childhood, Welfare and the State* (2002) and the forthcoming *Child Labour, Globalisation and Anti-Capitalism*.

Olga Nieuwenhuys has degrees in sociology and anthropology and is a Lecturer at the University of Amsterdam, the Netherlands. Her teaching and research interests include childhood and international development, participatory development, post-development and post-colonialism. She is the author of numerous articles and chapters and, among other books, *Children's Lifeworlds, Labour, Gender and Welfare in the Developing World* (1994). She is currently preparing a book that proposes a radical theoretical shift in the study of child labour.

Jens Qvortrup is Professor of Sociology at the Norwegian University of Science and Technology, Trondheim. For more than 20 years he has been involved in establishing social studies of childhood, for example, as director of the study Childhood as a Social Phenomenon (1987–1992) and as founding president of the ISA's Sociology of Childhood. He is currently also a co-editor of the journal *Childhood*. He has written extensively within the field, mainly from a macro-perspective, for example, as co-editor of *Childhood Matters* (1994) and *Childhood and Children's Culture* (2002).

Helmut Wintersberger has a PhD in social sciences and is a Lecturer in Political Sciences at the University of Vienna, Austria. As a director of the Programme on Childhood at the European Centre, Vienna, he played a major role in establishing sociology of childhood in its formative years. He is a consultant in child welfare and children's rights matters, Institute of Human Rights, Vienna, and a leading member of COST Action A19, Children's Welfare. He has written numerous books and articles on social, economic and political aspects of childhood. He was a co-editor of *Childhood Matters* (1994).

Viviana A. Zelizer is Lloyd Cotsen '50 Professor of Sociology at Princeton University, USA. She specializes in the study of economic processes, historical analysis and childhood. She has published books on the development of life insurance, the changing economic and sentimental value of children in the United States (*Pricing the Priceless Child*, 1985), and on the place of money in social life. Her forthcoming *Purchase of Intimacy* reports about her recent work on the interplay between economic transactions and different sorts of social relations.

1
Varieties of Childhood

Jens Qvortrup

Representations of children and childhood

Representations of children cover a wide range – from their non-existence to demands for their complete separation from adults. A few years ago an article in the *New York Times Magazine* (see Belkin, 2000) reported a new movement in the US, campaigning for 'child-free zones'. The main argument among its adherents was that childless adults had a right not to be bothered or pestered by other people's children. They felt emphatically that children were impermissibly and unacceptably visible – indeed, they had no larger wish than to make children disappear from their compass. In their view, children are a private matter; they should not disturb other people, and it should remain a parental obligation to keep children away from the public space, which apparently is regarded as an adult domain and prerogative. Advocates of child-free zones thus perceive children as a *private good* that is definitely none of their business; the idea of children as a *public good* hardly comes to mind. For them children should neither be seen nor heard, and should enter the societal arena only when they have matured. For them, children's intrusion into public arenas is thought of in terms of a 'status offence'. Among adults, they belong to 'free-riders' as far as responsibility for children or childhood is concerned.

It would be easy to denounce this new position as an absurd aberration. However, in Europe too we encounter advertisements for child-free holidays and restaurant visits, and perhaps this seemingly growing attitude should not come as a surprise, given a development in fertility rates where, for instance, 40 per cent of German women in academia are expected to remain childless. For better or worse, we may be facing a change in our norms.[1] Until recently women were expected – to the brink of stigmatization if not complied with – to bear and rear children. Currently, this option is merely one among others for young people to choose.

From this rather detached position towards children, there is historically and mentally a long distance to another extreme, namely the Arièsian vision

1

of children's representation in medieval and immediate post-medieval society. That was a vision of a society which was not short of children but which lacked childhood. Children were plentifully (and visibly) there, but they did not constitute a *conceptual category*, that is, there was no particular awareness of them. They were part and parcel of any local community; they were entrusted with duties like adults; they were not kept away from putative dangerous events – from sexuality to executions; no one prevented them from being witnesses to whatever took place because no one had the idea that children constituted a particular group, or that the child had particular needs. Thus, physically, children were conspicuously present in a society in which there was no clear idea about age-grading or a generational order;[2] no one realized or appreciated children's presence as such because childhood was invisible. Children were there. Not in their capacity as children, however, but rather in their toddler years as animal-like creatures and later as small adults.

The Arièsian vision was one in which children were a part of *public* life, that is, they were not confined to the privacy of a family. Indeed, it is doubtful that an idea of family privacy existed at all: 'sociability . . . hindered the formation of the concept of the family, *because of the lack of privacy*' (Ariès, 1962, p. 398, my italics; see also Brunner, 1980). Children were public in the sense that they were in the open[3] space, and to be in the open space implied large visibility, albeit not in the figure of children as a group or collectivity.

Interestingly, our vision of modern, democratic society is one that is informed by notions of openness (most famously propounded by Popper, 1966), while at the same time it has developed a large number of private forms – from private ownership of the means of production to private organizations and the privacy of families. Children in modern society basically belong to the private family, which is portrayed as a 'haven in a heartless world' or a retreat from the openness of public society. In this sense children have historically experienced a movement from visibility – as small adults – in open local communities to invisibility in public spaces in a modernity which is characterized by much more freedom and democracy – and in this sense more openness – than Arièsian societies.

These apparent paradoxes are resolved by suggesting that *childhood* has entered the historical stage. In fact, this was the gist of Ariès's famous thesis; children lost legitimate visibility in public as they were confined within a variety of forms of childhood: a family childhood, a school childhood, a kindergarten childhood, a leisure time childhood and so on. In short: even if children gained more and more visibility within these confines (see below), sociologically speaking, childhood had become severed from an encompassing encounter with adulthood. Children therefore came to lose visibility within, indeed they were excluded from, the increasingly dominant sectors of the social fabric, emblematic for adults, such as the world of business and labour, urban areas, and the political and administrative sectors.

The prominence of *the child*

Ariès wrote about family life in pre-modernity while the article in the *New York Times Magazine* is a product of recent individualized modernity. Historically, somewhere between these extremes, the concept of *the child* came to assume great influence. Perhaps Ariès's compatriot Rousseau conceived the concept in the eighteenth century, but it was only with the advent of the twentieth century that it was widely accepted.

Politically, the concept of the child was brought to public attention by the Swedish feminist and social reformer Ellen Key, who at the very beginning of the twentieth century published her famous book, *The Century of the Child*, which invoked a new visibility of the child in terms of a better informed and more caring attitude in the adult (Key, 1909). The timing of the publication of Key's political manifesto was hardly accidental. It coincided with the inauguration of a number of child sciences – first among them developmental psychology – through which the child gained scientific prominence. This child – in the singular – has been with us throughout the twentieth century, during which time the individual child has been seen as having got or having *taken* much more freedom to speak up, to have his/her own say, to be a negotiating partner, and so on – in other words s/he has in these ways become much more visible. But these freedoms and visibilities have to be contained within the particular spaces of childhood; they are rarely allowed to be expressed in public spaces, which seem to belong to adults.

Ironically, this child was hardly thinkable without the appearance of childhood in the Arièsian understanding of that term, that is, as a social space that was severed from the social space of adulthood. This psychological child (James et al., 1998) was in fact de-spatialized and de-contextualized in favour of being defined in terms of individual dispositions and was thus a truly universal child. Yet, the psychological concept of the child fitted well to Ariès's vision of childhood in that the latter was confirmed by its compartmentalization of age-groups: the child was not included in human kind but was on her/his way towards humanness and remained until then in a state of becoming and a stage of waiting. As such the child gained a high degree of visibility. Her/his particular needs were discovered and foreseen. The much larger likelihood for survival increased the attention to and protection of the child at the same time as s/he was increasingly seen as vulnerable. However, by the same token children were denied the kind, amount and scope of participation that they were previously granted.

It is one of the paradoxes of Ariès's work that children were much more visible when childhood did not exist. They were much more visible in the sense that fewer doors were closed to them and they had access to the same arenas as adults. However, children probably experienced much less in terms of permissiveness than is the case now. Of all we know, from deMause (1974) for instance, about previous societies, violence and harshness were wide-spread, and while the regarding of children as small adults (in the absence of any notion of childhood) meant a right and a duty for children to be participants in the community, it also implied that children were not particularly protected.

It is plausible to suggest that protection and participation, as we understand the terms, were hardly an issue at all in medieval society. They were neither part of a discourse, nor of a socialization or an educational agenda. If there was an idea of protection, it would most likely have been thought of in vague utilitarian terms. It was not primarily the child who needed protection; it was a prospective labour force that had to be nurtured. Therefore notions of opportunity were not grafted onto individual achievements, outcomes or successes but rather related to the survival of the community of which these children were an integral part.

Historically, the formation of childhood was not in the first place an effort to change the child, although this eventually did become the explicit project of both the child sciences and child savers' movements in terms of improving the child developmentally and rescuing children socially. It was, inadvertently, a process through which an ensemble of parameters was 'invented', the totality of which came to make up the architecture of childhood in structural terms. Childhood's very creation, however unwitting, did not leave children and their life conditions unaffected. In fact, one of the parameters was the creation of discourses about the child and her/his abilities as well as about children, who became increasingly private.

The conclusion so far, one might argue, is that the child has never in history been visible in public: in pre-modernity, because the category did not exist and therefore there was not seen to be a relationship to adults or adulthood. If childhood did not exist, adulthood did not exist either and thus a relationship between the two is logically excluded. In modernity, children are invisible in the public space because they have become marginalized from it, partly due to a new and now very conscious definition of the child as a person whose competences and capabilities are found wanting as a full-fledged member of the human community, partly because of a strong tendency to believe that the individual child and children as a group do not relate to adults in general, but only to their parents, teachers and supervisors. It is against this background that a 'child-free-zones' movement, as we saw, can emerge. We may find it repulsive, but its emergence is not contradictory to the position of children in modernity.

From contemporaries to next generation

Despite many historians' objection to Ariès's view of the non-existence of childhood in pre-modernity, it remains fruitful as a heuristic idea. It entails, among other things, the notion that young persons were basically seen as contemporaries with adults; they were living in the here and now, simultaneous with their elders. Adults did not spend much time and effort on contemplating a child's individual development, but nevertheless expected to be receiving support from their progeny in their own old age, if that was reached. Thus, although there was, conceptually, silence about the child, children and childhood, young persons were not silenced: indeed, they articulated and manifested themselves as indispensable participants in premodern public life; at the same time they were most certainly subjected to a harsh disciplinary regime on the side of their adult contemporaries – parents and other adults alike.

As already indicated, the cultural definition of children in modernity is quite the opposite. They have obtained the opportunity, if not a right, to speak up in the family, whereas their position in public has been weakened. In fact, their definition in modernity is strongly characterized by our expectations as to their futurity as adults. Colloquial expressions such as 'children are the future of society', 'children are the next generation' and 'children are our most precious resource' tend to deprive them of an existence as human *beings* in favour of an image of them as human *becomings*, thus underlining the suggestion that children are not authentic contemporaries of adults. They are here, as it were, to be invested in (see Davis, 1940; see also Esping-Andersen, 2002). This view reflects not only their changed position in the new mode of production, but also complies with and is substantiated by developmental psychology's portrayal of the child as progressing towards completeness, which renders the child regressively incomplete the smaller s/he is. The money and expectations invested by adults in children forces them into a waiting position. It is children's fate to be waiting – patiently waiting to become an adult, to have their contributions recognized, to have a say in societal matters, to be part of the citizenry. This eclipse of individuality, indeed of authentic participation, is likely to be thought of in terms of protecting the child and preserving and augmenting his/her potentialities for later use. In this sense it is a forceful parameter in creating childhood as a structural form and in constituting a generational limitation.

How did this change in the view of children come about? Was it a revelation in the minds of adults, a sudden affection brought to them with the waning of the Middle Ages (Ariès, 1962) or was it an impulsive sentimentalization at the turn of the twentieth century (Zelizer, 1985)? Ariès and Zelizer have both underlined the importance of changed attitudes in this reconstruction of childhood in people's minds; this view does not contradict my view that altered attitudes towards children were inherently connected to changes in modes of production and children's position in them. In other words, children lost their position as useful people as they were gradually transferred from manual activities in pre-industrial eras to mental activities in early industrialization's schools. From working side by side and simultaneously with adults, that is as contemporaries, their new position as pupils implied that only with many years delay could their school work be exploited as useful, if that connection was perceived at all (see Qvortrup, 2001). This new diachronic feature of their obligatory involvement required scientific justification, which was delivered by developmental psychology's claims that the child is preparing him/herself for adulthood. While schooling as such has become clearly appreciated as indispensably connected with a future qualified labour force, children have been deprived of a visible role in the (diachronic) social division of labour and instead reduced to receptacles of knowledge from adults – parents and teachers. The reverse side of their being sentimentalized therefore has been a silencing of their competences and capabilities, which apparently have all to be taught and learned as they grow up.

From participation to protection

Ariès has been accused of portraying medieval parents as not caring, affectionate or protective. However, I think his main message was about participation rather than protection, although the two notions are of course related. He did deplore what he saw as a decreasing role of children in the social fabric and he was critical of a protection which developed into domestication and institutionalization; a positive understanding of protection that increasingly turned into control of children and young people. Control is not a negation of protection, but rather its authoritarian or paternalistic version. What is more, moving towards this extreme version of protection at the same time degrades children's ability to employ their capacity and competence and reinforces an incipient lack of confidence among adults in the abilities of children.

The new and conscious emotionality or sentimentalization must be interpreted positively in terms of a child-friendliness previously unheard of in history. It implies a growing attention to the child, an appreciation of his/her needs, and at least in the family – to a certain extent also in kindergartens and schools – recognition of children as contemporaries, if not equals. In modern societies it has become the rule rather than the exception that it is unlawful to smack children; in families the development is slower – in only a handful of countries are parents not permitted to use corporal punishment (see UNICEF, 2003). I choose to interpret these developments optimistically, although one cannot completely ignore the hypothesis that they have been eased and facilitated by the increased conviction of a positive relationship between friendly and caring treatment of children and 'child outcome', as the productivistic term runs. I do not dare to think what would have happened, if the relationship had been negative.

Although these developments must be considered as encouraging and as a sign of the child's increased visibility, there is a price to be paid. In the first place, as we have seen, they harmonize with a new view of the child as an 'incomplete' or a 'not-yet' adult – a child who is, moreover, deemed more and more frail and vulnerable. Second, they go together with decreased options for children to participate in the broader areas of society. Thus, while children have obtained a greater say in the family and in some countries also in schools, and consequently we have reasons to believe in growing child-friendliness in these arenas, it is probably also true to suggest that such a friendliness is not obvious in society at large. It may not be pertinent, beyond the proponents of 'child-free zones', to speak of child hostility; I would not, however, hesitate to use Kaufmann's notion of 'a structural indifference' towards children and childhood on the part of corporate society, including, to varying degrees, the polity (Kaufmann, 1996). Indeed, indifference is one way of silencing or ignoring.

Given the characterization of the child as vulnerable, it seems appropriate to welcome a protective mood. The question is however what the limits of protection are and how protection and participation are offset against one other. Despite a growing tendency, for instance in social studies of childhood, to grant children competencies to the brink of omnipotence, it must be emphatically said that giving them anything close to equal rights would be an unwarranted risk. We have to admit that children are both physically smaller, and mentally and socially less experienced, and therefore Marx's contention that equal rights under unequal conditions are tantamount to unequal rights applies. On the other hand, an extreme emphasis on children's alleged vulnerability may be used by more powerful segments of society as a pretext for needlessly silencing and marginalizing them.

Schooling, as mentioned above, is a good example. There were undoubtedly many reasons for abolishing classical child labour, protection among them. However, these good reasons are not sufficient for overlooking or even devaluing children's new obligatory work in schools. It is not difficult to understand why influential advocates for schoolwork, such as the state and business, wanted to interpret schooling as a gift to children and parents and thus to ignore children's important input in the social fabric as a whole. Anything else would have entailed massive financial outlays to children or their parents. Stressing protection and socialization measures at the cost of interpreting schooling as children's participation in the social division of labour was therefore an irresistible temptation and interest, but nevertheless also a way of suppressing children's contributions.

There is no doubt either that it is right to introduce measures to protect children against modern society's urbanization and motorization and the increasing rapidity of transport and communication. Should one therefore not unanimously and unreservedly welcome a statistic from the UK, where it was shown that whereas in 1971, 1000 children were killed in traffic, in 1990 this figure was reduced to around 300? Indeed, this was the result of conscious efforts to protect children. However, as found in a study from

1970 and replicated in 1990, the number of children who were allowed access to the city without adult company was reduced accordingly. The share of children who were allowed to (1) cross the road alone, (2) go to leisure places alone and (3) use buses alone had decreased dramatically during the 20 years (see Hillman et al., 1990, pp. 44 and 131; see also O'Brien et al., 2000).

Although the reduction in traffic fatalities is of course welcome, is it permissible to suggest that the price for the positive result is by and large paid by children in terms of a decrease in their freedom of independent mobility? The price was certainly not paid by adults in terms of adapting to children's needs, or in acceding to their legitimate demands to be able to use the city as if it was theirs as well.

The example is not unique. The introduction of curfew bills in both the USA and the UK may be interpreted in the same way. Under the pretext of a wish to protect young children from danger, they are not permitted to be outside during specified periods, typically during the hours of darkness. It is however well known that these measures towards children are most welcomed by many adults who see themselves as disturbed by children.

In the light of such examples, we are forced to look dialectically at vulnerability, protection and participation. While it is relevant to regard children as vulnerable, it would be pertinent also to suggest that the adult world is vulnerable. Considering the investments made in the city, in its infrastructure to accommodate traffic, in factories and other business establishments, and one might add also the costs of adults' education, it is no wonder that great efforts are made to protect these investments against unruly children and their putative destructiveness. From this viewpoint, it is arguably adult properties, infrastructure and qualifications that must be seen as exposed and vulnerable; and accordingly it is logical to suggest that children are prevented from authentic participation in the life of the city in order to protect adult installations, rather than, or concurrently with, proposing that institutions for children are there to protect them against the dangers represented by the adult world.

A balanced view would imply that the severance of children from adults is explained dialectically, but the vulnerability of the adult world is seldom mentioned, and this imbalance is in fact one way of silencing children.

From public to private responsibility

Why should the adult world make concessions to the advantage of children, in terms of, for instance, adapting to their demands and needs and thus incurring costs? This question is, I believe, crucial for our understanding of the representation of children and childhood in modernity. It is a question, basically, about responsibility for children and/or childhood.

It can be deduced from what was said above, that responsibility for child-bearing and child rearing has changed from a public to a private responsibility. Privatization means in this context first of all familialization: parents make automous decisions to have children, when they want to have them, and how many they want to have. This was, one might argue, always the case. However, the more or less conscious presumption of generational inter-dependencies in pre-modernity had a profound impact on attitudes to the reception of new members of a community. Although the demand in numbers varied, the survival of a community depended cn reproduction of a new labour force, which at the same time was there to provide for both young and old. The perception of these tasks as common – and in this sense public – endeavours was supported by a social order in which reproduction and production could not be separated. Neither production nor reproduc-tion could be reduced to the private realm; both were transparently impor-tant for the whole community, including the contributions of children. No one could with impunity attempt to free-ride. Such were the principles as seen in retrospect. They did not, however, guarantee the smooth function-ing of community life and we know that tensions, frictions and poverty were frequent events in the past.

It is possible – indeed necessary – to argue that generations remain depen-dent on each other even in modern society. However, this insight seems to have gone astray as divisions of labour have intensified. First of all, it appears nowadays as common knowledge that production and reproduction are completely separate functions. Although business and the trades are com-pletely dependent on a renewal of a labour force, it is nowhere part of their, let alone a political, agenda that they assume any responsibility for its renewal. Even the state has reservations about getting involved in family decisions, unless life or welfare are jeopardized. No wonder, therefore, that individual adults regard it as a right to opt for a childless life, the extreme expression of which are movements such as those demanding 'child-free zones'.

As a result, parents – families with children – are left with reproductive responsibilities which have proven difficult for them to shoulder alone, as envisioned empirically in, for instance, disproportionate poverty rates for children and in low fertility rates. However, the privatization or familializa-tion of children – combined with their portrayal as incomplete, vulnerable and of no economic use – has additional consequences in terms of children being silenced or denied access to resources.

The historical development towards making children a private matter, as we have seen, coincides with a more caring attitude – a positive feature which however has rendered children increasingly dependent, the more so since they are also depicted as vulnerable and in need of adult protection. As such, their status as dependants is not exclusively a negative one, because leaving them with an independent status on par with adults would in fact be overlooking actual relations of power and endangering children. On the other hand this argument is not valid as a reason to hide significant aspects of children's lives. The good reasons for protecting children against exploitation and subjugation do not justify depriving them of a right to conceptual autonomy (Thorne, 1987), that is, an autonomy which allows them to be heard and seen in their own right. This is, as a matter of fact, what often happens – deliberately or thoughtlessly – in, for example, public statistics and social accounting about children.

Familialization also implies keeping children hidden in the family, inaccessible to the public gaze. For children, this can be detrimental. From a cultural point of view it must be regarded as a major shortcoming, which however seems consistent with the position of children in modern society, economically and symbolically.

The last decades have however seen an improvement in our understanding of children and childhood. We have, for instance, become much better informed about children's material conditions. The picture is not one in which children invariably lose, but it is nevertheless obvious that children belong to the more endangered groups in society. One major reason for this is – once again – that children are seen as belonging to the family or the household, and since parents are expected to share their incomes with children, it follows logically that income per household member will be lower than in households without children, even if economies of scale are taken into consideration. The situation of children is alleviated when the welfare state intervenes on behalf of children (or families with children), and it can be shown that children's poverty rates are systematically higher in countries (such as the USA and Italy) where the welfare state is more poorly developed than in the Nordic countries in Europe with a strong welfare state commitment.

It has to be said however that nowhere have children a constitutionally-based right to receive welfare support from the state (see Qvortrup, 2003). Even in welfare states, children are basically dependent on their parents. The reason for this is the unshaken ideology of the family, which perceives children as a parental responsibility.

Historically, children are arguably the last remaining group which has not yet been recognized as having a claim on current political and societal resources. The political and industrial revolutions of the West, Reinhard Bendix said, 'lead to the eventual recognition of the rights of citizenship for *all adults*, including those in positions of economic dependence' (Bendix, 1977, p. 66, my italics) – but not for children, who did not, as subjects, take advantage of these changes. In a sense, following Bendix's line of argument, children are still – politically and economically – part of a feudal system which accorded no immediate rights 'to subjects in positions of economic dependence such as tenants, journeymen, workers and servants: at best *they are classified under the household* of their master and represented through him and his estates' (ibid., pp. 66–7, my italics).

The criticism levelled here does not intend to hide the fact that children's material welfare has in general improved dramatically over the last centuries; but it is at the same time interesting to note that formally children remain by and large subsumed within the household – or perhaps more precisely, the family – without individual *rights* to *societal* resources. Despite much progress made and despite the advancement represented by, for instance, the United Nations Convention on the Rights of the Child, it remains a fact that children do not enjoy economic and political rights as autonomous citizens.

The chapters in this book

The introduction so far can be read as a symptomatic account of what social studies of childhood is about; or perhaps rather as the editor's idiosyncratic perspectives, which do not necessarily coincide with the views of the book's authors, let alone with the richness and complexities of children's life worlds. The chapters in this book do in fact demonstrate that childhood studies have gone a long way to broaden and deepen the analyses. A couple of decades ago these studies used to be labelled 'the new sociological paradigm of childhood' or 'the new social studies of childhood'. However, although the adjective 'new' is no longer considered appropriate, some would argue that there nevertheless remains a need for assuming something which is particular for childhood studies; something which distinguishes them from other branches of research dealing with 'child', 'children' and 'childhood' or from other departments of disciplinary studies of social science provenance. Others would underline the normality of childhood studies in the sense that children as human beings and childhood as 'their' social space should and must be studied with the same arsenal of theories and methods as other human beings and their respective social spaces. There were and remain tensions and ongoing discussions as to distinctiveness or sameness about the life worlds of children vis-à-vis the life worlds of other age groups or generations. These debates are reflected in intellectual arguments about the salience of focusing on one childhood or a plurality of childhoods, on perceiving children and childhood as anticipation of adulthood or as in the here and now, on weighting the activities and agency of children above the impacts upon them of close or distant societal forces, on childhood as confined to the family and the locality rather than as a societal or even a global phenomenon and so on.

Even if these arguments were and are indispensable constituents of ongoing discourses and (dis)agreements for coming to terms with the most fruitful access for understanding childhood, they are hardly, or with few exceptions, addressed explicitly in the chapters of this book; yet it should not be too difficult for those who want to find support for one view or the other to do so. Most chapters do carry 'messages', scientifically indeed, but also at the end of the day politically, since welfare and the well-being of children are not apolitical issues (see Mayall, 2002). They do have political antecedents and they do carry political implications. In this sense, as editor, I welcome engagement and involvement.

The introductory words above could be accused of being stuck in impermissible conceptual binaries, an example of which is an implied divergence between generations. As such Heinz Hengst's chapter could be taken on board as a criticism, given his reservations, to say the least, against dichotomous thinking. When a subheading (above) sketches a development in the perception of children from contemporaries to next generation one might (mis)understand Hengst's message about children nowadays as contemporaries as a conceptual return to an Arièsian dream world where generations are mixed up with each other. However, his use of the Mannheimian concept of contemporaries is in fact signalling or portraying a futurity that is already with us. Without sacrificing the reality of distinct generations, Hengst is nevertheless making a diagnosis of our current era as dominated by media and consumption. Our entry in this era has led to a cultural 'Freisetzung' (a loosening of traditional and normative bonds) which has equipped children and young people with insight to master and decode media messages and competence to act as consumers – at least on par with adults.

Drotner concurs with Hengst in the assessment of mediatization as crucial for understanding modern childhood, and she makes a forceful plea for heightening the attention of media studies to childhood and for increasing childhood studies' awareness of media. While underwriting a trust in the idea of the 'complex' society, her chapter is at the same time continuously searching for commonalities while balancing between acknowledging children's ability to deal with modern media in their most various forms and a recognition of the stakes held by proponents of knowledge on the one hand and entertainment on the other. The significant point is that children in both realms are subjects and objects. An important conclusion made by Drotner is that children are able to make choices of media on the basis of what is relevant for them in given contexts rather than being attracted by a particular medium as such. The almost global access to media tends to unite children over the world in a common identification, while at the same time 'intensifying users' recognition and reflection on local differences'.

Drotner's concluding caveat to avoid ingrained and opposing epistemologies of childhood innocence and childhood competence by transcending them serves well as a password into the two next chapters, which also deal with the media world. David Buckingham and Sara Bragg report about a study of children's and parents' responses to sex in the media and how they relate to each other in this context. The authors question the reasons for media panic about children who are said to be growing up too fast. Essentially, the authors find that children are largely well aware of their own knowledge about sex, and of the expectations that both culture and parents have as to what they should do or should know. They know about their 'territory' and about when they appear to reach its limits. Children are keen to present themselves as self-regulating. The study reported is an optimistic and positive account of children's insight and the authors find much support for understanding current cultural panic about children and the media as highly exaggerated. On the other hand a general act of empowerment of children such as the study might imply may entail costs in terms of burdens of full citizenship which may be heavier for some than for others.

The optimism of Buckingham and Bragg is not shared by Stephen Kline, who is much more reluctant to accept children's defensive capacities vis-à-vis the massive ammunition levelled against them from the media industry. Without denying the agency of children, he is rather inclined to understand the relationship between children and the media industry as a very unequal power relationship between partners whose interests do not coincide. The media world is thus seen by Kline as one among many other structural forces that children as well as adults have to contend with. Whether the media actually can or will result in violence or other unacceptable behaviour is obviously hard to prove; on the other hand profit-seeking companies are hardly to be seen in terms of benevolence or malevolence – perhaps they are better represented as indifferent to anything other than their own commercial interests. Everyone is likely to be a part of such a commercial ambience and children may eventually be as competent to meet the challenges as adults. Even if children and adults in this comparison may be seen as contemporaries, to use Hengst's phrase, nothing is said about the power relations between humans and the commercial world.

Media in all their varieties are a part of an ever-widening array of technological instruments at our disposal, and it is some of them which Cindi Katz takes to task. In Chapter 6, Katz, who has done so much in her earlier work to trace the common influences of capitalism in both the developing world (Sudan) and the modern world (New York), concentrates mainly on its most recent expressions of importance for children's everyday life in New York. The new developments, not least after 11 September 2001, in the USA, indeed eventually in many parts of the world, focused towards new regimes of surveillance are paralleled by an already flourishing industry dedicated to controlling children's movements and behaviour. Under the pretext of providing protection to children a plethora of monitoring and – in effect – disciplining measures are launched at the market while instrumentalizing parents' anxieties in the modern city. The chapter can also be read as another example of the way that children's participation opportunities are slighted with good parental intentions while serving the interests of the producers of hypervigilant products in amazingly, indeed disturbingly creative forms. One might suggest, given prevailing attitudes of sentimentalization, that corporate society is blatantly transgressing a moral agenda which has been with us for at least a century.

The questions raised here in the context of children's relationship with media and technology appear in various other contexts in the book; typical, of course, in social studies of childhood's attempt to find its identity or perhaps identities. They may be formulated in numerous ways, for instance in terms of protection and participation, constraint and opportunity, vulnerability and resilience, dependence and independence, adaptation and transgression or, most abstractly, structure and agency – all binaries or dichotomies, which never do completely justice to reality but nevertheless have some heuristic value and analytical utility.

Of course, it is the question of social order, which applied to childhood through a Parsonian optic, is the barbarian question (see Parsons, 1964, p. 208). Children are a challenge, not to say a provocation to the social order. They constantly seek to test the limits or even to transgress any normative agenda, as Chris Jenks suggests. They are the true, recurrent and joyful deconstructionists of an orderly social system that is understood as a continuous grand narrative, irrespective of whatever transformation society undergoes. It is the fate and/or tragedy of children that it is eventually them, as adults, who will be the corrective instance, entrusted with the prerogatives of socializing governance vis-à-vis never ending cohorts of transgressors. No social order will allow itself to accept a child's transgressive perseverance or persevering transgression since this will lead to anarchism. On the other hand, as Jenks suggests, some lessons about morality might be learned from even inarticulate voices of despair or resistance or optimism, since most systems also harbour more attractive responses to unorthodox demeanour than incarceration or institutionalization.

If childhood in general is transgression and entails numerous forms of institutionalizations, including childhood itself, this is even truer of orphanhood as a special case of childhood. Orphanhood is an embodied challenge to a patriarchal and familial social order. It is not the children as carriers of this status who aspire to challenge any prevailing consensus; rather it is the status itself which has become ascribed to children as a particular misfortune. In Judith Ennew's account, not much is left for orphans in terms of agency. Orphanhood is a double dependency: it is dependency on various forms of caretaking systems, and orphans are prisoners of their own dependency. The orphans are truly at the margin of any society, although typically tolerated for their value as investment objects. The continuity in orphanhood, historically and interculturally, is exactly its extreme marginality; orphans belong to nobody. The way orphanhood is approached as a problem varies, basically according to mode of production, and thus assumes different forms. However, as Ennew shows, different solutions cannot hide the fact that we are speaking about the same problem, which has only been quantitatively exacerbated due to the HIV/AIDS pandemic.

In various guises modes of production constitute the background for understanding the forms and expressions of children's life worlds in several chapters of this book. They encompass Ennew's chapter on orphanhood; Kline's chapter observes the subsuming of children's media use under capitalist firms' demands for profit; for Olga Nieuwenhuys and Michael Lavalette children's inclusion in the world of work in either the poor or the rich world is premised on relations of exploitation; while Katz's chapter offers an interpretation of what she calls 'the gravity of living in the shards of capitalist modernity'. Helmut Wintersberger also takes up this vocabulary while introducing notions of formal and real subsumption under capital in his analysis. Any simplistic references to reductionism or determinism – so typical when notions of capitalism are invoked – are unwarranted when in fact the realities of unequal relations of power are foregrounded. In the chapters, for instance, on children's work (including Viviana Zelizer's chapter), children are indeed granted important roles as actors, and none of the writers mentioned above are unaware of or not alert to the relationship between structure and agency. It remains important, though, to be attentive to the nature of this relationship; its continuous presence does not contradict its being typically represented as manifesting unbalanced power relationships.

Nieuwenhuys and Lavalette both write about child labour in the classical sense, but in two different parts of the world: Nieuwenhuys writes from the third world, while Lavalette deals with the issue in the modern United Kingdom. There are commonalities between them in the sense of understanding market capitalism or neo-liberalism as a threat to labouring children, but while Nieuwenhuys is inclined to accept children's active participation in work as necessary for survival (in India), Lavalette does not find much consolation or any excuses for letting children work in the UK, where sheer survival is not at stake. His main and classical trade union argument is that children must be protected against waged work because it exploits them, and that the neo-liberal economy and its influence on the British welfare state only exacerbate the problems. At the same time Lavalette critically implies an affinity between neo-liberalism and modern strands of social constructionism in the latter's alleged effort to 'liberate' children as competent agents, which only leads to their being 'adulterized'.

For Nieuwenhuys, in a third world context, the question is rather to acknowledge children as indispensable participants in intergenerational exchange relations. She is careful in distinguishing between paid and unpaid labour (or work), and makes it clear that children's unpaid work is indeed widespread, in fact it is by far the most common kind of children's useful participation. This work is of great importance since it forms a necessary part of a generalized reciprocity and thus finds an almost natural place within communities and localities in developing countries (and, one might add, in the history of the western world). Work performed by children is in fact their 'wealth' and has positive consequences as a part of the intergenerational wealth flows. It is suggested that children's work for wages also has negative effects since the surplus is 'siphoned off'; in that way it is exploitative. In a sense, therefore, there is agreement between Nieuwenhuys and Lavalette in their assessment of wage labour as exploitative; however, in modern societies Nieuwenhuys' 'unpaid work' does not have the same meaning as in developing countries, where the question of protection versus participation is not raised or contemplated.

This does not mean that unpaid work is not found in the modern world, as Zelizer convincingly points out, but again it carries a different meaning than in contemporary pre-industrial countries, and one may doubt that it is indispensable as a part of a generalized reciprocity. Nevertheless it is deemed extremely useful in its production, on the one hand, of transferable goods and services and, on the other, in its addition to existing capital. Zelizer's main examples are from care work, children as linguistic mediators and children in immigrant enterprises, and she demonstrates that 'meaning, organization, contribution and compensation of children's work' vary systematically from one social setting to the other. Although the work that Zelizer is exemplifying is useful in the contexts in which it is performed, it is to a large extent invisible; at the same time it is found meaningful for children. Zelizer concludes with an interesting flash-back to her famous book, *Pricing the Priceless Child*, and makes clear that in principle her new arguments are in line with the main tenets of that book.

Is there a historical development of children's useful participation in any mode of production? Wintersberger makes a bold effort to make sense of children's labour during history and even into the future, while combining it with its position in the division of labour. He describes and discusses the stages through which children's work so far has passed – from traditional to early-industrial labour, from human capital production to consumers – the latter being a role which children for the first time are negotiating without adult interference. The author partly uses a Marxist framework – formal subsumption (classical child labour) and real subsumption (for example, school work) under capital. It is further argued that while children through scholarization have obtained advantages, they have also been marginalized and affected negatively in terms of their position in the generational division of labour and generational distribution of resources. Even the most developed welfare states have suffered a child-blindness, and although the feminist movement can be seen as an inspiration for giving more visibility to children, it has not unequivocally been in favour of a generational perspective. Wintersberger, though, sees some hope in an – admittedly somehow speculative – future role of children, where they might assume a position as 'new post-industrial producers'.

In whichever form, there seems no doubt that children are performing useful activities. The question remains whether they are also rewarded for it. Are they also partakers in any system of distributive justice? Can they be seen as legitimate claimants on available resources in the communities or societies in which they live? Nieuwenhuys answers affirmatively as far as unpaid work is concerned in contemporary pre-industrial societies, while both she and Lavalette, by and large, regard children's paid work as exploitative. In her chapter, Bojer addresses the important issue of distributive justice for children. Rawls's famous work on justice does not address children's position and it is Bojer's aim to see if children can be conceptualized in Rawlsian terms. For this purpose she discusses the notions of children as public and private goods, and while she holds that children, strictly speaking, do not deserve a right to societal revenues, due to their age, they nevertheless must – as humans – have a claim on societal resources. Children are parents' responsibilities, but since they are also public goods with positive externalities it is only logical that parents can legitimately make claims for assistance in shouldering their responsibilities. In the light of Rawls's scheme, Bojer finds that it makes much sense to allow such claims: anything else would jeopardize life as a child.

The scope of children's activities is large indeed. In a historical and a global perspective, as we have seen, children have always been required to participate in a range of more or less useful activities. In this sense they are always, in one way or another, included in the social division of labour with adults. It is however important, as recent social studies of childhood have clearly demonstrated, also to deal with children as active in their relations to other children. For Bill Corsaro, who for decades has been a leading researcher on (mainly) young children in their meeting places, it is important to maintain that the level of analysis for studying childhood and children's life transitions must always be collective, that is, the individual in interaction with others within a cultural context. This distinguishes Corsaro's work from much psychological research, from which he nevertheless advises us not to disengage completely. Rather one should, as for instance through his own theory of interpretive reproduction, make attempts to bridge the micro–macro gap by stressing children's agency in their production of and participation in their peer cultures. Corsaro is careful in stressing the constraints of social structure and social reproduction, but finds that the nature of children's collective actions demands a more micro and temporally situated view of agency. To this effect, Corsaro is presenting his own qualitative empirical data, while drawing theoretically on Emirbayer and Mische's ideas about the 'triad of agency'.

Allison James also uses her own empirical data in an effort, as she says, 'to reclaim subjectivity for children'. She criticizes the schematic use of chronological age, which is so ingrained that even children themselves may be using it (as Ivar Frønes also suggests). There is a lot of 'nature' and 'mythology' to ideas of adulthood, which is in fact socially achieved. The widespread use of age schemes has led to policies which separate children and adults in their everyday lives and invokes a generational perspective. The power of developmental psychology is felt in both social practice and in parenting, which creates anomalies and renders children victims of a kind of 'ageism' – not only as objects but also in the sense that they internalize the schemes and use it on themselves. James's talks with children concentrate on their views of 'the future' and 'the past', and she argues that concepts of autobiography and of life history are relevant for children as well as for adults; through this the 'ageism' with which children are often saddled is questioned.

Frønes's chapter, finally, is an ambitious effort to theorize about the transition towards adulthood and the importance of age-phases. A particular significance is given to the impact of any child's future as adults – this next age-phase looms large not only in the minds and policies of adults, it is also significant in children's imagery of their own future. Frønes is critical of a one-sided structural approach, although he recognizes its importance. Children all assume particular positions at each age-phase. These are influenced not only by their situation in a generational structure, but also by gender, class and ethnicity. This means that any analysis of childhood must account for both structural influences and for differentiations that occur simultaneously. Despite the acceptance of a powerful structural influence on the formation of childhood, Frønes's chapter can be understood as an advocacy for the plurality of childhoods and for their internal differentiation. The chapter introduces a number of new concepts, such as paths, tracks, synchronicity and diachronicity and is, characteristically for the author, flavoured by an abundance of illustrative examples.

Ways ahead for childhood studies

Is there a historical continuity of childhood that can be extended into a future that may already be with us? As the chapters in this volume testify the study of childhood and therefore also the reality of children's life worlds covers a wide range and demonstrates large diversities. New nuances and gradations are added and oppositions to simplified dichotomies and binaries are boldly aired. Nevertheless, the old fronts between structure and agency are not discarded; indeed, while the constructive role of children is reiterated and made more visible in new areas, we are also witnessing the fact that notions of capitalism and modes of production are increasingly finding a place in the analyses.

The subheadings in the opening sections of this introduction may imply that some of the chapters seem inadvertently to suggest a continuation. As already indicated, it appears that we may again be talking about children as contemporaries in intergenerational terms after a long period in which notions of children as the next generation have been the reigning concept and conventional wisdom. This is particularly indicative within the chapters on media, where children are portrayed as harbouring competences that often match those of adults and indeed not infrequently surpass them. It is significant also to make visible new forms of participation by children, in terms of useful activities which for so long were hidden in the family, neighbourhood or school. Suggestions to this effect obviously raise questions about the salience of 'protection' as the 'king-P' among three Ps in the UN Convention on the Rights of the Child (the other Ps being provision and participation).

Yet, as cautioned by some and clearly demonstrated by others, children continue to be the less powerful part in an adult world – politically and economically. The real task remains that of combining a positive exploitation of children by making them and their life worlds visible while preventing negative exploitation of their weaknesses.

Making children's constructive roles visible, as well as laying bare the structural constraints that they are exposed to, would be one way in which childhood research might assist children in regaining status as members of the public without sacrificing the achievements obtained in modern societies of childhood as a protected position.

However, a re-appreciation of children as contemporaries, as participants and as reclaiming a status and a stake in the public and social fabric is in no way a return to an Arièsian lack of awareness. Rather, one would hope, it is a highly conscious effort to understand childhood as an integral part of society.

Notes

1. A search for 'child free' on Google produced a staggering 21,000,000 hits!
2. In fact, there was a generational order, of which, however, there was no awareness. O'Neill (1994) is therefore right in suggesting that we avoid speaking of a generational contract for these communities, but rather of a generational covenant.
3. In German (and in the Scandinavian languages, too) the word for 'the public' is 'die Öffentlichkeit', derived from 'Offenheit', the direct translation of which is 'openness' (offen = open). But 'Öffentlichkeit' is at the same time the antonym of private – 'die Privatheit' or 'das Private'.

References

Ariès, Ph. (1962) *Centuries of Childhood. A Social History of Family Life*, New York: Vintage Books.

Belkin, Lisa (2000) 'Your Kids Are Their Problem', *New York Times Magazine*, July 23, 30ff.

Bendix, R. (1977) *Nation-building and Citizenship: Studies of our Changing Social Order*, Berkeley: University of California Press.

Brunner, O. (1980) 'Vom "ganzen Haus" zur "Familie"', in H. Rosenbaum (ed.), *Seminar: Familie und Gesellschaftsstruktur*, Frankfurt a.M : Suhrkamp, pp. 83–91.

Davis, K. (1940) 'The Child and the Social Structure', *Journal of Educational Sociology*, 14 (4): 217–29.

deMause, L. (1974) 'The Evolution of Childhood', in *The History of Childhood*, New York: Psychohistory Press, pp. 1–73.

Esping-Andersen, G. with D. Gallie, A. Hemerijck and J. Myles (2002) *Why We Need a New Welfare State*, Oxford: Oxford University Press.

James, A., C. Jenks and A. Prout (1998) *Theorizing Childhood*, London: Polity Press.

Kaufmann, F.-X. (1996) *Modernisierungsschübe, Familie und Sozialstaat*, München: Oldenbourg Verlag.

Key, Ellen (1909) *The Century of the Child*, New York and London: G.P. Putnam's Sons.

Hillman, M., J. Adams and J. Whitelegg (1990) *One False Move . . . a Study of Children's Independent Mobility*, London: Policy Studies Institute.

Mayall, Berry (2002) *Towards a Sociology for Childhood*, Buckingham: Open University Press.

O'Brien, M., D. Jones, D. Sloan and M. Rustin (2000) 'Children's Independent Spatial Mobility in the Urban Realm', *Childhood*, 7 (3): 257–77.

O'Neill, J. (1994) *The Missing Child in Liberal Theory*, Toronto: University of Toronto Press.

Parsons, Talcot (1964) *The Social System*, New York: The Free Press.

Popper, K.R. (1966) *The Open Society and its Enemies*, London: Routledge & Kegan Paul.

Qvortrup, J. (2001) 'School-work, Paid Work and the Changing Obligations of Childhood', in Ph. Mizen, C. Pole and A. Bolton (eds), *Hidden Hands: International Perspectives on Children's Work and Labour*, London: RoutledgeFalmer, pp. 91–107.

Qvortrup, J. (2003) 'Kindheit im marktwirtschaftlich organisierten Wohlfahrtstaat', in R. Kränzl-Nagl, J. Mierendorf and Th. Olk (eds), *Kindheit im Wohlfahrtstaat. Gesellschaftliche und politische Herausforderungen*, Frankfurt a.M.: Campus Verlag, pp. 95–120.

Thorne, Barrie (1987) 'Re-visioning Women and Social Change: Where are the Children?', *Gender and Society*, 1 (1): 85–109.

UNICEF (2003) *A League Table of Child Maltreatment Deaths in Rich Nations*, Innocenti Report Cards, 5, Florence: Innocenti Research Centre.

Zelizer, V.A. (1985) *Pricing the Priceless Child. The Changing Social Value of Children*, New York: Basic Books.

2
Complex Interconnections: the Global and the Local in Children's Minds and Everyday Worlds

Heinz Hengst

Introduction

One of the aims of 'new social childhood studies', so-called, was (and still is) to identify its new collective subject, namely children. In the following, I would like to contribute to this endeavour. My approach is characterized by viewing today's children above all as *contemporaries*. That may seem a trivial way of identifying them, but I believe the implications are less trivial. For sociologists who are interested in treating children in the same manner as the members of other age groups, viewing children as contemporaries is a justifiable starting point and a rewarding approach.

My chapter is an appeal, to put it cautiously, for a kind of decentred childhood research. I am not maintaining that this approach can substitute for centred research on childhood matters, but am interested, rather, in developing a complementary perspective. I argue that studies which analyse children and childhood in a decentred manner have particularly good chances of delving into key experiences of children as contemporaries. Decentredness, in my view, is a perspective that transcends the dualism of childhood–adulthood distinctions and abandons any fixation on a presumed experiential space on the part of children that is primarily understood with reference to these distinctions. This also entails a rejection of dualistic thought. The latter is always at risk of failing to perceive complexities, simultaneities and periodicities. Binary codes, whether manifest or latent, are ill-suited in particular for perceiving and comprehending a globalized reality in which everything is intermeshed. My idea is that interesting and thought-provoking results would probably be yielded by investigating the changing identity (identities) of that population group we call children, with specific reference to their experience with a mediatized world of consumption. Even though their experience is shaped and influenced by many other factors, this specific experience stands out.

My approach is that of cultural analysis. I understand culture in the 'cultural studies' sense as a process involving the circulation of meanings. I think it makes sense to view the cultural, as Tomlinson (1999) does, not as an isolated sphere of human activity, but rather as a dimension of social life. I also believe that distinctions must be made in the construction of meanings – it is essential to gain an imagination, from and despite the complex web of (cultural), economic and political activities, in which the sense and purpose of culture is seen as attaching meaning to life. Existentially significant meanings characteristic for 'identity work' are the specific preserve of the cultural dimension. However, they are rather everyday in nature. Culture relates to the everyday thoughts, emotions and actions with which we 'spin' our lives.

To speak of the culture of a group (or a population) only makes sense when the members of that group are confronted with common existential challenges and approach them in a specific, distinct manner. To what extent children's culture can be distinguished from the culture of other age groups is an important question not only for children's culture research. The answer is highly dependent, quite obviously, on the sociocultural conditions under which childhood, youth and adulthood are lived. There is much to suggest that the present-day sociocultural framework no longer permits any easy distinctions to be made between the categories of childhood, youth and adulthood; put differently, that the significance of the childhood context for identity-forming experience (especially collective experience) has changed, been relativized and/or reduced.

Such notions are incompatible with ideas that associate culture with a fixed, recitable canon of fields, instances, materials, media, activities and aspects. Culture – in the sense I am outlining – develops through interaction and confrontation with the products, media, places, events, excerpts from reality and so on to which people ascribe meaning (for their own lives).

When *children's culture* is understood in this sense, it becomes tangible with regard to those excerpts from reality to which children ascribe meaning in their thoughts, emotions and actions, and in their specific forms of praxis. They act at all times in and through the symbolic worlds, bodies of knowledge, customs and so on that are present in a society – in other words, by using significant networks of meaning. These networks of meaning are not only the material from which they derive their orientations, but also the reference points from whose assumptions they distance themselves and to which they – not uncommonly – seek and find innovative access. What is typical for children – in the sense of a distinct quality – can only be specified (according to my concept of decentralized analysis) when one does not inquire exclusively into the cultural practices of children, or place them in relation to adults, but rather endeavours to differentiate and inquire into the cultural practices of their contemporaries. A decentralized perspective is open to new cultural 'relationships' between large groups in society.

My attention is primarily focused on those slices of reality and constructions of meaning in which present-day children become identifiable as 'children' of their (and our) time: as contemporaries. What I envisage is children's culture research that is both subject-oriented and sensitive to the specific features of the current age. I am interested in the (typical) 'answers' that children give to the challenges of the (globalized) environments and societies in which they are growing up. If these responses are confined to children is a question of research, it cannot be taken for granted.

The starting and leverage point for my ideas is the observation that present-day children and youth are involved in a process by which they are being socioculturally set free from historically given social forms and relationships to find their own destiny. To label this process Ziehe and Stubenrauch (1982) coined the term 'soziokulturelle Freisetzung' which is difficult to translate but could perhaps be understood as (a kind of) sociocultural dismissal.

The concept of children's culture that I favour is primarily geared to the analysis of (existentially important) constructions of meaning under the conditions of (socio)cultural dismissal in the sense of being set free from traditional bonds and dependencies. Such a concept harmonizes with key findings within the current debate on societal transformations. Manuel Castells, the US social theorist to whom we owe the most comprehensive analysis of contemporary social change, believes the key challenge lies in the fact that people must lead their lives these days without a 'route map', because the contours of new social, economic and cultural conditions are still relatively diffuse (Castells, 1998). Being socioculturally set free means not least that young people today can *or* must no longer refer in traditional fashion to the knowledge and experience – and hence the advisory competence – of adults.

When Castells refers to those who lead their lives without a 'route map', he is not thinking specifically of children or young people. I would suggest that his diagnosis is tendentially valid for all contemporaries in society. For that reason, too, it is a useful starting point for reorientation in (childhood and) children's culture research – social change has placed children and youth in a situation involving new commonhoods and differences. Under such conditions, it is appropriate to view children above all as 'new arrivals' in societies and cultures in which adults are not really at home either.

Sociocultural dismissal, being set free or leading one's own life without a 'route map' is an ambivalent process. On the one hand, it extends the range of options and hence the scope for disposition and action, but on the other hand it may threaten the ligatures, those firmly rooted cultural bonds that give people the capacity to assert themselves in a world of options. There is no question that the world of media and consumption acquires enormous importance in connection with cultural dismissal. It would be misleading to focus reflection on 'soziokulturelle Freisetzung' and people leading their lives without a route map, if one neglects the fact that, like all others, even the youngest of contemporaries can fall back on a plethora of 'templates' or 'set pieces' with which to interpret society and life in it.

The concept of 'soziokulturelle Freisetzung' bears similarities to that of 'cultural disembedding' used by researchers who culturalize Giddens' concept of 'disembedding' (Giddens, 1991) to refer to the ways in which the local is penetrated by remote influences (see Tomlinson, 1999). Cultural disembedding is, so to speak, the global–local variant of what is meant by 'soziokulturelle Freisetzung'. It refers to the fact that, although we all continue to live our local lives, in which 'the constraints of the body ensure that all individuals, at every moment, are contextually situated in time and space', this 'locality' is fundamentally different today from the 'self-contained localities of pre-modernity' (ibid., p. 59). The predominant experience of everyday life in the modern global world is that locally situated lifeworlds are penetrated by remote events, relationships and processes. Disembedding is a concept that can be applied in the analysis of culture. Without doubt, media and communication systems are disembedding mechanisms that Giddens does not at all discuss. The fact that television raises experience from the purely local context is patently obvious. And yet such disembedding is essentially performed by the entire commodified culture. The perception that remote events and processes are important for one's own life is becoming a routine experience of people to an increasing degree. The ever-broadening horizon of relevance in people's routine experience characterizes not only 'cultural awareness' in a (very) general sense, but also 'life planning' by individuals.

In this chapter therefore, I try to place new experience on the part of present-day children in relation to the influence exerted by markets and media. The chapter has two parts. In the first, I outline some very generalized ways of looking at changes on the side of our research subjects and objects. In the second section, I specify these perspectives in more detail, concentrating thereby on the complex interactions between the global and the local.

Changes on the side of research subjects and objects

1. On exploring the collective subject

In current sociological discourse on childhood, one is struck by a growing appreciation of the generation concept (see the review by Mayall and Zeiher, 2003). This concept has played a role in socio-structural research into childhood from the very outset, unlike in social-constructionist research, because as political sociology it raises the question of generational equity, for example, as an issue involving the distribution of resources and opportunities between children and adults, or between children and non-children. Giovanni Sgritta, for example, entitled his contribution to *Childhood Matters* (1994) 'The Generational Division of Welfare'.

Leena Alanen (1994) introduced a specific concept of generation into the discourse on childhood, namely that of a 'generational system' that organizes differences between children and adults in the same way that the gender system regulates differences between males and females. She coined the term 'generationing' (analogous to 'gendering') to characterize the processes in which people (learn to) act in a typically child-like or adult-like manner, and develop the corresponding identities. The transformation of childhood can be (re)constructed, with the help of Alanen's generation concept, as the analysis of 'generationing' processes. 'Beyond Mannheim' is the heading given by Leena Alanen to a section in 'Explorations in Generational Analysis' in order to distinguish and demarcate her generational approach from any concept in which generations are understood as historically positioned age groups or cohorts joined by common experience (Alanen, 2001, p. 17).

Whereas Alanen wants to go beyond Mannheim's concept of generation, I would like to introduce it (in a heuristic, pragmatic way) as an alternative to any recourse to the childhood concept when attempting to specify the collective subject of childhood research. In a famous essay on the 'generational problem' (1965), Karl Mannheim added new dimensions to the old topic of 'intergenerational relations', turning it into a macro-sociological concept. His new concept was a response to the rapid and sweeping transformation of modern society. In Mannheim's concept, the changing social structure determines not only the respective form and the fate of a generation, but also the differences and interactions between the generations that live contemporaneously in a society. Rapid and all-embracing modernization conditions a growing distance between the past and the future. This is paralleled by shrinkage of the knowledge gap between young and old, and of the latter's advisory competence. The trend in the distribution of competencies in society is tending towards reversal. The future is a matter for the younger generations, for those who can train themselves in and through the structures and elements of social change that are relevant for the future, without being weighed down by the ballast of tradition.

What is now presented (by Alanen) as 'generational order' and 'generationing' could gain from adding a Mannheimian dimension – ultimately in the sense of the decentring being sought. The point is to take into consideration, conceptually speaking, how the importance of 'generationing' for the constitution of childhood experience has varied historically. There are childhood experiences that essentially require recourse to the concept of generation, but which do not result from 'generationing' (and 'parenting') as Alanen uses the term. Children are confronted with processes of sociocultural change – also and especially under globalization conditions – that are not filtered in any decisive way by 'generationing'. Mannheim's approach is a way of including them in our analysis. Mannheim affirms the ('practical') importance of the generation concept, 'as soon as the aim is a more precise understanding of the accelerated transformations in the immediate present' (Mannheim, 1965, p. 31f.). The common positioning of cohorts 'in the historical stream of societal occurrences', the bonds forged by a 'shared, fate-like positioning in the nexus of economic power' leads, according to Mannheim, to selective (that is, generational) perception and processing of the world and the environment, fostering a collective tendency towards specific patterns of behaviour, emotions and thought.

Generations comprise cohorts characterized by sociocultural features, by specific '(life) orientations, attitudes and styles', and, last but not least, by the way they handle media, technologies and consumer goods. Media and consumer generations are created to an inflationary extent in the media and in (popular) scientific articles, with new labels being attached with increasing frequency: from the TV generation to the computer, Nintendo and Tamagochi generations to the network and cyber generations. However, it is obvious that the shared ways in which cohorts or age groups handle dominant new media or media products are not sufficient in themselves for labelling that cohort or age groups a generation (in Mannheim's sense). Neither do their members operate as collective actors in the public sphere, nor do they develop a specific (common) generational awareness. It should come as no surprise, then, that in the more seriously-minded analyses of sociocultural change as a process of mediatization, there is no fixation on specific media and innovations within (broadly conceived) media culture. It is evident from key studies how difficult it is to identify new patterns of selection, perception and processing, and to assign these to collectives in accordance with the generational approach. Schulze (1992), Kellner (1997) and Baacke (1999), for example, all assume (despite their other differences) that the relevant changes in the media landscape began as far back as the 1950s and 1960s (ushering in a gradual revolution). Other authors emphasize that the changes that the media and commercial culture have pushed for and borne in recent decades have not led to distinguishable generations, but to the diffuse identity of a new youthfulness. At the same time, fragmentation tendencies have been increasingly witnessed in recent years – processes of differentiation, pluralization and individualization are increasing, while overarching lines of cultural orientation are becoming lost in a myriad of foci (on media and commercial culture phenomena) whose duration and stability are obviously declining to a noticeable degree (see Baacke, 1999, p. 139).

Such assessments suggest that the concept of generation should be used as a search term rather than as an explanatory concept. Research in this field shows that the concept is being replaced by the thesis of a new, diffuse youth. As early as the 1980s, Hans-Jürgen Wirth noted that 'we find ourselves "en route to the adolescent society"' (Wirth, 1984, p. 71). Reference is made in anglophone research to 'extended youth' and 'elastic adolescence' (Mackay, 1997). What these analyses have in common – and this is particularly evident in Wirth's writing – is a dissociation of the concept of adolescence from a particular age-related phase, and its transformation into an attitude, a habitus, a lifestyle. Whatever view one takes of such assessments, there is enough empirical evidence to show that it is worth observing the constructions of meaning on the part of those we call children with reference to the idea that youth culture is not only opened biographically upwards (to adult age groups), but has also expanded downwards (to childhood age groups).

The present differences between generations cannot, for example, be determined by labelling today's students as a media (or consumer) generation. Their parents, too, were children moulded by consumption and media – and today they are living in a mediatized consumer culture. What distinguishes them from their children is the fact that they are (in the position of) parents. Therefore, differences between children and parents result from the primacy of responsibility (parents) on the one hand and the striving for autonomy (children) on the other hand. However, since they are themselves media and consumer children, today's parents increasingly look for media- and consumption-based solutions to their parenting problems. The same argument applies increasingly to teachers.

I shall use the concept of generation as a kind of reference model (heuristically, at most), as a concept with which, in the 1920s, the interdependencies of individual and social development, and the 'formation of consciousness' of birth cohorts in their encounters and conflicts with their respective and specific social condition, were conceived of in new ways. This was a response to the rapid and all-embracing transformation of modern societies, just as the renaissance of the generation concept since the beginning of the 1970s is first of all a response to the increasing acceleration and extension of sociocultural change.

2. Current societal and sociocultural changes

The question is raised as to the societal framework in which a repositioning of children as cultural players is taking place. In current debates, contemporary culture is sometimes defined as consumer culture (compare, among others, Featherstone, 1991; Slater, 1997). The concept of consumer culture is bound up, above all, with the assumption that characteristic social practices and cultural values, ideas, strivings and identities relate more to consumption than to the world of work. There are different ways of reading the genesis and establishment of consumer culture. I will confine myself to a few general remarks on the latest changes, whereby I would like to relate these to the social theory debate on societal transformations. That debate shows agreement among a number of sociologists that a new society is in the making. Manuel Castells, who has produced the most detailed analysis of this new process to date, has specified a set of conditions that must be met before it can make sense to speak of a new society. According to his line of argument, a new society comes into being when a structural transformation can be identified beyond doubt in respect of production, power and experience (Castells, 1998, p. 34). He dates the origins of the new societal formation that he diagnoses and calls the 'network society' to the period between the late 1960s and the mid-1970s.

The term 'post-Fordism' is often used to characterize the economically relevant change during the current period. Broadly speaking, post-Fordism stands for a transition from the mass, conveyer-belt production (of the Fordist era) to a flexible and decentralized organization of work that enabled further technological development. The characteristic features of post-Fordist relations include greater emphasis on 'choice', product differentiation, marketing and design, as well as the construction of consumer groups based on taste and lifestyle criteria. Post-Fordism is also bound up with important changes in international economies. Particularly relevant in this connection are the growth of transnational corporations, the internationalization of labour and financial markets, and the large-scale use of new information and communications technologies.

The post-Fordist paradigm is a controversial one. It is accused, in particular, of economic reductionism, which representatives of the cultural studies school refute with the argument that post-Fordism can equally be used to describe both cultural and economic change. Their interpretation of change implies culturalization, an upward revaluation of the cultural. They no longer view culture as mere superstructure, as a a reflection of other – economic and political – processes, but as something that is just as constitutive for the social world as economic and political factors. They place special emphasis on the cultural loading of production processes and the world of commodities (compare, among others, Slater, 1997). Under post-Fordist conditions, 'cultural technologies' (computers and periphery devices, telephones and so on), 'cultural goods' (games, toys, audiovisual media, sports equipment and so on) and many services are increasingly acquiring a barter value.

Growing dependence on consumption is a push factor driving the efforts of capital to expand existing markets and to create and develop new markets. This means the exportation of consumer capitalism to many third world regions, the commercialization of body, soul and identity by markets for sport, cosmetics and fashion, and the construction of a children's market of enormous scope and volume. In many (cultural) sociological writings, as a result of these trends, consumption is being seen as a factor that shapes lifestyles in the western world to a decisive extent. Continuing from Raymond Williams's definition of culture as a 'way of life', sociologist Steven Miles speaks of consumerism (although without explicit reference to Williams) as a contemporary 'way of life' (Miles, 1998). Difficulties in adapting to these new circumstances are partly due to the fact that the 'consumerism as a way of life' diagnosis means the abandonment of any notion of a consumer sphere that can be clearly demarcated from other phenomena and processes. In particular, the trend cannot be comprehended in terms of zero-sum games. It is rather the case that increase in market value is accompanied by, or runs parallel to the culturalization of products on offer. Consumerism, in the sense used by Miles, is a thoroughly cultural phenomenon. This makes it all the more difficult to identify the consumer. Using a typology generated by Gabriel and Lang, the consumer is identifiable in everyday discourses – those of academics and those of consumer organizations – as a voter, a communicator, a researcher, an identity-seeker, a hedonist or artist, as a victim, rebel and citizen (Gabriel and Lang, 1995).

There is no reason why children, as contemporary consumers, should not be conceived of in equally diversified forms. Consumption has become second nature to children in today's world. The list of buzzwords in support of that proposition extends from computers, fast food, bank accounts and mobile phones, to odd jobs, consumer boycotts, branded clothes, media, merchandising, fashion, separation of waste, surfing on the web, package holidays, shopping, toys, sports gear and equipment, from pocket money to consumer protection centres and advertising. Children of the present are buyers, multipliers, (sometimes) shareholders, very often savers and sometimes debtors. Beyond those roles, they are also addressees of many services – including those of banks and insurance companies. They are involved in a broad diversity of discourses pertaining to these objects, activities and memberships. And they appear more and more often on very different social stages. Their actions can no longer be allocated straightforwardly to the production and consumption side. Today, children's careers as consumers begin as early as babyhood, through contact with parts of an expanded range of media products.

For a couple of decades, the research activities and market strategies of the major corporations have primarily been aimed at making children (as consumers) increasingly independent of their parents and other adults. The dominant two-pronged strategy involves deliberately addressing children as non-adults, while at the same time labelling products and services as belonging outside childhood norms and structures, relating neither to school nor to education (see Hengst, 1996 and 2001). In other words, the media and consumer goods industries pitch their advertising at a non-hierarchical difference between children and adults. This is a decisive aspect of the cultural release of children, which can be observed around the world today.

In the image of childhood entertained by the increasingly reflective industries, the not-yet-adults are replaced by cultural actors whose games, enjoyments and wishes are taken seriously. Through what they stage for young people, the industries in question explore and mobilize the cultural and social capital with which children operate in the less educationally-focused zones of their everyday lives. Of decisive importance in this respect is the dissolution of traditional boundaries. Major proportions of these globalized cultural offerings are appropriated transversely to conventional genre distinctions, and in contexts that are not aligned with the systems of order in the industrial 'labour society' (Hengst, 2001). Another aspect that becomes evident – precisely here – is how little dualistic concepts can help one to understand what is actually going on (given the complex connectivity at work).

What can be observed, as far as the activities of those who engineer the market is concerned, is a dual strategy of adaptation to globalization and individualization processes. That strategy is aimed at segmentation and micromarketing, while also focusing on constant factors and on new commonalities when marketing to target groups. This leads to children's and youth culture(s) being increasingly dissociated from national and socioeconomic structures, to a differentiation of tastes, preferences and practices within a society which at the same time spreads across national and cultural boundaries.

Since the early 1990s, terms such as 'global generation', 'global teenager' and 'global child' have provided a clear indication of the framework within which these shared, common features are being increasingly thought and constructed. The target group of all efforts on the part of those who make the market is a doubly extended peer group. One extension relates to the age span (including its reinterpretation as a youth lifestyle or indeed as youth's attitudes and opinions), the other to the distribution of that peer group over the entire planet.

Globalization and (re)localization – three examples

In the second part of my chapter, I should like to discuss, with three examples, how children interact with globalization processes. I use the term globalization in the sense applied in recent research approaches that always include attempts at relocalization as well. These are dimensioned in very different ways. I would like to give at least some consideration to the latter aspects. It should go without saying nowadays that interactions with cultural options are always acts of hermeneutic appropriation. In the context of globalization, that (also) implies resisting the temptations of a totalizing critique of capitalism, and that caution must be exercised when dealing with ideas such as convergence, standardization and cultural imperialism.

1. Reconquering urban spots and spaces

My first example relates to some significant implications of globalized sport. New cultural spaces have come into being at the interface between sport and pop culture. The scripts of the lifestyle industries have taken up the need for unregimented activities, otherwise suppressed in organized sport, and opened it up for new cultural practices in which an intensive and highly diversified experience of the body is the centre of attention. Liberation from the physical regime of institutionalized sport is a kind of cultural release. It corresponds to a reconquering of the local, the street (see Hengst, 1997b).

The much-bemoaned 'sportification' of childhood, the features of which are isolation, moulding, regimentation and standardizing children's need to move, has resulted in a new observable counter-trend to institutionalized and educationalized sport – with innovative games involving movement of the body, they correspond today to a rediscovery of the street.

The people involved are mainly children and young people, but the trend is also spreading to adult cultures of play and movement. The actors are leaving the special spaces dedicated to sport and are discovering the public domain of the city as stages and activity areas for informal types of movement. Young people and children are making themselves publicly visible, thus opposing the cultural hegemony that adults wield over the street. By using public spaces for body-centred practices involving movement – without adults or even against their opposition – young people and children constitute their own public spheres, spaces that can be experienced directly and physically through joint play, and which cannot be engendered in private (micro)worlds or isolated ghettos. In the cultural spaces that ensue in this process, sport is only one element among many. The trend is going in two directions – on the one hand, sport is being somewhat deinstitutionalized, relative to conventional notions – yet body-shaping practices in popular culture games are becoming more important for recognition and success beyond the (non-serious) leisure domain.

The new (non-traditional) sport scripts were staged according to the pattern of commodity aesthetics. In other words, the sports activities congealed with elements of the individualized consumption and service society. Sport is aestheticized, and enters a symbiosis with the consumption of fashions, media and leisure. Negotiations in this field can always be reconstructed as interactions between global economic strategies and local everyday practice. The media and consumption industries process subcultural scripts to form 'style packages' for a global public. They set age- and generation-specific accents that are modified and rendered more concrete by the children within their respective peer groups (ibid.).

A special type of sociality arises outside or in confrontation with institutional, organized structures – a temporary and focused communitarianism based on a shared praxis, the sensuously perceptible collectivity of the movements, and the resultant conjunctive experience. Fragility in the institutional, organizational context and heavy investment in passion are then the two sides of the one coin. The less strongly that group membership is institutionally safeguarded and provided on a long-term basis, the greater the importance of personal and affective involvement obviously becomes (Alkemeyer, 2003).

The characteristic hybridization of cultures that leads Tomlinson (1999) to the conclusion that all cultures today are 'border cultures' is very well documented by the phenomenon referred to above. The fascination exerted by the new games is largely because they are games with limits and boundaries – with institutional and spatial boundaries, and with the limits of one's own body. In the new public domains for children and youth, there are also signs of societal transformations with more far-reaching implications. Not only do the new games compete with the events for children and young people organized by a wide variety of institutions, but they also shape features of the personality, patterns of community, and skills such as keenness to experiment, willingness to take risks, mobility and flexibility in handling space and time that harmonize very well with the changes occurring in key areas of modern societies, particularly the world of work, but also in private life.

Thomas Alkemeyer, a German sociologist, has pointed out 'that the new games are part of the context of radical changes in society since the 1970s, described in the social sciences with various concepts and slogans such as "de-statification", "deregulation" or "flexibilisation"' (Alkemeyer, 2003, p. 313). For all the important differences between them, these concepts address the same basic development, namely processes of de-institutionalization and hybridization. In different dimensions that can be seen particularly clearly in the new types of games, conventional, structural rules governing work, learning and living are thinned down, made fluid and fractured – in respect of time, space, form and content of activities, social organization, structures of meanings and values and so on. One consequence of this trend is that, although those involved are released from traditional institutions, compulsions and bonds, they can now also rely on external frameworks and structures that provide support.

The impacts of these economic, political and societal changes, here only intimated, extend as far as people's private lives. New demands in respect of 'key qualifications' for life are being imposed on actors in society, in different social milieus and to differing degrees. The changing social conditions under which people work, learn and live are making new requirements on the 'social form of personality'. The most important prefix in the list of competencies now required – long since sloganized in public debate – is 'self': self-control, self-organization, self-management, self-economization, self-sociation, self-motivation . . . and all this in combination with active 'marketing' of the individual and self with strategies for self-presentation and image management. These competencies link up with other reflexive skills, such as self-rationalization, self-cultivation and self-discipline that were already addressed to a degree in the classics of sociological literature.

The terms listed belong to a universe of discourse in which the structural change in society, described in empirical terms, is (ideologically) processed. It responds to that change and drives it forwards by constructing suggestive models of the 'flexible man' in the 'new critique of capitalism' (Sennett, 1998). These models include time- and self-management skills, adaptation to rapidly changing conditions, and project-like collaboration such as the willingness to 'check out' boundary zones of normality and to experiment creatively with what has been learned. The reverse side of an exaggeration of these skills is orientation to rigid norms and institutions that outlast all else and hold out the promise of security.

In many of the new games, the forms of self-organized community and the (neo-liberal) model of the 'self-entrepreneur', which are only gradually being manifested in other social fields, are already being anticipated through play. Although these movement games are welcomed, especially in some areas of sports education, as manifestations of a counter-culture that opposes the standardization and discipline of organized sport, this assessment would have to be revised if it is true that they manifest a historical trend. If that is the case, then the new movement games would be 'structural exercises' in which, separated from the serious areas of life, social forms of community and personality are embodied, staged and performed that correspond to 'post-Fordist' relations rather than those of a normal sports club. This does not mean that these games do not have any potential whatsoever for reflection and change. Every game also means distancing from social practice. As in all games, the new games of movement enable imaginary worlds to be discovered and one can experiment in them, purely for enjoyment's sake, with practices, elements and patterns (of perception) in social reality, without the pressures of circumstances and away from institutions and conventions. The game would then be a practical means of (re)discovering and learning to understand not only social practice but also the story of one's own body (Alkemeyer, 2003, pp. 312ff.).

2. 'Mangiare con calma'

My second example focuses on an interface between the global and the local (or national/regional) that illustrates the conditions under which the local is able to assert itself, as well as how and when ligatures steer the way that options are handled. In the mid-1980s, while reading a study about the leisure preferences and habits of Italian children, I came across an activity that would certainly not be encountered in a similar study in northwestern Europe. 'Mangiare con calma' ('eating in peace') was something that the majority of children in the study cited as a leisure activity that was important to them. Quite obviously we are dealing here with a distinct example of that significant meaning which is so characteristic for the cultural dimension.

Italian eating culture is (has remained) more Italian than German is German, and English is English. The topic of 'global food and local identity' must therefore be discussed differently with reference to Italy than to most other (not only) European countries. Italian food culture is first of all an example of how global advertising strategies are not always successful – here, among children as well as adults. On Italian television, especially on children's TV, US fast food chains try to interest children in their products. However, unlike in Germany, where the success of marketing efforts to pull children into fast-food restaurants is there for all to see, it seems that Italian children are able to resist such enticements. In this connection, I would like to note at least briefly that resistance to globalized, commercialized culture among Italians in general, and Italian children in particular, is not otherwise very marked.

When one knows the importance that is attached to food and eating in Italian families from earliest childhood on, then such resistance is no cause for astonishment. The attitude to food and eating is an expression of local cultural identity that cannot simply be broken down by advertising strategies (Müller, 2000, p. 82f.). This calls for explanation, both in fundamental terms and in respect of children. Firstly, it may be helpful to add a few comments and observations based mainly on the results of an ethnographic study that students from the Department of Cultural Studies at the University of Bremen carried out a few years ago on the Amalfi coast.

In order to provide at least a basic impression of the ligatures impacting in this field, I need to digress a little. In an essay on the social importance of eating in southern Italy, Dieter Richter (1999, p. 155) mentions the saying '*Chi non mangia in compagnia, è ladro o spia*' ('A person who does not eat in company is a thief or a spy'). This means that anyone who has no company while eating is outside the social community and for that reason suspect (see Müller, 2000, p. 45). The saying probably refers to the only guest in a medieval hostel, but it can also sensitise one to the important meaning ascribed to communal eating. Even today, shared meals have this important social meaning, especially for children. Nobody would seriously question the fact that eating is one of the earliest and most important 'socialization mechanisms'. Dieter Richter points out that in the south of Italy it is a commonplace that children 'hear others tell of the merits of the regional cuisine' from a very early age (Richter, 1999, p. 156). The regional specialities, how to prepare them, and their exact ingredients are discussed again and again at the dining table. What everyone who has ever been invited to eat with an Italian family with children knows, and experience during the ethnographic study mentioned above has shown, is that children and young people take part in these conversations and draw attention to the particular ways of preparation they like and which ones they like less, or not at all. The children learn from a very early age to participate in the discourse over food. They know how certain dishes are properly prepared. Having such knowledge and being capable of a differentiated judgement has an 'identity-forming function', according to Frank Müller (2000, p. 45). Individual taste is deemed to be an important element of personality. As Müller observed, people do not have to eat 'what is put on the table' (ibid., p. 46); each has the right not to like certain things.

I think it is this aspect, the recognition of the person by acknowledging his or her own taste that makes Italian food culture (even among children) so resistant to 'global food'. One factor that certainly needs to be taken into consideration is that, given the ease with which pasta dishes can be varied, there is little difficulty in catering to personal preferences. 'An extra sugo with a different ingredient is much quicker to make than, for example, an alternative to a cabbage dish' (ibid.). From a cultural-morphological view, the question as to what came first, the variety of dishes or recognition of a person's individual taste, does not arise. There are a number of noteworthy indicators in the way people conduct their lives that may be useful in a cultural-morphological analysis of Italian eating culture. 'Meal times structure the day. The arrangements that are made are centred, for example, on whether they are *"dopo pranzo"* (after lunch) or *"dopo cena"* (after supper)' (ibid.). However, there are also examples of global and local elements being combined. Shared meals contrast with the permanent presence of the mass media, especially from television sets that are never switched off.

3. Collective identities

My third, final and shortest example concerns traces of globalization in children's concepts of collective identity. In this connection it seems to me to make methodological sense to design research as exploration, so that it is an open process. It is essential to be prepared for experiences and reflections for which conventional questions, concepts and categories are of little use. When complex relationships are assumed, then there is little point in asking direct questions about membership of large-scale groups. A priority, it seems to me, is the identification of (and change in) the criteria by which present-day children gauge membership of a group and by which they distinguish between 'us' and 'them'. There is also the question as to whether a stable, collective 'we' is still present in their heads in the first place.

The results of a study I conducted in the mid-1990s (in Bremen and Manchester) show that it is difficult to gain a picture from survey material of the collective identity concepts of children today, and of the relevance of those concepts (see Hengst, 1997a and 2003). One outcome I find remarkable in the given context, partly because it was explicitly confirmed a couple of years later by a similarly designed study (Holloway and Valentine, 2000), is that, to a large extent, children identify similarities on the basis of western or, perhaps better, of consumption-centred lifestyles and ways of living.

That there is a tendency among children, across national boundaries, to view the members of western nations as similar was suggested by some pertinent studies in the 1960s (see Lambert and Klineberg, 1967). This tendency – towards identification with a western lifestyle – is also confirmed in later studies (see, for example, Werner, 1982). Whereas, in the large-scale study by Lambert and Klineberg, the Japanese were characterized by children from western nations as being different (Lambert and Klineberg, 1967) because the children focused primarily on physical features, western lifestyle as an orientation criterion has led to some children today discovering similarities with the Japanese. This is understandable in the light of Japan's presence on the world markets for media and commercial (children's) culture (from the Japanese cartoon film series of the late 1970s to Nintendo, Pokemon, TV and video equipment, from cameras and cars to computers and periphery). A comparison with the first two post-war decades also supports the assumption that the criteria for similarity applied by children are being increasingly culturalized.

That a major role must be attributed to the media and/or mediatized consumer culture – also and precisely in the context being discussed – is also shown by Holloway and Valentine (2000). They analysed the 'images' that British and New Zealand children had of the people and lifeworlds of one another's nations. This study, too, found that children from high-status, rich societies tend to define each other as similar, as 'us' and not as 'them', playing down or overlooking other features in the process. The study corroborates the influence of television, entertainment media and global consumption cycles on the manner in which children form a picture of everyday life in other societies.

Findings of this kind convey an impression of the dominance of consumer culture in contemporary societies; but that a particular culture dominates in a society is not contingent on all members of that society being able to participate in that culture in the same manner or at an identical level. Indeed, a culture can even be dominant when most people only aspire to participate in it: its dominance can be seen from the extent to which people express, in the concepts and terminology of that culture, their longings, their hopes and their anxieties, in the language that they use to express their reasons, motives and self-esteem, or – as in the context being discussed – their criteria for similarities and differences. There should be no questioning the dominance of consumer culture in present-day society.

There are indications here that globalization – as commodification, as the assertion of 'consumer culture' – not only exerts a critical influence on the structural flexibility of everyday life, but also provides a reference system in which people think, feel and dream. It is present all over the world, familiar to both rich and poor.

The orientations of children are quite obviously the result of (experiential) informal learning. They can sensitise us to the fact that sociocultural change is directly appropriated in many cases – that is, without having to pass the 'generation' filter – into the experience and constructions of meaning on the part of present-day children.

References

Alanen, L. (1994) 'Gender and Generation. Feminism and the "Child Question"', in J. Qvortrup, M. Bardy, G. Sgritta and H. Wintersberger (eds), *Childhood Matters. Social Theory, Practice and Politics*, Aldershot: Avebury, pp. 27–42.

Alanen, L. (2001) 'Explorations in Generational Analysis', in L. Alanen and B. Mayall (eds), *Conceptualizing Child–Adult Relations*, London: RoutledgeFalmer, pp. 11–22.

Alkemeyer, T. (2003) 'Zwischen Verein und Strassenspiel. Der Wandel jugendlicher Sportpraktiken und der Wandel der Gesellschaft', in H. Hengst and H. Kelle (eds), *Kinder, Körper, Identitäten*, Weinheim/München: Juventa, pp. 293–318.

Baacke, D. (1999) 'Die neue Medien-Generation im New Age of visual thinking: Kinder- und Jugendkultur in der Medienkultur', in I. Gogolin and D. Lenzen (eds), *Medien-Generation*, Beiträge zum 16. Kongress der Deutschen Gesellschaft für Erziehungswissenschaft, Opladen: Leske + Budrich, pp. 137–49.

Castells, M. (1998) *The End of the Millennium*, Oxford: Blackwell.

Featherstone, M. (1991) *Consumer Culture and Postmodernism*, London: Sage.

Gabriel, Y. and T. Lang (1995) *The Unmanageable Consumer. Contemporary Consumption and its Fragmentations*, London: Sage.

Giddens, A. (1991) *Modernity and Self-identity. Self and Society in the Late Modern Age*, Cambridge: Polity Press.

Hengst, H. (1996) 'Kinder an die Macht! Der Rückzug des Marktes aus dem Erziehungsprojekt der Moderne', in H. Zeiher, P. Büchner and J. Zinnecker (eds), *Kinder als Aussenseiter? Umbrüche in der gesellschaftlichen Wahrnehmung von Kindern und Kindheit*, Weinheim and München: Juventa, pp. 117–33.

Hengst, H. (1997a) 'Negotiating "Us" and "Them". Children's Constructions of Collective Identity', *Childhood*, 1: 43–62.

Hengst, H. (1997b) 'Reconquering Urban Spots and Spaces? Children's Public(ness) and the Scripts of Media Industries', *Childhood*, 4: 425–44.

Hengst, H. (2001) 'Rethinking the Liquidation of Childhood', in M. du Bois-Reymond, H. Sünker and H.-H. Krüger (eds), *Childhood in Europe. Approaches – Trends – Findings*, New York: Peter Lang, pp. 13–41.

Hengst, H. (2003) 'The Role of Media and Commercial Culture in Children's Experiences of Collective Identities', in B. Mayall and H. Zeiher (eds), *Childhood in Generational Perspective*, London: Institute of Education, pp. 111–32.

Holloway, S.L. and G. Valentine (2000) 'Corked Hats and Coronation Street: British and New Zealand Children's Imaginative Geographies of the Other', *Childhood*, 3: 335–58.

Kellner, D. (1997) 'Jugend im Abenteuer Postmoderne', in Arbeitsgruppe für Symbolische Politik, Kultur und Kommunikation (SpoKK) (eds), *Kursbuch Jugendkultur. Stile, Szenen, Identitäten vor der Jahrtausendwende*, Mannheim: Bollmann, pp. 70–8.

Lambert, W.E. and O. Klineberg (1967) *Children's Views of Foreign Peoples. A Crossnational Study*, New York: Appleton-Century-Crofts.

Mackay, H. (1997) *Baby Boomers, their Parents & their Children*, Sidney: Pan Macmillan.

Mannheim, K. (1965) 'Das Problem der Generationen', in Ludwig von Friedeburg (ed.), *Jugend in der modernen Gesellschaft*, Köln/Berlin: Kiepenheuer & Witsch, pp. 23–48.

Mayall, B. and H. Zeiher (2003) 'Introduction', in B. Mayall and H. Zeiher (eds), *Childhood in Generational Perspective*, London: Institute of Education, pp. 1–24.

Miles, S. (1998) *Consumerism as a Way of Life*, London: Sage.

Müller, F. (2000) 'Soziale Räume der Kinder. Fallstudie am Beispiel eines süditalienischen Dorfes' (unpublished master thesis from Studiengang Kulturwissenschaft der Universität Bremen).

Richter, D. (1999) *Fremdenverkehr und lokale Kultur – kulturanthropologische Untersuchungen an der Küste von Amalfi*, Bremen: kea-edition.

Schulze, G. (1992) *Die Erlebnisgesellschaft. Kultursoziologie der Gegenwart*, Frankfurt, and New York: Campus.

Sennett, R. (1998) *The Corrosion of Character*, New York: W.W. Norton.

Sgritta, G.B. (1994) 'The Generational Division of Welfare: Equity and Conflict', in J. Qvortrup, M. Bardy, G. Sgritta and H. Wintersberger (eds), *Childhood Matters. Social Theory, Practice and Politics*, Aldershot: Avebury, pp. 335–61.

Slater, D. (1997) *Consumer Culture & Modernity*, Cambridge: Polity Press.

Tomlinson, J. (1999) *Globalization and Culture*, Cambridge: Polity Press.

Werner, A. (1982) 'Geopolitisk sosialisering, miljøbakgrunn og fjernsyn. En kryssnasjonal sammenlikning av barn i Norden', *Tidsskrift for samfunnsforskning*, 23, 201–30.

Wirth, H.-J. (1984) *Die Schärfung der Sinne. Jugendprotest als persönliche und kulturelle Chance*, Frankfurt/Main: Syndikat.

Ziehe, T. and Stubenrauch, H. (1982) *Plädoyer für ungewöhnliches Lernen*, Reinbek: Rowohlt.

3
Mediatized Childhoods: Discourses, Dilemmas and Directions

Kirsten Drotner

Introduction

The discursive articulation of contemporary childhood takes many forms, and most of these have some connection to media and ICTs (information and communication technologies): children are variously called a zapper generation, a net generation (Tapscott, 1998, p. 3), a digital generation (Papert, 1996), cyberkids (Holloway and Valentine, 2003) and the thumb tribes (Rheingold, 2002). Both popular and more academic claims are often remarkably polarized into overly optimistic or pessimistic notions about the future of childhood: children are seen as harbingers of innovative competences and social interactions or they are regarded as potential victims of psychological and cultural demise. What these discourses indicate is that contemporary childhood is a mediatized childhood both in an empirical and a discursive sense.

In empirical terms, a complex constellation of mediated forms of communication is constitutive for the formation, expression and development of children's sociocultural practices. For example, 40 per cent of Danish children aged 9–16 use media and ICTs as pretexts for meeting with their friends – the boys playing computer games, the girls often watching films together or listening to music; and these results resonate with trends in many European countries (Drotner, 2001a, p. 164; Livingstone and Bovill, 2001). Thus, it is becoming increasingly difficult to harbour simplified views on children's social networks as prerequisites for and precursors of media and ICT uses.

In discursive terms, the polarized debates on mediatized childhood latch onto familiar patterns when new media technologies are appropriated by society (Jensen, 1990; Drotner, 1999; Critcher, 2003). Since the 1980s, a barrage of new media and ICT has been introduced into the homes of most western societies – satellite television, the VCR (video cassette recorder) and, of course, the computer and the internet with their diverse forms of interaction. In addition, we have witnessed a massive take-up of portable media and more personalized forms of communication – the gameboy, the discman, the MP3 player and, not least, mobile phones that are rapidly turning into PDAs (personal digital assistants, that is, minicomputers). These new gadgets become simple seismographs of complex sociocultural problematics, and they offer welcome projection screens for scenarios of the future. Since the younger generation is among the early adopters of new media and ICTs, the discursive dichotomies framing their introduction play into established discourses on childhood; discourses that since the eighteenth century have been characterized by an opposition between protection and autonomy (Gillis, 1974; James et al., 1998; Qvortrup, 2000).

The empirical mediatization of contemporary childhood is intensively studied by commercial and public players, both of which hold high stakes in the future of childhood, if for different reasons. Notably, large advertising agencies, private service providers and entertainment companies possess the financial muscle to carry out large-scale, longitudinal surveys on children's spending power, lifestyles and media preferences, a strength that few academic institutions can match. Media researchers, on the other hand, while carrying out empirical studies, of course, are rarely in a position to study the entire range of children's media culture, let alone its complex intertwinings. Thus, they often have recourse to theorizing childhood as particular sets of transmuting discourses; or they combine empirical studies of a single type of programme or medium, which is often television, with generalized claims for its implications for childhood at large. The commercial empiricists run the risk of under-theorizing and de-contextualizing their findings; while the more academically-inclined scholars easily mistake a single perspective for the entire picture.

What I propose to do in the following is to identify and analyse two major discursive approaches to mediatized childhood, namely the approaches that tie in with the respective claims that children live in a knowledge society and in an entertainment society. I compare these discourses with key empirical findings in the academic literature on (primarily European) children's media and ICT uses in an attempt to flag up possible fissures and contradictions for further reflection. On that basis I propose the concept of a complex society as an inclusive term whose appropriation allows more nuanced studies of mediatized childhood today. Finally, I sketch some of the scientific implications that such studies have for the future study of childhood more generally.

The distinction drawn below between discursive and empirical dimensions of reality is, of course, an analytical one. Public discourses, be they professional or popular, are selective articulations of sociocultural processes and practices which in turn the discourses feed into and help frame. What follows, then, is not a realist portrayal of mediatized childhood as if this can be studied as an empirical phenomenon unmarked by the role played by language in human knowledge acquisition. Nor is it a purely constructionist discourse analysis that tends to conflate ontological and epistemological levels of reality. Rather, the analytical position taken below is in line with what has been termed 'discursive realism' and which is defined as follows:

> The essence of discursive realism consists in the belief that there is a social reality that exists independently of language, but our only access to knowledge about this reality goes through language and other sign systems. This position is in contrast to both the empiricist belief in our ability to acquire true knowledge about a reality unaffected by the human understanding of it, and to the interpretativist belief that reality *is* our discursive understanding of this reality.
>
> (Schrøder et al., 2003, p. 45)

Such a position resonates well with Manuel Castells's remark that 'all realities are communicated through symbols . . . In a sense, all reality is virtually perceived' (Castells, 1996, p. 373). That all reality, as we understand it, is semiotically mediated, as it were, is a particular reminder to many scholars of children's culture who often set up an untenable distinction between direct, unmediated experience of interpersonal dialogues vis-à-vis symbolically mediated experience of, for example, computer gaming or television viewing.

First claim: children live in a knowledge society

Over the last two decades, contemporary societies have variously been defined as, among others, information societies, learning societies, knowledge societies and network societies (Masuda, 1980; Husén, 1986; Stehr, 1994; Castells, 1996). Irrespective of scientific traditions, these definitions focus on ICTs as the crucial technological preconditions for a knowledge production that can secure economic development and hence societal survival. In tandem with these theoretical deliberations, and indicative of their surmised implications, have been intensive economic, technological and political initiatives and interventions on a national as well as an international scale to help further what is perceived as a massive transformation from an industrial society to a society based on the digital production, processing and communication of signs – be they figures, text or images.

The discourse of the knowledge society, to pick one of the most widely used current terms, has had radical implications for the approach to childhood. Since children are tomorrow's wage-earners and citizens, some of the most hotly debated issues have centred on the definition of the skills that are necessary to carry out those future functions: do children need specific ICT literacies that are different from those trained through print media such as the book? Must schools engender new forms of cooperation through virtual networks and distance learning? What are the challenges posed to adults in general, and teachers in particular, when new modes of learning and forms of organization are required? The answers to questions such as these have mostly been provided by public bodies that, on a national scale, are often ministries of education and ministries of trade and industry; while on a trans-national scale, such as in the European Union, huge investments are made in studies of online and technology-enhanced education as new means of learning.

D. R. Garrison and Terry Anderson cogently sum up the rationale of online learning, or e-learning, when they state that 'for e-learning to have a significant place in education it must prove that it is more than a medium to conveniently access content. [It is] the context and process of e-learning that makes it unique' (Garrison and Anderson, 2003, p. 4). This statement is congruent with most online learning efforts that focus on the ways in which asynchronous, interactive and virtual learning environments may be formed as means of learning any subject. The computer and the internet (and to a lesser extent PDAs) are regarded as the technological motors for the development of new competences that focus on the rational elements of ICT uses.

The discourse of the knowledge society positions children in a key role both as objects of (new forms of) formal training, namely online learning, and as subjects of new sets of competences, namely digital or ICT literacies, that are supposed to result from these new forms of training. The two dimensions are discursively conflated when proponents stress the ways in which individual learners become empowered by the new learning modes, being in charge of the pace, place and practices of their own learning process. The empowerment-through-individualization claim is closely bound up with a related discourse, vigilantly put forward by commercial ICT industries, that ICTs are innovative 'lean-forward' technologies whose interactive properties enable active engagement, unlike old, 'lean-back' media such as television that position viewers as passive consumers. Such technological oppositions are routinely mapped onto another familiar notion about contemporary children, namely that they form a media-savvy generation outstripping their parents, and their teachers, in digital literacy. Thus, an ambiguous tension is set up between a range of oppositions: old and new media technologies, old and new literacies, old and young people. The overall result is a strong image of the empowered child masterminding the intricacies of new technology and transforming the overflow of information into rational, and useful, forms of knowledge that are of fundamental importance to societal advancement. The discursive dimensions of the knowledge society in terms of childhood are summarized in Table 3.1.

The discourse on the knowledge society is one of the most distinctive in the ongoing debates about contemporary, and by implication, future childhood. While it is obvious that the discursive definition of children as empowered individuals in their own right leaves room for adult recognition of children's resources and self-defined activities, it is equally evident that

Table 3.1: The discursive dimensions of the knowledge society in terms of childhood

Definition of society	Focus on economy
Definition of individual	Focus on rationality
Definition of childhood	Focus on empowerment
Definition of media	Focus on ICTs as distinctive technologies
Definition of learning	Focus on new technologies as means of learning
Definition of education	Focus on competences

this definition easily feeds into wider neo-liberalist trends that focus on individual rights rather than on collective responsibilities. The strong position of the knowledge society discourse is reinforced by its novelty both in terms of the very visible technologies around which it revolves and in terms of its opposition to a much older and persistent discourse on childhood, namely that of the vulnerable child.

Second claim: children live in an entertainment society

The enormous expansion of media and ICTs has been accompanied by an unrivalled intrusion of these technologies into nearly all spatial and temporal aspects of children's everyday lives. In the (post)industrialized parts of the world, the walkman, the discman and the photo-phone have been added to an already full menu of media which before consisted of more domestic and more stable media – television and radio, the computer and print media. Moreover, some of these new technologies are objects of heavy investments by families with children and illuminate the fact that even young children are fairly independent consumers and objects of marketing efforts. To this economic viability may be added that some media and ICTs act as catalysts to children's visible engagements in public. This is particularly evident with the mobile phone which operates as a lifeline between children and their parents, thereby extending even young children's public 'range' in malls and sports clubs, for example (Drotner, in press). Thus, media and ICTs are very visible properties of modern childhood, not only at school, but equally, and even more so, in children's leisure time spent with family and friends.

The expansion, immersion and visibility of media and ICTs into everyday life over the last two decades have spurred discourses that focus on the sociocultural implications of this development. Among the best-known proponents of this set of discourses is the US critic Neill Postman whose most popular books are *The Disappearance of Childhood* (Postman, 1982) and *Amusing Ourselves to Death* (Postman, 1985). The titles indicate the close connection he makes between social diagnosis and childhood definitions. According to Postman 'the decline of a print-based epistemology and the accompanying rise of a television-based epistemology has had grave consequences for public life . . . Entertainment is the supra-ideology of all discourse on television' (Postman 1985, pp. 24, 87). Society is described as over-flowing with all sorts of superficial entertainment that pervades children's lives and leaves little or no room for introspection and depth, properties that are perceived as being essential for healthy child development. Others speak with less cultural pessimism about the dream society (Jensen, 2001) and the sociable society (Hjarvard, 2003). All focus on a wide range of cultural, and mediatized, expressions as important preconditions of contemporary society, and all speak against the technological and rational logic underpinning the discourse of the knowledge society. It is argued that, judged by the time and money users spend on media contents, television viewing, computer gaming and listening to music on the radio or MP3 player are much more important activities than are rational information processing and intentional knowledge acquisition. Taken together, these and other publications lay claim to the notion that we live in an entertainment society.

The discourse of the entertainment society, particularly in its more cultural-pessimist versions, positions children in a precarious role as both subjects of public commitment and objects of professional care. Unlike the individualist focus of the knowledge society discourse, adherents of the entertainment discourse acknowledge societal responsibility for the social and cultural ramifications of childhood; as such, many are found to support welfarist rather than neo-liberalist policies. In Europe, this protectionist view of children is often bound up with a protectionist view of European culture as a set of superior values that is in danger of being devoured by US fast-food entertainment and trash media output (Kroes, 1996). US television series and computer games and Hollywood fiction films are rapidly becoming global norms, it is argued, that dumb down the lofty values and established cultural traditions underpinning old Europe. In wider terms, this discourse of national dichotomies feeds into a more general and pervasive notion of cultural hierarchies. According to this notion, print culture is at the pinnacle of a given nation's or individual's cultural resources, while visual culture in all its diversity ranks at the bottom, particularly when the output is fiction with the strong emotional appeal in which Hollywood excels.

The perceived threats to established values, print media and children concoct a powerful cocktail that it takes potent measures to countervene. The educational system, being one of the strongest pillars of the welfare state, offers a natural bulwark against the cultural attacks of Americanized leisure. It is in light of this mode of thinking that we may understand recurrent debates on curricular core contents, the search for essential national values and the mobilization of reading as the basis of learning. According to the entertainment discourse, children are defined not merely as present consumers or as future wage-earners in need of adequate competences, but rather as future citizens in need of proper norms and judgements of taste.

Table 3.2: The discursive dimensions of the entertainment society in terms of childhood

Definition of society	Focus on culture (hierarchy)
Definition of individual	Focus on emotionality
Definition of childhood	Focus on protection
Definition of media	Focus on print media as cultural norm
Definition of learning	Focus on print media as ends of learning
Definition of education	Focus on character formation as particular (national) norms and values

Historians of childhood will easily recognize how this definition latches onto romantic notions of the innocent child and to German idealism of the late seventeenth century with its Enlightenment focus on *Bildung*, or general character formation. What is striking, however, is that the Enlightenment ideals of universality (*general* character formation) are currently being transformed into ideals of particularism (*national* character formation). The discursive dimensions of the entertainment society in terms of childhood are summarized in Table 3.2.

As is evident, the discourse of the knowledge society and the discourse of the entertainment society in fundamental ways act as oppositions defining one another. But they equally share crucial characteristics. Most importantly, both are normative discourses that speak to particular tensions and fissures in contemporary childhood and in society at large. Moreover, both are selective discourses, focusing on aspects that operate as self-fulfilling prophesies. As such, both construct what Roland Barthes called a 'reality effect': we begin to understand and articulate our experiences and activities within their discursive ramifications. In that sense, and with reference to the introductory remarks to this chapter, it may be argued that we are all discursive realists. Still, precisely because of the selective character of the two discourses, they also generate contradictions and ambiguities that make them open for further inspection. Let us take a look at some important trends in European children's media uses to gauge how these tensions are played out in contemporary childhood.

Frameworks of the future: convergence and globalization

That children when they leave school have spent more time on media than in the classroom is a much-tooted fact that is often claimed as a primary reason for professionals to harbour an interest in children's media uses. However, two recent trends serve to reframe the justifications of that 'quantitative' interest, namely media convergence and media globalization. Taken together, these trends point to the fundamental ways in which mediatized forms of communication have become constitutive to modern childhood both seen from the individual child's point of view and from a societal point of view. Thus, our justification for studying children's media uses are moving towards what may be termed a more 'qualitative' interest in this constitutive domain.

We are currently witnessing a gradual merging of our television sets and radios, our print media, mobile phones, computers and the internet. This convergence between media, telecommunication and ICTs is enabled by the technological possibilities of digitizing all signs – text, sound, live and still images – and combining all of these signs through the computer. Technological media convergence has been accompanied by financial convergence in the form of transborder mergers and acquisitions between large news corporations, internet providers, broadcasters and entertainment industries, of which the Time/Warner fusion in 2000 is a prime example.

Taken together, technological and financial convergence serve to blur existing boundaries between what is often named 'new' and 'old' media. Thus, ICTs, or new media, no longer develop in isolation from old media such as television, newspapers or radio. Hence, it becomes increasingly untenable to analyse and understand ICTs as distinct phenomena. Moreover, the rapid domestication of these technologies in many parts of the world serves to shift people's interest from the new gadgets themselves onto their function, and this is particularly true of children. For example, they rarely buy a new mobile phone because of a more advanced technology, but because they want to communicate in new ways, at different times and locales (Drotner, in press; Ling, 2004). Hence, in addition to a more holistic approach to the study of new and old media, it becomes increasingly important to focus such studies on contents, forms of expressions and users' appropriations, rather than on technological developments as such. And these aspects may illuminate how technological and economic convergence develops in tandem with distinct divergences of content production and uses.

Together with convergence, the last two decades have seen an intensified globalization of media and ICT production, distribution, formats and applications. It is commonly agreed that today media are constitutive of cultural globalization: the accelerated global flows of signs and cultural commodities by communication technologies serve to increase what John Tomlinson calls 'complex connectivity' (Tomlinson, 1999, p. 2), that is, global, or transnational, media accentuate the interconnectedness of distinct cultures and modes of existence. So far, a top-down perspective on globalization has prevailed; a perspective that focuses upon the economic, technological, political and legal aspects of this complex connectivity. Studying children's uses of media, genres and formats that traverse geographical and temporal boundaries is one way of approaching media globalization from a bottom-up perspective, which may serve to substantiate and nuance the often very generalized top-down theories about cultural globalization, theories that also tend to be formulated as dichotomies between national and transnational (that is, US) culture; between homogenization and heterogenization.

Convergence and divergence of children's media uses

In the late 1990s, several large studies were conducted on children's appropriations of the emerging media landscape. Not surprisingly, these studies focused on North America and Europe, continents with a long-term interest in children and media and a rapid, if uneven, take-up of new media. In the US, a major investigation was made of the full range of media uses among two nationally representative samples of children aged 2–18 (Roberts et al., 1999). Also, an independent report was issued on current research into children's new media uses (Wartella et al., 2000). In Europe, a comprehensive, academic study was conducted in the late 1990s (*European Journal of Communication*, 1998; *Reseaux*, 1999; Livingstone and Bovill, 2001). It involved informants aged 6–16 in twelve countries and investigated interactions between uses of new and old media through a mixture of quantitative and qualitative methodologies. Both home and school uses were included. Several of the overall results demonstrate that the evidence to support the main contentions found in the discourses of both the knowledge society and the entertainment society remains fairly thin on the ground.

First, the discourse of the knowledge society is challenged by both the European and US studies, which clearly demonstrate that contemporary children are what may be termed a multimedia generation in the sense that most of them apply a variety of media and modes of address. Only about 2 per cent are PC specialists (Johnsson-Smaragdi, 2001). Even if this percentage has grown since the data was collected, the results go to demonstrate that in terms of time use, TV is still the primary medium; there is a close fit between access and use, and as such TV may be termed the most democratic medium. New media do not displace old, but are integrated into existing media uses. The young already tackle the beginnings of media convergence through their mundane day-to-day combinations of and interactions with a multimedia environment of new and old media, an environment in which choices and combinations are made on the basis of social and textual relevance, not the media applied.

Second, the European study indicates that children s media uses in their leisure time are more diverse and more advanced than are their media uses in school. This challenges the discourse of the knowledge society as well as the entertainment society both of which make a clearcut distinction between proper learning at school and more general formation of experience outside the classroom. For example, while European children use school computers mainly for information processing, composition and arithmetic, at home a good number of them make their own homepages, edit music and images and a few boys do some programming (Drotner, 2001a). Through these activities, children train what we may term informal media competences, that is intuitive and personal knowledge about the ways in which media 'work' both in a technical sense (this applies mostly to boys) and in more substantive and aesthetic senses. For example, 11-year-old Tasha tells about one of her favourite animation films *Toy Story* in the following manner:

Tasha: I like it a lot that you, yourself, are a kind of toy; you look at it from the ground many times, and that I really like.
Interviewer: Yes,
Tasha: That you enter the movie sometimes. That you, yourself, are there running along the characters and so on, this is what I like a lot.
(Drotner, 2003, p. 84)

Tasha's repeated viewing of the Disney video has made her aware of what in professional terms is called subjective camera. Of course she does not know the word, but she recognizes the substance of the concept when she sees it. This attentiveness is a good example of informal media learning – that children learn something in their leisure time, when they least expect it. Other examples of informal media learning include aesthetic comparisons of, for example, the narrative differences between computer game and film versions of the same format.

Third, the large-scale studies offer no substantiation of the widespread claim that the young make up a media-wise generation which knows what there is to know about media and ICTs and therefore is beyond the need for public regulation and adult control. Informal learning does not equal competence in a more formal sense. As David Buckingham cogently stresses we must be careful to distinguish between children's active media engagement and technical know-how and their media competences, or discerning media literacy (Buckingham, 1998). As do all other forms of learning, media competence involves systematic training and a development of tools for analysis, expression and evaluation. Still, the documentation in the large-scale studies that many children possess intuitive knowledge about a range of media and ICT aspects in itself mobilizes a particular tension in current debates about future competence development.

Fourth, several studies indicate children's widespread, if uneven, content production through media and ICTs (for example, Sefton-Green, 1999; Drotner, 2001a; Drotner, 2003). The opportunities created by interactive media such as the internet and mobile (photo-)phones to produce, for example, home pages, to take and edit images or participate in blogs, chats and short messaging imply a blurring of boundaries between content production and reception, and hence between professional and lay (or mass) spheres of mediatization. Naturally, few of today's children are tomorrow's film-makers or internet designers. But children's wider options to experiment with the expressive dimensions of media content open up new vistas for creating media competences and, perhaps, even a possibility of demystifying some production processes.

Crucially, children's expressive experiences are important levers for citizenship in an age when the public sphere is thoroughly mediatized (Dahlgren, 1995). More than in previous generations, all citizens' options for and abilities to handle a variety of media are crucial to their democratic engagement and participation. What may be a new tenet in contemporary childhood is that children in many parts of the world now have the options to enter the public sphere through a variety of interactive media. Even the many children around the world who lack those options are often aware of the possibilities that they seem to miss. This awareness is a result of media globalization which serves to accentuate the interconnectedness of distinct cultures and modes of existence.

Global and local dimensions of children's media uses

The European study indicates how this interconnectedness works in contemporary childhood. Most importantly, the results demonstrate that through the juxtaposition of cultural difference, global media constantly evoke for young users what Anthony Giddens describes as 'absent others' (Giddens, 1990, pp. 18–21). At a very basic level, media globalization both enforces and facilitates our encounters with symbolic expressions of otherness. In so doing, media globalization serves to intensify users' recognition of and reflection on local differences precisely because they are identified in relation to an understanding of the world as a 'single place' (see Robertson, 1992, p. 6). The mediatized evocation of absent others offers a fundamental challenge to a central tenet in the discourse of the entertainment society, namely its focus on character formation through national print culture, that is, book fiction and, to a lesser degree, national newspapers.

First, informants in the European study generally recognize and remark on visual signs of difference (for example, different street signs, decor and dress, labels on food cans). But it is one thing to note that children recognize traits of difference, what they make of these traits is another matter. Here, the results show that European children do not necessarily consider that domestic media products belong to the domain of the known while foreign media products belong to domains of the unknown (Drotner, 2001b).

For many youngsters, hugely popular TV series such as *Ally McBeal* or *Friends*, may be readily incorporated into a known everyday world: their genre concepts are so conventional as to be perceived as generic. And their conflicts are immediately recognizable. What Ien Ang has termed the emotional realism of soaps (Ang, 1985) makes the seemingly exotic world of Australian beaches and American suburbs into a domestic norm. Conversely, domestically produced narratives demonstrating unusual formal traits or focusing upon characters and narrative modes not normally depicted in the media may seem more outlandish and strange to young audiences than a soap opera produced abroad. Results such as these should caution against making simple analogies between domestic culture as a homogeneous and known domain of experience that may be neatly contrasted to foreign culture as an equally homogeneous unknown whose exoticism is defined and delimited through its complete difference from the domestic. The comparative, European study shows that mediated globalization may be as much about exoticizing the seemingly well known as about acculturation to the seemingly foreign.

So far, theories of otherness in media and cultural studies have focused primarily upon what is termed diaspora cultures, that is distinct immigrant cultures and their symbolic and material collisions and collusions with the cultures they encounter. In the words of British media ethnographer Marie Gillespie these encounters of subaltern cultures nurture 'the strategy of familiarising one's "otherness" in terms of other "others"' (Gillespie, 1995, p. 5). The results of the European comparative study endorse such strategies. But it equally highlights the necessity to complement the notion of diaspora with conceptualizations of what, for want of a better term, I will call a *mundane character formation of othernesses*, that is, the often imperceptible processes of negotiating signs of otherness within seemingly homogeneous cultures. Such a character formation of otherness offers a reworking of the normative concept of *Bildung* that attunes it to the demands and possibilities of mediatized globalization.

Second, both the US and European studies are in line with earlier findings that children, like many adults, favour fiction over fact. These findings substantiate the claim made in the entertainment discourse that people do, indeed, prefer emotional engagement over intellectual acumen. Still, the results challenge the discursive distinctions made between global (that is, US) and local (that is, national) forms of expression. Remembering that TV is the dominant medium in terms of time use, let us take a closer look at the origins of European children's favourite TV programmes (Table 3.3).

In Denmark, Finland, Israel and Switzerland a solid majority of informants prefer TV programmes of foreign origin. These are all small countries and two of them, Israel and Switzerland, comprise quite separate language communities. And, unlike large countries, small countries have difficulties allowing for, or prioritizing, a varied domestic output of programmes that appeal to the young of both genders and various ages and ethnicities. Unlike the claim made by proponents of the entertainment discourse that children take mostly to Hollywood and thus become Americanized, the European study demonstrates that young informants prefer foreign fiction, not because it is foreign, but because it appeals in style and content.

Table 3.3: Origin of six- to sixteen-year-old Europeans' favourite TV programmes (%)

		CH	DE	DK	ES	FI	GB	IL	SE
6–7 years	National	43	54	46	29	46	14	–	52
	International	NA	58	54	46	71	54	86	48
9–10 years	National	10	55	42	66	29	57	59	63
	International	90	45	58	35	72	43	41	37
12–13 years	National	7	66	27	72	25	61	30	52
	International	94	34	73	28	75	39	70	48
15–16 years	National	7	69	30	75	22	59	19	46
	International	93	31	70	25	78	41	81	54
Average	National	8	60	36	68	26	57	29	53
	International	92	40	64	32	74	43	71	47

Source: Drotner (2001b, p. 290).

Foreign fiction is also primarily commercial fiction. Conversely, factual genres such as news and documentaries are still a mainstay of national, public-service media. Thus, young European media users tend to develop a chain of associations in which the concept of media globalization is linked to fiction, which is perceived as entertaining and engaging while the concept of public-service media is linked to the nation and to boring but necessary facts. These results serve to nuance the entertainment discourse. A major challenge in the general character formation of the young may be not to secure their reading of approved national fiction, so much as to safeguard their engagement with a diversity of mediatized expressions.

Discursive challenges: the complex society

As should be evident from the above, the respective discourses of the knowledge society and the entertainment society provide us with selective bases for understanding contemporary relations between childhood and mediatized culture. As we have seen, children's media and ICT uses are at once more diverse, advanced and nuanced than the discourses would lead us to believe. In order to analyse and evaluate these uses, we need a more holistic discursive framework. Such a framework may be found with social theorists such as Anthony Giddens (1990) or Ulrich Beck (1997) who focus on teasing out the complexities of modernity. Others speak about late modernity (Fornäs, 1995) and the hypercomplex society (Qvortrup, 2003). Irrespective of important theoretical differences, a key element in these authors' theoretical frameworks is an acknowledgement that the empirical complexity of contemporary societies must be matched by a similar theoretical complexity. The term 'complex society' therefore seems an apt choice if we wish to grasp this theoretical commonality. Moreover, the authors all acknowledge that mediatized forms of communication are transformative social resources, not merely cultural embellishments on social and economic phenomena (Fornäs and Qvortrup most directly), and they do not restrict their analyses to either 'new' ICTs or 'old' mass media.

Such an approach has decisive consequences for the ways in which child-hood is defined and delimited. In a complex society, people's ability to handle signs is a fundamental prerequisite for their economic, social and cultural engagement; and ever more sign systems are mediatized. Thus, in a societal perspective a fundamental challenge is to train what may be termed children's semiotic abilities so that the young may function as full members of society. Moreover, when complex societies rest on democratic principles such training must involve an inclusive perspective of engaging children not merely as future wage-earners, citizens and consumers, but equally as present stakeholders in society.

That this democratic perspective speaks to a particular set of tensions in the other two discourses that we have identified is illuminated with parti-cular clarity in the British policy debates about media literacy. While this concept has a long discursive tradition within education (Hobbs, 1998), it moved toward the centre of political debate in Britain when a new media regulator, Ofcom, in 2003 was given a remit under a new communications act to promote media literacy to the population at large. One year later, Ofcom published its strategy and priorities in this respect and defined media literacy as:

> a range of skills including the ability to access, analyse, evaluate and produce communications in a variety of forms . . . With these skills people will be able to exercise greater choice and be able to better protect themselves and their families from harmful or offensive materials.
>
> (Ofcom, 2004, p. 4)

This definition takes an inclusive approach to media and ICTs that accords well with the existing technological and economic moves towards conver-gence and with the regulator's comprehensive responsibilities across televi-sion, radio, telecommunications and wireless communications services. Speaking of social members as 'citizen-consumers', the regulator at one and the same time addresses the discourse of the knowledge society ('exercise greater choice') and the entertainment society ('protect themselves and their families'), but without acknowledging the inherent contradictions between the two discourses.

That media literacy, at least in some countries, is moving from the spe-cialist field of education into the wider field of policy-making is indicative of the ways in which mediatized learning and competences hold crucial stakes in the development of contemporary societies. The term literacy denotes the specification of competences as having to do with mediated forms of communication. Viewed from the perspective of a complex society, it becomes clear that these competences encompass both the more specific abilities flagged up by the discourse of the knowledge society and the more general character formation that is highlighted in the discourse of the entertainment society. As evidenced by the trends in media uses described above, contemporary children are well on the way to training both. Navigating the complexities of old and new media have become a primary means for children of knowing about themselves, interacting with others and appropriating the world around them. Through this navigation children gain competences, mostly of an informal kind, that are of fundamental importance for the development of media literacy both in its specific sense of accessing, analysing and producing mediatized forms of communication and in the wider sense of acquiring what I have termed a mundane character formation of otherness.

Comparing the discursive dimensions of the complex society in terms of childhood with those of the knowledge society and the entertainment society we may gauge the challenges posed to the future of childhood learning and literacy (see Table 3.4).

As is seen in Table 3.4, the discourse of the complex society takes a deliberative position: ambiguities and tensions must both be acknowledged and

Table 3.4: The discursive dimensions of the complex society in terms of childhood

	Knowledge society	**Entertainment society**	**Complex society**
Definition of society	Focus on economy	Focus on culture (hierarchy)	Focus on interaction between sites
Definition of individual	Focus on rationality	Focus on emotionality	Focus on rationality, emotionality and their intersections
Definition of childhood	Focus on empowerment	Focus on protection	Focus on specific balancing of empowerment and protection
Definition of media	Focus on ICTs as distinctive technologies	Focus on print media as cultural norm	Focus on new and old media as forms of communication
Definition of learning	Focus on new technologies as means of learning	Focus on print media as ends of learning	Focus on means and ends of learning
Definition of education	Focus on competences	Focus on character formation as particular (national) norms and values	Focus on specific competences and general character formation

handled through concrete discussions and actions. Perhaps the most important professional challenge to face in terms of handling mediatized childhood in the future rests on acknowledging its fundamental structural
paradox: the informal learning processes of children's leisure are crucial to
the development of semiotic competences that they need in a complex
society, while at the same time the educational systems neglect or limit the
basis on which these informal learning processes may be transformed into
formal competences through joint learning. The educational systems around
the world still rest on the traditions of a print culture which, at best, offers
pupils selective literacies and learning resources (Luke, 1989; Bentley, 1998;
Tyner, 1998). Through an intensified dialogue with public and commercial
stakeholders in the communications industry, Ofcom and others may
advance people's informed media choices in accessing media and ICTs. But
the results will be limited as long as people do not possess adequate tools
for transforming such choices into relevant resources for social action. The
discrepancy between access and appropriation seems to be most striking in
relation to new media such as the internet, as is evidenced in recent studies
on domestic uses of online forms of communication (Livingstone and
Bober, 2004).

The future of studying mediatized childhood

Studying mediatized childhood from the perspective of a complex society
poses particular problems both to media and childhood studies. For media
scholars, their first challenge is to face the trend towards technological convergence of ICTs and mass media. This calls for an intensified cooperation
between scholars from the arts (including history, design, literary studies),
the social sciences (including anthropology, economy) and the natural and
technical sciences (including soft engineering and interaction design). All of
these hold decisive stakes in the development of media convergence but
none of them hold the key to a full understanding of its implications.
Second, the development of technological and economic convergence in
tandem with social and cultural forms of divergence makes it imminently
important for media scholars to develop a joint analytical focus that encompasses a media as well as a user perspective (Drotner, 2000). If we focus only
on the media perspective we may risk overemphasizing the convergent
aspects involved in multimediated communication (the computer as a
super-medium combining all other mediated forms). Conversely, if we focus
on the user perspective we may see only social and cultural divides. What
we need to do is to apply a joint perspective on the entire media landscape
and the intricate interstices between different formats, genres, appropriations and institutions. Because it is often at the intersections that innovation germinates. Third, increasing globalization of media production and
reception calls for comparative studies across sites and settings, the results

of which may help caution us against inflated claims on the generality of local findings. It is obvious that the scientific appropriation of a joint perspective and of comparative studies goes well beyond the scope of individual scholarly attention, even if individual researchers can be attentive to their necessity. In order to unfold these perspectives we need systematic international cooperation that reaches well beyond occasional conferences and workshops.

For childhood scholars, most of whom are not media scholars, the demands made by studying mediatized childhood in a complex society are no less daunting. The first, and perhaps the most decisive, challenge is to acknowledge that a media perspective is at all relevant to childhood studies which have primarily been defined by sociologists and historians – if rarely in cooperation. To meet this challenge implies acknowledging the constitutive character of media and ICTs in contemporary childhood. Indicative of the task ahead is William Corsaro's standard work *The Sociology of Childhood* (Corsaro, 1997); taking a synchronic approach to the study of childhood, of its 304 pages three touch on media (television and books). Conversely, historians of childhood, taking a diachronic approach to childhood, will describe the importance of book reading, often noting its affiliation to adult inculcation of discipline and character building. But few define books as media whose production and distribution is as commercial as comics and newspapers; and no one, to my knowledge, makes sustained efforts in analysing the implications such insights would have for an understanding of children as consumers, even, for example, in the nineteenth century. Thus, Colin Heywood's *A History of Childhood* (Heywood, 2001) devotes seven pages out of 230 to an analysis of wet-nursing and two pages to children's books – no mention of more popular fare such as comics and magazines.

This omission points to the second challenge that childhood scholars face if they want to study mediatized childhood in a complex society, namely the integration of diachronic and synchronic perspectives. While this challenge applies more generally to childhood studies, perhaps a focus on mediatization flags up the need for integrative approaches. This is because children have often constituted pioneer media audiences – and such a role has been, in many cases, very visible to the public eye. Thus, they were among the earliest and most avid consumers and readers of so-called 'penny dreadfuls' (Drotner, 1988), and in Britain after World War I juveniles made up about 30 per cent of the cinema audiences (Richards, 1984). Such mediatized processes beg immediate questions concerning continuities and differences in children's culture that can most usefully be studied by a combination of synchronic and diachronic approaches. For example, the very pioneering status of children as media audiences is open to analysis: does this persistent position hide differences in terms of gender, power relations and types of media and contents? The answers to this question offer a fundamental starting point for a reasoned assessment of the many claims, mentioned in the introduction to this chapter, that children's relations to media are currently undergoing a qualitative change.

Both media and childhood scholars, then, need to develop more integrative research perspectives and more sustained and systematic forms of co-operation in order to advance childhood studies for the twenty-first century. In my own experience, such approaches harbour an extra asset in that they facilitate the formation of an epistemology which transcends the two main epistemological positions that have framed the study of childhood, namely that of childhood innocence and childhood competence. As we have seen in this chapter, proponents of childhood innocence will position themselves as responsible adults at a secure distance from their objects of attention and in control of defining what children need protection from. Conversely, many advocates of childhood competence – often in explicit reaction to the former tradition – will take the insider's empathic position and trust children's abilities of self-regulation. In each case, the result is a partial picture that may be increasingly untenable for interpreting childhood in complex societies. As researchers, we may wish to escape each of these positions, but we cannot escape positions of power dependent on age vis-à-vis children; and our studies will always reveal particular priorities and positions of address. The scientific dialogues that are shaped through actual cooperation or at least committed interest in different research traditions and approaches, by sharpening our professional reflexivity, may help develop a more integrative epistemology of empathic understanding and distanced evaluation whether speaking about, for or with children.

References

Ang, I. (1985) *Watching Dallas: Soap Opera and the Melodramatic Imagination*, London: Methuen.

Beck, U. (1997) *Risk Society: Towards a New Modernity*, London: Sage.

Bentley, T. (1998) *Learning beyond the Classroom*, London: Routledge.

Buckingham, D. (1998) 'Introduction: Fantasies of Empowerment? Radical Pedagogy and Popular Culture', in D. Buckingham, *Teaching Popular Culture: beyond Radical Pedagogy*, London: UCL Press, pp. 1–17.

Castells, M. (1996) *The Rise of the Network Society. Vol. 1: The Information Age: Economy, Society and Culture*, Oxford: Blackwell.

Corsaro, W.A. (1997) *The Sociology of Childhood*, Thousands Oaks, CA: Pine Forge Press.

Critcher, Ch. (2003) *Moral Panics and the Media*, Buckingham: Open University Press.

Dahlgren, P. (1995) *Television and the Public Sphere: Citizenship, Democracy and the Media*, London: Sage.

Drotner, K. (1988) *English Children and their Magazines, 1751–1945*, rev. edn, New Haven: Yale University Press.

Drotner, K. (1999) 'Dangerous Media? Panic Discourses and Dilemmas of Modernity', *Paedagogica Historica*, 35 (3): 593–619.

Drotner, K. (2000) 'Difference and Diversity: Trends in Young Danes' Media Cultures', *Media, Culture and Society*, 22 (2): 149–66.

Drotner, K. (2001a) *Medier for fremtiden: børn, unge og det nye medielandskab* [Media For the Future: Children, Young People and the Changing Media Environment], Copenhagen: Høst og Søn.

Drotner, K. (2001b) 'Global Media through Youthful Eyes', in S. Livingstone and M. Bovill (eds), *Children and their Changing Media Environment: a European Comparative Study*, Mahwah, NJ: Lawrence Erlbaum Associates, pp. 283–305.

Drotner, K. (2003) *Disney i Danmark: at vokse op med en global mediegigant* [Disney in Denmark: Growing Up with a Global Media Giant], Copenhagen: Høst og Søn.

Drotner, K. (in press) 'Media on the Move: Personalised Media and the Transformation of Publicness', in S. Livingstone (ed.), *Audiences and Publics: When Cultural Engagement Matters for the Public Sphere*, Bristol: Intellect Books.

European Journal of Communication (1998). Special issue on 'Children, Young People and the Changing Media Environment', edited by S. Livingstone and M. Bovill, 13 (4).

Fornäs, J. (1995) *Cultural Theory and Late Modernity*, Thousand Oaks, CA: Sage.

Garrison, D.R. and T. Anderson (2003) *E-Learning in the 21st Century: a Framework for Research and Practice*, London: RoutledgeFalmer.

Giddens, A. (1990) *The Consequences of Modernity*, Cambridge: Polity Press.

Gillespie, M. (1995) *Television, Ethnicity, and Cultural Change*, London: Routledge.

Gillis, J.R. (1974) *Youth and History: Tradition and Change in European Age Relations, 1700–Present*, New York: Academic Press.

Heywood, C. (2001) *A History of Childhood: Children and Childhood in the West from Medieval to Modern Times*, Cambridge: Polity Press.

Hjarvard, S. (2003) *Det selskabelige samfund: essays om medier mellem mennesker* [The Sociable Society: Essays on Media among People], Copenhagen: Samfundslitteratur.

Hobbs, R. (1998) 'The Seven Great Debates in the Media Literacy Movement', *Journal of Communication*, 48 (1): 6–32.

Holloway, S.L. and G. Valentine (2003) *Cyberkids: Children in the Information Age*, London: RoutledgeFalmer.

Husén, T. (1986) *The Learning Society Revisited*, Oxford: Pergamon Press.

James, A., C. Jenks and A. Prout (1998) *Theorizing Childhood*, Cambridge: Polity Press.

Jensen, J. (1990) *Redeeming Modernity: Contradictions in Media Criticism*, Newbury Park, CA: Sage.

Jensen, R. (2001) *The Dream Society: How the Coming Shift from Information to Imagination Will Transform Your Business*, New York: McGraw-Hill Education.

Johnsson-Smaragdi, U. (2001) 'Media Use Styles among the Young', in S. Livingstone and M. Bovill (eds), *Children and their Changing Media Environment: a European Comparative Study*, Mahwah, NJ: Lawrence Erlbaum Associates, pp. 113–39.

Kroes, R. (1996) *If You've Seen One, You've Seen the Mall: Europeans and American Mass Culture*, Urbana/Chicago: University of Illinois Press.

Ling, R. (2004) *The Mobile Connection: the Cell Phone's Impact on Society*, San Francisco: Morgan Kaufmann.

Livingstone, S. and M. Bovill (eds) (2001) *Children and their Changing Media Environment: a European Comparative Study*, Mahwah, NJ: Lawrence Erlbaum Associates.

Livingstone, S. and M. Bober (2004) *UK Children Go Online: Surveying the Experiences of Young People and their Parents*, www.children-go-online.net (consulted August 2004).

Luke, Carmen (1989) *Pedagogy, Printing, and Protestantism: the Discourse on Childhood*, New York: State University of New York Press.

Masuda, Y. (1980) *The Information Society*, Tokyo: Institute for the Information Society.

Ofcom (2004) *Ofcom's Strategy and Priorities for the Promotion of Media Literacy: Consultation Document*, www.ofcom.org.uk/consultations/past/strategymedialit/strategymedialit/annex4/?a=87101 (consulted August 2004).

Papert, S. (1996) *The Connected Family: Bridging the Digital Generation Gap*, Atlanta, GA: Longstreet Press.

Postman, N. (1982) *The Disappearance of Childhood*, New York: Delacorte Press.

Postman, N. (1985) *Amusing Ourselves to Death: Public Discourse in the Age of Show Business*, New York: Viking.

Qvortrup, J. (2000) 'Macroanalysis of Childhood', in P.H. Christensen and A. James (eds), *Research with Children: Perspectives and Practices*, London: Falmer Press, pp. 77–97.

Qvortrup, L. (2003) *The Hypercomplex Society*, New York: Peter Lang.

Reseaux (1999) 'Les jeunes et l'ecran', D. Pasquier and J. Jouët (eds), 17: 92–3.

Rheingold, H. (2002) *Smart Mobs: the New Social Revolution*, Cambridge, MA: Perseus Publishing.

Richards, J. (1984) *The Age of the Dream Palace: Cinema and Society in Britain, 1930–1939*, London: Routledge & Kegan Paul.

Roberts, D.F. et al. (1999) *Kids & Media @ the New Millennium: a Comprehensive National Analysis of Children's Media Use*, Menlo Park, CA: The Henry J. Kaiser Family Foundation, www.kff.org/entmedia/1535-index.cfm (consulted July 2004).

Robertson, R. (1992) *Globalization: Social Theory and Global Culture*, London: Sage.

Schrøder, Kim et al. (2003) *Researching Audiences*, London: Arnold.

Stehr, N. (1994) *Knowledge Societies*, London: Sage.

Tapscott, D. (1998) *Growing Up Digital: the Rise of the Net Generation*, New York: McGraw-Hill.

Sefton-Green, J. (ed.) (1999) *Young People, Creativity and New Technologies: the Challenge of Digital Arts*, London: Routledge.

Tomlinson, J. (1999) *Globalization and Culture*, Cambridge: Polity Press.

Tyner, K. (1998) *Literacy in a Digital World*, Mahwah, NJ: Lawrence Erlbaum Associates.

Wartella, E., B. O'Keefe and R. Scantlin (2000) *Children and Interactive Media: a Compendium of Current Research and Directions for the Future*, New York, NY: Markle Foundation, http://search.markle.org/cgi-bin/ts.pl (consulted August 2004).

4

Opting in to (and out of) Childhood: Young People, Sex and the Media

David Buckingham and Sara Bragg

Introduction

Children today are growing up much too soon, or so we are frequently told. They are being deprived of their childhood. Their essential innocence has been lost. Indeed, some would say that childhood itself is effectively being destroyed. For many people, perhaps the most troubling aspect of this phenomenon is to do with sex. Young people seem to be maturing physically – and showing an interest in sex – at an ever-earlier age. Even quite young children appear to adults to be alarmingly knowledgeable about the intimate details of sexual behaviour. Children, it is argued, are being prematurely 'sexualized'.

Much of the blame for this supposed loosening of sexual boundaries and the subsequent 'loss' of children's innocence has been placed on the media, and on consumer culture more broadly. These arguments are traditional territory for right-wing moralists. It is perhaps not surprising to find a conservative newspaper like Britain's *Daily Mail* fulminating about the media's 'sick conspiracy to destroy childhood', as ten-year-olds are apparently 'bombarded on all sides by pre-teen make-up, clinging clothes and magazines encouraging them to be Lolitas' (24 July 2002). Likewise, its columnist Peter Hitchens (2002, p. 49) paints a picture of a culture saturated and depraved by uncontrollable sexuality, most of it derived from the media:

> It is very hard to be innocent in modern Britain. Advertising on television, on posters and on the radio, is drenched in sexual innuendo. Television programmes rely almost entirely on sex and violence to raise their drooping audience figures. The playgrounds of primary schools echo with sexual taunts and jibes. Rock music, which is now almost compulsory in the lives of even the youngest, is full of sexual expression and desire.

Yet this image of childhood innocence debauched by media and consumer culture also appeals to more liberal commentators. Thus, Yasmin Alibhai-

Brown of the *Independent* (18 March 2002) laments her 'innocent' daughter's impending corruption at the hands of a 'sordid popular culture'. 'Powerful, immoral people', she argues, will 'manipulate her desires and appetites', pressurizing her to transform herself into a 'sex machine'. According to Alibhai-Brown,

> the next campaign for British feminists needs to [be] directed at those advertisers, broadcasters, celebrity pedlars, newspapers, magazines, pop stars and others who have made this carnal hell for our young ones, and who still insist that this is nothing at all to do with them.

Even liberationists like the gay activist Peter Tatchell, who argue for the importance of 'honesty' about sexual matters and advocate 'sexual rights' for young people, tend to dismiss the 'half-baked and sensationalist' information which they perceive in the media (2002, p, 70). From this perspective, 'good parenting' necessarily entails regulating and restricting children's access to the media – and not doing so is tantamount to child abuse.

Within the terms of this debate, therefore, children are effectively seen as lacking any independent agency whatsoever: they are merely innocent victims of the media's evil attempts at manipulation. Yet the recurrent claim that children are being 'sexualized' at the hands of the media obviously implies that they were not sexual in the past, and have now become so. Likewise, the view that children's relation to sexuality is being 'commodified' or 'commercialized' also seems to presume that there was an earlier time in which childhood was somehow free from commercial influences. As ever, we are encouraged to look back to a Golden Age of innocence, well before the media led us all to 'carnal hell'. This narrative of decline is one which many historians of childhood would certainly dispute: the lives of children, even as recently as the nineteenth century, were far from insulated from the influence of sexuality, or indeed from the economy (for example, Cunningham, 1995; Hendrick, 1997). Here, as in many other areas, the notion of childhood comes to be used as the vehicle for much broader concerns about the social order: moral entrepreneurs of both Left and Right tend to invoke threats to children as a means of justifying much more extensive forms of regulation (Jenkins, 1992).

To some extent, it is possible to distinguish here between broadly 'conservative' and 'liberal' perspectives. Thus, conservatives hold sexual permissiveness partly responsible for what they perceive as social or moral decline; while liberals argue that sexual repression leads to a whole range of social ills. Yet these views overlap in complex ways with different perspectives on childhood. On the one hand, children's awareness of sexuality can be seen as a healthy, natural phenomenon, which is distinguished from some of the more distorted or corrupted conceptions of adults. On the other, it can also be viewed as precocious or unnatural; and the acquisition of sexual knowledge can be seen to weaken the boundaries between childhood and adulthood, which are apparently designed to protect children. Both 'sides' in this debate invoke ideas about the 'natural' form of sexuality, and about children's inherent needs or interests; and in doing so, they inevitably define them in particular ways. While they may purport to speak on behalf of children, they also construct 'the child' in ways that reflect broader social and political motivations.

Researching children's perspectives

In general, children's views are conspicuous by their absence from these debates. By contrast, in this chapter we report on the findings of a research project that aimed to explore children's own perspectives on these issues.[1] During 2001 and 2002, we conducted over one hundred interviews with 120 young people (aged from nine to seventeen) and approximately 70 parents, and surveyed nearly 800 young people. We worked with young people in state schools in the south-east and the north of England. Participants completed a 'scrapbook' or 'diary' about their media consumption and thoughts on media images of love, sex and relationships, watched a video compilation, and were interviewed at least twice, both in friendship pairs and in groups. (In this chapter, all interviewees have been given pseudonyms. In parentheses after their names, we refer to N or S to indicate whether they were interviewed in the north or south; numbers indicate their age; and P, G or D refers to whether data comes from pair interviews, group interviews or diaries.)

Our research clearly demonstrates that children are aware of the public debate about their relationship to sexual media; and this inevitably shapes the stories and presentations of self they offer in interviews. Children construct their own 'counter discourses' in response to adult concerns. As Carol MacKeogh has noted, young people construct images of themselves as 'media-savvy' to counter the 'discourses of vulnerability' adults apply to them (MacKeogh, 2001). These were also a feature of our interviews; and in this context, children were often keen to appear 'sex-savvy' as well. Children frequently presented themselves as 'knowing it all', and sometimes as 'needing to know' things in relation to sex, while their parents apparently remained ignorant both of the extent of their knowledge and of their (revealing) thirst for it. Both in turn help to explain their accounts of why they particularly valued the media as a source of learning about sex and relationships.

Yet the media do not have 'effects' in isolation from the particular contexts in which they are used. The regulation of the media provides a powerful set of definitions about what is 'appropriate' for children and for children at particular ages; and while these definitions may be disputed, they are nevertheless widely acknowledged. Family media consumption, especially around the television, also often appears to be an occasion for attributing knowledge or ignorance, and hence for defining child (and adult) identities. The children in our study often resented or tolerated parental assumptions of their innocence and presented evidence of how they had outwitted attempts to restrict their viewing. At the same time, however, they protected their parents from accusations that they were lax and therefore uncaring, by arguing that they as children were particularly mature and trustworthy.

Both in themselves, and by virtue of the ways in which they are distributed, regulated and used, the media provide yardsticks against which children can measure their development and decide whether they are 'fast at growing up' or not. Responses to the prominence of sexual content in the media – while they are often exaggerated – thus inevitably provide powerful indications of the changing meanings of modern childhood. Children today may or may not know more about sex than previous generations, but in their dealings with the media, they are increasingly called upon to make choices about whether they want to remain a 'child'.

Constructions of competence

The children in our research repeatedly claimed to 'know it all'. As Courtney (N, 12, P) told us, 'My mum doesn't say anything about it [sex on television], because she knows I know everything about sex and relationships.' From the age of eleven, most children claimed to enjoy a state of absolute knowledge:

> Kelly (N, 14, P): My mum has spoken to me about bits, but it's embarrassing. And we kind of know it all already, don't we?

Indeed, for some, much of the embarrassment here seemed to derive from having to pretend that they did *not* know about such things, in order to keep their parents happy. While some, like Kelly, believed that their parents were content for them to 'know it all', others felt that parents might be disturbed to discover the full extent of their knowledge. In our survey, 69 per cent of children responded positively to the statement 'I know more about sex than my parents think I do.' (In fact, one fourteen-year-old who piloted the survey suggested that the statement should read 'I know more about sex than my parents.')

Of course, it would be easy to mock the idea that twelve-year-olds (or even fourteen-year-olds) could possibly know 'everything' about sex and relationships. Whether or not we can claim to 'know it all' partly depends upon what we mean by 'it', the nature of which was defined in various ways here. 'Knowing it all' implies a position untroubled by uncertainty or contradiction. Yet there are all sorts of paradoxes here. You may believe that you know everything, but it may simply be that you are not aware of the existence of what you do *not* know. You may feel you know all you 'need' to know; but this depends upon being completely confident about the extent of your needs. You may believe you know more than your parents think you know, but it may be that this is precisely what they would like you to think. For Courtney's mother, assuring her daughter that she already knows everything might be a good way of avoiding some of her own embarrassment in discussing such matters; and Courtney herself might well choose to go along with this for the same reason.

Moreover, our interviews threw up many instances where children clearly did not 'know' particular aspects of the 'facts of life', although this did not diminish their desire to present themselves as if they did. Some of them failed to understand some of the sexual content in the media we discussed – particularly where this was merely suggested, or in the form of innuendo. Some striking gaps in their knowledge were revealed: Bea (N, 10, P), for example, assured us that lesbians could not really have sex because 'to be able to have sex . . . a man's penis has to go into the lady's belly button to send the sperm in'. In other instances, we were probed for more specialized information, as when one of the authors was asked to explain to Sharmaine and Noelle (S, 12, G) why anybody would need to use flavoured condoms. Certainly, it would be hard to claim that these children represented a generation obviously more corrupted or more knowledgeable about sex than previous ones.

In other cases, children presented themselves as having desire for knowledge that their parents did not recognize. Indeed, this was almost as embarrassing as already knowing it, because even curiosity about such matters could be seen as 'precocious'. As Danielle (N, 10, P) put it, 'you feel embarrassed about asking your mum because your mum might not know that you know about [these things], and you might feel embarrassed about asking her'. Rachel (N, 10, P) agreed:

I know it sounds weird – but you sort of like *want* to watch it to learn about it. But like you're scared . . . you're sort of like embarrassed in watching it in front of your mums because they sort of say like 'turn away' and if you like say 'no', and they sort of like go 'well it's a bit rude and I think you should like go to bed'. And I say like, 'but we've got to learn about it', but she doesn't know that I sort of know about it yet . . . but I do and I want to learn about it but she doesn't know that I want to learn about it.

As we explore further below, the media can often provide the occasion for the revelation by children of 'inappropriate' knowledge or curiosity within their families.

Learning about sex

As the comments above imply, the children in our sample significantly preferred the media to other potential sources of information. According to our
interviewees, sex education in schools taught them nothing new; while
parents' efforts in this respect were generally seen as quite misplaced. Even
where children were prepared to admit that sex education might have taught
them something, there was a sense that the focus was much too narrowly
'medical' or 'scientific'. They might have learnt about 'the insides and all
that' (as Glenn (S, 17, P) put it), or about different forms of sexually trans-
mitted disease, but they argued that the 'really useful knowledge' they
actually needed had to be obtained elsewhere. Several young people also
perceived there to be a moral agenda in sex education which was fundamentally about 'just saying no'. Pleasure and fun, they argued, were not
mentioned here: as Chantel (N, 14, P) asserted, 'school puts like a downer
on things, 'cos they just make it sound so serious and like . . . it should be
something that you like!'
   If school was not very positively rated as a source of sex education, neither
were parents. A few did express a positive preference for finding out about
sex from their parents: Rollo (S, 12, P), for example, claimed 'I can talk freely
with my mum about sex. Some parents get shy [but] my mum's not, 'cos
she knows that sex is part of life, I'll find out about it.' Nevertheless, this
matter-of-fact approach appeared to be rare. In some situations, children felt
that parents were likely to 'hold back' from a full explanation, or be unduly
formal. Like teachers, parents were sometimes accused of trying to teach
children things they already knew. Kelly (N, 14, P), for example, expressed
exasperation at her mother's constant warnings to her when she went out
with her boyfriend – 'they just underestimate us!' And, as we shall see, family
discussions of sexual matters – at least in relation to the media – were frequently characterized by a great deal of mutual embarrassment.
   In turn, the inadequacies of home or school helped to account for the
appeal of the media as a key source of information and ideas about love, sex
and relationships. Soap operas and (for the girls at least) teenage magazines
were frequently mentioned in this respect (compare Kehily, 1999). Although
it was accepted that, like parents, the media could be evasive and that (as
Neville (N, 14, P) put it) 'they don't always show you that much', they often
addressed topics directly that many children found embarrassing to discuss
with their parents or teachers, or that parents might feel they were not
'ready' for. In some cases, this included information about physical development: for example, Bea (N, 10, P) described how she had been 'helped'
by reading a four page feature 'all about boobs' in the girls' magazine *Shout*.
For the older children, the media also offered information on sexual 'techniques' which was harder to obtain elsewhere: as Chloe (N, 17, P) pointed

out, sex education in schools did not tell you '*how* to have sex', whereas magazines would tell you 'anything you wanna know'.

In this respect, as in many other areas of children's media (see Buckingham, 2000), there is now a strong aversion on the part of producers to appearing to patronize young people. The media increasingly seek to address young people 'on their level', as already 'savvy' and 'mature'. Thus, a positive quality of teenage magazines, and to some extent of soap operas as well, was that they often took a humorous approach, and avoided the preacherly tone that was often seen to characterize sex education in school, being instead informative but not unduly 'serious'. As Phoebe (N, 14, P) argued, the magazines didn't 'tell you what to do . . . they just put it in and see what you think about it'.

The media also seemed to offer the benefit of anonymity, particularly if they were consumed privately. As Courtney (N, 12, P) put it, when you are reading a magazine, 'it's as if someone's having a conversation with you but they don't know who you are and you don't know who they are. So you're just finding it out but no one knows about it. No one has to find out.' Unlike school, media did not have the element of compulsion: as Reena (N, 14, P) put it, 'it's there if you want to read about it', but 'they don't go on about it so much'. And, as Lara (S, 14, P) pointed out, reading a magazine privately meant that you could avoid the 'mickey taking' that occurred during sex education classes in school. In general, the children were keen to reject any suggestion that there was 'too much sex' in the media – even if they did express concern about its possible impact on children younger than themselves. While some of the older children accused the media of 'glamorizing' sex, others argued that they also showed 'the negatives' – and that the media were just as inclined to warn children about the dangers of sex as to encourage them to engage in it 'prematurely'.

From the children's perspective, then, learning about sex and relationships appeared to entail a considerable degree of independent agency: it was a matter of actively seeking information from several potential sources, and making judgements about a range of potentially conflicting messages. It was also often a collective process, conducted among the peer group. Chantel (N, 14, P), for example, described how she and a friend had bought a book called *A Girl's Guide to Sex*, and would talk about such matters at sleepovers. In general, girls appeared to find this process easier than boys: many boys agreed that they were less likely to discuss such things with their friends, for fear of more 'mickey-taking' – particularly if they were to do with their own relationships. Yet while children would certainly talk things through with friends or older siblings (and sometimes parents) if they were in doubt, they were generally keen to work things out for themselves.

One of the most interesting expressions of this view came from Will (S, 10), who wrote in his diary in response to a 'sexy' advertisement for beer, 'I think I should know about it, but not right now, because I think I am too young to understand.' He could not really understand, he said, why beer adverts should feature 'girls in bikinis':

> Will (S, 10, P): I shouldn't know about them right now. When I know a bit more about them [I'll be ready] . . . Well, when I get a little bit older and I've learnt about the body a bit more and I know what happens. And about people who want to do this and why they want to do it.

When we asked whether he would expect to find out about all this from school or from his parents, Will replied:

> Neither. I think I've got to work it out myself . . . By doing research and then eventually when I get older I'll find out.

Will's curiously academic notion of 'research' seems to encapsulate something of the gradual, even haphazard, nature of sexual learning. 'Finding out' was not a once-and-for-all event, but an ongoing process, which involved 'piecing it together' from a variety of sources. Will's insistence on 'working it out himself' was typical of the independent approach many of the children adopted, or sought to adopt.

Opting in to childhood

As this implies, living in a media-saturated world may require a certain degree of reflexivity or self-consciousness about the position of being a child. The children in our research frequently sought to calibrate themselves in terms of age, and in relation to assumptions about what children of different ages *should* know about or be able to see or do. The pressure to 'grow up fast' was certainly a powerful one – although what 'growing up' *meant* was defined in some quite diverse ways. Whilst most looked forward to the freedom they imagined would come a few years hence, some of the younger interviewees claimed they were happy to remain children. Nevertheless, this seemed to require a conscious decision on their part. For instance, several of the younger children argued quite strongly that they were not yet ready to learn about sex, or that they did not need to know. Tania and Lucy (S, 10, P), for example, argued that they did not really need the advice about snogging they had found in *Mizz*, a teenage girls' magazine, because 'we're not the age to do that yet'. Likewise, Kim (N, 12, P) argued that 'in this age group', she did not want to watch all the 'picturing' of sex in programmes like *Coronation Street*; and she even resisted her mother's attempts to teach her about sex on similar grounds:

> Kim (N, 12, P):Like when she's telling me what's going on, like, and explaining that when you're a teenager, like . . . when you're a teenager,

do you know [about] your hormones? right. She's doing that and I'm going 'oh, I don't need to know this right now'.

Even among the fourteen-year-olds, there were those who argued that there were things they did not 'need' to know – although there was also a kind of shy excitement about these responses, which was accentuated by the difficulty the girls seemed to encounter in discussing sexual pleasure. Lara and Jody (S, 14, P), for example, claimed not to enjoy reading stories about sexual 'positions' in their magazines, or seeing sexually explicit content in documentaries: as Jody said, 'I don't watch it because I don't feel that I need to know about that yet. Because it's not something I'm planning to do until later.'

As these observations imply, children appear to locate themselves within developmental narratives, in which particular kinds of knowledge are 'needed' at particular ages. They calibrate themselves in terms of what is seen as appropriate or necessary to know. In the process, they negotiate with, resist and reproduce dominant adult constructions of the *meaning* of childhood itself. Yet they can no longer be so easily sheltered from material that some adults might deem inappropriate for them; and so they may have to positively 'opt in' to childhood, rather than experiencing it as a state from which they cannot escape.

'It's so embarrassing . . .': family viewing

This process of negotiation was particularly apparent in the children's accounts of family television viewing. For many children, family viewing was a key occasion on which attributions of sexual knowledge, desire or ignorance could be made and contested. The ways in which television was interpreted and used by different family members thus provided opportunities for proclaiming and disavowing childhood and adult identities.

The appearance of sexual content on television – at least in the public space of the family living room – was frequently described both by parents and children as generating embarrassment. Many children described the physiological experiences of such embarrassment and the responses it provoked – sweating, shuddering, getting 'all shy' or 'squirming', feeling 'uncomfortable', staring ahead as if transfixed, sitting in complete silence, and so on. These tales sometimes sounded almost ritualistic, in that participants recounted them with relish and in similar terms, without necessarily being able to provide many specific examples of problematic material. We need to emphasize that we are dealing here with *accounts* of embarrassment, not actual events. Claims to feel embarrassment are conventionally structured in order to make claims about identity, status within the family, and maturity; they may represent a demand for recognition of sexual identity or for its invisibility. Indeed, parents and children appear to construct their identities through what we might call 'embarrass-ment exchanges'.

Thus, parents and older siblings could assert their authority or greater status within the family by teasing children: 'the jokes'll come in . . . just cause we're there' (Flora N, 17, P). In fact, some parental responses as reported by their children were far removed from the maturity to which the parents in our focus groups laid claim. Thus, Rebecca (N, 10, P) said that 'when people kiss on TV my mum goes "ooh look Rebecca they're kissing" . . . as a joke. 'Cause I used to always look away when people were kissing on television.' Sometimes such teasing provoked considerable resentment or indignation from interviewees, who claimed that their embarrassment was engineered by others. Naomi and Phoebe (N, 14, P) identified this as something mothers did:

> Phoebe: The dads don't . . . they're all right. They just let you watch what-ever you want. But your mum . . . If your mum's there, they look at you and you're like. 'What, just let me watch TV!' They keep just staring at you. You're like . . .
> Naomi: 'Mum!'
> Phoebe: 'OK. I'm going to go upstairs now. Because you all keep staring at me' [laughs] . . . They just keep staring till you get a reaction.

One can only speculate here whether parents might be projecting their embarrassment onto their children or vice versa. However, such teasing and staring not only creates an unwelcome visibility for their recipient, but implies that their response to sexual material might be somehow inadequate or problematic. The indignant tones of these accounts counter such implicit accusations by transposing the alleged inadequacies onto parents instead.

However, descriptions of parental embarrassment enabled some young people to demonstrate their own greater sophistication. Seamus (N, 14), for instance, described in his diary 'one particular moment [in the drama *Foot-ballers' Wives*] where Jason Turner had sex on the snooker table with another footballer's mum, which doesn't affect me but for some reason my parents'. Likewise, Melanie (N, 10, P) presented herself as more able to cope with such material than her parents: 'They keep being stupid about things like that, I'm like "mum and dad, it's not that rude. I mean, get a grip, it's not that rude!" [laughs].' She claimed both that she thought it was 'just entertain-ment' and that in any case she knew about 'it' already – 'Huh. Four brothers, one sister. I think I do!' Of course, it may have been particularly necessary for Melanie, as the youngest in her family, to assert her sophisti-cation in this way.

Some young people, however, did describe their own embarrassment, claiming that it was inherent to the situation of watching with parents: they often had to remove themselves from the scene or from the sight of the source of the embarrassment, so they recounted covering their eyes, hiding behind cushions, leaving the room on the pretext of getting a drink, and so on. Some engaged in moralistic discourse as a defence:

> Nancy (S, 17, P): Go make a drink. 'Cause you can't watch it. Even though you could watch it by yourself, when your parents there it just feels . . . Even now sometimes. Now it's a bit . . .
> Olivia: Yeah. I still get embarrassed now.
> Sara: Do you. Mm. So what do you do now if you get embarrassed?
> Olivia: Go 'Oh god there's too much sex on TV now'. And she'll go 'yeah, you're right'.
> Nancy: Yeah – 'That's disgusting' [all laugh].

Where some younger children claimed they did not want to watch sexual material in the media at all (and many interviewees referred to this as something that had been the case in the past rather than the present), their rejection seemed to represent a refusal of the world of adulthood itself. Embarrassment, however, came to mean something different, confirming children's identity as different from that of their parents, but at the same time often representing a demand for recognition of their growth towards adulthood.

Collective viewing thus served as a forum in which revelations of knowledge could be made or suppressed. Ceri (N, 17, P) remarked 'some of the things that you'd laugh at, your parents go "Why do you know about that?" . . . I would rather leave them with a nice little mental image of me being twelve, if that is what they want.' Similarly, Gareth (S, 14, P) remarked 'on *They Think It's All Over* or something, when they say something, I'll laugh and my mum just looks at me thinking like "oh, he knows what that means" . . . Sometimes when I watch it upstairs with my brother, I laugh then, but when I'm downstairs I try to not laugh at some of the things which I shouldn't really know.' In some instances, children's media choices and active display of choosing potentially embarrassing media seemed to constitute a 'coming out' to one's parents as sexual. Thus, Chloe (N, 17, P) described her mother's shock the first time Chloe bought a teenage girls' magazine at the age of ten: 'she just didn't realise that I wanted to read more about stuff like that, rather than comics like the *Beano* and stuff'.

A consequence of embarrassment was that young people developed definite preferences about which programmes they would watch with parents, and which they would watch in their own rooms if they had a television there. Whilst it was generally agreed that the main living room contained the best quality television, and many young people sought out the pleasures of watching with others, at other times it was not worth the embarrassment of doing so. On many occasions, such decisions would have to be made during a programme, where children would disappear upstairs to continue watching in peace. It seemed that parents would operate a 'don't ask, don't tell' policy on this, where they knew what was happening but preferred not to challenge it.

'Over-protective parents': accounts of parental regulation

Children's accounts of their parents' attempt to regulate their viewing had to negotiate a kind of 'ideological dilemma' (compare, Billig et al., 1988). On the one hand, as we have seen, the children were keen to condemn parental over-protectiveness – not least as a way of proclaiming their own maturity. Yet in the light of public discourses about 'good parenting', they were also loath to accuse them of irresponsibility. Parents might thus be regarded as touchingly ignorant and out of touch, but nevertheless as well-meaning.

So for instance, they argued that parents were unaware of how much they knew: many echoed Krystal's (S, 14, D) argument that 'parents would *die* if they knew half the things kids talk about!' As Melanie (N, 10, P) put it, 'they want to keep me a child for ever'. or as Eve (N, 17, P) argued, 'they think you are six until you are twenty-six, don't they?' They emphasized the gulf between the older generation and theirs in this respect: Neville (N, 14, P) argued that today: 'You get more freedom . . . 'Cause they used to not get any freedom at all . . . When they were young they didn't really get to do much 'cause they were told not to, and they obeyed.' Several children claimed that their parents were too 'protective', and that this made it difficult for them to discuss such issues together. Older interviewees tended to recognize their parents' concerns as touchingly benevolent, even if misplaced. As Jon (N, 17, P) remarked of his father: 'I think he's just laying rules as all good parents do, they've gotta set standards and they expect you to abide by them.' Yet others were more forthrightly dismissive and impatient, such as Alicia (N, 10, P): 'Mums and dads, they're like *eighties* kind of thing, oh God! . . . They think it's all rude and they think I shouldn't be knowing about this until I'm about thirteen or fourteen or something like that . . . They wanna keep me a child forever!'

However, children were aware that not regulating TV is tantamount to admitting to being a bad parent and would be viewed negatively by others. Clint (S, 10, P) explained that his mother didn't like him watching sexual material because 'she just thinks you're gonna go round at school like and talk about it and everything', which would mean, Leo added, that 'your mum and dad aren't very nice people'. While some took a libertarian position, many upheld parental rights to regulate children's viewing: as Noelle (S, 12, P) remarked: 'I think my mum should tell me if she thinks it is [suitable] because she's been my age and she's been older and she knows what's better for me.' Children often presented a picture of relative harmony; for instance, where rules could be bent if adults were watching later programmes with them, making the occasion something of a treat. Rebecca (N, 10, P): 'Me and my mum normally like watching the same things. So when there's a programme on that we've been waiting for ages then I'm allowed to stay up late and watch it . . . If it's after quarter to ten and I'm not going to bed . . . She like tells me not to look 'cause they're doing more dirty stuff.' Mindful of the notion that the good parent is the regulating parent, children were careful to explain any laxity in a positive light, arguing that they themselves were exceptionally mature, that their parents trusted them, and so on.

Nevertheless, they also described various strategies they had evolved for evading parental scrutiny, recounting scenarios in which they pitched their wits against their parents to watch the forbidden material they desired. For instance, Caitlin (N, 12, P) exploited her grandmother's deafness to watch *Sex and the City* when her parents were out; others would watch with older siblings or at friends' houses; they would capitalize on differences between their parents to persuade one to let them watch what the other would not. Lysa (S, 10, P) recommended plying adults with Baileys to encourage them to relent over such issues; while Bea (N, 10, P) had found simple emotional blackmail effective in persuading her mother when she was reluctant to let her take *Bridget Jones's Diary* to a party: 'I sort of say like, "yeah but *everyone*, you'll let the *whole* party down" . . .' They would disguise what a text was really about, for instance by hiding cases that showed classifications. They would watch disapproved material from behind settees, on staircases, or upstairs on another television, swiftly changing channels when they heard their parents approaching. It was clear from our interviews with parents that they were aware of some of their children's subterfuges in this respect, but preferred not to pursue the matter. As David Buckingham has pointed out (Buckingham, 1996), children are not powerless within the family, although they may also relish exaggerating the amount of power they do have.

'Too young to understand' or 'fast at growing up'?

Like the parents we interviewed, children were generally hostile to external regulation. People who actively complained about particular representations were dismissed (in symptomatically sexist and ageist terms) as 'opinionated middle aged women', 'old ladies who are so moany . . . wasting their pensions using the phone and complaining because ages ago they didn't have stuff like this. And now they're jealous!' All our participants knew the classification categories for videos and most knew how the watershed functioned, even if the meaning of the term itself was obscure. However, they were quick to point to what they saw as anomalies in classifications, particularly in relation to computer games, but also films. The older children asserted that they were old enough to watch sexual material, pointing out that at sixteen they could engage in heterosexual sex and so should be allowed to see it. Some rejected any regulation at all, on the basis that it should be 'your choice' or pragmatically because regulations had little practical force anyway. Some drew parallels between their active decision-making in other areas of their lives and their rights to do so in relation to the media. Neville (N, 14, P) pointed out that young people were being invited to take responsible decisions about their lives at relatively early ages – his example was selecting subjects to study, which required developing a sense of what life would hold in the future beyond school. Externally imposed regulation came to seem anomalous where they were being encouraged to see themselves as active meaning-makers and decision-takers elsewhere (compare Rose, 1999b). To the extent that the idea of regulation suggested that they were 'unfree', they saw it as an affront.

However, regulation also played a productive role in children's identities and media practices. Regulation helped mark out material that was desirable or where they would expect to find more graphic material. Todd (S, 10, P) proudly enumerated his collection of 'over-age' videos: 'I got like twenty 12s, one 18 and four 15s.' They had also developed a degree of media literacy that made them aware what to expect of a programme from its title, scheduling, credits, and so on, and thus to cope with its potential sexual content. They understood the fictionalized nature of portrayals, for instance that actors 'are allowed to kiss but they are not actually having sex, making a baby. They are allowed to kiss though' (Rory, N, 10, G). If they did encounter sexual material later in the evening they were aware that it was 'for adults' and that they were encroaching on their territory. Lysa (S, 10, P) who listed as one of her hobbies 'watching films over my age limit', described watching a Channel 4 programme on 'Sex Gods and Goddesses', which featured 'people humping on the back of a fire engine, naked': 'I thought it was okay, but as it was like, it's on like twelve o'clock at night, there wouldn't be so many like little children running about the house.'

As this implies, regulation provides at least some of the terms within which children think about their relations with the media. To this extent, they have a stake in preserving its categories. Regulation gives children a norm against which to calibrate their own developmental levels – albeit mostly discovering that they are in advance of the stages that seem to be set out for them by the regulators. Bea (N, 10, P), for example, described how she bought girls' magazines because she was 'fast at growing up'. Growing up, in her account, is not something that happens to her, but something that she can achieve – and her media consumption is a measure of her speed and success in doing so. We might call this the 'Just 17 principle', according to which media companies target the age-based aspirations of their audiences: despite (or because of) its title, *Just 17* was a magazine whose primary readership was among girls aged between eleven and fourteen.

Some children even anticipated a time when they would be strict with their own children and shocked by what they watched – which Jon (N, 17, P) described in a tone of cheerful resignation as the 'festering of getting old'. Many spoke of 'other' audiences, invariably younger than them, for whom regulation was necessary and whose putative existence served to underpin their own claims to be mature and competent. For instance, Ethan (N, 12, P) acknowledged that the guidelines were useful, referring to them as 'good rules for your children'; Joseph (S, 12, P) commented that 'if there's not a Watershed you don't know what time the kids should not be watching'. These formulations – 'the kids', 'your children' – suggest that in discussing regulation both Joseph and Ethan temporarily assumed an 'adult' position. Children were also able to rehearse for adulthood by practising censorship on younger siblings. Thus, Will (S, 10, P) argued that, although children of his age needed to know about 'such things' at quite a young age, its downside was that younger children (below seven) might get to see it. He solemnly reported that his five-year-old sister hadn't seen 'it' (that is, sexual material of one sort or another) but had got 'very close to seeing it'. Fortunately, he reassured us, 'I always manage to get the control off her.' For Will, seeing material over his age was a mark of adulthood; but so too was regulating material on behalf of even younger viewers.

The children were, overall, keen to present themselves as self-regulating. In the case of sexual material, many younger children in particular often chose actively not to watch it and were very definite about not wanting to see what they referred to as 'full frontal views' or nudity. When they did seek it out, or even came across it inadvertently, they often gave the impression that they fully expected to find it repellent; and they employed a range of strategies for coping with material they thought was 'too much'. For instance, Theo (S, 12, P) claimed that when sex came on, even when watching on his own, he would 'just face the other way and just relax'. Others described how they could remind themselves that it was fake – that if two characters kissed, for instance. 'it's not like they're really going out, is it?' Occasionally young people proved to be sterner censors than their parents. As Noelle (S, 12, P) remarked of *At Home with the Braithwaites*: 'it was just like showing how like people can be lesbians and that. And I think that I shouldn't be watching this! I think maybe my mum or dad should've watched this a couple of times!'

The dilemmas of autonomy

Our research reflects the broader emphasis in childhood studies on the importance of recognizing children's competence and agency. However, it also points to some of the limitations of this approach – and in particular to the dangers of celebrating children's capacities as 'self-regulating' media consumers. In conclusion, we would like to draw attention to some of the dilemmas and tensions that arise for children in this new environment.

None of our young participants presented themselves as dependent for moral guidance on the authority of religion, traditional morality, or established experts such as teachers, even where they came from strongly religious family backgrounds. Nevertheless, all the young people to whom we spoke were involved to some extent with the secular expertise provided by 'pedagogical' media texts, such as magazines and soap operas. These texts constitute their audiences in ethical terms – that is, they invite them to engage actively with the dilemmas and issues they portray and to take responsibility for their responses and views. Our interviewees were often sceptical about such material as well; and they repeatedly expressed a preference for more open storylines or forms of presentation that appeared to allow them to 'make up their own minds'. Yet audiences' scepticism about more overtly 'pedagogical' texts does not necessarily imply that they are immune to them. The fact that young people were almost unanimous in claiming that they did not read the advice on problem pages, but only the letters, for example, does not mean that they have no influence. Problem pages may be less significant for the solutions they offer than in the ways they define certain kinds of behaviour as problematic in the first place, or encourage readers to imagine themselves (for instance, as individuals in control of their sexual identity and conduct). Similarly, many young people spoke of completing the quizzes in these magazines – which, albeit in frequently parodic or joking ways, are designed to yield information about the self for the purposes of self-assessment and judgement. Such media may help to habituate audiences to the rituals of assessing their own desires, attitudes and conduct in relation to criteria set out by experts (Rose, 1999a). Again, it is less relevant that they often rejected the conclusions the magazines reached for them: they nevertheless echoed the discourses of such magazines as they spoke of working out 'what kind' of a person they were, where their desires lay, and of the importance of reaching 'their own' decisions about matters of sexual conduct.

To some extent, we can see this as evidence of the success of a process of engendering a sense of 'hyper-responsibility': children today have been bound to become self-regulating media consumers, and (more broadly) responsible for their own ethical self-development and well-being (compare, Rimke, 2000; Rose, 1999a). As we have shown, these responses were also to some extent shaped by the wider public debate. Children are aware that they are positioned as innocent, as especially vulnerable, or as media-incompetent, both in the domain of public debate (and media regulation) and often in the family. Their response is to emphasize their knowingness, be it about sex or the media, and thereby to construct a (powerful) counter-position to the (powerless) one that is marked out for them. When Will

(S, 10, P) describes how he will 'find out for himself' about sex through 'doing research' (see above) he positions himself very much as an autonomous, calculating entity in control of his personal quest for enlightenment and information – and this position was, we would claim, relatively typical. This preferred self-image significantly complicates the business of research – and indeed of education – in this field.

The emphasis our interviewees placed on their self-governing capacities may help explain the particular dilemmas of regulating sexual material. Media regulation, we have argued, actively constitutes the meanings of media texts. In particular, it invites audiences to consider texts in terms of their social acceptability – for example, as when an age classification on a video implies that it may be inappropriate for younger audiences. However, sex appears more problematic as an issue here than does violence. There is a long-established tradition of research into so-called violent media that focuses on their 'social harm'. Whilst it is certainly contentious (Barker and Petley, 2001), it is nonetheless well-known and often attains the status of common sense wisdom in popular debates. In previous research, David Buckingham found that children were aware of these arguments (for instance, about the 'copycat' effect or 'desensitization' to violence in real life) and fully able both to rehearse and to challenge them (Buckingham, 1996). However, it was notable that our interviewees – both children and parents – were much less sure of themselves when discussing the possible harmful effects of sexual media. Their statements were often confused and seemed unconvincing even to themselves: for instance, young children and even some older teenagers speculated that nudity might make children want 'to wear no clothes', whilst parents seemed undecided about whether promiscuity was the effect of the media or of 'peer pressure'. One possible explanation here might be that sexual media material has been increasingly drawn into the domain of personal ethics, as an occasion for individuals to scrutinize their own desires, conduct and responses, rather than that of social harm. For this reason, it may be harder for regulatory bodies to obtain the degree of consensus that is necessary to win legitimacy, at least when it comes to controlling sexual material.

We have pointed to children's insightfulness, to their ability to contribute to public debates about matters of morality and ethics, and to their competence as media consumers. Our conclusion, in effect, is that children should be considered as active consumers rather than only the passive objects of interventions from above. In this sense, we are proposing that the definition of the modern citizen and the privileges of self-government should in certain (limited) ways be extended to young people to a greater degree than at present. This might be seen as a form of 'empowerment' – a transfer of power to individuals who were previously denied it. Yet it might equally be seen as a matter of simply extending the technology through which government creates self-regulating and responsible individuals.

Certainly, there are costs to this process. Our interviewees spoke frequently of the structured inequalities of power they experienced (although not in those terms); for instance, when girls described forms of harassment by boys, or when boys both enacted but were also critical of the divisiveness and aggression within homophobic male culture. They were also aware of the limits of their capacity to manage their own lives, caught as they were between conflicting pressures. Yet the discourses of voluntarism, autonomy and individuality that are so dominant today provide little space for other explanatory frameworks that might offer different ways of making meaning of their lives. If children are to be allowed to enter the sphere of modern citizenship, they must also conform to its norms and rituals; and these impose burdens which, we would argue, may well prove heavier for some than for others.

Note

1. This project was entitled 'Young people, media and personal relationships'. It was funded by a consortium of British broadcasting and regulatory bodies: the Advertising Standards Authority, the British Board of Film Classification, the BBC, Broadcasting Standards Commission and the Independent Television Commission. A report based on the research can be downloaded from www.asa.org.uk or from www.mediarelate.org; and we have also published a book based on the project, David Buckingham and Sara Bragg, *Young People, Sex and the Media: the Facts of Life?* (Basingstoke: Palgrave Macmillan, 2004).

References

Barker, M. and J. Petley (eds) (2001) *Ill Effects: the Media / Violence Debate*, London and New York: Routledge.

Billig, M., S. Condor, D. Edwards and M. Gane (1988) *Ideological Dilemmas: a Social Psychology of Everyday Thinking*, London: Sage.

Buckingham, D. (1996) *Moving Images: Understanding Children's Emotional Responses to TV*, Manchester and New York: Manchester University Press.

Buckingham, D. (2000) *After the Death of Childhood: Growing Up in the Age of Electronic Media*, Cambridge: Polity Press.

Cunningham, H. (1995) *Children and Childhood in Western Society since 1500*, London: Longman.

Hendrick, H. (1997) *Children, Childhood and English Society, 1880–1990*, Cambridge: Cambridge University Press.

Hitchens, P. (2002) 'The Failure of Sex Education', in E. Lee (ed.), *Teenage Sex: What Should Schools Teach Children?* London: Hodder and Stoughton, pp. 49–61.

Jenkins, P. (1992) *Intimate Enemies: Moral Panics in Contemporary Britain*, New York: Aldine de Gruyter.

Kehily, M. (1999) 'More Sugar? Teenage Magazines, Gender Displays and Sexual Learning', *European Journal of Cultural Studies*, 2 (1): 65–89.

MacKeogh, C. (2001) 'Taking Account of the Macro in the Micro-politics of Family Viewing – Generational Strategies', *Sociological Research Online*, 6 (1): U109–U126.

Rimke, H.M. (2000) 'Governing Citizens through Self-help Literature', *Cultural Studies*, 14 (1): 61–78.

Rose, N. (1999a) *Governing the Soul: the Shaping of the Private Self*, 2nd edn, London and New York: Free Association Books.

Rose, N. (1999b) *Powers of Freedom: Reframing Political Thought*, Cambridge: Cambridge University Press.

Tatchell, P. (2002) 'The ABC of Sexual Health and Happiness', in E. Lee (ed.), *Teenage Sex: What Should Schools Teach Children?* London: Hodder and Stoughton, pp. 63–79.

5
Is it Time to Rethink Media Panics?

Stephen Kline

Introduction: the roots of media effects debates

As social historians have noted, in post-war America television was at first apprehended as the harbinger of social progress and democratization. Hope was especially strong among progressive educators that television's 'window unto the world' would provide the next generation with a universal access to knowledge and culture and help forge a more democratic family institution (Minow and LaMay, 1995). And in many ways it did. At the vortex of a burgeoning consumer culture, television became the preferred source of entertainment and information for all sectors of the population – but especially loved by children for its up-beat visual storytelling and for its acknowledgement of them as consumers. Yet as 'low brow' popular entertainments flooded the airwaves, the progressive dream of a media educated citizenship dissolved into an anxious fretting about the crisis of socialization in the mediated world. America, perhaps slightly before other advanced industrial nations, was in the midst of traumatic and confusing sociocultural changes. The transitional Spock generation – although happily indulged by their parents – were also regarded suspiciously as potentially spoiled and feckless brats. Given the crucial symbolic space that childhood occupies in western cultures, and the conflicted perspectives on childrearing, it is hardly surprising that children's fascination with commercial TV was discussed ambiguously by the American public at large (Spigel, 1998). Did TV function as a universal cultural treasury for the nation or did it produce a generation of ignorant couch potatoes hooked on violent fantasy?

So, shortly after its introduction, children's television became the flashpoint of a protracted political struggle over post-war childrearing that grew ever more controversial with children's growing enthusiasm for it. Media had become part of the 'matrix of socialization', handing to advertisers and networks responsibility for the cultural curriculum (Kline, 1993). At the centre of this controversy was the question of what children learned while watching. Social commentators worried that commercial TV was responsible for hastening the moral decline of the nation, the breakdown of the family, the waning of literacy and a rising tide of libertine values unleashed by affluence.

Sociologists waded into the debate suggesting that the norms (and value systems) that had maintained public order in the past were being eroded by the new regimes of socialization (Goodman, 1956; Riesman, Glazer et al., 1961). The controversy quickly moved beyond the low-brow values and aesthetics represented in popular programmes to its impact on children's well-being. In an increasingly risk-averse society, television became one of the toxic elements. Psychologists worried mostly that children might identify with and emulate the repeated acts of crime and violence they saw on TV.

The emerging public debates about the 'negative effects' of the media put pressure on government to throw a regulatory cordon sanitaire around children's film and television to control the threat. Policy-makers were forced to assess these claims scientifically. Giving testimony to the Kefauver inquiry (Hoerrner, 1999), leading media researcher Paul Lazarsfeld admitted to the limitations of the fledgling science of communications: there simply wasn't enough research to evaluate the impact of TV programming on children. It was within this politically charged context that the scientific study of the 'effects' of children's exposure to media violence became one of the central missions of media research. Needless to say, many studies, scientific reviews, inquiries and commissions have been convened on the topic, not only in the USA but around the world. And since Klapper (1960) first reviewed the evidence, most have only provided qualified proclamations of limited media effects (Surgeon General's Report, 1972; NIMH, 1982; Huston et al., 1992). And this lack of definitive evidence became the rallying cry of the media industry's opposition to regulatory control that has echoed through the years in successive controversies about the impact of media violence on children (Murray, 1995).

Anyone interested in this question must now confront shelves of books, mountains of empirical data, and endless summarizing reviews of the literature assessing the impact of media violence on children's learning of aggressive and anti-social behaviour. As in most complex scientific questions there is no definitive answer. Although the evidence is contradictory and limited, there is a broad, if qualified, consensus among psychologists and physicians that some children in some situations seem to be affected (Paik and Comstock, 1994; APA, 2003; Surgeon General's Report, 2001). Having reviewed this literature recently, I must agree with the often repeated provisos about the complexity of answering this difficult question (Kline, 2003). Instead of doing so here, this chapter sets out to explore the contested role that this science of media effects has played in the public discourses on youth aggression in the media saturated world.

Media violence in the age of moral panic

Throughout modern history, youth aggression has been at the forefront of the public concerns about social control and order. But during the 1960s apprehension about the widening generation gap between pre-war parents and the TV generation were propelled into the limelight by the threatening prospect of an indulged TV cohort growing into juvenile delinquents, smoking dope, having sex and constantly battling authority in the streets. This much talked-about 1960's fear of 'youth beyond control' was agitated not only by drug-taking hippies and anti-war protestors, but also by spectacular instances of youth violence, such as the Charles Manson cult slaying of Sharon Tate in August 1969 which provoked widespread alarm about the imminent social breakdown of authority. And unlike the drug-taking protestors, Manson's defence had an ironic twist of bitter lemon for those trying to explain these brutal killings: violence was what the nation should expect when it allows its children to watch constant killings in TV cartoons, cowboy shows and crime dramas. He declared. 'I am only what you made me. I am only a reflection of you . . . You spoon fed us Saturday morning mouthfuls of maggots and lies disguised in your sugary breakfast cereal. The plates you made us clean were filled with your fears. These things have hardened in our soft pink bellies. We are what you made us. We have grown up watching your television. We are symptoms of your Christian America, the biggest Satan of all. This is your world in which we grow. And we will grow to hate you' (Manson, 2004). Although Manson was imprisoned for life, his brutal creed had a disturbing explanatory value for a nation worried that their children had grown restive and dissatisfied watching the tube.

Thinking about these intensifying generational conflicts, in 1972 sociologist Stanley Cohen observed that modern societies appear to be subject to periods of what he called 'moral panics' about youth aggression. Cohen's study traced in the media reporting of the public confrontations of the 'mods and rockers' the social process underlying anxious public discourses on youthful aggression: 'A condition, episode, person or group of persons emerges to become defined as a threat to societal values and interests; its nature is presented in a stylised and stereotypical fashion . . . the moral barricades are manned . . . socially accredited experts pronounce their diagnoses and solutions; ways of coping are evolved or (more often) resorted to; the condition then disappears, submerges or deteriorates and becomes more visible' (Cohen 1987, p. 9).

'Moral panic' is the adroit term which Cohen coined to characterize the 'sudden and overwhelming fear or anxiety' which seemed to seize the public debates about youth as generational conflicts erupted into violence. As in anthropological accounts of collective social phenomenon such as witchhunts, inquisitions or public hangings, the modern discourses on youth violence seem propelled by hysteria and a need to blame 'folk devils' for perceived threats to the social order. The word panic itself derives from the young god Pan whom the Greeks imagined unleashing the powers of irrational fear as he played his pipes. In this light, ongoing debates about youth disturbances reveal a very modern mistrust of young people as the visible edge of social change. Cohen believed that, caught up in panic, public policy often turned to repressive policing and restraint on youth cultures to control the threat. He suggested that the same dynamics applied to many aspects of youth cultures – drug-taking, binge drinking, turf wars and rock and roll – with a similar consequence of a growing spectre of social regulation.

Cohen's theorizing of the public panics about the youth movements of the 1960s was quickly assimilated into the canon of the fledging cultural studies whose analysis of cultural politics sided with youth in their struggles against the oppressive censorship and controlling interest of the dominant bourgeoisie. Media industries were at the centre of these struggles because in responding to youth aesthetics and taste, they became the enemy of the more restrictive mores of the older generation. The idea of a 'moral panic' began to be used by cultural studies' scholars to deride all public 'over-reactions' to the emerging youth taste cultures. These scholars celebrated even the angry and anarchistic elements in popular culture as spunky signs of young people's refusal to be entertained by the bland and sanitized nanny-state culture foisted on them by over-controlling parents. As Kirsten Drotner commented, generational conflicts over culture came to be expected: 'Children and young people are prime objects of "media panics" not merely because they are often media pioneers; not merely because they challenge social and cultural power relations, nor because they symbolise ideological rifts. They are panic targets just as much because they inevitably represent experiences and emotions that are irrevocably lost to adults' (Drotner, 1992, p. 59). Yet it was also clear that counter-culture movements were not the harbinger of unravelling social unrest. Moreover, by the mid-1980s the baby boomers who had grown up with TV were parents themselves and their concerns about TV seemed tempered with the knowledge that their children weren't that different. And so the public hand-wringing about juvenile delinquency and youth violence out of control gradually waned as exaggerated violence became the acceptable domain of normalized youth transgression. In the USA, Ronald Reagan's Republicans even deregulated children's media, casting aside the codes and conventions developed during the 1960s and 1970s (Kline, 1993). Moreover, the growing popularity of violence and horror genres among youth were taken by some media scholars as indications that young people's own tastes, aesthetics and even psychological needs were finally being recognized by the industry (Cumberbatch, 2001; Fowles, 1999; Goldstein, 1998).

The rise of panic politics

While the threat of youth out of control seemed subdued for a while, parental concerns about violence in children's programming never entirely dissipated. There were three reasons for this. First the amount and the graphic intensity of media violence in the cultural market continued to increase. Content analysis of television indicated that youth and child programming continued to be punctuated with violence (Wilson et al., 1997; 1998). To this the popularity of games such as 'Street Fighter', 'Mortal Kombat' and 'Doom' elicited new public anxieties about young people's (boys') growing fascination with experiencing virtual violence (Provenzo, 1992). Perhaps things were different for this Nintendo generation after all argued some media researchers (Funk, 2000; Dill and Dill, 1998). Second, the incidence of youth crime, bullying, fighting and violence in the schoolyard continued to rise through the early 1990s and was widely reported. For example, Dorfman et al.'s (1997) content analysis of 214 hours of local television news from California found that violence dominated local television news coverage of youth, that over half of the stories on youth involved violence, while more than two-thirds of the violence stories concerned youth. Widespread news coverage of kids killing kids in the playground seemed to touch a raw 'mean world' nerve accentuating parental anxieties about their kids walking home in communities rife with guns, drugs and gangs (Sorenson et al., 1998; Maguire et al., 2002). And third, after 30 years of violence research, the scientific community was growing more confident in the evidence they had of a complex link between media violence, attitudes towards violence and anti-social behaviour (Huston et al., 1992; Murray, 2001).

During the 1990s, concerns about the effects of violent entertainment resurfaced, figuring ever more prominently in the public discourse on postmodern childhood. Pressure mounted on the Clinton government to do something about the cultural industries, not only television but also digital media, which seemed to be pushing gratuitous sex and violence to new limits. In America, where media producers had successfully opposed government regulation because of their special constitutional standing, the problem was to do so without violating media freedoms. This was accomplished by a new Children's Television Act (which mandated more educational programming) and the Telecommunications Act which included the V-chip legislation, intended to bring children's choice of programming under individual parental control. In the face of growing Congressional calls for legislation, the video game industry (and the recently commercialized internet) needed to mollify parental concerns too. Rallying behind the twin flags of freedom of expression and corporate responsibility they put on the mantle of self-regulation, developing an age-related code similar to that for films, and a body called the ESRB which classified games according to their violent and anti-social themes.

By 1997 the media violence issue seemed to be back under control, until a particularly nasty school massacre, at Jonesboro, brought the issue of media-inspired violence back to the front pages: America was again seized by media panic. The news was again filled with children's advocates blaming drugs, parents, families, teachers and of course video games for the rise of school shootings. Perhaps ironically Jonesboro was also the place where Dr

Dave Grossman, author of *On Killing* (1995) and a leading critic of violent video games, had retired. Grossman was a retired US army lieutenant colonel who had built a career figuring out how to train soldiers to kill. As such, he seems well-positioned to comment on the similarity between the tactics used in the army to train soldiers and the use of violent video games by children. The US military has long used simulation training for its soldiers because the repetition and desensitization of simulated killing affects kill rates (the actual percentage of soldiers who will pull the trigger in real life combat). Recently he has become a leading US advocate of restraining the American entertainment industries, arguing that 'the main concern is that these violent video games are providing military quality training to children'. Grossman believes that violent video games may have a similar effect on young people who play them a lot to the simulation training of soldiers, not because they create models or templates for children's behaviour, but because they help break down the psychological barriers that prevent killing: 'children don't naturally kill; they learn it from violence in the home and . . . from violence as entertainment in television, movies and interactive video games'. Grossman persuaded many Americans that it was time to do much more about the 'virus of violence' infecting American youth culture (Grossman, 1998, p. 32).

After the shootings at Columbine High School in Littleton in 1999, Congress was prodded by the growing public outcry to hold new hearings on media violence. Grossman expressed his strong views to the committee. So too did a number of psychologists who summarized the scientific evidence proving video games were harmful. The ISDA (Independent Software Developers Association) president submitted the industry's view that video games did no harm to children. In the course of these hearings psychologists such as Goldstein, Funk and Anderson all offered their expert opinions on whether video games have effects on children's behaviour. Headed to Washington to testify too, cultural studies scholar Henry Jenkins was worried that reasonable parents were being gulled into panic by a powerful coalition of right-wing moralizers and effects psychology (Jenkins, 1999): 'Suddenly, we are finding ourselves in a national witch hunt to determine which form of popular culture is to blame for the mass murders and video games seemed like a better candidate than most.' Jenkins rebuffs the growing hysteria about video game violence, arguing that the scientific debate was turning into a witch hunt mobilized by misplaced anxieties: 'We are afraid of our children. We are afraid of their reactions to digital media. And we suddenly can't avoid either.' Seized by moral panic we were in danger of escalating the surveillance and monitoring of children's play. Jenkins articulated the cultural studies' suspicions of the effects-research tradition. Social science was misleading, and presented exaggerated evidence to scare the trusting public into accepting more regulation of children's media. He particularly ridiculed those researchers who study media violence in laboratories by counting how many times a child hits a Bobo doll. He argued that media consumption is a voluntary behaviour undertaken by active audiences that is much enjoyed by young people and not a passive assimilation of contents. Children know that video games are simply environments for playful exploration of a sometimes difficult 'adult' world. Moreover children's play and game play is a very complex learning process because it is imaginary: we can't assume children make literal sense of the violence in their video games. Jenkins rejects the simplistic media-effects assumption of vulnerability, arguing that rather than harm, media provide children with a rich cultural 'resource' that they explore, interpret and appropriate in their own way. They choose to watch horror films or play fighting video games for many reasons, including the potential to fantasize 'empowerment' and 'transgression' and to experience 'intensified emotions' or reinforce 'ideological' understandings of the grown-up world. Legislation amounts to control of children's pleasure. So he claims, eliminating violence from the screens will have absolutely no impact on aggressive and antisocial behaviour, because it doesn't affect children in the first place. As media sociologist Todd Gitlin (1994) argues: is it not far better to recognize that the roots of aggressive behaviour lie with dysfunctional families, drugs and impoverished communities rather than media violence – or to regulate guns rather than channel changers?

British media scholar, David Buckingham, similarly claims that the scientific study of media effects had become morally and epistemologically aligned with right-wing ideologues: 'The media effects industry is, of course, largely driven by moral and political panics about the harmful influence of media on children. Within Cultural Studies, there is a long tradition of damning this work, not just as positivist and empiricist, but also for conceiving of children (and audiences generally) as merely passive victims of the media' (Buckingham, 2000a, p. 55). Buckingham similarly asserted that not only are parental anxieties baseless, but the effects-researchers have failed to respect children's genuine quests for more varied and less conventional forms of recreation and amusement. TV is after all only storytelling, a fantasy resource which children choose willingly and, accordingly, should be a matter of 'taste' and not regulation. However ribald and aggressive popular cultural products are, what children watched reflected their own values, tastes and needs. Psychological theories of media effects simply failed to understand the robustness of children's culture he argued, or to acknowledge that children are active and savvy audiences who can tell the difference between fictional violence and news, play and reality – even if their parents can't (Buckingham, 2000b). Buckingham goes on to critique both the bourgeois elite who programmed and regulated children's television, and media-effects academics who studied it, as if children were helpless victims of the media. 'Ultimately, there is a denial of children's agency at the heart of this approach; and these criticisms apply just as much to more apparently "critical" research about the effects of advertising or consumer culture as they do to research about media violence' (Buckingham, 2000a, p. 124). He advised adults to lighten up a bit, preferring to grant to children's cultural industries more autonomy to serve their child audiences free from the invasive interference of the moralizers. At least the commercial producers didn't talk down to them in nannyish tones of sanitized blandness.

So too when the brutal Jamie Bulger child murder in Britain once again returned the question of media violence to the public agenda, and horrified child psychologists called urgently for regulation of media violence, there was a different voice heard from the academic community. In response to the media coverage of the killing, a group of cultural studies' scholars rallied against this threatened censorship of children's culture proclaiming that the public was being 'panicked' by pseudo-science. Published in a collection of essays edited by Barker and Petley (1997) these media theorists challenged the validity of the scientific evidence which 'proves' media effects, and questioned the motives of social scientists' calls for social regulation of media, declaring *there are no 'ill effects' of media violence.* Citing scientific critiques of media-effects research they argue that a varied diet of popular entertainment has never been shown to be harmful to children. The evidence that childhood is in crisis, or that TV influences aggression is weak and based on mindless positivistic effects-theory that fails on close examination to demonstrate that media are to blame for the social diffidence of youth. So the moralizing claims of the effects brigade are not only 'false and misleading' but also 'daft' and 'mischievous'. It is false because there is 'no such thing as violence in the media which can have either harmful or beneficial effects' in the first place. Mischievous because the 'alarmism' precipitated by 'effects science' contributes to public censorship of children's culture by pumping up the anxiety of parents. They argue that the public's fears arise from their reactionary traditional values and not from *real effects of media* (Barker and Petley, 2001).

Panic theory goes to court

Confronted by the spectacular media coverage of repeated schoolyard slayings and constant political pressure from congressional headline grabbers, the video game industry has repeatedly had to defend itself at public hearings, in community enquiries, in the courts, in the legislatures and in scientific arenas – wherever the effects of violent media and video games were being called into question by angry critics. One recent example is the contested St Louis ordinance which would restrict the sale of violent video games to children. A similar ordinance had been successfully defeated by the industry in Minneapolis when the ISDA convinced the judge to declare that since violence has been part of children's literature throughout history that it 'would not only be quixotic, but deforming to shield children from the very graphic violence in new media like television and video games'.

Needless to say, the ISDA intervened again in St Louis to prevent legislated restrictions on the sale of video games to children there.

What is different in this instance, is that the ISDA have been willingly assisted by some academic friends of the court – including prominent cultural studies scholars Henry Jenkins, Jib Fowles, Todd Gitlin and David Buckingham – who have taken up their cudgels against a local community whose elected officials are trying to place legal restrictions on the sale of violent and horrific media products to children (to whom the industry itself claims not to be selling them). Their brief submitted as Amici Curiae (expert witnesses who have standing as friends of the court) argues that the previous court judgements have unwittingly succumbed to the 'commonly held but mistaken beliefs about a proven causative link between violent entertainment and violent behavior to uphold a censorship law'. Yet they worry that the St Louis court too will mistakenly accept the 'effects hypothesis' as proven on the basis of psychologist Dr Craig Anderson's testimony that 'there is a causal connection between viewing violent movies and TV programs and violent acts' and that the trial court relied on the claim that video games 'provide a complete learning environment for aggression'. They warn that 'researchers who attempt to reduce the myriad effects of art and entertainment to numerical measurements and artificial laboratory experiments are not likely to yield useful insights about the way that viewers actually use popular culture', citing recent reviews by individual scholars Jeffrey Goldstein (2001), Mark Griffiths (1999) and Jonathon Freedman (2002) whose methodological critiques of effects science are intended to 'assist the court in understanding the media effects debate'. In the following sections I wish to examine the political, scientific and moral issues underwriting the Amici Curiae's wholesale dismissal, as another moral panic, of parental concerns about a relationship between violent entertainment and antisocial behaviour.

Proof of cause

In their brief, these Amici Curiae acknowledge that 'the relationship between entertainment and human behavior is multi-faced and complex'. In so far as the Amici's critical reviewers (Durkin, 1995; Goldstein, 2001; Griffiths, 1998) point out the inconsistent frameworks, dubious findings and design shortcomings of the experimental literature on video gaming they are on solid ground. All three are scathing about the design and measurement issues plaguing the video game literature: 'all the published studies on video game violence have methodological problems and that they only include possible short-term measures of aggressive consequences' (Griffiths, 1998, p. 208). The early experimental studies conducted in labs and lecture halls with psychology students are particularly problematic and what is meant in them by aggressive behaviour is confusing: studies include hitting and fighting, verbal taunts, feelings of hostility, moral judgements of other's behaviour, as well as playful enactments of conflict. Moreover, a ten-minute exposure to a Space Invaders game or a questionnaire conducted in a lecture hall provides limited understanding of the complex processes of internalizing representations of imaginary conflict in video games. Griffiths is particularly concerned about lumping together cartoon-like violence and more realistic games (as in TV shows) and also in the absence of differentiation between games where conflict is competitive hostility (sports or racing) as opposed to aggressive contest (fighting, shooting). Overlooking these distinctions in risk factors however, makes it less likely for researchers to have found a significant result (Potter, 1997).

Which is why Griffith reaches the conclusion that: 'the question of whether video games promote aggressiveness cannot be answered at the present because the available literature is relatively sparse and conflicting, and there are many different types of video games which probably have different effects' (Griffith, 1998, p. 208).' I totally agree: of the 25 or so studies, at least half are out of date. Experimental comparisons of playing Space Invaders for ten minutes can provide no insight into the consequences of playing Soldier of Fortune for ten hours a week for a year: many of these early studies are so badly designed and out of date that one wonders why they are still being discussed (Kline, 2000). Goldstein (1998) maintains that what these studies actually show is that boys enjoy playing-out action adventure fantasies. Since male aggression is so deeply embedded in our contemporary culture, positive findings are best explained by the tendency of those predisposed to aggression to enjoy violent games more. Since most experiments are so inadequate, there is no reliable evidence to prove the causal hypothesis over and above this male fascination with human conflict (Goldstein, 2001). Goldstein concludes that unless experiments show consistently that after playing a murderous video game a significant number of children jump up and kick or hit another child, the researchers cannot claim there is an effect on behaviour.

To concede these limitations of psychological lab research is not however tantamount to confirming that these experiments reveal 'absolutely nothing' about children's use of violent video games. Goldstein criticizes the video game research for demonstrating that at most, video games only influence the way children talk and play together aggressively. Griffiths too goes on to say that 'one consistent finding is that the majority of the studies on very young children – as opposed to those in their teens upward – tend to show that children do become more aggressive after either playing or watching a violent video game' (1998, p. 209) when the research observes children's 'free play'. In short he believes their influence on play, knowledge and skills has been demonstrated, but not precisely enough to specify the consequences of a particular game on different kinds of children. Griffiths's reading of this literature has convinced him that video games can have both positive and negative consequences for children's learning: 'If care is taken in the design, and if games are put in the right context, they have the potential to be used as training aids in classrooms and therapeutic settings, and to provide skills in psychomotor coordination in simulations of real life events, for example, training recruits for the armed forces' (ibid.). It appears as if Grossman and Anderson are in agreement after all because both see video games as 'environments' in which players can learn about aggression.

Weight of evidence

The Amici's brief does not confine its rebuttal of effects-research to the video game literature however, claiming that there is no scientific proof that any violent entertainment has any harmful effects. The brief cites Jonathon Freedman's (2002) recent substantial and complex book-length review of the TV violence studies. They probably should have read it more carefully, because Freedman, being a cautious empiricist, does not claim there is *no proof of harmful effects*. Rather, he suggests that the amount of research has been dramatically exaggerated, that the weight of evidence has been overstated and that there has been a biased criterion used in the evaluation of the findings. Freedman, the behaviourist psychologist, finds for example that many measures of aggression (attitudes, reported feelings, judgements, play) are 'dubious' indicators of a causal hypothesis. Moreover he finds social psychologists' acceptance of any effect among interacting factors unscientific. If they only do so under some of the experimental conditions – for example, a significant relationship to boys' heroes and not girls', or a strong correlation in the USA data but not in Finland – then he thinks the null hypothesis has been confirmed. Freedman proposes instead that studies must demonstrate a *direct causal relationship* between violent representations and aggressive behaviours to be counted as evidence.

Freedman's behaviouralist corset results in a very biased tally of the evidence. Moreover, in many cases it misrepresents the actual hypotheses proposed by the researchers who often aspire to evaluate the interacting influences on the socialization of aggression. Having recently written on effects-research traditions, I take issue with Freedman's use of this behaviouralist yardstick which ignores the actual goals of the research and excludes studies of intervening variables (identification, attitudes, desensitization) as contributing any understanding of the media's effects. No self-respecting effects-researcher proposes that every kid who plays Mortal Kombat is going to become a killer. In fact, I can't think of many researchers who have pursued such a simplistic version of the direct causal hypothesis, at least since Bandura, Ross et al.'s (1963) Bobo doll experiments (performed in a nursery school not a lab).

Their interest in the mechanisms of learning leads many researchers to use indirect measures of the effects of violent programming. Take for example Bandura's study. Freedman is derisive of this Bobo doll (and all play) study because he claims that hitting a doll is 'not a measure of real aggression'. But does that mean it makes no contribution to our understanding of the causal connection between media and aggression? Especially when, as Bandura clearly states, the purpose of the study was to examine observational learning processes through which children imitate adult models, whether they are on television or not? As Bandura points out, peer aggression is not common in supervised situations like the nursery school environments so he chose a measure of learning that might be expected in free play. Hitting of the Bobo doll is never interpreted by Bandura as a measure of aggression per se. Rather the hitting of Bobo indicates the degree to which the child, having observed the particular pattern of modelled behaviour, incorporates that behavioural construct into their play routines. His study indicates that they are not less likely to do so when the behaviour is modelled on television.

Bandura's quasi-experimental research tests specific learning theories about how (and in what circumstances) the media can contribute to children's acquisition of antisocial attitudes and behavioural scripts. Most contemporary social psychologists and clinicians do not theorize aggression as a direct response to stimuli, but as a learned social behaviour that becomes enacted in different situations which have implicit rules and sanctions. Psychologists know that there are many things besides media which also contribute to children's learning about conflict and aggression in social relations. Personal experience, peer relations, identification with role models, intelligence, sex roles, and parenting styles are obviously important factors in the development of social skills and aggressive dispositions. The propensity to act aggressively therefore will vary across individuals depending on their experience and circumstances, their peer relations and communities. But many also believe that media representations of conflict and interpersonal aggression can make a contribution to the cumulative formation of those mental constructs, representations and feelings which prevent or privilege aggressive behaviour. What is learned from media will depend on children's interest in, patterns of use, identification with and interpretation of the violent narratives (Eron, 1997; Huesmann and Guerra, 1997).

Learning to be aggressive and antisocial involves developing interests, attitudes and emotional responses over the course of a lifetime: it is reasonable to hypothesize therefore *both* that violent content contributes to aggressive attitudes and that children who are aggressive may become more fascinated with violent entertainment. Nor do they assume there is only one kind of cognitive, emotional or social mechanism involved. What matters in the long run is whether the patterned use of media contributes to their attitudes, feelings, and ultimately to their social interactions with peers and others. The difference between the causal hypothesis of the behaviourists and the learning model of the social psychologists then is that the latter does not predict a uniform consequence of heavy viewing of violence in the child population. In fact, the research conducted by psychologists is often more concerned with distinguishing the circumstances and processes which explains why some heavy viewing individuals become violent and others don't. For this reason sweeping assessments about direct effects of media violence are bound to be of limited value.

Risky analysis

The Amici contend that effects-researchers have been beating the panic drum without solid proof that violent entertainment *'causes – or is even a risk factor for actual violent behavior'*. Absolute proof of general harm may be a legal requirement in USA courts under their constitution (compare the battle over tobacco), but a careful scientific researcher would rarely claim to have proven that there are harmful effects from violent entertainment. Rather they would explain that the process of scientific evaluation of data is a process of weighing various kinds of evidence based on statistical techniques that help us distinguish probable outcomes based on assumed conditions. Anderson therefore may be faulted if he did not explain the rules of scientific evidence and the meaning of significance to the judge, but he is right in claiming that many psychologists looking at this evidence have come to reject the proposition *that there are no consequences of heavy exposure to violent video games*.

In fact most large-scale surveys indicate a consistent relationship between heavy viewing/playing of violence and aggression. Murray has suggested that the 'risks' associated with violent media use approach those which link smoking to lung cancer – about 10–15 per cent (Murray, 2001). Freedman's own estimate is that heavy viewing accounts for at most 10 per cent of the variance of aggressive behaviour, a level he regards as 'vanishingly small'. But these estimates depend on the population being sampled, because the risks are higher for some populations – that is children growing up poor, in abusive homes, hanging with aggressive peers and growing up in high crime neighbourhoods experience escalating risks. Slightly lower risks are found therefore in broad samples like the Youth Risk Behaviors Survey (YRBS). For example in the 2001 survey of approximately 13,000 teens, the evidence shows that risks of fighting at school among teens are rather high (25 per cent of girls and 42 per cent of boys reporting fighting during the last year). When the data are broken down by the respondent's media use, it is found that those who view more than four hours of TV daily are 7 per cent more likely to get in a fight during the year than those who watch less than one hour. Yet those are estimates are for the whole population. For example the relationship between watching TV and fighting found in the YRBS data is much stronger for girls (8.4 per cent) than for boys (3.8 per cent). So although there is less fighting among girls than boys, it seems that television watching compounds it more than for boys.

We know that aggression is a complex form of social interaction which is learned within peer groups, schools, families, communities – and not just from TV. And there are strong social restraints on hurting others in our culture. Mitigating factors in the socialization of aggression are well established empirically, ranging from family modelling and mediation to zero tolerance schools and public advocacy programmes. Aggressive individuals or those who experience abusive or brutal family and peer relations may develop a preference for violent entertainment, which in turn reinforces templates of human relations which privilege violence as a way of solving conflict. Other families monitor, limit and co-view media, exerting a moderating influence over the way children use and interpret media conflicts. These are just a few of the reasons why effects-researchers do not expect even a majority of children will be negatively influenced by media violence. It all depends on circumstance and context. Garbarino (2001, p. 13) for example has noted that once the research accounts for these 'developmental assets' the media's role in the socialization of aggression becomes clearer. Among asset-rich children the rate of violence is low while among asset-poor children the rate is high. 'Assets are found throughout the social ecology of the child – family, school, neighborhood, and community. The rate of demonstrating significant violence is 6% for kids with 31 to 40 assets bracket, 16% for those with 21 to 30, 35% for those with 11 to 20, and 61% for those with 0 to 10. Risk and opportunity accumulate.' Which is why, Garbarino says 'an accumulation-of-risk model is essential if we are to understand where televised violence fits into the learning and demonstration of aggressive behavior.' By accounting for mitigating risk factors psychologists hope to better understand why not all heavy consumers of violent entertainment grow up to be aggressive and anti-social. Their key question in risk factor research is *to determine what it all depends on*.

Beyond panic

It is true that we don't know much about how video game violence will affect children's lives in the long run. The Amici suggest that since harm has not been proven we can expect *no positive outcomes* from the regulation of media. But the same lack of evidence about computers' contribution to learning didn't stop us from investing billions in classroom technology. The Amici have also dismissed learning theory's analysis of the various factors that mitigate a steady diet of aggressive entertainment. Far from inconsequential, these studies have provided insights into the possibility of reducing the risk factors encountered in heavy media consumption. This has been nicely illustrated by two recent field experiments undertaken at Stanford by Robinson et al. (2001) which demonstrated that reducing young children's overall exposure to media (TV and video games) can have very positive effects on their health and aggressive behaviour. Robinson points out that correlational evidence indicates that avid TV viewers, especially girls, are at risk of obesity and boys of violence. It is true that these correlations don't tell us whether aggressive and fat children watch more TV, or whether heavy TV viewers fight and eat more and exercise less. But since we are really interested in reducing obesity and antisocial behaviour it is possible to test these directional relationships by reducing the risks associated with heavy TV viewing.

Applying Bandura's social learning models, Robinson reasons that reducing children's media exposure could lessen their identification with aggressive heroes and reduce their enactments of domination scripts in their playground interactions. In the case of obesity three media-related mechanisms have been found in the literature: first that children substitute watching TV for more active play; second that in watching more TV children will be exposed to more snack and fast food advertisements; and third that children develop a particular habit of eating while they watch. Robinson developed a schools-based media education programme for reducing those media risks. At the test school, researchers found children in the media risk reduction intervention had reduced their TV viewing by about one-third. They also found that after six months the Body Mass Index (BMI) gain in the treatment schools was significantly lower. Moreover, based on ratings of playground aggression, frequencies of bullying and rough and tumble play were about 25 per cent lower in the treatment school than those at the control school.

This is why many medical and psychological researchers believe that a multi-factorial risk analysis will ultimately help us make sense of this complex question of the media's long-term influence on children's socialization. Although the risks and explained variances are relatively small, there is a growing ability to explain why some heavy viewers in some circumstances are more likely to be aggressive and antisocial. Scientists obviously need to find out more about which kids and why. With this in mind the Surgeon General's summary of this controversial evidence is optimistic:

> Although our knowledge is incomplete, it is sufficient to develop a coherent public health approach to violence prevention that builds upon what is known, even as more research is under way. Unlike earlier Federal research reports on media violence and youth (National Institute of Mental Health, 1982; U.S. Surgeon General's Scientific Advisory Committee on Television and Social Behavior, 1972), this discussion takes place within a broader examination of the causes and prevention of youth violence. This context is vital. It permits media violence to be regarded as one of many complex influences on the behavior of America's children and young people.
>
> (Surgeon General, 2001)

The Surgeon General concludes that researches to date 'justify sustained efforts to curb the adverse effects of media violence on youths'. The report therefore ends by recommending a multilayered solution to address aggressive and violent behaviour including a precautionary principle when it comes to media policy. Perhaps parents shouldn't be panicked about the effects of video games on their kids. But neither should we ignore the evidence of health and safety risks to those who consume them incessantly.

Coda: rethinking panic not effects?

Over the last half century, an escalating youth crime rate has fuelled increasing public attention to the problem of youth aggression, as is shown by Dorfman et al.'s (1997) content analysis of local Californian television news. Especially during the 1990s, the coverage of a series of schoolyard slayings generated an impression of North American communities rife with guns, drugs and gangs (Sorenson et al., 1998; Maguire et al., 2002), raising concerns about the primary causes of youth aggression which since the 1950s have erupted as public controversies about the effects of media and the breakdown of the family. Urging a precautionary view of all risk factors, the US Surgeon General has suggested repeatedly that it is unwise completely to ignore the media's contribution to crime and aggression in our society (Surgeon General, 2001). With this in mind, this chapter has examined the recent academic controversy over media effects which have led two schools of media scholarship to a face-off in the courts over the labelling of video games in the USA.

Generalizing from empirical studies, psychologists like Craig Anderson have testified that those children who watch and play with violent programmes over a long period of time and identify with aggressive characters are more likely to become aggressive adolescents in the absence of mitigating familial, peer and community resources. Yet concerned that such scientific pronouncements were misleading the courts, a group of media scholars have sided with the video game industry in their opposition to the 'regulation' of children's cultural industries. Suggesting that protectionist psychologists were fanning the flames of public 'panic', this group of scholars have challenged both the evidence and methods offered by these researchers, claiming that their experiments have failed to demonstrate 'harmful effects'. Worried that Americans were going on a witch-hunt, they have argued that any *'efforts to address real-world violence by censoring entertainment are profoundly misguided'.*

It must be said that Cohen was not entirely pleased by the way cultural studies' scholars appropriated his theory of moral panic. In the introduction to the 1987 edition, he condemned those who read his work as a wholesale enthusiasm for the youth counter-culture movements. Cohen was particularly uncomfortable with these scholars' 'constant impulse to decode the style in terms only of opposition and resistance' which he thought 'seeks to elevate delinquents into the vanguard of the revolution' (Cohen, 1987, p. xxvi). He refused to view young people through such liberal glasses believing that 'for many or most of the kids walking around with swastikas on their jackets, the dominant context is simple conformity, blind ignorance or knee-jerk racism'. Moreover he was not convinced that youth transgressions bubbled up autonomously from the grass roots and that 'commercialization and co-option are something which just happens afterwards' (ibid., p. xxv). Noting that various corporate interests also mobilized to 'exploit' deviance, he complained that cultural analysis privileged a type of sociology which 'implied that everything would be all right if only the kids were left alone' in the market (loc. cit.). Cultural studies' scholars, he felt, were in danger of reducing the politics of working-class youth culture to issues of taste and freedom of choice in the market.

It is also worth remembering that Cohen himself believed that what distinguishes modern panics from witch-hunts is the role that media play in priming the pumps of hysteria. Cohen's analysis pointed out how sensational news coverage of youthful conflicts mobilized a variety of social agencies with a stake in youth culture – some progressive and some less so. Although journalists don't create panic out of nothing, their focus on the issue elicits a strong reaction within the community – especially among those groups (religious, educational, judicial) whose role it is to preserve the moral order. As these various experts interpreted the growing threat of violence, the youth rebels were demonized as posing a threat to the whole social fabric. And as Peter Horsfield (1997) has concluded from his case study of moral panic about church child abuse, this theory can be as readily 'invoked by those in positions of power in society and in situations where it doesn't apply, in order to discount and defuse legitimate challenges to their power' – and interests. A full analysis of the politics of media panics therefore must chart the competing interests within the justice establishment, scientific community, religious groups, social theorists and commercial entities in this debate – all of whom claim a stake in the ongoing struggle over who has what rights to communicate to children.

After 50 years of controversy, it should be clear that a politicized struggle is taking place over the youth media industries which will continue to be agitated with each story of murder in the classroom. I agree with the Amici that clamping down on children's media may not be the best solution to playground murders since such cases are a very minor part of the underlying risk factors associated with heavy viewing. But I also think it is far from useful to dismiss, or even pathologize the concerns that American parents and educators have about bullying and fighting and its relationship to media culture. In this respect the main benefit of moral panic may be that the issues of youth violence continue to be aired. Yet as Murray's (2001) analysis of news coverage of explanations of aggression shows, the voice of media researchers is all too rarely heard within the media's reporting of youth violence. He claims that rather than feeding panic, news reporting of media effects research has *consistently understated the amount of evidence and magnitude about media risk factors* (Murray, 2001). Perhaps because the media have something at stake, or perhaps because they apply simplistic news values in framing stories, there is simply very little contextual discussion of the socialization of aggression in the news (Maguire et al., 2002). So if anyone is to be blamed for the growing fear parents feel about or for their children, perhaps it is the media, which sensationalize crime, and not the effects-researchers who study it, who should be in the spotlight. With the media eye fixated on youth out of control, the scientific arguments about media as risk factors is being marginalized in the public discourses on youth aggression.

In the USA, where freedom of speech has come to mean the freedom for corporate interests to dominant public discourses, even requests for mandated ratings have been opposed by the video game industry. In this political struggle over children's gaming industries, the Amici are voluntarily intervening on the side of an industry which has lobbied hard for more than ten years to resist having any kind of legislation imposed on the promotion, sale and distribution of digital entertainment – even for the under-sevens – against the general drift of American popular opinion. So is the Amici's brief written as an expert opinion clarifying what is known about the role played by media in the socialization of aggression or is it a political intervention supporting the video game industry's legal argument that any legislation attempting to deal with marketing and sale of violent entertainment to children *is tantamount to censorship*? In the appeal court finding, aided by the Amici's brief, the judge decided that parents' interest in their children's health and safety do not override the industry's rights of commercial speech. Well, that is the American way. But the political struggles over children's media regulations are decided differently in Canada, Britain, Sweden and France where community standards guidelines and mandated warnings on risky products (that is, tobacco, genetically modified food) have been regarded as legitimate and helpful ways in which the state can balance market choice with parental responsibility for their own children.

Although their media flacks blithely declare that this is the best of all possible worlds and that of course the kids are OK, perhaps there is even a glimmer of hope for democracy as media panics about violence, and now fast foods, galvanize parents to challenge corporate complacency.

References

Amici Curiae (2002) *Interactive Digital Software Assn. et al. v. St Louis County et al.*, United States Court of Appeals for the Eighth Circuit. Access on line through Particip@tions website 2004, http://www.participations.org/.

APA (American Psychological Association) (2003) 'Violence on Television – What Do
 Children Learn? What Can Parents Do?', http://www.apa.org/releases/media_
 violence.html.
Bandura, A., D. Ross et al. (1963) 'Imitation of Film-mediated Aggressive Models',
 Journal of Abnormal & Social Psychology, 66(1): 3–11.
Barker, M. and J. Petley (eds) (1997) *Ill Effects: the Media/Violence Debate*, Communi-
 cation and society, London: Routledge.
Barker, M. and J. Petley (eds) (2001) *Ill Effects: the Media/Violence Debate*, Communi-
 cation and society, London: Routledge.
Buckingham, D. (2000a) 'Studying Children's Media Cultures: a New Agenda for
 Cultural Studies', in B.v.d. Bergh and J.v.d. Bulck (eds), *Children and Media: Multi-
 disciplinary Approaches*, Leuven: Garant, pp. 49–66.
Buckingham, D. (2000b) *After the Death of Childhood: Growing up in the Age of Elec-
 tronic Media*, London: Polity Press.
Bushman, B.J. and C.A. Anderson, (2001) 'Media Violence and the American Public.
 Scientific Facts versus Media Misinformation', *American Psychologist*, 56(6–7):
 477–89.
Cohen, S. (1987) *Folk Devils and Moral Panics: the Creation of the Mods and Rockers*,
 Oxford: Blackwell.
Cumberbatch, G. (2001) *Video Violence: Villain or Victim?* Video Standards Council,
 UK.
Dill, K.E. and J.C. Dill (1998) 'Video Game Violence: a Review of the Empirical Liter-
 ature', *Aggression and Violent Behavior*, 3(4): 407–28.
Dorfman, L., K. Woodruff et al. (1997) 'Youth and Violence on Local Television News
 in California', *American Journal of Public Health*, 87(8): 1311–16.
Drotner, K. (1992) 'Modernity and Media Panics', in M. Skovmand and K.C. Schrøder
 (eds), *Media Cultures: Reappraising Transnational Media*, London: Routledge, pp.
 42–62.
Durkin, K. (1995) *Computer Games: their Effects on Young People*, Sydney, NSW: Office
 of Film and Literature Classification.
Eron, L.D. (1997) 'The Development of Antisocial Behavior from a Learning Perspec-
 tive', in D.M. Stoff, J. Breiling and J.D. Maser (eds), *Handbook of Antisocial Behavior*,
 New York: Wiley, pp. 140–7.
Fowles, J. (1999) *The Case for Television Violence*, Thousand Oaks, CA: Sage Publica-
 tions.
Freedman, J.L. (2002) *Media Violence and its Effect on Aggression: Assessing the Scientific
 Evidence*, Toronto: University of Toronto Press.
Funk, J.B. (2000) Testimony Regarding the Impact of Interactive Violence on Children
 before the United States Senate Commerce Committee, 2003.
Garbarino, J. (2001) 'Violent Children: Where Do We Point the Finger of Blame?',
 Archive Pediatric Adolescent Med, 155(1): 13–14.
Gitlin, T. (1994) 'Imagebusters: the Hollow Crusade against TV Violence', *American
 Prospect*, 5(16): 42–9.
Goldstein, J.H. (1998) *Why We Watch: the Attractions of Violent Entertainment*, Oxford:
 Oxford University Press.
Goldstein, J.H. (2001) 'Does Playing Violent Video Games Cause Aggressive Behav-
 ior?', conference paper, Cultural Policy Center, University of Chicago.
Goodman, P. (1956) *Growing Up Absurd*, New York: Random House.
Griffiths, M.D. (1998) 'Violent Video Games and Aggression: a Review of the Litera-
 ture', *Aggression and Violent Behavior*, 4(2): 203–12.

Grossman, D. (1995) *On Killing: the Psychological Cost of Learning to Kill in War and Society*, Boston: Back Bay Books.

Grossman, D. (1998) 'Trained to Kill', *Christianity Today*, 10 August 1998: 31–9.

Hoerrner, K. (1999) 'The Forgotten Battles. Congressional Hearings on Television Violence in the 1950s', *The Web Journal of Mass Communication Research (WJMCR)*, 2 (3 June 1999), http://www.scripps.ohiou.edu/wjmcr/vo102/2-3a-3.htm.

Horsfield, P. (1997) 'Moral Panic or Moral Action? The Appropriation of Moral Panics in the Exercise of Social Control', http://www.vic.uca.org.au/ecrp/papers.html.

Huesmann, L.R. and N.G. Guerra (1997) 'Children's Normative Beliefs about Aggression and Aggressive Behavior', *Journal of Personality and Social Psychology*, 72(2): 408–19.

Huston, A.C. et al. (1992) *Big World, Small Screen: the Role of Television in American Society*, Lincoln: University of Nebraska Press.

Jenkins, H. (1999) 'Professor Jenkins Goes to Washington', http://web.mit.edu/21fms/www/faculty/henry3/profjenkins.html.

Klapper, J. (1960) *The Effects of Mass Communication*, Glencoe Ill.: Free Press.

Kline, S. (1993) *Out of the Garden: Toys, TV and Children's Culture in the Age of Marketing*, Toronto: Garamond Press.

Kline, S. (2000) 'Moral Panic and Video Games Research in Childhood', in *A Collection of Papers. Sociology, Culture and History Conference*, Odense University, Denmark: Department of Child and Youth Culture.

Kline, S. (2003) 'Media Effects: Redux or Reductive?' *Particip@tions*, 1(1), www.sfu.ca/media-lab/risk/.

Maguire, B., G.A. Weatherby et al. (2002) 'Network News Coverage of School Shootings', *Social Science Journal*, 39(3): 465–70.

Manson, Charles (2004) http://www.quotemeonit.com/mansonc.html.

Minow, N.N. and C.L. LaMay (1995) *Abandoned in the Wasteland: Children, Television, and the First Amendment*, New York: Hill and Wang.

Murray, J.P. (1995) 'Children and Television Violence', *Kansas Journal of Law & Public Policy*, 4(3): 7–14.

Murray, J.P. (2001) 'TV Violence and Children's Brains: More Reasons for Advocacy and Policy Reform', *The Child, Youth, and Family Services Advocate*, 24(2): 1–4.

NIMH (National Institute of Mental Health) (1982) *Television and Behavior: Ten Years of Scientific Progress and Implications for the Eighties: Vol. 1. Summary Report* (DHHS Publication No. ADM 82-1195), Washington, DC: US Government Printing Office.

Paik, H. and G.A. Comstock (1994) 'The Effects of Television Violence on Antisocial Behavior: a Meta-analysis', *Communication Research*, 21(4): 516–46.

Potter, W. James (1997) 'The Problem of Indexing Risk of Viewing Television Aggression', *Critical Studies in Mass Communication*, 14: 228–48

Provenzo, E. (1992) 'What Do Video Games Teach?', *Education Digest*, 58(4): 56–8.

Riesman, D., N. Glazer et al. (1961) *The Lonely Crowd*, New Haven: Yale University Press.

Robinson, T.L., M.L. Wilde, L.C. Navacruz, K.F. Haydel and A. Varady (2001) 'Effects of Reducing Children's Television and Video Game Use on Aggressive Behavior: a Randomized Controlled Trial', *Archive Pediatric Adolescent Med*, 155: 17–23.

Sorenson, S.B., J.G. Peterson Manz et al. (1998) 'News Media Coverage and the Epidemiology of Homicide', *American Journal of Public Health*, 88(10): 1510–14.

Spigel, L. (1998) 'Seducing the Innocent: Childhood and Television in Postwar America', in H. Jenkins (ed.), *The Children's Culture Reader*, New York: New York University Press, pp. 110–35.

Surgeon General's Scientific Advisory Committee on Television and Social Behavior (1972) *Television and Growing Up: the Impact of Televised Violence* (DHEW Publication No. HSM 72-9086), Washington, DC.

Surgeon General of the USA (2001) 'Youth Violence: a Report of the Surgeon General', http://www.surgeongeneral.gov/library/youthviolence/.

Wilson, B.J., D. Kunkel, D. Linz, J. Potter, E. Donnerstein, S.L. Smith, E. Blumenthal and T. Gray (1997) 'Violence in Television Programming Overall: University of California, Santa Barbara Study', in M. Seawall (ed.), *National Television Violence Study*, Vol. 1, Thousand Oaks, CA: Sage Publications, pp. 3–184.

Wilson, B.J., D. Kunkel, D. Linz, J. Potter, E. Donnerstein, S.L. Smith, E. Blumenthal and M. Berry (1998) 'Violence in Television Programming Overall: University of California, Santa Barbara study', in M. Seawall (ed.) *National Television Violence Study*, Vol. 2, Thousand Oaks, CA: Sage Publications, pp. 3–204.

YRBS, http://www.cdc.gov/HealthyYouth/yrbs/index.htm.

6

The Terrors of Hypervigilance: Security and the Compromised Spaces of Contemporary Childhood

Cindi Katz

Introduction – 'gravity's rainbow'

On 11 September 2001 'a screaming came across the sky'.[1] The events of that horrific day laced into the United States's insular presumptions of security, and the ongoing responses to the attacks and what they signified in the US imaginary have made clear the imperial privilege and xenophobic rancour upon which that security is built. I have been resistant to talking about 11 September in part because so much of my intellectual project has been to draw links between the lives of children and the prospects for young people in rural Sudan and racialized working-class New York City, and these events seemed to collapse that connection into a fatal arc that at the moment of their occurrence reminded me of the phrase Thomas Pynchon used to describe the parabolic arc of Germany's V2 rockets in World War II, 'gravity's rainbow'. Given my commitments to young people in New York and Sudan and the sorts of connections I have spent my career drawing between them – which I have come to call 'countertopographies' – I feel compelled to address the dangers of the reductionism that enables the binaries of 'us' and 'them' when the construction of otherness – and similarity or connection – is so much more complicated and potentially productive than that. This endeavour is loaded with a different kind of 'gravity': the gravity of living in the shards of capitalist modernity. It is the gravity of this situation that links young people in New York and Sudan, among many other places.

The 'gravity' in this sense is the gravity of US globalism and the populations it sheds at its margins. It is the scrambling, and at times despair and hopelessness, of those who are excluded and marginalized by the conditions produced by an increasingly globalized and neo-liberal capitalism, and the non-accidental racialization, gendering, and obvious class-based and imperialist nature of the divisions between those who are included and excluded, or those who 'have' and those who 'have not' at all levels. Among the effects of these processes is a growing number of young people excluded from the prospects – or even the fantasy – of a meaningful work future. The gravity for me is worked out most forcefully in the relationship between production and reproduction, and how the globalization of capitalist production has altered, ruptured, and at times rendered moot the promises associated with the social wage or the hard-won ability to ensure human growth and development along with the conditions of production for capitalist expansion. The relationship between production and reproduction is compromised in the global south by the excesses of primitive accumulation and by the structural adjustment programmes imposed on debtor nations by the International Monetary Fund, and in the globalized north, by the neo-liberal practices associated with privatization, welfare reform, and public disinvestment in social reproduction, even in Northern Europe where the welfare state has been long venerated.

Globalization, insecurity and hypervigilance

It is these sorts of shifts in the US that have provoked a real sense of insecurity – personal and ontological – and this insecurity has all too frequently been mobilized against targets quite different from its actual sources. Rather than targeting shortfalls in the social wage or the offloading of responsibility for it, individual and public actors may focus on such flattened categories of people as 'terrorists', 'the homeless' or 'urban youth', for example. These mobilizations, against stereotyped and homogenized 'others', often take the form of 'security' measures – surveillance, bunkering, fortressing and the like – that may allay the anxieties prompted by ontological insecurity but do nothing to reduce the sources of that insecurity, which I am arguing have more to do with things like broad-scale disinvestments in the social wage and the visceral presence of globalized violence. Ontological insecurity, in other words, seeps from the sorts of reconfigurations of daily life associated with new relationships between capital, the state and civil society in the accomplishment of social reproduction; rescalings of the relationships between political, economic and cultural forms and practices in everyday life; and a widespread retreat from the promises of a secure social wage.

If personal and ontological insecurity is an effect of economic restructuring, job insecurity, environmental hazards, war, militarism and state violence, economic and political marginalization and reductions in support for social welfare, why is the response to it more often than not meted out through all manner of 'revanchist' policies and practices mobilized against poor, homeless and racialized people at the local and state levels, or against 'terrorists' and 'rogue states' at the national and international levels (compare Smith, 1996). Apart from the disciplinary practices that are associated with such things as 'welfare reform' or structural adjustment programmes, all manner of state and other organizations are increasingly engaged in measures that buffer against 'outsiders'. These measures not only can be seen at a variety of levels from the home to the nation, but also, increasingly within the home as well, particularly around children's lives. If one response to these concerns, then, might be the fortressing of public space such as was seen in New York City following 11 September; and another the state violence that has become commonplace in Sudan, whether in its recently ended but decades-long civil war or more recently its genocidal mobilizations against another enemy within, the non-Arab (but Islamic and Arabic-speaking) residents in Darfur; and a third the state violence brought to bear against external enemies such the US's 'war on terror' fought in Afghanistan and Iraq, another site of response to these anxieties at least in the global North is the home. In recent years in the US, for instance, there has been an intensification of interest in securing the home and its inhabitants, particularly children. My argument here is that hypervigilance within the home parallels hypervigilance in public space and by extension the spaces and boundaries of nations. Their common grounds and effects merit some scrutiny. While elsewhere I have drawn comparisons between New York and Sudan in confronting the insecurities of children's futures, this chapter will focus on the practices of hypervigilance in US homes and the time-space of childhood in New York and the US, and only touch on these comparisons in the discussion of countertopographies in the conclusion (compare, for example, Katz, 2002; 2004a, b).

As capitalist production has become increasingly globalized, producers tend to construct their investments as placeless, or at least unmoored from the specificities and demands of any particular place. At the same time, financially strapped governments – at all levels from the municipal to the national – try to lure increasingly mobile producers to their regions with a battery of incentives, among them low wage rates and reduced taxes. Under these conditions neither producers nor governments have much incentive to pay for the costs of social reproduction, and the spaces in which children come of age are often among the first things to be jettisoned under such conditions. Yet it is in these everyday environments such as playgrounds, schoolyards and recreation centres, that children acquire the skills and knowledge they need to maintain and reproduce the matrix of social relations within which they come of age as well as the wherewithal to construct both their identities and the cultural forms and practices associated with them.

The withdrawal of support is particularly evident in the spaces of working-class and poor neighbourhoods; a function of the predictably uneven nature of declines in the social wage coupled with the inability of poorer families to compensate for the loss of public support for their children's well-being and sustenance over time. These conditions reflect, starkly at times, the expendability of this population from the perspective of capitalists and an increasingly fawning capitalist state. Crudely put, the reproduction of this population may represent a loss to capital both in the present and over the long term, because in a global economy with labour-saving innovations and virtually limitless international labour migration, their labour may be unnecessary to ongoing production. However crude and cruel a metric this might be, it abets if it doesn't drive the disinvestments in the public environment that have become the hallmark of contemporary neo-liberal capitalism. Public schools, housing, parks and playgrounds suffer in their wake. While production is increasingly fluid and mobile, social reproduction – grounded in the reproduction of people and place and the social relations that bind them – is inevitably more rooted (Katz, 2002). These circumstances take a toll in various deteriorations in children's health and well-being.

In the often mundane spaces of the public environment children and teens have opportunities to play in open-ended or organized ways, to engage with other children serendipitously or by design, and literally to get their hands dirty as they engage with the physical environment and its various resources. The often unheralded public spaces of everyday life are crucial to the processes of social reproduction, but they rarely garner the attention of other sites of social reproduction such as schools, childcare centres, the home or, more troublingly, prisons. The relative inattention to these spaces is in marked contrast to the early years of the twentieth century in the US when Progressive Era reformers focused on the streets, playgrounds and gymnasiums as settings wherein working-class immigrant children might be scooped up and 'Americanized'. As often as not this imperative was driven by a desire to tame the potential unruliness of these young people and to channel their boredom or oppositional impulses to what the reformers saw as more productive ends, including education and stable if not riveting employment (Rainwater, 1922; Goodman, 1979; Nasaw, 1985; Gagen, 2000). Reformers encouraged urban park and playground construction and staffing, and municipal governments quickly caught on, readily seeing the advantages of providing play and recreation opportunities for children and youth, especially those living and working in overcrowded conditions.

By the end of the twentieth century such imperatives were much harder to come by. With state budgets constrained by the effects of right-wing spurred tax rebellions, exacerbated by the tendency of many governments to offer businesses tax abatements in exchange for capital investment, there was little money to provide for play and recreation. In most localities these limited funds went to maintenance and occasionally construction projects, and were rarely channelled to programmatic development or staffing. Even with the trend towards privatization associated with neo-liberal capitalism globally, there has been relatively little private support for the unglamorous spaces and routine activities associated with children's play and recreation. Most of the highly vaunted public–private partnerships interested in open space in New York City are involved in capital improvement and infrastructural maintenance rather than routine staffing or programmatic activities. Even then, these conservancies and organizations associated with 'business improvement districts' tend to be much more deeply involved in highly visible public spaces rather than those in poor and working-class neighbourhoods where wealthy residents, corporate leaders, and tourists rarely visit (Katz, 1998).

If the early twentieth-century reformers supported play leadership and the development of play spaces to draw children from the streets and other unsupervised and unsafe public environments, the current absence of such support for the public spaces of children's everyday lives does not mean that children are back on the streets in large numbers. Quite the reverse. Indeed, thanks in part to the deteriorations in the social wage associated with neo-liberalism, particularly in combination with some of the cultural and technological changes of the last couple of decades, children and young people are increasingly withdrawn from the public environment through more private means. Televisions, computers, video games and the internet can be seen as strategies of privatization in the ways that they draw people away from the common physical spaces of their everyday lives (Wood and Beck, 1994). But in this realm, as on the streets, parents frequently restrict their children's autonomous mobility, although they do find one another through 'instant messaging' and other electronic social forums.

Apart from techno-cultural forms of privatization, and the privatization of public spaces themselves, there are still other ways that children's access to the outdoor environment has been privatized. For instance, while children, of course, still occupy and take advantage of the public open spaces of their communities, they commonly do so supervised by an adult care-taker, even in suburban and rural environments and well into adolescence. While wealthier families are more easily able to afford either the presence of a parent or a paid childminder, poorer and single-parent households often have little choice but to keep their children home alone after school. The cutbacks in after-school programmes and other publicly-sponsored community programmes exacerbate these problems. In the name of safety, then, young people are subject to greater supervision, face increasing amounts of surveillance, are kept home alone, and tend to participate in more regulated rather than spontaneous activities with their friends or peers. Parental restrictions on children's autonomous mobility promulgate and often mask the troubling consequences of the privatization of their lives; all in the name of their safety.

The spaces of children's everyday lives in New York City

Yet these circumstances notwithstanding, the public spaces of children's everyday lives matter deeply, of course, and many remain woefully neglected in New York City. As more visible parks in the city are lavishly attended through public–private partnerships such as the Central Park Conservancy and the (Brooklyn) Prospect Park Alliance, many public spaces in the less visible parts of the city have faced enduring budget cuts and been left to deteriorate. Not surprisingly, playgrounds in poor neighbourhoods, which tend to be under-served by park facilities to begin with, are often worse off. But the pattern of attention and neglect is no less serious for being pre- dictable. In the places of neglect there are few opportunities to restore or otherwise address the declines in services and reductions in funding for public open space, and when school or community groups organize around these issues the results can be frustrating because they lack the political clout and 'cultural capital' to accomplish even modest goals.

The case of New York City's community gardens is a notorious example of such frustrations. In many poor and working-class neighbourhoods, residents – often with the assistance of non-governmental organizations such as the Green Guerrillas – turned vacant lots (frequently owned by the city) into thriving community gardens growing vegetables and ornamental plants. These gardens – oases for children and others – often encompassed simple gathering places such as a gazebo, mini-amphitheatre, picnic table or 'casita' (a small house resembling those in Puerto Rico and other Caribbean islands). Yet despite community dedication and intensive use these spaces were not secure. In 1998 then-mayor Rudolph Giuliani autho- rized the transfer of 741 community gardens from Project Green Thumb to the city's development agency to pave the way for housing development. There was widespread and vociferous opposition to these bold moves. Many of the gardens selected for auction and demolition were in the neighbour- hoods most poorly served with open or green space. Most galling was that many times there were vacant lots or landlord abandoned properties nearby. When Giuliani authorized the auction of more than 100 gardens in the spring of 1999 his efforts were thwarted by 'divine' intervention. The singer Bette Midler funded and managed to secure private means to purchase the gardens so that they might be held in trust for community use. Unfortunately, this intervention was too late to save the Children's Garden of Love in central Harlem, which was bulldozed in front of a number of schoolchildren's eyes, giving them a civics lesson they were not likely to forget.

In another less dramatic instance, also in Harlem, my colleagues at the City University of New York and I collaborated with two community schools concerning the reconstruction of their schoolyards from banal and poorly maintained patches of asphalt – which afforded little but selected organized sports, running around, and certain ad hoc activities that required little space – to differentiated, vegetated, pleasant multi-use environments. We were brought into the project by a schoolyards committee organized by parents, teachers and administrators in the school district. We worked with neighbourhood and school groups in a participatory design process that cul- minated in an international student design competition, which produced several splendid and workable designs for each of the two yards – one for early primary and the other for late primary students (Hart et al., 1992). Yet it took more than a dozen years for there to be any significant changes on the grounds. The previously allocated school construction budget remained elusive throughout our work despite – or maybe because of – other school-yards being improved in more prosperous areas of the district during the same time period. These latter initiatives were made possible in part because of private initiatives by parents and others, while our community self-help measures seemed of little avail until the principal of one of the schools finally succeeded in garnering funds from the Manhattan Borough President's Office.

Central Park is only two blocks south of these two schools, and during the 1990s – exactly the same period during which we were struggling to change the schoolyards – Central Park was completely renovated thanks to the massive and extraordinarily well-funded efforts of the Central Park Conservancy. Not only does this point to the contradictions at the heart of contemporary neo-liberalism, but there were more local and poignant political implications as well. Children in this south-central Harlem neighbourhood, so close to Central Park, were not allowed to visit the park unaccompanied because of parental fears for their safety. Its fabulous resources, which in the immediate vicinity included a skating rink, a pond, a nature study centre, and beautiful forested hills and ravines, were all too often unavailable to them. Yet while the schoolyards were at the children's disposal either because they were occasionally staffed during after-school hours or because they were visible (or at least audible) from many apartment windows, they remained unimproved, unsightly and in places unsafe, because the schools were not able to find the modest sums required to improve them. At the same time the Central Park Conservancy, awash in funds, was unable to provide assistance outside of the park boundaries although its staff did suggest that they might be able to provide some gardening assistance if we got the garden beds in place.

As I have suggested, the early years of the twentieth century were vastly different in terms of both the attention to playground and park development, and the support for play leadership and other forms of staffing in poor neighbourhoods of the city. The reformers and their municipal partners saw team sports, calisthenics and other activities as pleasurable means of inculcating respect for authority, self-discipline, and adherence to rules; goals not coincidentally connected to making a willing and pliant labour force and ensuring some measure of 'security' for the capitalist state. The rise and fall of New York's industrial economy during the course of the twentieth century is echoed in the investments and disinvestments in public space and recreational programming. When the city relied on a home grown workforce it and private philanthropists made a range of provisions for their social reproduction (and disciplining), including recreational spaces and activities. The disinvestments in public open space by the end of the century inverted the investments at its start, but the fulcrum of both was the reproduction (or not) of a domestic labour force.

This argument about the investments and disinvestments in public open space is necessarily oversimplified and even a bit crude. Investment decisions concerning these and other spaces of social reproduction were influenced by broader considerations of class, race and gender as much as by shifting perspectives on such things as urban life, the role of the state, children's lives and role in society, immigration and the imagined future. All that notwithstanding, economic data suggest there is a disturbingly straightforward relationship between the importance of producing a differentiated labour force and investment in the spaces associated with social reproduction by governments and non-governmental groups associated with civil society. This relationship came into stark relief in New York City following the fiscal crisis of the mid-1970s when virtually all of the public spaces of the city from the least to most visible deteriorated dramatically in the course of years of erosive budget cuts that precluded capital investment and all but the most important maintenance work. Public–private partnerships, such as the Central Park Conservancy were established to compensate for these losses and redeem at least the prominent parks of the city. These partnerships tended to concentrate on the landscape rather than recreational activities, and so improved the visible city of wealth and privilege over and against the everyday city of children. If in the past privileged groups and individuals advocated the public provision of high quality open space accessible to all, the tendency now is to care for their own backyards. This tendency is part and parcel of the neo-liberal ethos spurred and enabled by capitalist globalism, which not only has unhinged the commitments of producers to particular places and the reproduction of a localized workforce, but has authorized a shrill and often venomous discourse against shared public responsibility for social welfare and reproduction. These altered commitments take their toll in the undramatic but nonetheless serious degradation and reduced operations of all manner of play environments, from parks and playgrounds to recreation centres and neighbourhood pools. These must be counted among the effects of 'globalization' for young people and their families.

Household hypervigilance

If public–private groups such as the Central Park Conservancy offer spatialized responses to socioeconomic problems that reflect largely bourgeois interests, what happens closer to home, in the household itself? Here the question of security arises again. In the face of the everyday deteriorations marked above, exacerbated by an easily tapped fearfulness and insecurity following the attacks of 11 September, there has been an intensification of domestic fortressing and what I call parental hypervigilance (Katz, 2001a).

This hypervigilance parallels that of the contemporary 'anti-terrorist' state in that it guards against and may forestall the effects of certain well-developed but polymorphous anxieties, but does little to protect against or redress the problems that underlie and provoke these anxieties. And it is these problems that need serious social tending.

In the face of these concerns, made more visceral by the fear stoked and manipulated by governmental offices and agencies in the US and their allies in the mass media and security industry, a growing number of parents are drawn to an array of strategies – usually private – to protect their children from perceived (but generally quite rare) threats to their well-being. Among these strategies are private play corrals such as 'Discovery Zone' or those provided by fast-food establishments; home surveillance systems including child monitors and 'nannycams' (concealed video cameras that provide a visual record of the activities of children, childcare workers and others); web-camera systems that allow parents to access real-time video recordings of childcare centres and schools through the internet; school-based closed-circuit camera systems, and, more ominously, monitoring devices attached to children that allow parents and others to locate them using GPS (geographic positioning systems). As these novel strategies become the norm, the assault on social reproduction and the social wage proceeds, instating a kind of terror about children's everyday lives that is not in the least redressed by these measures even if it calls them forth. These measures, which can be quite invasive, respond to the symptoms and not the root causes of the serious problems at hand. In other words, insecurity is impelled and fostered in part by widespread and increasingly deep disinvestments in social reproduction. The gap between privileged and disadvantaged families in developing ways to respond to these problems is large and growing and presents its own set of problems and concerns. Hypervigilance is in part a response to these discomfiting facts, and plays out differently in households of different means. All of this notwithstanding, it is simply not possible (nor desirable) to protect children from everything, and hypervigilance along with other forms of 'hyperparenting' misses this point completely. Indeed, as Jean Gottmann expressed it, what makes terror terrifying is its utter unpredictability, and this, of course, is what cannot be completely protected against. Focusing on the insecurities provoked by fear and stoked by terror channels too many resources away from addressing less dramatic problems, which actually have a chance of being redressed, toward troubles that almost by definition transcend resolution. The gap between rich and poor is widened in the process and the responses in each realm in turn produce their own anxieties.

The parallels here between the urban, national, and global levels are direct. Just as in the domestic sphere, it is a fiction that security measures can protect the population from everything; and promulgating an ever-widening charade of 'security' puts extraordinary resources at the service of military destruction, surveillance and policing. Moreover, in the home, as in the US state, some of the most serious threats to security, to say nothing of well-being, are often from within. If these resources expended for 'security' were spent on the goods, services and spaces associated with the social wage, for instance, it might curb some of the free-range insecurity – ontological and more material – that permeates contemporary life in the United States. The terrors of globalization, or more aptly of capitalist-driven US global hegemony, are witnessed in the mundane ravages of everyday life that I have been addressing here. Not only is there a great and growing divide between rich and poor households, but in the former childhood is often fetishized while in the latter just securing the means of children's existence can be elusive. Under these circumstances too many young people are evicted from the promises of the future, and with the war in Iraq even the possibility of a future is tragically foreclosed for some. The means to redress these concerns require not piecemeal private strategies that are largely compensatory for an absent social strategy, but a politics of social justice that is translocal, internationalist, and encompasses the uneven relations of power and privilege across differences of nation, race, gender and class.

But here I want to stay focused at the domestic and community scale to draw out the consequences for children and young people of domestic hypervigilance. The discourse of fear centred on children's well-being has called forth an increasingly serious and even militarized domestic response to perceived dangers in the local and distant environment. Beyond the fortressing and alarming of the domestic environment, a growing number of households are enlisting the wares associated with the burgeoning 'child protection industry'. This industry purveys all manner of technologies from the increasingly familiar, such as nannycams, to the still mercifully bizarre, such as wrist rockets or child-size mace sprays. While the industry taps into the anxieties traced above, it papers them over with more prosaic claims about family life, suggesting for instance that parents will be able to ensure that their childcare providers – whether in the home or outside of it – are doing good work, that their children are engaged and well-tended, and that they themselves know what's going on in their children's everyday lives (Katz, 2001a). These laudable attributes do not get around the fact that these businesses have also exploited a battery of sensationalized tales of childcare misconduct and child injury to develop their market. All of which, in conjunction with other social, political and economic processes such as the backlash against feminism, fans the flames of parental insecurity and contributes to a sort of creeping privatization of children's everyday lives.

The industries associated with child protection and security more generally not only foster this privatization, but their very existence and attractiveness suggest a proclivity for technocratic solutions to social, political and economic problems. While such solutions may always be 'easier', at least for those with means, there have been times when alternative political logics held more sway than the current neo-liberal impetus to provide for social goods and services through private means (compare, Hayden, 1980 for examples from a different era). In the 1960s–1970s, for instance, there was more widespread interest, especially among feminists, in the social and more democratic organization of childcare and community spaces for children and families. The shifts, especially under present economic and political circumstances, are easy to understand. Purchasing services (and the mechanisms that ensure that they are of adequate quality) takes financial resources but considerably less effort (and probable frustration) than organizing their social provision, especially in an inhospitable social climate. At the same time those with little money, who might find the social provision of childcare a more attractive alternative than its purchase, often have little time and fewer resources to accomplish this work without governmental assistance and a more broad-based constituency involved in the project.

The sales of nannycams in the USA have been increasing steadily in the last few years. While still used by a minority of households with young children, in a recent poll by the marketing research firm, Parks Associates, 19 per cent of households (with young children) indicated that they would purchase such a device to keep an eye on their babysitters or nannies (Tarkan, 2004). Scripts of conversations on parent websites suggest an ambivalent embrace of the technology among web loggers. Many parents expressed a hesitance to spy on their nannies but this was often coupled with acclamation of the peace of mind such devices offer. Other technologies include ambulatory child monitors and various electronic locating systems invented for the warehouse and shipping industries, and using satellite technology in the form of GPS as means for locating children in either enclosed spaces such as large recreational facilities or the broader public environment. Most startling among these devices is the 'digital angel', a chip that was intended to be subcutaneously implanted in children so that they could be located anywhere. While privacy concerns thwarted the merchandising of these patented devices, they were quickly retooled in two directions. For children, the chips were placed in various friendly-looking accessories so that they could be worn around their necks or wrists, albeit sometimes the bands used require a special tool to remove. A mechanism with sobering similarities to those used on low risk prisoners under 'house arrest'. In other realms, the subcutaneous chip found a new home in animals. Chips have been successfully marketed to pet owners, first so that their animals' medical history might be easily retrieved, but also so that they might be located if they strayed or were stolen. Their use with children might not be too far behind. Cell phones, of course, have become almost a rite of passage among younger and younger children in families with means to afford them, and serve fairly innocuously as a means of keeping tabs on children (and parents). Mobile phones have made electronic tethering among family members fairly routine.

While many would argue that these devices enable greater mobility for children in the public environment and reassure parents that their children are safe in the home or various childcare environments – and I don't disagree – I am concerned about their implications for family life, how they take fear and distrust for granted, and the ways in which they are recreating the state in miniature form in the home (Katz, 2001a). These devices, among others, offer technocratic solutions for economic and social problems, such as the withering of the Keynesian state, the persistence of a gendered division of labour that holds women more accountable than men for the provision of childcare, and the reworking of everyday geographies in ways that have reinforced the dispersal of extended families and put greater distance between the workplace and home. In communities distant from both families and work, not only can it be more difficult for parents to secure the congeries of goods and services associated with social reproduction or the social wage, but also in such places there is greater exposure to – and perhaps a deeper sense of vulnerability toward – strangers in the settings of everyday life, from the home, neighbourhood and school, to the workplace and nearby commercial areas. In this hard and still relatively novel place a growing number of parents not only hire people to assist with the upbringing of their children and maintenance of their domestic environment, but also substitute social engagement with technological interventions.

The effects of these shifts are not well understood. At their most benign these displacements and substitutions seem to foster a relationship between parents and children that is more akin to 'parallel play' than interaction; in other words parents and children are in touch and may have a sense of what one another are up to, but they are not really engaged with one another socially or psychologically. More serious, perhaps, is that in pursuing these material social practices, parents are not only compensating for the diminished state in their home environments, but responding to the vulnerabilities it provokes by instating themselves as domestic spies and community police. Parents not only spy on the workers in their homes, most centrally childminders, but on their children as well. Quite separate from the technologies I have been discussing such as child monitors, 'digital angel' devices, nannycams, and web cameras in daycare and school settings, a small but growing number of parents appear to be drawing on other sectors of the 'child protection industry' through the acquisition and use of such surreptitious technologies as home drug-testing kits, automobile speed monitors which provide a read-out of the speeds attained by young drivers, and keystroke monitoring systems that can reprise all messages, websites, and passwords entered by children on their home computers. Drawing on these technologies batters common notions of familial trust, however fraught this might have been in the past, and creates a home environment in which children may grow up taking for granted that they are under surveillance even in the most intimate spaces of their lives. Worse than parallel play between parents and children, these circumstances of distrust and limited privacy seriously alter the grounds for the development of personal autonomy and responsibility among young people. These developmental consequences are graver than the conditions that provoke parental hypervigilance.

Hypervigilance is, of course, a response to many things. It is a response to common fears and anxieties around children's welfare and well-being that is part and parcel of the swirl of fear that increasingly characterizes contemporary life in the United States if only because it is stoked by the media and various government agencies. Hypervigilance – or hyperparenting more generally – is also a response to the guilt and anxiety that many parents feel as a result of being absent from their children for much of each week, usually for work. These feelings are often exacerbated and inflamed by a range of discursive practices that associate women with children, and discipline them, in the Foucauldian sense, to stay at home. Hypervigilance, particularly around childcare workers, also must be provoked at some level by employers internalizing the great gaps in wealth and privilege that enable them to hire others to care for their children. These exchanges of money for love and love for money, especially when they require childminders to leave their own children in the care of others, often in their countries of origin, reflect the painful unevenness of the global economy and may spur feelings of anxiety and vulnerability on both sides of the equation (Hochschild, 2003; Parreñas, 2001). But the strategies associated with hypervigilance, such as those detailed above, can never be up to the task. Indeed they sidestep and obscure the deeply problematic issues underlying the free-range insecurity which provokes parental hypervigilance in the first place. As I have indicated, these underlying issues include the political and economic assault on the social wage associated with neo-liberal globalism. The shrinking social wage and the fraying of social reproduction associated with today's highly mobile modes of capitalist production produce a much larger kind of 'insecurity' at the heart of children's lives. And this insecurity is not easily redressed through hypervigilant parenting, whatever form it takes.

It is not possible – or desirable – to protect children from every possible harm; they really do need to learn how to make assessments of risk and danger on their own. But even if this fantasy of parenthood were a viable option, all of the micro-management strategies in the world would fall short. For one, children (over the centuries and all over the world) have proven to be pretty crafty in the face of parental restrictions and monitoring of various sorts. But second, and more serious, is the obdurate fact that children are most commonly harmed by or at risk from members of their own families and households. Indeed there have already been instances of nannycams catching family members abusing young children. But most significantly, as this piece has tried to underscore, the most pernicious and persistent dangers to children are from an entirely different source. If these problems are social, economic and political, so too must be the strategies that respond to them. The privatized 'state' that is the citadel home and its extensions may well cope with the symptoms of an eviscerated social wage, but they do virtually nothing to change the conditions that produce it.

Securing the future – a political response

These concerns call for responses well beyond private means of securing everyday life, however anxiety-reducing these may be. They call for rejuvenating a broad politics of social justice focused on the concerns of social reproduction and the diminished social wage; a politics that aspires to internationalism and works translocally around issues of education, childcare, housing, health and public space would begin to get at these deeper concerns and their effects on children's and families' everyday lives. And so I want to return to 'gravity's rainbow', both the gravity and the rainbow. Along with the globalization of capitalist production – and the tolls it takes on myriad localities – is also a globalization of knowledge, culture and media, and these circulate with and against capital, labour and other global movements. Under these conditions, the promises of modernity are made more apparent to people who can't necessarily share in them. Michel-Rolph Trouillot (1996) has developed the notion of 'fragmented globality,' wherein some parts of the world are more firmly connected while others are hurled further apart. Geographical contiguity is less important for access to wealth, power, services and the like than other factors such as technology, resources, knowledge and skills under these circumstances. This fragmentation can be seen in households (namely, home workers and employers) as much as at the urban, national and global scale. But other kinds of connections are possible, and it is important to find and make something of these. The 'fragments' of globalization and of those scrambling to 'secure' their lives and futures can refuse the policing and other divisive and distrustful strategies associated with hypervigilance whether within or outside the home, and work toward making connections that strive to restore the promises of the social wage for all. International coalition-building such as that associated with Jubilee 2000 or the World Social Forums makes clear the potential (and arduousness) of this sort of political work.

But other geographical imaginations might be called forth as well. Elsewhere in my work I have developed the idea of 'countertopographies' as a means of abstractly linking disparate – and even unlikely – places by virtue of their particular relationship to issues connected with the social wage, such as the deskilling of young people or the absence of childhood play environments (compare Katz, 2001b; 2004b). The project of mapping (and then politically organizing around) the 'contour lines' that link these dispersed sites, the countertopography, is one that attempts to make good Marx's admonition to theorize 'up' from the abstract to the concrete. Producing countertopographies takes an abstraction such as capitalist globalism or the shifting relationship between production and social reproduction, traces its effects on multiple grounds, highlighting specific issues such as children's everyday lives, and then works out a geography at once imaginative and concrete for responding politically to these circumstances. The politics such connections might spur refuse the bait of privatization, objectification of others, and hypervigilance. Tracing a trajectory similar to that of neo-liberal globalism and focused at the heart of its strategies around social reproduction, this sort of political practice might respond to some of the many insecurities it provokes. Securing the future of modern childhood and contemporary children, whether in the global north or south, or from over-privileged or underprivileged households, requires no less.

Note

I am grateful to Jens Qvortrup not only for his fabulous work concerning childhood and for inviting me to the seminar for which this piece was originally prepared, but for his engaging wit and extraordinary patience as I missed deadline after deadline.

1. The phrase is the opening line of Thomas Pynchon's extraordinary novel, *Gravity's Rainbow*.

References

Gagen, E. (2000) 'An Example to Us All: Child Development and Identity Construction in Early 20th-Century Playgrounds', *Environment and Planning A*, 32: 599–616.
Goodman, C. (1979) *Choosing Sides: Playgrounds and Street Life on the Lower East Side*, New York: Schocken Books.
Hart, R., C. Katz, S. Iltus and M.R. Mora (1992) 'International Student Design Competition of Two Community Elementary Schoolyards', *Children's Environments*, 9 (2): 65–82.
Hayden, D. (1980) 'What Would a Non-Sexist City Be Like? Speculations on Housing, Urban Design and Human Work', *Signs: Journal of Women in Culture and Society*, 5 (3) Supplement: 170–87.
Hochschild, A.R. (2003) *Commercialization of Intimate Life: Notes from Home and Work*, Berkeley and Los Angeles: University of California Press.
Katz, C. (1998) 'Whose Nature, Whose Culture? Private Productions of Space and the Preservation of Nature', in B. Braun and N. Castree (eds), *Remaking Reality: Nature at the End of the Millenium*, London and New York: Routledge, pp. 46–63.
Katz, C. (2001a) 'The State Comes Home: Local Hypervigilance of Children and the Global Retreat from Social Reproduction', *Social Justice*, 28 (3): 47–56.
Katz, C. (2001b) 'On the Grounds of Globalization: a Topography for Feminist Political Engagement', *Signs: Journal of Women in Culture and Society*, 26 (4): 1213–34.
Katz, C. (2002) 'Stuck in Place: Children and the Globalization of Social Reproduction', in R.J. Johnston, P.J. Taylor and M.J. Watts (eds), *Geographies of Global Change: Remapping the World*, 2nd edition, Oxford: Blackwell Publishers, pp. 248–60.

Katz, C. (2004a) 'Reconfiguring Childhood: Boys and Girls Growing Up Global', *Revista: Harvard Review of Latin America*, 32 (2): 12–15.

Katz, C. (2004b) *Growing Up Global: Economic Restructuring and Children's Everyday Lives*, Minneapolis: University of Minnesota Press.

Nasaw, D. (1985) *Children of the City*, Garden City, NY: Anchor Press/Doubleday.

Parreñas, R.S. (2001) *Servants of Globalization: Women, Migration and Domestic Work*, Stanford, CA: Stanford University Press.

Rainwater, C. (1922) *The Play Movement in the United States*, Chicago: University of Chicago Press.

Smith, N. (1996) *The New Urban Frontier: Gentrification and the Revanchist City*, New York and London: Routledge.

Tarkan, L. (2004) 'The Nannycam Diaries', *Child*, May: 67–70.

Trouillot, M.-R. (1996) 'Theorizing a Global Perspective: a Conversation with Michel-Rolph Trouillot', *Crosscurrents in Culture, Power and History: a Newsletter of the Institute for Global Studies in Culture, Power and History, Johns Hopkins University*, 4 (1): 1–4.

Wood, D. and Beck, R. (1994) *Home Rules*, Baltimore and London: Johns Hopkins University Press.

7
Childhood and Transgression

Chris Jenks

This chapter is a piece of social theory inspired by the challenges that children present to the social order. Educational psychology and pedagogic theory more generally have, over the past three decades, proliferated categories of childhood pathology. In turn the vocabularies of parenting have assumed a much broader range of accounts that seek to mitigate for any perceived gap between actual child behaviour and desired or 'ideal' child behaviour. Now it may be that our children are becoming increasingly complex as we enter the twenty-first century or, more likely, we are becoming more complex in the way that we understand and articulate identity and difference. Whatever, the starting point of this chapter is the proposition that pathology, difference and transgression are things that children do and as social theorists we must attend to the messages encoded in such behaviour.

Conventional structural sociologies begin from a premise of order, its maintenance and reproduction. Such order is guaranteed through values shared at the highest level of abstraction, normative constraint and processes of governance and control. As a consequence binaries are sustained between crucial elements of the social structure and social process. Understood, entrenched and oppositional values are devised between the centre and the periphery, normative behaviour and deviant behaviour, sacred symbols and profane symbols, and that which is pure is distinguished from that which is dangerous by processes and conditions of defilement. Further transitional concepts are developed to account for the transition of individuals (or judgements concerning their behaviour) from one zone to another. So, for example, we have van Gennep's (1960) original concept of a *rite de passage*, which in Victor Turner's (1974) hands develops into a consideration of the liminal zones in human development and identity change. Nevertheless, from its inception sociology has rested on deep-seated humanistic or indeed altruistic philosophies (or fictions) which sustain these narratives which defy the contemporary recognition of complexity in human affairs.

The Enlightenment and Nietzsche's challenge

In a strong sense the boundaries that mark out the supposed segments or places within social life are, in effect, entrenched ways of understanding different moral spaces in social life and, more cynically, justifications for mechanisms of power and control. These contradictions arise to a major degree from the confluence of the Enlightenment ideals that fed social theory and the Nietzschean philosophical revolution that has, more recently, threatened to bring it down. Whereas the Enlightenment insisted upon the ultimate perfectibility of human kind – a goal to be achieved by privileging calculative reason, Nietzsche's sonorous announcement that 'God is dead' insisted upon radically less.

The Enlightenment ideal has come to mean three things: (i) that we systematically confuse change with progress; (ii) that we have experimented with human excellence through various flawed political policies; and (iii) that we have become intolerant if not incredulous towards excessive or transgressive behaviour. Nietzsche's obituary for the Almighty, on the other hand, has given rise to three different but contributory processes: (i) it has removed certainty; (ii) it has mainstreamed the re-evaluation of values; and (iii) it has released control over infinity.

Post-structuralism has released us from the necessity of binary thinking and has relativized the notion of boundary, previously so essential to order and orderly thinking. The tradition inspired by Nietzsche looks at this constant re-evaluation of values and seeks to free us from what it regards as the totalizing rationalist legacy stretching back to Hegel that sees all life as balanced, progressive and thus evolving towards the end of history.

George Bataille and heterology

George Bataille presents an extraordinary figure whose ideas have been most instrumental in the project of this chapter. Although he could claim no monopoly over the term, his work, perhaps beyond all others, is closely associated with the concept of transgression. Bataille seemed obsessed by and wrote erratically on topics such as 'death', 'excess', 'transgression', 'eroticism', 'evil', 'sacrifice', 'Fascism', 'prostitution', 'de Sade', 'desire' and other more conventional topics, but always in an unconventional manner. There was an intense energy, wildness and vandalism about Bataille, which he manifested to the full, that make his medieval scholarship, Marxist studies, association with surrealism, involvement in secret societies, rumours of human sacrifice, writing pornography, and drunkenness and fornication, all coherent parts of his total persona. Hussey (2002, p. 86) summarizes this clearly when he tells us that:

> Bataille was a distinguished and influential figure, editor of the respected journal *Critique*, whose long rivalry with André Breton had established

him and his circle as a rallying point for dissident Surrealists. Bataille, who combined a diligent career as a librarian at the Bibliothèque Nationale with a thirst for excess and violence in philosophy and politics, also had a reputation as an eroticist. Bataille's fictional writings were notorious for their blasphemy and sadistic content; Bataille's own personal life was alleged to match anything found in his fictions.

So, larger than life, decadent, depraved, fêted in his own time by a small but highly influential group of friends including Jacques Lacan, Michel Leiris, Maurice Blanchot, Pierre Klossowski and Roger Caillois, nevertheless, Bataille remained a minor figure on the European intellectual landscape. Ironically, after his death and in the later part of the twentieth century Bataille has been resurrected as the new intellectual avatar, the unspoken father of heterology and the 'post-', the 'prophet of transgression' (Noys, 2000). The literature by, on or about Bataille has proliferated and he is now seen, increasingly, to be a central and seminal figure – a fame that he would have resented for mainstreaming his maverick thoughts. However, despite the modern preoccupation with his capture Bataille's ideas remain labyrinthine, obscure, multiply-fuelled, fierce, neglectful of tradition and simultaneously poetic and repulsive. He does not warm, welcome or seek either agreement or consensus. Bataille appears often to be working through the obligations of a Sadean 'sovereign man', the reader can 'take it or leave it' and the pursuit of inspiration is clearly more important than that we should join hands and applaud his achievements. His topics are dictated by no agenda other than his own libidinal force and his desire will be heard. Leiris, his friend for many years, described him as 'the impossible one, fascinated by everything he could discover about what was really unacceptable' (Leiris quoted in Habermas, 1984, p. 79). However, this does not mean that he is without a trajectory; his work is coherent but the narrative is very much internal. He is intensely engaged in the Hegelian struggle for recognition and yet stands somewhere on the cusp of such political action sliding from an address of the community, the collective, to the decentred manifestation of difference that inhabits contemporary 'identity politics'. His rage is with the economics of capitalism and the economics that this mode of production inserts in the relationships between people, yet his fear stems from the loss of God and the subsequent threat to individual sovereignty. He has exhausted the limitations of Marxism. He wants to counter the negation of Hegel with the revaluation of values recommended by Nietzsche. He seeks to replace dialectics with genealogies. And he wants a focus on the unconscious. The pornographer that he is sometimes formulated as 'goes to the limit', exposes his interiority, ironises the pornographic tendencies of capitalist social structures, plays with metaphors that reveal the patterns of exclusion and expulsion and dehumanization that are rife within the twentieth century (including both Fascism and Stalinism). He writes so as not to be followed, which truly the transgressive never can be. So, for example, when Bataille writes about bodily excrement and the politics of excrement he is talking about shit because it is rude, because it figures in some advanced sexual fetishism, because it was a preoccupation of de Sade's, but he is also talking about the body of collective social life and those excreted, excluded, expunged, like the bad, the insane, the deviant, the poor, the marginal, the dispossessed. The transgressor or the transgressive act can take us to these places without obeying the niceties of manner, politeness or style.

> For Bataille, transgression was an 'inner experience' in which an individual – or, in the case of certain ritualized transgressions such as sacrifice or collective celebration (*la fête*), a community – exceeds the bounds of rational, everyday behaviour, which is constrained by the considerations of profit, productivity or self-preservation. The experience of transgression is indissociable from the consciousness of the constraint or prohibition it violates; indeed, it is precisely by and through its transgression that the force of a prohibition becomes fully realized.
>
> (Suleiman, 1990, p. 75)

Transgression – a childhood urge?

Foucault (1977) provides a brilliant prolegomenon to Bataille's concept of transgression even though it was written a year after Bataille's death. It was part of a homage to Bataille and contributed to his newly collected works. It is a piece of writing one suspects would achieve the grudging approval of its subject. Foucault begins with modern sexuality, the new age delimited by Sade and Freud and freed from the grasp of Christianity. And yet the old vocabulary of sexuality provided depth and texture beyond the act's immediacy. With the absence of God, with morality no longer obeisant to a spiritual form, we achieve profanation without object. The godless vocabulary of modern sexuality achieves limits and prescribes ends in the place previously held by the infinite. 'Sexuality achieves nothing beyond itself, no prolongation, except in the frenzy which disrupts it' (Foucault, 1965, p. 30). Freud further prescribes our limits through sexuality by employing it as the conduit to the unconscious. Our vocabulary of sexuality today shows no continuity with nature but rather a splitting enshrined in law and taboo. As God is dead then there is no limit to infinity, there is nothing exterior to being and consequently we are forced to a constant recognition of the interiority of being, to what Bataille calls sovereignty – the supremacy, the rule, the responsibility, and the mono-causality of the self. This experience is what Foucault describes as the limitless reign of limit and the emptiness of excess. So there are wonderful possibilities bestowed on humankind and on human thought through the death of God but there are also difficulties posed that appear insurmountable. The only way that a limitless world is provided with any structure or coherence is through the excesses that transgress that world and thus construct it – the completion that follows and accompanies transgression. Transgression has become a modern, post-God initiative, a searching for limits to break, an eroticism that goes beyond the limits of sexuality. God becomes the overcoming of God; limit becomes the transgression of limit. The nothingness of infinity is held in check through the singular experience of transgression.

> Transgression is an action which involves the limit, that narrow zone of a line where it displays the flash of its passage, but perhaps also its entire trajectory, even its origin; it is likely that transgression has its entire space in the line it crosses. The play of limits and transgression seems to be regulated by a simple obstinacy: transgression incessantly crosses and recrosses a line which closes up behind it in a wave of extremely short duration and thus it is made to return once more right to the horizon of the uncrossable. But this relationship is considerably more complex: these elements are situated in an uncertain context, in certainties which are immediately upset so that thought is ineffectual as soon as it attempts to seize them.
>
> (Foucault, 1977, pp. 33–4)

There exists then, an absolute contingency between a limit and a transgression, they are unthinkable, futile, and meaningless in isolation. The meaning derives from the moment of intersection between these two elements and from all that follows in the wake of this intersection. There is an inevitable violence in the collision and a celebration in the instantaneous moment at which both limit and transgression find meaning. Limit finds meaning through the utter fragility of its being having been exposed, and transgression finds meaning through the revelation of its imminent exhaustion. This is an orgasmic juxtaposition. But equally clearly the power and energy of both elements derives from the perpetual threat of constraint or destruction presented by the other.

> Transgression, then, is not related to the limit as black to white, the prohibited to the lawful, the outside to the inside, or as the open area of a building to its enclosed spaces. Rather, their relationship takes the form of a spiral which no simple infraction can exhaust. Perhaps it is like a flash of lightning in the night which, from the beginning of time, gives a dense and black intensity to the night it denies, which lights up the night from the inside, from top to bottom, and yet owes to the dark the stark clarity of its manifestation, its harrowing and poised singularity; the flash loses itself in this space it marks with its sovereignty and becomes silent now that it has given a name to obscurity.
>
> (Foucault, 1977, p. 35)

All that's solid melts into air

This startling visual image throws light on our earlier considerations of limits where the rule, that which it contained and its occasional penetration all appeared much more clearly drawn. The comforting certainty of structuralist binaries has been painfully relativized and exposed in the Foucauldian exposition above. We find other sustained examples of such critiques in post-structuralist work. Deleuze, for example, invokes the metaphor of a 'rhizome' (*mille plateaux*) in relation to social process indicating that it is possible for phenomena to be both surface structural and deep structural in an undulating fashion, their grammar does not have to remain captured in one register. He also employs the notion of 'the pleat' (*le pli*), a fold in a map that enables new conjunctions, crossings, juxtapositions and coincidences of contours, places and features in much the same way that contemporary consciousness both disaggregates and re-orders the social according to different structures of relevance. In many senses such theoretical tropes serve to crystallize the central characteristics of the post-structuralist 'differance' which have been summarized by Mouzelis (1995) as threefold: (i) it is anti-foundationalist, it defies origin accounts and mono-causality, it resists fixed, orienting binaries and explodes them at least into continua if not randomness, it broadens the gap between the signifier and the signified; (ii) it de-centres the subject, if not the 'death of man' thesis then certainly the sense that self, subjectivity and personhood are not the causal initiations of social action, process or event; and (iii) that it disposes of the idea of representation or empirical referent.

To return to Foucault's account of transgression. The relationship between transgression and limit is both blindingly simple, like the lightning flash, but also overwhelmingly complex, like the spiral which relates the two. The event of their intersection cannot therefore stand within a code, it is essentially outside, it is amoral. Foucault insists that the relationship must therefore remain free of notions of scandal or the subversive, anything negative; and in abstraction this is so. As Bataille himself tells us: 'evil is not transgression, it is transgression condemned' (Bataille, 2001, p. 127). In practice, of course, all contemporary transgressions relate to the mad, bad and dangerous because pre-post-structuralist life, that is, everyday life, is riven with code, binary, law, opposition and negation and indeed, anything but genealogy as its method. Paedophiles, children who kill children, or indeed Osama bin Laden cannot be seen as either outside of or ahead of their time, they are oppositional manifestations, they are significations of evil and darkness, we claim their limits as our consensus and we actually fight for the right of such recognition (in a way that Hegel would have understood). Nevertheless, Foucault persists; his role is not as apologist for everyday life. For him (and Bataille) transgression is not oppositional, disruptive or transformational: 'Transgression is neither violence in a divided world (in an ethical world) nor a victory over limits (in a dialectical or revolutionary world)' (Foucault, 1977, p. 35).

Transgression announces limitation and its obverse. This is the beginning of what Foucault calls the 'nonpositive affirmation' of contemporary philosophy; one can detect the early traces of a postmodern manifesto. This is also heralding what Bataille had called the 'inner' or 'interior experience', that is, an experience free of disciplinary, professional, moral constraints which, like his own work, can relentlessly question, aggravate and unsettle all things certain. Bataille has become Nietzsche and the questioning of limit in the face of certain limitlessness can be seen as a kind of secular rediscovery of the sacred, the arbiter of the end of experience.

Foucault continues to vaunt the transgressive turn in contemporary thought; he sees Bataille's writing as confronting the issue of language and language use in philosophy in a way that resonates with the important idea about Wittgenstein's *Philosophical Investigations* being actual investigations in progress. Bataille, then, is invoked as a transgressive method, a transgressive challenge, a messenger of transgression, and the new post-Hegel, post-Kant, post-limit, way forward.

> 'the philosophy of eroticism' . . . the experience of finitude and being, of the limit and transgression? What natural space can this form of thought possess and what language can it adopt? Undoubtedly, no form of reflection yet developed, no established discourse can supply its model, its foundation, or even the riches of its vocabulary. Would it be of help, in any case, to argue by analogy that we must find a language for the transgressive which would be what dialectics was, in an earlier time, for contradiction? Our efforts are undoubtedly better spent in trying to speak of this experience and in making it speak from the depths where its language fails, from precisely the place where words escape it, where the subject who speaks has just vanished, where the spectacle topples over before an upturned eye – from where Bataille's death has recently placed his language.
>
> (Foucault, 1977, p. 40)

This is quite a claim and a hard one to affirm, even in nonpositive ways!

Madness is childhood

This chapter, though theoretical in its concerns, turns upon an account of a particular demographic group within all societies but, and much less concretely, it topicalizes a status of personhood to which we are all subject – namely childhood. Childhood's drama is that such nomination is definitionally tainted by unreason, disruption, creativity, confrontation and what educational psychologists now call 'challenging behaviour'.

> The absence of constraint in the nineteenth century asylum is not unreason liberated, but madness long since mastered. For this reason which reigns in the asylum, madness does not represent the absolute form of contradiction, but instead a minority status, an aspect of itself that does not have the right to autonomy, and can live only grafted onto the world of reason. Madness is childhood. Everything in the Retreat is organised so that the insane are transformed into minors. They are regarded 'as children who have an overabundance of strength and make dangerous use of it. They must be given immediate punishments and rewards; whatever is remote has no effect on them. A new system of education must be applied, a new direction given to their ideas; they must first be subjugated, then encouraged, then applied to work . . . For a long time already, the law has regarded the insane as minors.
>
> (Foucault, 1977, p. 252)

This is an interesting inversion, 'madness is childhood', but it does throw an interesting light on our understanding of a major collectivity within society, but also upon a compulsory segment of each of our life courses. There is a sense in which children are both destined and required to transgress in a way that tests both society and social theory. They are placed in the powerless and strangely disadvantageous situation of always being required to submit to the violence of the existing socio-historical order, but they have not been pre-warned. Children 'learn the hard way' which is another way of saying that they consistently, either willingly or unwillingly, flout the norms, rules and conventions of their adults' society. Adults call it learning, maturation or socialization but whatever, its outcome is largely predictable. Children explore and exceed limits on a constant basis; indeed, when they cease to behave in this manner they are deemed no longer to be children. Contemporary liberal thought may regard their transgressions as benign but this is not the full story, as we shall see. Childhood transgressions can expose the fragility of adult power, as crystallized in the familiar response to a challenging question 'because I'm your father, that's why!' Repetitious threats to the sacredness of 'having respect for your elders' can reveal adult rationalizations which make recourse to explanations in terms of childhood wickedness, or even children's proximity to the unconscious.

The idea that the child might be inherently evil stems from an earlier historical period but is not without trace elements in contemporary moralizing, criminology and debate over pedagogic practice. This image rests upon the assumption of an initial evil, corruption, baseness, disruption and incompetence as being primary elements in the constitution of the child. Childhood, then, is found in the exercise of restraint upon these dispositions or, more intrusively, in the exorcism of these dispositions by programmes of discipline and punishment. In the manner later analysed and extrapolated by Foucault (1977) into a metaphor for the form of solidarity and social control within the *ancien régime*, correct training gave rise to docile bodies. And docile bodies are pliant members and good citizens – a utility emergent from docility. This resonates strongly with Durkheim's legal code of 'retribution' as providing an external index of the condition of mechanical solidarity. Within this classical model, which contains no theory of the interior or inner life, the body became the site of childhood and its correction. As Foucault put it:

> The classical age discovered the body as an object and target of power. It is easy enough to find signs of the attention then paid to the body – to the body that is manipulated, shaped, trained, which obeys, responds, becomes skilful and increases its forces.
>
> (Foucault, 1977, p. 136)

The image of the evil child found its lasting mythological foundation in the doctrine of Adamic original sin. Children, it was supposed, entered the world as a wilful material energy; but their wilfulness is both universal and held in an essentialism, to that degree it does not constitute a theory of intentionality. Children are demonic and harbour potentially dark forces. Such thinking has provided a powerful theme in contemporary literature and cinema, but also a useful media resource in explaining childhood transgression as, for example, in the abduction and murder of Jamie Bulger in the UK in 1993; he was aged two and his two killers were both ten (James and Jenks, 1996). These primal forces, it was supposed, would be mobilized if, by dereliction or inattention, the adult world should allow them to veer away from the 'straight and narrow' path that civilization has bequeathed to them. Evil children must be made to avoid dangerous places. They will not, therefore, fall into bad company; establish bad habits; develop idle hands; and be heard rather than just seen. Such dangerous places are those contexts which will conspire in the liberation of the demonic forces within. Any such escape threatens the well-being of the child itself but, perhaps more significantly, it threatens the stability of the adult collectivity as well. Jenks (1996) has likened this model of the child to Dionysian mythology:

> The child is Dionysian in as much as it loves pleasure, it celebrates self-gratification, and it is wholly demanding in relation to any object, or indeed subject, that prevents its satiation. The intrusive noise that is childhood is expressive of a single-minded solipsistic array of demands in relation to which all other interests become peripheral and all other presences become satellites to enable this goal.
>
> (Jenks, 1996, p. 71)

The philosophical antecedent for the evil child is to be found in the work of Thomas Hobbes, not that he dedicated his time to accounting for the condition of childhood but he certainly produced an implicit specification of its content through his highly publicized conception of the human actor. Although not a Puritan himself Hobbes's initial scholarly education was within a Puritan tradition and he shared some of their beliefs in terms of their bland materialism, an unostentatious minimalism that he extended into an empiricism, a reductionism that propelled his interest in geometry, and finally a commitment to the view that what is of most importance is good conduct. These elements combine in Hobbes's *Leviathan* which proffers a powerful advocacy of absolutism. The power of the monarch, and thus the power of parents, are absolute and stand over and above the populace or children who have no rights or power. The source of this power is knowledge which children could only attain by eventually becoming parents themselves. The powerful ogre of the state or the parent is omnipotent and the individual is saved from the worst excesses of him or herself by contracting into the society or the family. The life of the child without parental constraint is anarchistic; indeed, its childhood would surely be 'solitary, poor, nasty, brutish and short' without such control. When Hobbes does call the child by name he is rather disparaging:

> Likewise children, fools, and madmen that have no use of reason, may be personated by guardians, or curators, but can be no authors, during that time, of any action done by them, longer than, when they shall recover the use of reason, they shall judge the same reasonable. Yet during the folly, he that hath right of governing them, may give authority to the guardian.
>
> (Hobbes, 1651, p. 127)

Old Testament Christianity provided perhaps the most significant contribution to the image of the evil child. Parental, God-parental and loco-parental guidance consisted in a forceful introduction of the young to the humourless ways of the Almighty. This sedimented a lasting tradition in child-rearing even though, as Shipman (1972) has pointed out, the dramatic fall in infant mortality through modernity appears to have reduced our urgency and collective anxiety concerning the infant's state of grace, as has the inexorable process of secularization. Previously Ariès (1962) had, in his discovery of the genesis of childhood, described its sixteenth-century manifestation as a form of weakness. This weakness referred to the child's susceptibility, the fact that it had little resolve and was easily diverted and corrupted. Such belief gave rise to the widespread practice of 'swaddling' that is a binding and constraining of the child's body. Swaddling can also be treated instructively as a metaphor for a style of parenting that is confining of the child's urges and desires; a distant, strict and physical direction of the young. With the formalization of the evil child in the sixteenth century, the practice of socialization most certainly took on the form of a contest. This combative relation between adult and child had close parallels with the way that people treated domestic animals and 'broke' them or tamed them in order to integrate their naturalness into the adult human world of culture. This harshness and indeed brutality in child-rearing gained a powerful ideological bedrock from the zeal for greater reformation that accompanied the religious Puritanism of the sixteenth and seventeenth centuries. As with the most oppressive social movements, the control and constraint exercised on the subject (in this case the child) was for its own good. Puritanism was determined that rods should not be saved in order to save children and it was equally certain that the child should be grateful for the treatment it received. Though exhausted as a formal church, elements of the Puritan morality extended with an evangelical zeal into the nineteenth century, creating the Poor Laws and the campaigns against drunkenness, while still regarding children as being in need of correction. Much of the literature of the period employs the evil child as a symbol of the outmoded and hypocritical morality that continues to buttress an anti-democratic state. Dickens's novels are a great source of reference for our institutionalized violence towards the young, and Coveney's (1957) later critical work gathers many of the ways in which children have been portrayed in literature, setting such harsh treatment against the romantic images of Blake and Wordsworth.

At the turn of the twentieth century the sudden impact of the Freudian edifice and the new growth of interest in the human psyche produced something of a volte-face in our thinking about the child. After a long series of concerns with the idea of development and a continuous but unconcerted attention to futures, childhood became the province of retrospectives. Whereas children had become firmly established in both theory and everyday consciousness as pointing in the direction of tomorrow, Freud opened up a concern with the child centred on adult pasts. In one sense Freudian theory is dedicated to an account of human maturation and it has lodged a battery of incremental concepts in the modern language of becoming. The critical difference, however, is that Freud's elements of personality, stages of development and complexes are all dedicated to an understanding of the building blocks in the architecture of adult psychopathology. Freudianism and its variety of modern tributaries instigated a search from surface to depth in a manner later emulated by structuralism. The search of psychoanalysis is, however, dedicatedly diachronic, the surface being the present and the depth being the past.

Freudian development is a familiar process of the compatible bonding of the elements: *id*, *ego* and *super-ego*. The id comprises an elementary and primal broth of essentially libidinal drives; it is wholly expressive and utterly inexhaustible. The id can be visualized as a reservoir of the instinctive energies, it is uncontrolled and thus dominated by the pleasure principle and impulsive wishing. Here is a potential source of creativity but it is wholly incompatible with a collective life and thus needs to be curbed. Successful development is, for Freud, the proper management of this 'curbing' or repression. The id awakens all of the images and resonances of the model of the evil child but at a later historical moment; here again is a childhood predicated on constraint, management and the fear of an evil that resides within, this time in the form of the unconscious. The ego assumes the role of interaction in childhood, it enables the self to experience others through the senses and thus begins an adjustment in behaviour through which the id is monitored. Consciousness and rationality are finally wrought through the supremacy of the super-ego, the experience of the collective other which regulates the presentations of self and integrates the child into the world of adult conduct. What has become evident through the growth of psychoanalytic influence in contemporary thinking is that Freud successfully generated a new source of causality. The explanation, and in many cases the blame, for aberrant adult behaviour is the child. The resource for accounts of the deviant, the criminal and the abnormal through late-modernity has developed into equations of parental–child relationships. The child has thus become transformed into the unconscious itself and all adults, it would seem, transport their childhood like a previous incarnation, from action to action. Although this model has opened up a vast potential for adult self-exploration in line with the many journeys towards belief that modern society has spurred (Giddens, 1991), it has done little to broaden an understanding of the child as other than a state of unfinished business or becoming. Childhood, within this view, is dispossessed of intentionality as this is absorbed in the vocabulary of drives and instincts. Sexuality becomes the major dimension in the development of self and amnesia emerges as the key to successful socialization (or the supposed end of the transgressive urge).

> Let us leave to psychoanalysis then the task of curing badly spent childhoods, of curing the puerile sufferings of an indurate childhood which oppresses the psyche of so many adults. There is a task open to poetico-analysis which would help us reconstitute within ourselves the being of liberated solitudes. Poetico-analysis ought to return all the privileges of the imagination to us. Memory is a field full of psychological ruins, a whatnot full of memories. Our whole childhood remains to be reimagined. In reimagining it, we have the possibility of recovering it in the very life of our reverie as a single child . . . the theses which we wish to defend . . . all return to make us recognize within the human soul the permanence of a nucleus of childhood, an immobile but ever living childhood, outside history, hidden from others, disguised in history when it is recounted.
>
> (Bachelard, 1971, pp. 99–100)

Childhood becomes an interesting metaphor for a post-structuralist, post-modern identity at both an analytic and a concrete leve. Analytically children have become, through our burgeoning contemporary studies, a way in which we explore missing, unexpressed and disempowered aspects of ourselves. Concretely children are seen to present with an increasing complexity of 'challenging' behaviours and adult populations respond with increasingly complex and penetrating means of control. All conducted through an ideology of care.

If we are truly committed to childhood as an active expression of human being should we not be listening to the challenges they present as critiques of the current order rather than as disruptions of a properly normative life. Their transgressions should not merely complete and affirm our constraints; they might better make us think again about the moral basis of our social bond. This is not a romantic and outmoded plea for us to be led by the 'innocent creativity' of children but perhaps a recommendation that we might employ their disruption as a source of critical examination of our dominant means of control. Children explore the very limits of consciousness and highlight, once again, the indefatigable, inherent and infinitely variable human capacity to transgress.

References

Ariès, P. (1962) *Centuries of Childhood*, London: Jonathan Cape.

Bachelard, G. (1971) *The Poetics of Reverie*, Boston: Beacon Press

Bataille, G. (2001) *Eroticism* (Introduction C. MacCabe), London: Penguin.

Coveney, P. (1957) *The Image of Childhood*, Harmondsworth: Perguin.

Foucault, M. (1965) *Madness and Civilization*, London: Tavistock.

Foucault, M. (1977) *Language, Counter-Memory, Practice* (contains the 1963 essay 'Preface to Transgression'), New York: Cornell University Press.

Giddens, A. (1991) *Modernity and Self-identity: Self and Society in the Late Modern Age*, Oxford: Polity.

Habermas, J. (1984) 'The French Path to Postmodernity: Bataille between Eroticism and General Economics', *New German Critique*, 33: 79–102.

Hobbes, T. ([1651] 1962) *Leviathan*, New York: Collier.

Hussey, A. (2002) *The Game of War: the Life and Death of Guy Debord*, London: Random.

James, A. and C. Jenks (1996) 'Public Perceptions of Childhood Criminality', *British Journal of Sociology*, 47: 315–31.

Jenks, C. (1996) *Childhood*, London: Routledge.

Mouzelis, N. (1995) *Sociological Theory: What Went Wrong?* London: Routledge.

Noys, B. (2000) *Bataille*, London: Pluto.

Shipman, M. (1972) *Childhood: a Sociological Perspective*, Slough: NFER.

Suleiman, S. (1990) *Subversive Intent: Gender Politics and the Avant-Garde*, Cambridge, MA: Harvard University Press.

Turner, V. (1974) *Dreams, Fields and Metaphors*, New York: Cornell University Press.

Van Gennep, A. ([1902] 1960) *Les Rites de Passage*, London: Routledge & Kegan Paul.

8
Prisoners of Childhood: Orphans and Economic Dependency

Judith Ennew

Children who have lost one or both parents are usually among society's most vulnerable members and dependent on wider society for their safe passage through childhood. The customary estimate is that, in developing countries, the 2 per cent of children who are orphaned can be absorbed into the extended family and community. However, when the Joint United Nations Programme on HIV/AIDS (UNAIDS) announced in 2001 that orphan numbers would increase by 200 per cent because of HIV/AIDS mortality, it was clear that finding the necessary resources to protect orphaned children must be a priority for the international community (UNAIDS, 2001). Although this unprecedented rise in the number of children living without parental care appears to be a problem for children, in reality it highlights a historical tendency for 'the problem of orphans' to be an economic issue for adults.

Whether in an institution or a substitute family, orphans are prisoners of their own dependency. In this paper, I argue that orphanhood is a form of detention, in which children are treated exclusively as objects of concern and items in socioeconomic accounting, rather than as subjects of human rights. Despite the rhetoric of kindness and concern about orphans, no one wants to pay the cost of their upbringing. I shall illustrate this using historical examples, as well as recent research in Bosnia and Herzegovina, Tanzania, Thailand and Viet Nam.

Who is an orphan?

An orphan is assumed to be a dependent child, however child is defined culturally, although according to international law a child is a person less than 18 years of age. 'Orphan' is not a unitary category, nor is there a single agreed definition. Within the general classification, special categories receive attention from time to time within international aid discourses. These include AIDS orphans and street children, as well as historically specific groups constructed by the media such as 'Biafra babies' in the 1960s and 'Romanian orphans' in the early 1990s.

Although the most usual global definition of 'orphan' used in international work is a child with two deceased biological parents, this is by no means universal; orphans may have one or both parents alive, absent or continuing to care for them. It is common, especially in cultures in which women do not have full economic and political independence, to refer to a child whose father is dead and mother alive as an 'orphan'. This is the case in many parts of Africa, as is reflected in the definition of the Tanzanian Ministry of Labour and Youth Development (1995): 'An orphan is a child below the age of 18 years whose *one* or *both* parents have died of any cause' (my emphasis). This definition recognizes the fact that children who have no living parents face many of the same economic and social problems as children of widowed mothers: 'A married woman here is no different to a widow', as one woman put it to Tanzanian researchers (*Mwanamke alieolewa hapa, hana tofauti na mjane*). What this definition does not take into account is that many of the problems of biological orphans are shared with children who might be called 'social orphans', who have been abandoned by both parents, or whose fathers have abandoned them to the sole care of their mothers, whether or not they are wives (Ahmed et al., 1999).

Thus a child who has no father is frequently regarded as having a disadvantage equal to a child who has no parents at all, particularly in socioeconomic and cultural contexts in which the value of women is low and they cannot be regarded as household heads. Because of their low participation in formal labour markets, women are not regarded as household breadwinners, even if they generate a viable income through home-based or informal sector work. This is not exclusive to developing countries. At least until the late 1980s, UK census enumerators would not accept a married woman as a head of household, even if she were the house owner and only income earner. In Bosnia and Herzegovina current social work policy is to award custody to fathers when parents divorce, because women cannot be household heads and return to their father's house, to which custom dictates that they cannot bring a child with a different surname (Čehajić et al., 2003).

Whatever their actual economic status, women and children are de facto social dependants ('widows and orphans' being a frequent joint classification, especially in the religious texts of Abrahamic religions; Arole, 1998). The implication is that they cannot survive without the social and economic protection of an adult male. This is why the 'orphan' category encompasses children of widows, bi-parental orphans, abandoned children, children whose fathers have abandoned their mothers and many illegitimate children. Malinowski's famous definition of illegitimacy could equally be applied to orphanhood: 'No child should be brought into the world without a man – and one man at that – assuming the role of sociological father, that is guardian and protector, the male link between the child and the rest of the community' (Malinowski in Goody, 1971, p. 39).

Yet this patriarchal definition of orphan is not always used in the context of AIDS orphans who, until recently, were defined by the United Nations as children less than 15-years-old whose mothers have died of AIDS.[1] The emphasis on loss of a mother, rather than a father, or on children who are 'double orphans' because both parents have died, also implicitly acknowledges something about the importance of female links between child and community. Societies are not uniformly patrilineal. A Thai proverb sums this up: 'Without a father, a child's life will be hard; it will have no direction. Without a mother, the situation is even worse – the same as a sinking boat or a drifting ferry' (quoted in UNICEF, 1997, p. 45).

Mainstream Thai society is traditionally matrilineal and matrilocal. Inheritance and authority reside with maternal relatives (maternal father and uncles) and residence after marriage is also with kin of the wife. Fathers became more important during the twentieth century, as descent through the maternal line declined gradually in response to the enforcement of the Surname Act of 1913, which ensured that a man's wife and children should bear his name. This effectively transferred to paternal relatives (fathers in particular) rights that had previously been invested in a wife's family, and accords with the global tendency to treat patriarchy and nuclear families as the traditional and natural norm.

In the traditional Thai matrilineal system, children whose mother died would have been adopted by maternal relatives, because they belonged to her kinship group and therefore had rights to matrilineal land and other resources. Children over 12 years of age would have cared for themselves and younger siblings, under the overall management of maternal kin who would provide a social and economic safety net. The combination of reduced fertility, increased paternal authority (without accompanying paternal kin resources) and the move from matrilocal to nuclear households, has exacerbated the impact of maternal death, resulting in an increased demand for 'orphan care' outside families (UNICEF, 1997). Children in poor rural families may now find themselves suffering from the negative effects of both matrilineal and patrilineal systems, lacking effective support from either kin or state.

Matriliny and matrifocality are not unique to Thailand of course. And it is not only in matrilocal kinship groups that maternal deaths can have greater consequence than paternal. In a patrilineal, polygamous society mothers may be all that stand between their children and the jealousy of co-wives. Indeed it is often to protect their children from this real or imagined malevolence that African mothers send their children to be fostered, sometimes at a very young age, by a maternal grandmother (see for example, Bledsoe and Isiugo-Abanihe, 1987).

Cultural and social histories of orphanhood

Throughout western history, orphans have played a pivotal role in two domains – mythology and social welfare provision. In modernity and postmodernity the social construction of the nation-state world is increasingly based on the image of nuclear family units. By living outside 'the family', orphans challenge the necessities of patriarchy, thus their vulnerability and dependency are emphasized as the rationale for their institutionalization and other forms of control. If they live outside families or adult care, they threaten the consensus that family is necessary. However they are defined, children labelled as orphans have to surmount the symbolic obstacle of the 'orphan' of the popular western imagination; a mythology that is both historical and current, which is constructed by, inscribed in, and used by, various discourses of governance and planning.

The role of parentless children in popular stories is not new in European thought. In classical Greek and Roman mythology, for instance, there was a tendency for hero figures who were the biological sons of kings to be brought up by humble foster parents. Only later in life these mythical figures discover their true identity and bring about a destiny that is frequently related to killing their fathers (Rank, 1964). This is a constant theme in European narratives. As the author of a study of lost and found children in English Renaissance literature points out, 'The reader of a fairy tale or a novel by Dickens has a generic faith that its orphan hero will turn out to be royal or at least wealthy, that he will discover his legitimate ancestors and reject his substitute family' (Estrin, 1985, p. 14).

Reality does not always follow mythology. In early-modern Europe, children who lived in the increasing numbers of public 'orphanages' are reported to have operated their own form of internal stigmatization; orphans whose parentage was known 'sometimes actively despised' children of unknown parents (Pullan, 1989, pp. 5 and 22). Far from being regarded as a potential hero, an abandoned child became seen as 'the creature who stands utterly naked before the charity of strangers' (ibid., p. 6), requiring the care of public institutions and paid for out of public funds. This change in attitude towards children who do not enjoy the care and economic support of their parents parallels the epistemological break in the history of childhood identified by Philippe Ariès and others, in which the figure of 'the child' was a construction necessary to the development of capitalism. Forms of care for orphans underwent a change from 'a generalised societal investment in informal fostering and welfare mechanisms within kinship-based societies' into 'institutionalised abandonment in early modern states' as the result of the need to account for the costs of upbringing (Ennew, 2000, p. xiv).

Initially, because children's labour was valued, the model of institutional care for abandoned children ('foundlings'), which began in Renaissance Italy and spread to most of the rest of Europe, actually encouraged child abandonment because 'Foundlings constituted a stock of children at society's disposal and the money spent on them was an investment' (Panter-Brick, 2000, p. 15). A spate of new legislation ensured that minimal investment was made in children who lacked parental care. Even in their own homes, children in pre-modern and early-modern Europe were working and thus not entirely dependent during their upbringing. For example, beginning in 1576 with the first legislative provision for the illegitimate children of the poor, local authorities (parishes) in England ensured that orphaned, vagrant and begging children were forced to work. The main concern was to ensure that such children did not become a burden on parish funds, raised from local taxation. If parents could not be forced to pay for their own children's upkeep, the cost to ratepayers was reduced by apprenticing them at an early age. Progressive 'Poor Laws' between the sixteenth and nineteenth century enabled parishes to rid themselves of economic responsibility by returning any unwed mother and/or her child to her parish of origin whenever possible (Pinchbeck and Hewitt, 1969; 1973, pp. 207–13; Teichman, 1978, pp. 24–5).

Despite these provisions, by the mid-nineteenth century the number of abandoned children was growing out of control, while children were being forced out of the labour market through an unholy alliance of trade unions, industrialists and philanthropists. As 'public' care gradually devolved more upon the institutions (and costs) of emergent states, orphaned children began to share the stigmatization of the poor in general. Poverty was associated with moral failure, which made the poor a burden on public funds. Categories such as 'indigent poor' and 'abandoned orphan' became fixtures in the statistical accounts of European states and their colonies, together with schemes either to include them in the labour force as rapidly as possible or to hand them over to philanthropic, charitable organizations if they were unable to work. From being an investment, a parentless child was increasingly seen as a cost, with the result that children were regularly shuffled between parishes and municipalities, their upbringing entrusted to charitable organizations if at all possible. They were rapidly trained in very basic skills and might even be shipped off to colonies.

The modern concept of childhood has changed all this. As Viviana Zelizer points out, western twentieth-century children were priceless; no longer valued for their labour but because they bring happiness to parents (Zelizer, 1987). If they are careless enough to lose one or both parents, however, the costs to governments, international agencies, charitable organizations and donors are considerable. Funds have to be found to pay for children outside parental care. From the mid-nineteenth century onwards orphans became, and continue to be, the focus of charitable pity. As Patricia Holland points out, 'Without the image of the unhappy child, our contemporary concept of childhood would be incomplete . . . they figure in imagery as the most vulnerable, the most pathetic, the most deserving of all of our sympathy and aid' (Holland, 1992, p. 148). This imagery of distress drives policies and programmes for orphans, although still underscored by the questions 'Whose child is this?' and 'Who can, should or would take responsibility for the economic cost of rearing a dependent orphan child?'

The state is not a willing parent

The assumption in international human rights instruments is that families are the best place for children's rights to be secured, while the duty of a state is to support families to do this through providing accessible social services and social protection (Articles 18, 26 and 27 particularly), as well as ensuring family integrity (as for example in Articles 7, 8, 9 and 10). Other Articles in The United Nations Convention on the Rights of the Child (CRC) establish standards for the care of children without parents:

> Article 3: Establishing the requirements for the 'best needs' of children, rather than adults or helping agencies, to be the primary consideration in planning for children;
> Article 9: On the conditions under which children should be separated from their parents and the right to continued contact with parents when in the care of the state;
> Article 10: On family reunification if children and parents become separated by national borders;
> Article 20: On state responsibilities and alternative forms of care for children separated from their parents;
> Article 21: On adoption;
> Article 25: On the need for periodic review of placement for children without parents placed in institutional or alternative care.

States thus have considerable and detailed responsibilities for the care of orphans set out in international law. Yet, in practice, provision for parentless and homeless children depends to a large extent on the relative development of structures of governance and available resources, as well as on attitudes to 'orphans'; and the answer to the question 'Whose child is this?' may often be 'Nobody's'.

One convenient response from impoverished states is to hand over responsibility to extended families, with increasing attention paid to ever more distant kin. In wealthier countries, traditional fostering is largely ignored as an option as it does not fit easily into state-sponsored schemes. Among the Innupiat of Alaska, for example, children themselves choose new foster homes where they feel more comfortable than in their natal homes, and settle in over time, retaining their links with their birth family as a matter of course, a system that does not accord with US social work models of removing parental rights from one set of parents and investing them in a new mother and father (Bodenhorn, 1988). On the other hand, in a post-conflict situation, where orphan numbers increase without a state fostering system securely in place, social workers may rely so heavily on kin-related foster placements that they forgo the checks on suitability and monitoring that are made necessary by the provisions of the CRC. This appears to have happened in post-conflict Bosnia and Herzegovina (BiH), where nearly 90 per cent of foster placements are with members of the extended kin group, with no consistent criteria applied for suitability, little or no economic support and virtually no periodic review of placement. The advantage of foster care with family members is that it is cheap. In many cases, the BiH Centres for Social Work responsible for making payments to foster families lack even the funds to pay their own staff. Financial support for fostered children is not available, which means that foster families (kin or non-kin) cannot be easily recruited. The obligations of extended families, already over-stretched by refugee movements during and since the 1992–95 war, are further relied upon to care for children whose upkeep is in fact a state responsibility (Čehajić et al., 2003).

Who makes the decisions about what happens to children whose parents are no longer able to care for them? Despite the provisions of Article 12 of the CRC, it is very rarely children. The Innupiat case is unusual even among traditional fostering systems. Modern state systems do sometimes include adults to speak on behalf of children, 'in their best interests', but there is still little evidence of children routinely speaking their views *as of right.* Indeed, there is no precedent in history for them to do so. Under international human rights law, and in much domestic legislation, the assumption now is that states should intervene to support, dismantle or replace parent/child relationships. In the absence or inability of state powers to do this, communities not only have performed and do perform this role, but they also absorb children without parents into the group as a whole. The distinction can be summed up in two diagrams illustrating who in society takes the decisions about the definition and fate of orphans. In both cases, agency is not allocated to the orphaned child (figures 8.1 and 8.2).

These polarities show different relationships between children, biological parents and governance. In Figure 8.1 the welfare of an individual, rights-bearing child is shared between biological parents and a state that has the power to intervene, through the mediation of child experts, in 'the best interests of the child' to support, but also to dismantle families (Donzelot,

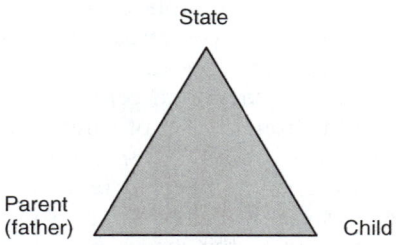

Figure 8.1:   Responsibility for children in nation-states

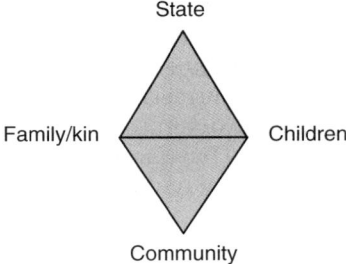

Figure 8.2: Responsibility for children in 'traditional' communities

1981). 'Family' consists of two biological parents and their child or children with grandparental and uncle/aunt/cousin relationships unmarked until and unless they are needed. Nuclear families function to raise children during the first 18 years of life – as temporary as birds' nests. And indeed the period immediately after a child leaves home for the 'world of work' is often accompanied by what psychologists call the 'empty nest syndrome'. If biological parents die, abandon their offspring or are judged (by state experts) to be incapable of proper child-rearing functions, parental rights are assumed by the state and may be delegated to a number of different agencies, including orphanages, remand homes, foster and adopting parents or perhaps biological kin. The degree of state intervention varies according to the efficiency of governance, the extent and resources of a welfare state, cultural norms about the privacy of family life, and the relative values of parental rights and children's rights.

When orphan numbers rise and state resources decrease, as in the case of Bosnia and Herzegovina, states may be forced to revert to family care, with little or no supervision. It is also typical for many orphans effectively to disappear from state records and controls by being handed over to unlicensed, unsupervised charitable institutions. In Bosnia and Herzegovina, for example, at least one of the current 16 institutions for children outside parental care has no formal ties with the state authorities, but operates under the independent auspices of the Roman Catholic Church, with children referred to it by the Catholic community. Researchers found that state authorities did not know about, or monitor, the activities of this institution (Čehajić et al., 2003).

In Figure 8.2, children are bearers of rights as a social group, rather than as individuals. They are members of a community, for which they are a resource and within which they have responsibilities. Child-rearing is a joint responsibility for biological parents, the wider kin group and the community itself. Some anthropologists have referred to this as a 'joint management system' (see for example Weisner, 1969). The term 'parent' (together with the associated authority and responsibility) may include paternal and maternal aunts and uncles, or anyone of the same age set as one's biological parents. Even breast-feeding may be shared between a number of women. Older siblings may also take a considerable role in childcare. Children are the responsibility of the extended family together with other community members. Although the state may have legal rights to intervene, it may have neither the human nor the material resources to do so. Under weak systems of governance, the extended family, with the approval of the community, intervenes when parents are unwilling or unable to care for their children. Whatever decision is taken is likely to be endorsed or condoned by the wider kin group and/or the community. This accounts for the recorded/expected absorption into the community of the estimated 2 per cent of children who become orphans under 'normal' circumstances.

In practice, the decision for child placement may be a process rather than a single decision. According to data collected in a study of Tanzanian orphans, whether children are social or biological orphans, the care they receive tends to be situational and arbitrary. Communities and families appear to be willing to assume responsibility but not to plan for the care of these children, even though the research found a definite stated preference for community care over institutional orphanages. Orphans are seen as an economic cost rather than welcomed for the present or future economic benefits of their labour, as might have been the case in the past. This is related to the imperative for schooling, which reduces the economic gains possible from child work and increases the costs of childcare. Nevertheless, researchers were impressed by the caring attitudes of caretakers of both social and biological orphans, which did not appear to be based on the assumption that investment in these children in the present would provide for future support of caretakers in old age. Indeed, care seemed to be provided in the face of considerable economic difficulties (Ahmed et al., 1999).

Orphans redistributed

Shifting the economic burden for parentless, homeless and stateless children has been a consistent way of dealing with orphans, from the ancient practices of exposure, so often retold in western myths, to shuffling children across administrative borders through the English Poor Laws. As long as children are regarded as an economic benefit it is not too difficult to find a placement. In the redistribution systems of eighteenth- and nineteenth-century Europe, as well as in current rural/urban girl domestic servant chains of most developing countries, the movement was and is underpinned by fictive family relationships in which a fostered child is structurally positioned in a family somewhere between a servant and legitimate offspring. As numbers of orphaned/abandoned children rose towards the end of the nineteenth century, and began to assume the proportions of a 'surplus population', orphanages and charitable organizations in Europe began the progressive export of children, including what would now be called 'street children', to people the 'empty' colonies of North America and Australasia. This process did not end until the 1960s and was romanticized in novels such as *Anne of Green Gables*, although in reality the boys and girls shipped to Canada and Australia were more likely to encounter servitude, abuse and isolation (see for example Bagnell, 1987).

About the same time that child export halted, in a parallel movement in the opposite direction, inter-country adoption became a strategy through which some developing countries deal with their own 'surplus' child population. In 1999, adoption was stated by the Vietnamese Ministry of Labour, Invalids and Social Affairs to be the primary means by which the estimated 155,757 orphans in Viet Nam could be provided with a home. Several thousand children are adopted annually by foreigners. Once again this is an estimate, partly because many such adoptions are privately arranged, but mostly because accurate orphan numbers are something few countries seem to be able to produce. Of course a surplus population of children does not correspond to an accurate demographic reality. These children are surplus to requirements, rather than a sign of overpopulation. They are children of the poor, or children with no one to care for them, who would otherwise be a burden on state or community funds. Children of the wealthy are not put up for adoption any more than the illegitimate children of the aristocracy were shuffled across parish borders in early-modern Europe.

There is a direct economic connection between increase in international adoptions from Viet Nam and the transformation from command to market economy (*Doi Moi* or 'renovation'), which began in Viet Nam in 1986, resulting in some immediate improvements in socioeconomic indicators, which nevertheless decreased after 1997. Although the growth rate in 1995 was 8–9 per cent a year, by 2000 it had fallen to around 4.8 per cent (UNICEF Viet Nam, 1999), and by 2001 had only risen to 6.5 per cent (UNICEF Viet Nam, 2001). Even before this, the Committee on the Rights of the Child expressed concern about the negative effects of the transition on children and women (quoted in UNICEF Executive Board, 1995, p. 2). By 1995, *Doi Moi* had resulted in decreased income for 10 per cent of the population and no improvement at all for 20 per cent, particularly in remote and ethnic areas. Families now have a greater responsibility for meeting children's needs than they did before, including cost sharing for basic social services. For the poor (especially women) this represents an extra burden with few benefits (UNICEF Executive Board, 1995). Public spending on health and education is reduced. Pre-schools run by cooperatives have closed. New pressures have emerged for children, particularly those from the poorest groups, to become contributors to family income and even, in the worst cases, to provide entirely for their own welfare. Children have also come to be seen as commodities. They are traded between families for their labour, and sold abroad for labour as well as for adoption. In some reports it is noted that, as a coping strategy, the urban poor decide to have babies precisely in order to offer them for adoption to foreigners – for a price (Bond and others, 1999).

There is, of course, no supply without demand. In the face of a rising demand for Asian children among western childless couples, biological families from Viet Nam are put under pressure to give up their babies. The trade is underpinned by illegalities and forged documents (UNICEF, 2000, p. 74, and personal observation). Likewise, the Thai Ministry of Labour and Social Welfare openly states that the preferred placement for abandoned and orphaned children whose identity is known is adoption – although many abandoned babies in both countries are those with disabilities, who tend not to be attractive to potential adopters. Neither Thailand nor Viet Nam has ratified the Hague Convention on international adoption, indeed they are not among the 62 member states of the Hague Conference.[2]

The attractions of inter-country adoptions are linked to ideology, geographical distance and legal practicalities. In the first place, adopting a child from a poor country can appear to be a personal solution to the problem of 'world poverty' for a couple (or individual) from a wealthy country. It requires no major change in lifestyle, or commitment to challenging global inequalities. It is also a romantic route to parenthood; an impoverished child from another race and place is more attractive than a disadvantaged child from one's own ethnic group and home town. This is not just due, I would suggest, to the exotic appeal of a foreign baby. For couples who have not been able to have children of their own, the journey to a distant place is a metaphor for pregnancy and birth.

The final factor underpinning the preference for inter-country adoption is practical. Baby 'orphans' available for adoption are becoming rare in developed countries, while rules for selection of adopting couples are becoming more strict. Older couples, same sex couples, couples with histories of poor health or divorce are likely to be ruled out by social workers. Even 'ideal' couples may be faced with an unacceptably long wait until a baby becomes available. Thus adopting a 'surplus' baby from a poor country, where legal rules are not so clear, or not so rigorously applied, becomes an attractive option. Nevertheless, couples may find themselves falling foul of legislation that requires adoption to be repeated in their own country, and some children have found themselves stranded in foreign orphanages because of this, or because their new parents cannot cope with an older child from another country, who may have been traumatized by institutional care or other life experiences. The unseemly rush to adopt Romanian orphans, after television coverage following the collapse of government in 1989 revealed unbelievably squalid orphanage conditions, had this long-term result in some cases, as placements broke down irretrievably. Likewise the confusion of armed conflict and natural disasters has frequently led to unaccompanied children being sent overseas for adoption as the first option, rather than being reunited with their own, living parents. UNHCR guidelines for dealing with refugee children were drawn up to prevent these occurrences (Wressler, 1992). Yet the general public still prefers to read in popular magazines such as *Hello* about celebrities who have adopted exotic children from countries practising 'orphan' export, which fortifies the new romance of orphanhood.

Prisoners of childhood: the institutional model

What to do with children who do not have family and community support is the same dilemma that faces government with respect to any dependent population; the elderly, the infirm, people with disabilities and mental illnesses, in short the non-productive economic burden that must be borne by the economically active population. Of all these groups, investment in children is perhaps the easiest to rationalize because of their future potential for economic contribution. This was the rationale behind medieval encouragements to abandon children to orphanages, which was a relatively short-term investment, because childhood did not last long in those days, and the orphanages produced the early-modern version of an industrial reserve army at a time when most economic activities were labour-intensive. Now that childhood is more prolonged and economies require greater investment in education to produce skilled workers, a longer period of childhood is required. Moreover, dependency ratios have changed, and the position of children is counterbalanced by increasingly larger, more costly, populations of the aged – who, unlike children, have voting power. Even in advanced industrial nations childhood appears to be an onerous burden for both state and (nuclear) family. Childlessness and small family size become positively valued. Institutional care, even for severe psychiatric cases, is reduced, in favour of care in the community, and welfare provision for the elderly largely handed over to the private sector with pressure on families to bear the costs. Children without parents, however, remain a cost to the public sector, with the result that substitute family placements are preferred to the more costly option of institutional care. Twentieth-century regulation, in industrial societies, of previously informal or non-existent forms of fostering and child adoption is one indication of this trend.

It is clear that, whereas institutional care for orphans is often described as the 'traditional option', it is not in fact the preferred option. Instead it is the option of last resort, because it is expensive to provide even basic shelter and food. As long as orphans were regarded as labour-force investment, orphanages could be regarded as cost-effective in the long run. But building, equipping and managing a closed institution for children is not cheap and is frequently handed over, by local and national authorities, to charitable and religious institutions that, like the religious home in Bosnia and Herzegovina mentioned earlier, keep children out of sight, out of mind, out of accounts and outside any form of monitoring. Although the number of institutions for children outside parental care trebled during and immediately after the war, most of the new institutions were built and are run by foreign charities, which operate according to their own regulations and are not systematically monitored by the state (Čehajić et al., 2003).

One encounters three universal features in orphan policies and programmes. In the first place, being the object of 'orphan' programmes and policies does not necessarily mean a lack of living biological parents, but it can mean lack of contact with parents and other family members. This may not be because parents do not wish for contact. Homes for children with disabilities may be too far from the parental home for frequent visits, and visits to orphan facilities are often governed by a considerable number of rules, or set at times that are difficult for parents but convenient for institutional staff. Strangers from foreign voluntary organizations may have greater access to children than their own parents.

In the second place, orphans are often categorized and housed according to what one might call secondary orphan characteristics, such as age, gender, type of disability or social status. Provision tends to be service-orientated, rather than needs-based or rights-oriented. In the main Thai facility for children with disabilities, there are separate buildings for 'blind', 'deaf', 'cerebral palsy' and 'mentally handicapped' children, each receiving both financial and human resources from a different foreign donor. Although convenient for staff, this robs children of their identity and deprives them of varied experiences. This type of organization can result in siblings being separated, for institutional convenience, breaking kinship bonds and, paradoxically, developing peer groups in which strict orphanage rules can still prevent supportive friendships developing. Children's capacity may also deteriorate in the absence of appropriate stimulation. Life skills fail to develop in larger, strictly-organized orphanages, in which food is provided, clothes and rooms cleaned, so that young people leave at 18 years of age not only having no family to support them but also without being able to shop, cook, wash their clothes and keep their personal space clean. It is a consistent research finding that teenagers in orphan homes and projects fear the future after 'orphan' care (Ahmed et al., 1999). Teenagers in Bosnia and Herzegovina deliberately chose to go to trade school, rather than to academic secondary school, because they knew they had to be economically dependent when they became too old for orphanages (Čehajić et al., 2003).

Prisons without walls

Most research and policy-making would agree that substitute family care is better for children than institutional arrangements, as well as being cheaper. However, there are two further modes of orphan care available, both of which claim to be non-institutional – children's villages and 'drop in' street children projects.

In the narrow social science sense, the term 'institution' is defined as a purposeful organization fulfilling a public need, which is generally residential and requires special buildings, staff and equipment in order to function properly. Institutions also tend to use bureaucratic means of reaching their objectives and establishing rules for the lives of the group of people for whom they operate. In the case of care for children without parents, the term 'institution' is associated with orphanages and sometimes has negative connotations. The best known of the children's village organizations, SOS Children's Villages, strongly resists the label of 'institution', yet can only be defined this way in sociological terms. SOS Villages are highly bureaucratic and internationally governed. The female-headed cluster of households around the family of a male director is not even a facsimile of either family or community care, nor is the separation of young teenagers into youth houses (although this coincidentally mirrors some pre-industrial forms of organization). Many modern orphanages also organize children in genuine facsimiles of 'family groups' that include both genders and children of different ages, often with both mother and father figures, and retain children in these groups until the age of 18 years or older. Of course the villages are well funded, the houses well built, mothers receive training and services usually surpass those provided by the state. But in many cases the villages are among the forms of orphan care operating outside state supervision.

One of the most crucial aspects of the modern notion of childhood is that its location is inside – inside society, inside a family or institution, inside a private dwelling, inside school. As children are increasingly conceptualized as vulnerable dependants, in danger from and unable to deal with influences outside families, they have correspondingly been banished from the streets. State policy is to get them out of sight – in modern states, streets are for circulation rather than for social life. Street children are often confused with orphans and described as 'abandoned', but not all are outside family. Research worldwide has shown that street children are seldom abandoned, most have taken the decision to leave home for reasons that may range from lessening the burden on parents to escaping abuse or simply because they are bored (see for example the summary in Ennew and Swart-Kruger, 2003).

What street children share with orphans is that they are objects of concern, around whose actual lives and bodies a rhetoric and practice of rescue and redemption is constructed (Ennew, 2000, p. xv). Dependency is forced on them. Younger street children were and are institutionalized into orphanages, while older ones often find themselves in detention in juvenile or adult prisons.

Challenges to this institutionalization of street children arose in the 1980s during the period in which discussions about children's dignity and freedom were taking place in the context of the CRC, and at a time when numbers that were gross overestimates were developed to raise public awareness about this 'ever increasing' problem (Connolly and Ennew 1996). In response, there was an increase in the number of street children projects run by a specific type of civil society organization – non-governmental organizations or NGOs – to the extent that one could almost define a street child as 'a child alone on the street completely surrounded by NGOs' (Ennew, 1998; see also the introduction to Hecht, 1999). NGOs developed a new 'non-institutional' model of provision, in which the watchwords were 'participation' and 'respect for children'. The practice is often a drop-in centre, to which children are encouraged to go for safety and services by the street educators, and from which, ideally, they graduate to various forms of 'alternatives', ranging from institutional homes, through children's villages to vocational training schemes. Once past the first hurdle of the drop-in centre, where their decisions are respected to a large extent, the tendency is for the project to regress into fairly traditional institutional provision for children outside families. The result, as recorded in many countries is that street children 'shop around' the available projects, manipulating identity in different domains (Ahmed et al., 1999, p.171; Lucchini, 1996; Turnbull, 2000).

Aids orphan: victim or threat?

Just at the point at which the freedom model was recognized as being as problematic as institutional models, the AIDS orphans crisis made both models redundant through sheer weight of numbers. The construction of the 'AIDS orphans' problem has resulted in a fairly sudden break with historical continuity with respect to orphan care. The narrative of the popular construction of orphans has been overlaid by the narrative of 'the scourge of AIDS', which as many pointed out in the late 1980s is a new construction of old histories of disease, such as the Black Death of the European Middle Ages and the 'pox' of syphilis in early-modern Europe. One UNICEF UK campaign referred to an 'epidemic' of 'children growing-up-alone' and stated that 'Any credible estimate . . . suggests that their numbers must run to well over 100 million' (UNICEF UK, 2000) thus repeating an unsubstantiated figure used by UNICEF for two decades for street children numbers. It is clear that the international aid community feels it is faced with a potentially unmanageable welfare cost.

The solution cuts across patriarchal, nuclear family models of organization and throws children back into extended family care in the community – any family and any community will do. This accords with the consensus of international development practice that 'community-based solutions' based on 'community participation' are good practice (Ginzberg, 2002, pp. 8–9). The generalized solution, which has also been espoused by SOS Children's Villages in the East Africa region, is to support extended families by using existing community-based structures, especially in high risk communities (see for example, Foster et al., 1995; Donahue, 1998). Community solutions are also current international policy (fuelled by the Bretton Woods

organizations) for developing democratic governance through decentralization. In practice, decentralization implies displacement of state obligations
and reduction of state powers – both to intervene and to have to pay –
because communities take on the administration, management and implementation of works and services of collective interest. Yet this drive towards
development of responsible citizenship and good governance at local level
is forcing vulnerable, economically-fragile communities to assume greater
responsibilities than they have the capacity to fulfil. With respect to orphan
care in particular, I would argue that, despite the rhetoric of good governance, this is just a means of abandoning both children and communities,
in a repeat of age-old public accounting systems, which regard people who
are dependent as costly objects of charity and pity rather than as subjects
of rights.

By way of conclusion

My argument in this rapid description of orphan care in different times and
places has been that the form it takes is a response to economic necessities.
The rhetoric may be kindness, but reality is harsh. The logic is that children
of the poor, whose parents cannot care for them, are a burden on the public
purse, for which the cheapest solution is best. The key characteristic of these
children is their economic dependency. The longer childhood lasts, the
greater the need for education in life and livelihood skills, the higher the
cost of institutional care and the stronger the argument for substitute family
care. The form of family, and the monitoring of the care it provides is infinitely variable, according to the resources a state is willing, or able, to invest.

Fostering, in its many forms, has probably always been the most common
way of caring for social and biological orphans in most societies, and
remains largely informal in most societies. Despite its disadvantages in
human and financial terms, institutional care can raise considerable charitable funding and is probably the first idea in the general public conception
of orphan care. It is a relic of historical care based on the idea that it is economically worthwhile to invest in parentless children. Like formal fostering
systems, formal adoption of minors largely developed through state and
legislative changes in the nineteenth and twentieth centuries, with inter-
country adoption becoming popular in the last half century. Both fostering
and adoption are cost-effective ways of dealing with a dependent population that appears to have no economic return, for whom responsibility
is only reluctantly assumed, and whose agency must therefore be denied.
Children in state care are seldom consulted about their views, and their
placements are usually inadequately monitored. Both non-institutional and
freedom models are, at base, as institutional as institutions. The potential
economic costs of the AIDS orphans crisis is leading to a new approach that,
in the name of democracy, throws all responsibility for children without

parental care onto communities that are unprepared for, and under-resourced to bear, the burden of these children's upbringing and fulfilment of their rights.

Notes

This paper would not have been possible without the research and analytical inspiration of colleagues in Bosnia and Herzegovina, and Tanzania: Siham Ahmed, Suada Buljubašić, John Bwana, Sabina Čehajić, Vera Cvijetić, Ivana Đarmati, Asja Dupanović, Eric Guga. Maja Hadžiosmanović, Demere Kitunga, Albert Mgulambwa, Pili Mtambalike, Lazarus Mtunguja, Eunice Mwandayi, Suleman Sumra and Suzana Srnić Vuković. Thanks are also due to Mark Connolly, Elma Kurnitz, Gitte Liebst Robinson and Heather Montgomery. The paper is dedicated to the memory of Vera Cvijetić and Albert Mgulambwa.

1. Although the UN definition of 'child' in documents such as the Convention on the Rights of the Child and International Labour Organisation Convention 182 is a human being less than 18 years of age, UNAIDS continued to provide figures for 'AIDS orphans less than 15 years old' until 2004, ignoring the 16–18-year-olds (UNAIDS, 2004).
2. The Convention on the Protection of Children was adopted in 1993 by the Hague Conference and came into force in 1995. By 2001 over 40 countries had ratified.

References

Ahmed, S., J. Bwana, E. Guga, D. Kitunga, A. Mgulambwa, P. Mtambalike, L. Mtunguja and E. Mwandayi (1999) *Children in Need of Special Protection Measures: a Tanzanian Study*, Dar es Salaam: UNICEF Tanzania.

Arole, W. (1998) *Religion and Rights of Children and Women in South Asia*, Kathmandu: UNICEF South Asia Regional Office.

Bagnell, K. (1987) *The Little Immigrants*, Toronto: Macmillan.

Bledsoe, C. and U.C. Isiugo-Abanihe (1989) 'Strategies of Child Fosterage among Mende Grannies in Sierra Leone', in R. Lesthaeghe (ed.), *African Reproduction and Social Organisation*, Berkeley: University of California Press, pp. 442–74.

Bodenhorn B. (1988) 'Whales, Souls, Children and Other Things that are "Good to Share": Core Metaphors in a Contemporary Whaling Society', *Cambridge Anthropology*, 13 (1): 1–19.

Bond, T. and others (1991) *Poverty in Ho Chi Minh City: Results of a Participatory Poverty Assessment in Three Districts*, Hanoi: Save the Children UK.

Čehajić, S., V. Cvijetić, I. Đarmati, A. Dupanović, M. Hadžiosmaović and S.S. Vuković (2003) *Children and Institutions in Bosnia and Herzegovina: First Report of Capacity Building Research*, Sarajevo: UNICEF Bosnia and Herzegovina.

Connolly, M. and J. Ennew (1996) 'Introduction: Children out of Place', *Childhood*, 3 (2): 131–46.

Donahue, J. (1998) 'Community-based Economic Support for Households Affected by HIV/AIDS', Discussion Papers on HIV/AIDS Care and Support, USAID, Washington DC.

Donzelot, J. (1981) *The Policing of Families*, New York: Pantheon.

Ennew, J. (1998) 'Entournés par les intervenants', unpublished paper for the Graduate Seminar in Sociology, University of Fribourg.

Ennew, J. (2000) 'Preface', in C. Panter-Brick and M.T. Smith (eds), *Abandoned Children*, Cambridge: Cambridge University Press, pp. xiii–xvi.

Ennew, J. and J. Swart-Kruger (2003) 'Introduction: Homes, Places and Spaces in the Construction of Street Children and Street Youth', *Children, Youth Environment*, 13 (2): peer reviewed electronic journal, http://cye.colorado.ed.

Estrin, B.L. (1985) *The Raven and the Lark: Lost Children in the Literature of the English Renaissance*, Lewisburg: Bucknell University Press; London and Toronto: Associated University Press.

Foster, G., R. Shakespeare, F. Chinemara, H. Jackson, S. Gregson, C. Marange and S. Mashuba (1995) 'Orphan Prevalence and Extended Family Care in a Peri-urban Community in Zimbabwe', *AIDS Care*, 7 (1): 3–17.

Ginzberg, O. (2002) 'Building Projects on Assumptions: Trip Report for Laos, June 10–20, 2002', UN Inter-Agency Project to Combat Trafficking in Women and Children in the Mekong Sub-region, unpublished.

Goody, J. (1971) *Kinship*, Baltimore: Penguin.

Hecht, T. (1999) *At Home in the Street*, Cambridge: Cambridge University Press.

Holland, P. (1992) *What is a Child?* London: Virago.

Lucchini, R. (1996) 'The Street and its Image', *Childhood*, 3 (2): 235–46.

Panter-Brick, C. (2000) 'Nobody's Children? A Reconsideration of Child Abandonment', in C. Panter-Brick and M.T. Smith (eds), *Abandoned Children*, Cambridge: Cambridge University Press, pp. 1–26.

Pinchbeck, I. and M. Hewitt (1969 and 1973) *Children in English Society*, Volumes I and II, London: Routledge and Kegan Paul.

Pullan, B. (1989) *Orphans and Foundlings in Early Modern Europe* Reading: University of Reading Stenton Lecture 1988.

Rank, O. (1964) *The Myth of the Birth of the Hero and other Writings*, New York: Vintage Books.

Tanzanian Ministry of Labour and Youth Development (1995) 'Guidelines on Care of Orphans', Ministry of Labour and Youth Development, Social Welfare Department, Dar es Salaam.

Teichman, J. (1978) *The Meaning of Illegitimacy*, Cambridge: Englehardt Books.

Turnbull, B. (2000) 'Street Children and their Helpers: a Social Interface Analysis', unpublished PhD dissertation, University of Sussex.

UNAIDS (2001 and 2004) Fact sheets on children orphaned by AIDS in Sub-Saharan Africa.

UNAIDS (2004) *Children on the Brink: a Joint Report of New Orphans Estimates and a Framework for Action*, UNAIDS and UNICEF.

UNICEF Executive Board (1995) *Country Programme Recommendation – Viet Nam*, United Nations document E/ICEF/1995/P/L.20

UNICEF (1997) *Children and Families in a Changing Thai Society*, Bangkok: UNICEF Thailand Country Office.

UNICEF (1999) *Annual Report*, Hanoi: UNICEF Viet Nam Country Office.

UNICEF (2000) *Situation Analysis of Women and Children in Viet Nam*, Hanoi: UNICEF, Viet Nam Country Office.

UNICEF Viet Nam (1999) *Annual Report*, Hanoi: UNICEF Viet Nam Country Office.

UNICEF Viet Nam (2001) *Annual Report*, Hanoi: UNICEF Viet Nam Country Office.

UNICEF UK Committee (2000) Growing Up Alone, campaign materials.

Weisner, T. (1969) 'One Family, Two Households', paper for East African Social Science Council 5th Annual Conference, Nairobi.

Wressler, E.M. (1992) *Evacuation of Children from Conflict Areas: Considerations and Guidelines*, Geneva: UNHCR and UNICEF.

Zelizer, V.A. (1985) *Pricing the Priceless Child: the Changing Social Value of Children*, New York: Basic Books.

9
'In Defence of Childhood': Against the Neo-Liberal Assault on Social Life

Michael Lavalette

Introduction

Writing a chapter entitled 'In Defence of Childhood' no doubt seems provocative, especially in a book of essays overwhelmingly drawing on theorists from within the traditions of the 'new sociology of childhood'. It is common for writers within this approach to stress the fact that childhood is a social construct, one that has the effect of constraining and restricting children's social activities. Within the British academy, such themes have been shaped by both postmodernist and cultural relativist approaches – which further emphasize the 'liberationist' concerns of writers on childhood (for a critique see Goldson et al., 2002, and Lavalette, 1999b). Childhood is viewed as a 'cultural constraint', a historical creation that imposes limits on children's social roles and activities. A position that has led some radical rights advocates (Holt, 1974, and to a lesser degree Franklin, 1995) to argue that we should liberate children from childhood – a position James, Jenks and Prout come close to endorsing in their important intervention to the debate *Theorizing Childhood*.

In general terms, the first of these claims – that childhood is socially constructed – is a perspective I agree with, though I would always emphasize that social constructs are formed in specific historical circumstances (modern childhood is for me, therefore, a development of capitalism and of capitalist social relations; see Lavalette and Cunningham, 2002, and Lavalette, 1999b). Thus the importance, for me, of the chapter subtitle. What we are witnessing – in Britain in particular – is a neo-liberal assault on social life that involves a reduction in the state's role as provider of services. For neo-liberals this involves greater freedom, 'liberation' from the state and various authoritarian and restrictive welfare agencies. But this is a 'freedom' for the few who have the means to access whatever services they require; it condemns the majority to harder, more constrained and narrower lives and this especially impacts on those with the greatest needs, for example the poor, the elderly and children. Thus the second of the 'British' new sociologists' claims – that we should liberate children from childhood – is more complex.

'Liberating children from childhood' is a nebulous phrase that implies removing restrictions on children's lives and giving them the full range of rights that adults take for granted. As Holt (1974, p. 15) puts it: 'I propose ... that the rights, privileges, duties, responsibilities of adult citizens be made available to any young person.' In the abstract most readers will agree with the sentiment behind these words – but what happens when we try to operationalize such conceptions within the contradictions of modern global capitalism?

As someone whose research background is into child labour I have always felt uneasy at adopting an uncritical call for children to have the 'right to work' – to be 'liberated' into employment – a call that can be found on a number of children focused NGO websites. In most European countries the Industrial Revolution 'liberated' children from some of the restrictions of familial life and patriarchal authority. As Anna Davin notes, working-class children in Britain in the nineteenth century 'were prepared for adult life through participation, and their early experiences equipped them for responsibility and independence at an age when their *betters* were still in the schoolroom' (Davin, 1990, p. 60). But such 'liberation' was achieved by being drawn into employment, and children worked long hours in atrocious conditions for little monetary reward. To paraphrase Marx, their political and social liberation came at the cost of economic compulsion under the forced yoke of capitalist social relations. As I have argued elsewhere, the regulation and abolition of child labour from the main sectors of employment marked a significant victory for children and their families (Lavalette, 1998, and 1999a). Similarly today, when I see images of young people working down mines, or children employed on building sites or factories, my impulse is to advocate greater protection and regulation as a means of liberating children from the consequences of unregulated economic compulsion.

Such concerns are particularly pertinent at present. It seems to me that unwittingly there may be a possible coincidence of interest between 'liberationists' and neo-liberals. At the present historical juncture it does seem to give a hostage to fortune to advocate freedom from state provision of services, or even freedom from interference from welfare professionals. In a very real sense, these have been the goals of neo-liberals in government for the last twenty-five years or so. As neo-liberals have pursued their goals they have adopted a range of strategies, such as the use of an apparently 'progressive' language based on the notion of giving individual rights to people against the monolithic provisions of the state.[1] But the realities of such processes are far from sanguine. Behind the rhetoric of individual rights is the erosion of social networks, provisions and spaces that makes social living more brutal and more alienated (see Jones and Novak, 1999, and Davies, 1998).

In this chapter I want to locate issues about children's 'right to work' within broader policy developments. I want to argue that there have been some fundamental shifts in both policy and social discourse (and practice) about and affecting children in Britain. In particular I want to argue that we must not confuse 'liberation' from childhood with policy developments which thrust adulthood and 'adult responsibility' onto young people, what Goldson (2002) in a rather awkward phrase, describes as attempts to 'adulterize' children.

With regard to children's work I think it means posing two sets of questions. The first deals with the experience of work. How central is work to children's experiences? What do they do and what kind of rewards do they obtain? When children work, who benefits? What is the context of that work?

The second set of issues relates to the context within which work takes place. The imperative to work – in a world where choices are narrowing as a 'welfare gap' emerges – can be the signal of a loss of freedom, of finding oneself more deeply embedded in the cash-nexus and the labour-capital relationship. As the welfare state withers, as poverty gains a greater hold, as children become the target of advertisers and niche marketers, the imperative to work becomes greater. But to what extent is this an attack on a welfare-orientated childhood which is being replaced by an 'adulterized' childhood, liberated (or abandoned) by the state (at least in its caring role) and left to the vagaries of the market?

At the present moment, it seems to me, we need to defend and argue for the reinstatement of important *elements* of a welfare-orientated childhood against the retrenchment of services which produces the 'forced freedoms' embodied within 'adulterized' processes. But by saying this I am not arguing that we should return to a world where various welfare professionals had 'paternalistic' authority over the activities and lives of young people; we cannot go back to some (mythical) golden age. I am merely suggesting that some of the *goals* of earlier 'reformers' – and here especially with regard to the notion of children's freedom from labour – are worthy of consideration in the context we find ourselves at the start of the twenty-first century.

To set the context the following section looks at some developments in childhood in modern Britain.

Childhood in modern Britain

Britain is presently the fourth richest country in the world. It has never been wealthier and its economy has never been as large. Yet despite this, poverty and inequality are pervasive. In 1999/2000 the Households Below Average Income statistics revealed that 14 million people (25 per cent of the population) were living below 50 per cent of mean income after housing costs. In 1979/80 the corresponding figures were that five million people (9 per cent of the population) found themselves in such dire straights (CPAG, 2001).

Growing national prosperity has not reduced poverty because of the pattern of income inequality in Britain (see Ferguson et al., 2002). Over the last 25–30 years the wealth of the wealthiest has increased at the expense of the poorest in society. According to the Child Poverty Action Group (CPAG) between 1979 and 1999/2000 the real income of the poorest 10 per cent of the population grew by a mere 6 per cent, for the richest 10 per cent it grew by a massive 86 per cent (CPAG, 2002). During the 1980s and 1990s Britain experienced a massive increase in income and wealth inequalities as a result of conscious government policy and corporate greed. As Novak (2002, p. 60) argues:

> The imperatives of a market system and the reassertion of the privileges of social class, of wealth and power, that was epitomised in the governments of Margaret Thatcher brought an abrupt end to the limited achievements of the welfare state.

Changes to tax policy, privatization of various welfare services and public utilities, labour market deregulation and the substantial hiking of top pay levels (to the point that British company board members now pay themselves more than any of their equivalents in Europe) helped reverse the (albeit slight) redistributive trend that characterized the period between 1949 and 1976 (Pantazis and Gordon, 2000). On coming to power in 1997 the New Labour government of Tony Blair inherited a country more unequal than at any time since 1945. Yet it has not reversed these dismal figures on inequality. As Lakin (2001) notes, since 1997 earning inequalities between the richest and poorest deciles have continued to move further apart. For a variety of reasons, children have been most affected by this growing divide. Although children make up 22 per cent of the whole population, 29 per cent of children are in the lowest income fifth of the population, and (we should not forget, because all children are not the same!) 11 per cent are in the richest fifth. This puts Britain at the bottom of the European Union table for child poverty:

> the most shaming fact is that while child poverty remained stable or increased only slightly across most OECD countries in the last twenty years, it tripled in Britain ... Child poverty in Britain is twice as high as France or the Netherlands and five times higher than Norway or Sweden.
> (UKPHA 2000, pp. 1 and 12)

As Micklewright and Stewart (2000, p. 23) argue, on the basis of these figures the UK is 'a serious contender for the title of worst place in Europe to be a child'.

While the wealthy were rewarded with tax cuts to boost their already spiralling incomes, the welfare services on which the majority relied were reduced, abolished, or stripped of their helping role (Jones and Novak, 1999). During the 1980s and 1990s government policy, rather than softening the effects of free market inequalities, added significantly to the growing divide between rich and poor. Working-class children have been affected in myriad ways by the erosion of the welfare state. Let's look at some examples.

The schooling system in Britain is presently facing one of its regular crises. Schools across the country are threatening to make teachers redundant because they have no money. Damian Green (2003), Conservative shadow education spokesman has claimed that: 'Consultation letters on teacher redundancies have already gone out in Gloucester, Devon, Bristol and other areas. Phoning around the top 25 secondary schools as listed by The Sunday Times revealed that almost all were facing cuts ranging from £60,000 to £300,000.'

Green rather disingenuously goes on to suggest the problem is teachers' pay – actually the real problem is rooted in the marketization of schooling that developed after the Education Reform Act of 1988.

This Act introduced sweeping changes to the education system in Britain. It centralized the curriculum, restricting what teachers could teach, and introduced regular testing of children via Standard Attainment Tests (SATS). In England and Wales children are now examined at the ages of 7, 11, 14, 16, 17 and 18. By the time they enter university they are the most tested children in the world.

The Act also paved the way for schools to 'opt-out' of local authority control, giving more powers to governors and parents, and allowing head teachers far greater control over school budgets. The link between these two elements was the introduction of school league tables (in 1993) based on exam scores and truancy rates and 'parental choice' over the schools their children attended. Budgets followed pupils, so 'good' schools (defined almost exclusively in terms of examination results) got more resources and 'bad' schools spiralled into decline (see Timmins, 1995 for an overview). As Maitles notes:

> Educational disadvantage is intrinsically linked to socio-economic disadvantage ... the higher ranked schools are usually private, specialist, grammar or comprehensives (usually oversubscribed) in middle class areas ... The paradox is that money follows the 'successful' schools in the league tables as parents are keen to get their kids, where feasible, into these schools. This leads to the development of over-subscribed schools close to 'sink' schools.
>
> (Maitles, 2002, pp. 82 and 85)

The consequence was to open up divisions – under the guise of competition – and further solidify disadvantage within the schooling system.

But the system as a whole is restrictive to all children. According to a recent report about older pupils 'Some 8% of teenagers say they have had suicidal thoughts brought on by the stress of exams' (Curtis, 2003). More worryingly is a report that suggests exam stress and fear of failure now affects children as young as seven. As Morris (2002) notes:

> Pupils in their second year of primary school show signs of anxiety such as appetite loss, insomnia, bed-wetting, forgetfulness, and depression. [R]esearchers found . . . 55% of seven-year-olds preparing for standard assessment tests (SATS) showed signs of stress . . . [And] 88% of teachers said pupils started dreading the tests at the start of the summer term, though guidelines say they should be introduced in a way that does not cause worry.

Individual school budgetary concerns have also led to cuts in various ancillary services. For example, there is concern over school meal provision with increasing worries raised about the standard and quality of food provided for children and their long-term health consequences (Penketh, 2005). Although there are now recommended nutritional standards for school meals, these are failing to be adequately implemented. As school meal services are put out to tender, price is still the dominant factor when contracts are awarded – and this has consequences for quality.

A recent diary survey of 246 children carried out by the consumer magazine *Which?* found 'children between the ages of 10 and 15 are surviving on a diet of crisps, chips and chocolate bars washed down with soft drinks. Fruit and vegetable consumption is inadequate, and many of them are not getting vital nutrients.' When it came to school meals the diaries:

> were repetitive and often read like fast food menus. Pizza, chicken nuggets, and fishcakes were among the most popular main courses. Chips and potato-based smiley faces were the most frequently eaten starchy food, with baked beans the most common vegetable. The children ate an average of just two portions of fruit or vegetables a day, despite government advice that they should eat five to reduce the risk of cancer or heart disease. The older boys in the sample managed only 1 portion. School meals contributed less than one portion of fruit and vegetables a day to the children's diets, which were high in fat, sugar and salt, and low in fibre, iron, folate, zinc and other nutrients essential to growth.
>
> (Lawrence, 2003)

Unhealthy eating outside school also has wider social causes. As Will Hutton notes:

Few families can manage regular family eating times; both parents are working typically long and increasingly unpredictable hours, and children are fed as they demand rather than at regularly spaced family meals. The food needs to be quickly prepared; inevitably, it has a higher fat content. Distracted parents, forced to crowd household chores into less leisure time, gratefully allow their children to divert themselves with sedentary computer games. In any case, local authorities, prohibited from taxing by central government for fear it would offend 'business', have not the wherewithal to provide sports facilities. Result – an explosion of child obesity. The overwhelming majority of obese people are victims of the crushing social and economic forces that deny us control of our time.

(Hutton, 2002)

Back in schools – and again with potential long-term health consequences – school sports activities are in deep decline as stretched and underpaid teachers withdraw from a range of extra-curricula activities and school sports fields are sold off by schools and local authorities at a rate of almost one a week. Since 1982 it has been estimated that:

6,000 sites have been sold, many for supermarkets, housing developments and car parks ... The loss of playing fields has been felt most keenly in the inner cities. In the London borough of Camden, which has a population of 300,000 there is not a single grass pitch available for use by children.

(Kelso, 2002)

It's not just school parks. Public space in general has been restricted and is inadequate. Ken Worpole (2002) calls Britain the 'dirty man of Europe' because of the shabby quality of its public realm, but it is also, he suggests, 'one of the least child-friendly'. A survey conducted by the Children's Society and the Children's Play Council suggested most children thought their local parks were 'boring'. The results indicated that children were not allowed to play with water (45 per cent of child respondents), not allowed to climb trees (36 per cent), not allowed to play on climbing equipment (27 per cent) and not allowed to ride bikes or use skateboards (23 per cent). Worpole (2002) notes:

A combination of parental anxiety, local authority penny-pinching and cuts in non-statutory provision is in danger of producing a culture of childhood which leapfrogs from playschool to chatrooms, bypassing street games, adventure play and the freedom of the city which comes with territorial independence.

A linked aspect here is the development of what Frank Furedi (2001) calls 'paranoid parenting'. Furedi discusses the 'culture of fear' that 'has led parents to restrict their children's independent outdoor activities'. He notes that this has impacted on children's play, a range of formerly unsupervised activities and even getting to and from school and recreational activities as children are ferried back and forth by their parents. 'In 1971, eight out of ten 8-year-olds were allowed to walk to school alone. Now it is fewer than one in ten.'

Behind such developments is a socially constructed fear and anxiety about children's vulnerability. Furedi notes the findings of a System Three survey on the safety of children in Scotland in 1998. It suggested an

> overwhelming sense that children were far less safe than 20 years ago. Although the incidence of child murder by a stranger in Scotland is very low and has shown no change in the past 20 years, 76 per cent of respondents thought that there had been an increase in such tragedies, while 38 per cent believed that the increase had been 'dramatic'. A large majority – 83 per cent – also thought that more children were now being knocked down by traffic on the roads of Scotland. In fact the incidence of road injuries to children had decreased by 60 per cent during the previous 20 years.

The gap between adult perceptions and the reality of the risks faced by children is dramatic, and it leads some parents to restrict their children's activities; according to the Children's Play Council in 1997, it means some children have 'become virtual prisoners in their own homes' (ibid.).

Such 'paranoid parenting' is derived from a fear of modern living, a reflection of the deep alienation many individuals face in the modern world, and an exaggerated fear of 'criminals' and 'strangers' (see Ferguson and Lavalette, 2004). But it is also partly derived from the erosion of the social and public world and the increased pressure on 'time-poor' parents for life with children. As parents are drawn into the labour market, and as hours increase (4 million people in Britain work more than 48 hours a week because Britain opted out of the1998 European Working Time Directive, and British workers – women and men – work the longest hours in Europe) family leisure has become a highly structured commodity, undertaken (overwhelmingly) on out of town or edge of town sites.[2] The consequence is that family life has become more compressed, and more restrictive (for more on this see Ferguson et al., 2002).

As the state's role of provider of services has declined or been abolished – including the range of services that were beneficial to children's lives – it has increased its role in the surveillance and control of young people, especially those young people from the poorest communities in Britain who find themselves increasingly criminalized for 'hanging out' with friends on the streets of their communities. Over the last ten years there has been a significant authoritarian backlash within the criminal justice system in Britain. The result is increasingly to treat children and young people as adults within the system and subject them to adult forms of punishment. In a sense, then, they have been 'liberated' from childhood and treated as adults.

A key point in this process were the events that surrounded the 'Bulger case'. In 1993, two 10-year-old boys abducted and killed a two-year-old near the city of Liverpool. Although very unusual, children killing children is not a unique phenomenon. In Trondheim, Norway, in 1994 for example, a five-year-old girl was beaten unconscious by three six-year-old boys and left to die of hypothermia (Franklin and Petley, 1996). But the response of the media, the public and the criminal justice system in Britain to the Bulger case was extreme (Morrison, 1997).

The case in Britain marked a significant turn towards retributive 'justice', and children, especially poor working-class children, were targeted for harsher and more punitive treatment by the law. In the same year, the then Home Secretary, Michael Howard, argued that young people needed to feel the force of the law and be treated like adults, facing adult punishments. He referred to a problem with: 'self-centred arrogant . . . young hoodlums . . . who are adult in everything except years . . . [and who] . . . will no longer be able to use age as an excuse for immunity from effective punishment . . . they will find themselves behind bars' (quoted in Goldson, 1997, p. 130).

It was a trend that New Labour was to follow. Legislation passed over the last decade, such as the Criminal Justice Act 1993, the Criminal Justice and Public Order Act 1994, the Crime and Disorder Act 1998 and the Youth Justice and Criminal Evidence Act 1999 (the first two under the Conservatives, the latter two under New Labour) have combined to establish an increasingly 'tough' regime structured around retributive and punitive 'justice' (see Goldson, 2002). The consequence is that increasing numbers of children are treated and punished like adults.

For the present New Labour government in Britain, this trend is partly justified by reference to a variety of communitarian values, wrapped up in the ideology of 'Third Way' new social democracy. Here, while children and young people have increased rights in society (via legislation such as the Children Act 1989, it is claimed) these come with a series of responsibilities and obligations to community and society. These are 'obligations' and 'responsibilities' that are defined and outlined by the state and various policy formulators (for example, policy centres, political parties, the media) and are not necessarily built upon accepted universal values (Lavalette and Mooney, 1999). These are contested concepts and reflect a particular world outlook, defining social policy problems primarily in terms of individual behaviour rather than emphasizing the social and structural causes of those problems.

The consequence has been that the state has stepped in to regulate and control young people by targeting their supposed 'anti-social behaviour', by imposing 'curfews on kids'[3] and ensuring that children from the age of 10 can face criminal charges and be treated as responsible for their actions.

The final aspect shaping modern British childhood has been the growth of a range of private companies offering services and commodities for children. Inadequate state nursery provision has led to the growth of private pre-school nursery provision which is among the most expensive in Europe. This creates a huge financial burden for those working-class families on average, or even slightly above average incomes. For poor families it leaves them stressed by having to balance and manage childcare by relying on grandparents, relatives and friends. The perception that schools are stretched and under-resourced has led to an expansion of the private school system, with middle-class parents using their increased purchasing power to try and enhance their children's life chances.

Beyond the school gates there is an extensive leisure and service industry focused on children. This includes mass-produced children's parties, children's eateries (for example McDonald's and Burger King) and children's food (the mass-produced children's foods – pizzas, chicken nuggets, fish fingers – which are increasingly cooked separately for children at their meal times). And then there are the chain stores focused on young people (like Claire's Accessories – part of the multinational Clairestores group with revenue in 2002/2003 of $1.01 billion – where young girls can buy the latest fashion accessories, make-up and jewellery, as the company website puts it 'what's hot for our pre-teen 7–12 year olds').

What we are witnessing in Britain is an assault on childhood, a process which has its roots in a series of neo-liberal values based on 'consumerism', 'self-reliance' and marketization. The consequence has been to increase inequality between children; to restrict public and social space; to make schools more competitive, and concerned with narrow 'academic success' at the expense of broader notions of education and child well-being; to justify restrictions to state social welfare and 'caring' activities while increasing the state's control function over young people; and to turn children into both commodities and a potentially lucrative market for multinational corporations.

Where does child labour fit into this picture?

Child labour in modern Britain

There is now a substantial body of literature establishing the extent, nature and form of child labour in modern Britain. In the post-World War II era, child labour was thought to be a relatively harmless, minority experience. But a number of studies from the 1980s onwards have shown the phenomenon to be extensive, and increasing.

The studies which have taken place have originated from diverse sources including NGOs, academics and some government-funded work.

The Low Pay Unit has undertaken and published a series of studies from across the UK. Together these studies established that child labour was not a marginal activity. In 1980 MacLennan's findings indicated that in London 35 per cent of children (in their last school year) were involved in part-time employment. The study was later expanded to include Luton and Bedford where findings indicated 40 per cent of children were working (MacLennan et al., 1985). While in 1991 a study in Birmingham indicated 43 per cent of schoolchildren in the city were working, again during their later school years (Pond and Searle, 1991). Although these studies were quite large in scale they were criticized for being restricted to local job markets and for not being representative of the UK as a whole.

However support for their findings was found in two studies that were conducted in Scotland in the 1990s by academic researchers (Lavalette et al., 1991, and McKechnie et al., 1994). These studies, covering urban and rural areas, found approximately one-third of children in their last year of compulsory schooling were involved in part-time employment at any one time. In addition, the Scottish researchers assessed not only the part-time jobs that children had at the time of the study but also any jobs that they may have had in the past. When this perspective is taken there is evidence that as many as two-thirds of children have experience of part-time work by age sixteen. In 1995 the findings of a nationwide survey supported the findings of the various regional studies (Hibbett and Beatson, 1995). Of course, comparisons between studies can be problematic because of variations in definitions and methodology (see Hobbs and McKechnie, 1997). However, a consistent picture does emerge. It is the norm for children to have experience of paid employment outside of the family before they reach the end of compulsory education: it is the majority experience. When it comes to the types of jobs children perform, there are two things worth noting. First the majority of children work at tasks that are perceived as suitably 'children's'. This means that the majority will be engaged in delivery work (like newspaper or milk delivery to customer's homes), shop and café work – serving behind a counter or waiting at tables – and some agricultural tasks. But the second element is that there will always be children working in a range of tasks that are viewed as 'unacceptable' for children. They will work in garages, factories and warehouses. In fact they will work wherever they get the opportunity. Jolliffe et al. (1995), for example, recorded children working in over twenty different job categories.

The majority of children who work break the law and the regulatory system is inadequate. Children work before the legal minimum age of 13, they start before they are allowed to in the morning (7 a m.) and finish later than they are allowed to at night (7 p.m.). Most children do not have the required work permits (on most studies over 90 per cent of workers do not possess a work permit) and they often work in areas where they are specifically barred from employment (MacLennan et al., 1985; Lavalette et al., 1991; Hobbs and McKechnie, 1997).

Children's working conditions are poor. They are overwhelmingly employed in the more 'marginalized' sectors of the economy: in small shops and cafés, for newsagents and in door-to-door delivery work, on farms, and at garages. There is little inspection and regulation of their health and safety situation. They do not get specialized clothing appropriate to their work needs (appropriately designed bikes for news deliverers or waterproof clothing, for example). Their wages are pitiful – on average several pounds an hour less than the minimum wage.

Even in the 'children's' jobs, we should not assume that these are harmless, light activities carried out for a little bit of extra pocket money. Here are three examples drawn, not from factory or warehouse work, but from 'classic' types of children's jobs – newspaper delivery, milk delivery and work at a fast-food outlet.

Our first example concerns newspaper delivery work. In 1988 the *Observer* carried an article about the weights carried by newspaper deliverers (Cooper, 1988). Young people delivering Sunday newspapers were estimated to be carrying 'anything from 21.5 lbs to 68.5 lbs – nearly five stones' (1 kg is equal to 2.2 lbs). An agreement between the Post Office and the Communication Workers Union in Britain restricts weights carried by 16–18-year-old postal workers to 20 lbs on foot and 26 lbs on a suitably adapted bike. This means that newspaper deliverers could be carrying almost three times the agreed limit of (older) postal workers.

The second example is the milk round. In 1991 journalist Ken Oxley reported the story of two brothers Anthony (13) and John (12) who worked on a local milk round. They got up each morning at 2.30 a.m., started work loading the van at 3.30 a.m. and set off on the delivery round at 4.15 a.m. Their work would finish at about 7.30 a.m. when they would go home, have breakfast and then go to school. They worked for 73p an hour. If their school day was an average five and a half hours (excluding breaks) then their work day was nine and a half hours. On several counts (John's age, the starting time, the number of hours worked, the type of activity) this work breaks the law, and at 73p an hour few would argue against the depiction of this work as cheap child labour.

Yet there is something else worth noting about this example. When the employer was questioned by the reporter he replied that 'I know it's against the law to employ kids but all the milkmen . . . do it', and then he went on: 'The dairy sent me a leaflet about the dangers of cheap labour but they don't know the competition.'

It may not be obvious or well known, but this employer is alluding to the effects of privatization, deregulation and outsourcing on labour practices in this field. In the past the big dairy firms employed their own delivery workers, but during the 1980s there was increasing pressure brought to bear on the milk supply industry by government (leading to full deregulation and the privatization of former Milk Marketing Boards between 1991 and 1995). One consequence was that milk delivery was outsourced; 'milkmen' now had to bid for milk rounds, the cheapest bid winning the contract. One way to make your bid cheap was to squeeze labour costs and to extend the size of the run. The consequence for successful bidders was to 'speed up' the work process (they had to start earlier and work more intensely and faster), and to employ labour as cheaply as possible – and children have always been cheap.

Thirdly, let's take an example from one of the iconic 'logo' companies of the modern global era. In July 2001 two McDonald's restaurants in Surrey were fined £12,400 for what Morris (2001) described as 'exploiting child workers'. They had been employing schoolchildren illegally, forcing them to work overtime and late (illegally so) on school nights. Morris went on: 'Ten schoolchildren, including a girl who worked 16 hours on a Saturday and another who worked until 2 a.m. on a schoolday, were found to be illegally employed.' This example includes young people working in the frenetic McDonald's atmosphere, on minimum wage rates and for incredible working days – some working until 2 a.m. and expected to be in school at 9 a.m. the following day.

These last two examples show that the jobs children undertake are subject (like the jobs adults do) to processes of deskilling and degradation. Children at work find their tasks increasingly fragmented and controlled (by both supervisors and machines which embody managerial control). They sell their labour power – often very cheaply – on the labour market. They have no control over the process of production, or the products of their labour. In the work process they find themselves vulnerable (with few rights at work), in competition with other workers and with no collective representative (from a trade union). Their work is an example of alienated labour.

Who benefits from child labour?

Yet despite these examples, is it the case that child labour is harmful or a negative experience, and what do children themselves want? We can start to address these questions in a number of ways, each reflecting a variety of approaches to the child labour issue.

First, over the last few years a number of social psychologists have looked at the impact work has on individual development (see Hobbs and McKechnie, 1997). The key text in this line of research is Greenberger and Steinberg's *When Teenagers Work* (1986) though it has been added to and developed by a large number of writers, creating what is almost an academic 'sub-discipline' of child labour research. Reviewing this literature

Marsh (1991) has argued that there are two general approaches within this writing, the 'zero sum model' and the 'developmental model'. Essentially the zero sum model suggests that work will have a series of negative impacts on young people's academic achievements (crudely, that time spent at work reduces that available for homework or academic concerns), while the developmental model argues that working is 'character-building' (it teaches children the value of money, it allows the transfer of a range of skills and practical knowledge, it encourages responsibility and an adult outlook).

Now there is an immediate problem with this approach that we need to note. Work is a social activity and workers are located within social relations of production. These approaches, however, are concerned to look at work as a more or less isolated psychological experience. Moreover expressed in this individualized way there is a danger of viewing these alternatives as 'getting to the heart' of the child labour issue: that if research evidence supports the zero sum model then work is 'bad', but if it supports the developmental model work is 'good'. The problem, however, is that the evidence is not clear-cut and indeed the questions are often posed in quite 'ideological' ways.

Let's look at some of the evidence from the 'costs and benefits' debate. First, there is the question of work's impact (or otherwise) upon educational performance. In the 'zero sum model' all work is 'bad' because it impacts negatively on schooling. However if work is detrimental because it eats into time available for 'academic' work then what is being argued over is essentially a time allocation issue, but interestingly there is no claim that those taking part in sport or various other leisure activities are damaging their education.

The problem for 'zero sum' advocates is that the evidence is not clear. There are some research findings that suggest a limited amount of work will not have a negative impact on schooling. Indeed some evidence suggests that part-time work, providing it does not last more than 10 hours a week, can lead to improved academic performance, though work that lasts more than 10 hours a week does seem to have a detrimental impact on education (compare Hobbs and McKechnie, 1997, and Mortimer et al., 1996).

These findings may be thought to lend some support to the 'developmental model'. Further studies can be found that suggest that work helps develop 'personal responsibility' (Steinberg et al., 1982), an awareness of the 'value of money' (Greenberger and Steinberg, 1981), social responsibility and autonomy (Steinberg et al., 1981) and greater appreciation of the realities of the world of work (Green, 1990). But supporters of developmentalism may feel less secure when work is also identified as having a negative impact on family and peer relations, seems to be linked with increased cigarette, alcohol and drug use, and produces a degree of 'occupational cynicism' as young people learn about the realities of work on the modern labour market (Hobbs and McKechnie, 1997; Lavalette, 1994).

For almost every claimed 'benefit' work brings there is a balancing 'cost' that has to be acknowledged. Further, much of the research in this field fails to take account of significant background elements – such as class, poverty, types of employment – which might help unpick some of these confusions. So it is not clear – in terms of individual psychological development – whether and to what extent children benefit from work.

There is a second issue. Do employers benefit from child labour? It might seem strange that we have to ask this question but there has been a suggestion made in some quarters that employers get little out of employing children. The suggestion is that children are an 'inefficient' source of labour power, that they don't have the required skills, knowledge or strength of adult workers. In the 1980s and 1990s in Britain a number of politicians, philosophers and employers suggested that child labour was actually a form of education or training carried out by (almost) philanthropic employers. In 1993 Michael Forsyth (at the time British Minister of State for Employment) and Gerry Malone in 1994 (at the time Minister for Health) both made statements reflecting the view held by the then Conservative Government on this issue. They suggested child employment was healthy and light. That it was well-regulated and provided some beneficial experiences for the young people involved (see Lavalette et al., 1994/95). Right-wing philosopher Roger Scruton was reported in the *Guardian* as saying that, in his opinion, 'Many a 14 year old, set to work as a builder's apprentice, an electrician's mate or a stable hand, will learn more than he could ever at school' (*Guardian*, 13 February 1990). Finally, one employer in north-west England, who employed children illegally at his box-making factory, suggested that he was providing a kind of social service. If the children were not at work in his factory they could, he suggested, be getting into trouble or mischief on the streets (Channel 4, 1994). This employer was so convinced of the benefits of his social role that he had helpfully removed safety protectors on the guillotines to enable the smaller children to get their hands up close to the moving blade.

This is all clearly reflective of a particular ideological perspective on child employment, one that views it as a light, harmless activity carried out in beneficial circumstances. As argued above, this ideological depiction has little connection with reality.

When we move beyond the ideological claims, we are left with a much clearer picture. Children get jobs (albeit often ones that are thought particularly suitable for children to perform) because employers want particular work tasks fulfilled and children are the ideal workforce for their needs. Even in those typical children's jobs – in milk or newspaper delivery – they provide a service that enables their employers to obtain or hold onto customers. They work within the general circuit of production and provision of goods and services and they do so as an exceptionally cheap and flexible workforce, with fewer worker rights and no history of work-based collective organization and representation. Further, in some sectors children are used to replace adult workers, or are used by employers to place pressure on adult wages. In these circumstances we should be clear that employers benefit from the exploitation of child labour.

But, of course, there is one other aspect that we need to take account of: many young people want to work. Work gives them a certain feeling of social worth, it brings a degree of independence, and, of course, it brings money and from this, access to many of the symbols of the increasingly pervasive youth cultural market. Should this surprise us?

Work is one of the central values of capitalist society. From a very young age children are taught to think in terms of their future occupation and place within the division of labour. In Britain under New Labour the poor, those on benefits, lone parents, and the disabled, for example, are all told that the way to avoid 'social exclusion' is via working – at any job, no matter what pay and conditions it may bring with it. Work also gets tied up with a whole set of 'common sense' ideas about development. So it fits with common sayings such as work 'teaches children the value of money', or 'it lets them see what the world is like' or 'it never did me any harm'. Finally, given the competitiveness and narrowness of the British education system, the decline in open and social space (and linked to this the decline in team sports provision, and a variety of youth organizations), and the increasingly insular and isolated (and expensive) pastimes that children and young people engage in, work not only provides money but often social contact.

Given all this it is not at all surprising that children want to work. Indeed it would be surprising if they automatically threw off the ideological pressure and rejected the legitimacy of commodified labour.

But does this alone mean that we should promote children's 'right to work' no matter what the circumstances may be?

The problem is that often we are not comparing like with like. The combined research evidence of educationalists, sociologists and psychologists suggests that a small amount of work (less than 10 hours a week), in well-regulated circumstances (with appropriate enforcement of health and safety regulations and starting and finishing times), with collective representation available for young workers (like all workers children should have access to trade unions and have representatives who can express their collective interests) and appropriate levels of pay (if minimum pay levels exist why should they not apply to children?) may be beneficial to children in terms of their development. But the further we move away from these conditions the more exploitative and dangerous work becomes.

Children, of course, do work in these less than ideal circumstances but this is the result of several factors. Family poverty, decline of social and welfare services, unscrupulous employers, inadequate regulation and lack of government will (to treat the problem seriously and enforce regulation) all create conditions in which children enter work. But when children work in these circumstances it is not an example of their 'liberation' but rather, an example of them obtaining the 'freedom of economic compulsion'. The pressure to work, and the conditions and experiences whilst at work, are shaped by the social relations of capitalism and, in recent years in Britain, by the neo-liberal commitments of both Conservative and New Labour governments. Working children in Britain (as they are in other parts of the globe) are overwhelmingly the victims of these processes, not their beneficiaries. Work is not an example of 'liberation' but of 'adulterization'.

Conclusion

The primary concern in this chapter has been to look at the impact of neo-liberal policies in Britain on children; in particular to focus on the various examples where there have been attempts to 'adulterize' children's activities. These developments are important to all those who work, write and research with children and young people.

Within the new sociology of childhood there has been – correctly in my opinion – a focus on children's rights and one trend within this broad set of concerns has been to advocate 'liberationism', the notion that children should be freed from the restrictions of childhood. However, on the basis of the above discussion I suggest we need to be more nuanced in our advocacy of any such approach. Calls for children to have the right to work, or to be liberated from educational restrictions, or be freed from welfarist prescriptions are in danger of being manipulated by neo-liberal advocates of deregulation as a means of further opening up the social world to the interests and domination of free-market capitalism. The conclusion is that 'adulterizing' children is not liberation but instead represents a regressive attack on children's basic social rights.

Notes

1. Perhaps the best example here is the word 'empowerment'. This is a nebulous word with contested meanings. For a number of academics and welfare practitioners it has been used to assert the right of a range of social and user groups to determine their own needs and services; fine in theory, but a set of demands that have rarely been fulfilled in practice. Instead the word has become part of the lexicon of welfare 'managerialist-speak' and reflects strategies aimed at privatizing and marketizing services. Here clients or 'customers' are 'empowered' to choose from a limited range of service providers who often only meet minimal service provision criteria (on much of this see Harris, 2003).
2. And as an aside – mass-produced leisure for families really has all the hallmarks of 'Fordism' – a look at the 'kids' parties' run by most chains emphasizes this point perfectly.
3. On one large working-class estate in Hamilton (just south of Glasgow) police have maintained a dusk till dawn curfew for under 16s. This policy was first implemented in 1998.

References

Channel 4 (1994) *Look Who's Working*, Undercover Britain Series, Channel 4 Television.

Child Poverty Action Group (2001) *Poverty: the Facts*, 4th edition, London: CPAG.

Child Poverty Action group (2002) 'Poverty: the Facts – Summary', *Poverty*, 111: 1–4.

Clairestores, www.clairestores.com/company/profile.html.

Cooper, E. (1988) 'Paper Weight Lifters', *Observer*, 18 December.

Curtis, P. (2003) 'Teenagers "Suicidal" over Exams', *Guardian*, 14 May.

Davies, N. (1998) *Dark Heart*, London: Vintage.

Davin, A. (1990) 'When is a Child not a Child?', in H. Carr and L. Jamieson (eds), *The Politics of Everyday Life*, Basingstoke: Macmillan, pp. 37–61.

Ferguson, I. and M. Lavalette (2004) 'Beyond Power Discourse: Alienation and Social Work', *British Journal of Social Work* (April): 297–312.

Ferguson, I., M. Lavalette and G. Mooney (2002) *Rethinking Welfare*, London: Sage.

Franklin, B. (ed.) (1995) *The Handbook of Children's Rights*, London: Routledge.

Franklin, B. and J. Petley (1996) 'Killing the Age of Innocence: Newspaper Reporting of the Death of James Bulger', in J. Pilcher and S. Wagg (eds), *Thatcher's Children?* London: Falmer, pp. 134–54.

Furedi, F. (2001) 'Paranoid Parenting: Making Sense of Parental Paranoia', *Guardian*, 26 April.

Goldson, B. (1997) 'Children in Trouble: State Responses to Juvenile Crime', in P. Scraton (ed.), *'Childhood' in 'Crisis'?* London: UCL Press, pp. 1–33.

Goldson, B. (ed.) (2000) *The New Youth Justice*, Lyme Regis: RHP.

Goldson, B. (2002) 'New Labour, Social Justice and Children: Political Calculation and Deserving–Undeserving Schism', *British Journal of Social Work*, 32: 683–95.

Goldson, B., M. Lavalette and J. McKechnie (eds) (2002) *Childhood, Welfare and the State*, London: Sage.

Green, D. (2003) 'Cuts Both Ways', *Guardian*, 9 April.

Green, D.L. (1990) 'High School Student Employment in Social Context: Adolescents' Perceptions of the Role of Part-time Work', *Adolescence*, 25: 425–34.

Greenberger, E. and L. Steinberg (1981) 'The Workplace as a Context for the Socialization of Youth', *Journal of Youth and Adolescence*, 10: 141–57.

Greenberger, E. and L. Steinberg (1986) *When Teenagers Work: the Psychological and Social Costs of Adolescent Employment*, New York: Basic Books.

Harris, J. (2003) *The Social Work Business*, London: Routledge.

Hibbett, A. and M. Beatson (1995) 'Young People at Work', *Employment Gazette*, 103: 169–77.

Hobbs, S. and J. McKechnie (1997) *Child Employment in Britain: a Social–Psychological Analysis*, Edinburgh: HMSO.

Holt, J. (1974) *Escape from Childhood*, Harmondsworth: Penguin.

Hutton, W. (2002) 'Fat is a Capitalist Issue', *Observer*, 27 January.

James, A., C. Jenks and A. Prout (1998) *Theorizing Childhood*, Cambridge: Polity.

Jolliffe, F., S. Patel, Y. Sparks and K. Reardon (1995) *Child Employment in Greenwich*, London, Borough of Greenwich: Education Social Work Service.

Jones, C. and T. Novak (1999) *Poverty, Welfare and the Disciplinary State*, London: Routledge.

Kelso, P. (2002) 'Despite Pledge, Labour Fails to Slow Sales of School Playing Fields', *Guardian* 16 December.

Lakin, C. (2001) 'The Effects of Taxes and Benefits on Household Income, 1999–2000', *Economic Trends*, 569, April, London: HMSO, pp. 667–80.

Lavalette, M. (1994) *Child Employment in the Capitalist Labour Market*, Aldershot: Ashgate.

Lavalette, M. (1998) 'Child Labour: Historical, Legislative and Policy Context', in B. Pettitt (ed.), *Children and Work in the UK*, London: CPAG, pp. 22–40.

Lavalette, M. (ed.) (1999a) *A Thing of the Past? Child Labour in Britain in the Nineteenth and Twentieth Centuries*, Liverpool: Liverpool University Press

Lavalette, M. (1999b) 'The "New Sociology of Childhood" and Child Labour: Childhood, Children's Rights and Children's Voice', in M. Lavalette (ed.), *A Thing of the Past? Child Labour in Britain in the Nineteenth and Twentieth Centuries*, Liverpool: Liverpool University Press, pp. 15–43.

Lavalette, M. and S. Cunningham (2002) 'The Sociology of Childhood', in B. Goldson, M. Lavalette and J. McKechnie (eds), *Childhood, Welfare and the State*, London: Sage, pp. 9–28.

Lavalette, M. and G. Mooney (1999) 'New Labour; New Moralism: the Welfare Politics and Ideology of New Labour under Blair', *International Socialism*, 85, Autumn: 27–48.

Lavalette, M., J. McKechnie and S. Hobbs (1991) *The Forgotten Workforce: Scottish Children at Work*, Glasgow: SLPU.

Lavalette, M., J. Lindsay, S. Hobbs and J. McKechnie (1994/95) 'Child Employment in Britain: Policy, Myth and Reality', *Youth and Policy*, 47, winter: 1–15.

Lawrence, F. (2003) 'Junk Food Diet Still Served up at Schools', *Guardian*, 6 March.

MacLennan, E. (1980) *Working Children*, London: Low Pay Unit.

MacLennan, E., J. Fitz and J. Sullivan (1985) *Working Children*, London: Low Pay Unit.

Maitles, H. (2002) 'Children and Education: Inequalities in our Schools', in B. Goldson, M. Lavalette and J. McKechnie (eds), *Childhood, Welfare and the State*, London: Sage, pp. 73–86.

Marsh, W.H. (1991) 'Employment during High School: Character Building or a Subversion of Academic Goals?' *Sociology of Education*, 64: 172–89.

McKechnie, J., S. Lindsay and S. Hobbs (1994) *Still Forgotten: Child Employment in Rural Scotland*, Glasgow: SLPU.

Micklewright, J. and K. Stewart (2000) 'Child Well-being and Social Cohesion: is the UK the Oddball in Europe?' *New Economy*, March: 21–5.

Morris, S. (2001) '£12,400 Child Labour Fine on McDonald's', *Guardian*, 1 August.

Morris, S. (2002) 'Primary Pupils Stressed by Exams', *Guardian*, 30 December.

Morrison, B. (1997) *As If*, Granta Books: London.

Mortimer, J.T., M.D. Finch, S. Ryu, M.J. Shanahan and K.T. Call (1996) 'The Effects of Work Intensity on Adolescent Mental Health, Achievement and Behavioral Adjustment: New Evidence from a Prospective Study', *Child Development*, 67: 1243–61.

Novak, T. (2002) 'Rich Children, Poor Children', in B. Goldson, M. Lavalette and J. McKechnie (eds), *Childhood, Welfare and the State*, London: Sage, pp. 59–72.

Oxley, K. (1991) '3.30 a.m. . . . and 12-year-old John Fletcher starts work', *Sunday Sun*, 2 June.

Pantazis, C. and D. Gordon (2000) *Tackling Inequalities*, Bristol Policy Press.

Penketh, L. (2005) 'Social Policy and the Politics of Food', in M. Lavalette and A. Pratt (eds), *Social Policy: Theories, Concepts and Issues*, 3rd edition, London: Sage.

Pond, C. and A. Searle (1991) *The Hidden Army: Children at Work in the 1990s*, London: Low Pay Unit.

Steinberg, L.D., E. Greenberger, A. Vaux and M. Ruggier (1981) 'Early Work Experience: Effects on Adolescent Occupational Socialization', *Youth and Society*, 12: 463–22.

Steinberg, L.D., E. Greenberger, L. Garduque and S. McAuliffe (1982) 'Effects of Working on Adolescent Development', *Developmental Psychology*, 18: 385–95.

Timmins, N. (1995) *The Five Giants: a Biography of the Welfare State*, London: Fontana.

UKPHA (2000) *Report: Newsletter of the UK Public Health Association*, 4 Summer.

Worpole, K. (2002) 'Come Out To Play', *Guardian*, 7 August.

10
The Wealth of Children: Reconsidering the Child Labour Debate

Olga Nieuwenhuys

1. Reconsidering the child labour debate[1]

The past two decades' re-emergence of child labour has been explained as the outcome of the globalization of the world economy which has made the work of young children available for exploitation on a previously unknown scale. But how this work is exploited and by whom exactly remains a matter of debate. Dominant economic approaches see in local entrepreneurs the main exploiters and place the responsibility with both governments and parents. Parents, being either risk-averse or lacking in altruism, would offer their children as cheap labour power to profit-hungry entrepreneurs. Detailed anthropological studies, far fewer in number, suggest that this view fails to account for the reciprocity that informs long-term intra-familial exchange relationships and the pivotal place of children therein. Both approaches have their merits, but are unsatisfactory.

My own anthropological work on children's work in a Kerala village supports the centrality of reciprocity in the day-to-day exchanges that take place locally between children and their surrounding (Nieuwenhuys, 1996 and 2000). But this is only part of the story. Reciprocity carries a price: propertyless children – who form about half of the population of the village – can only service their reciprocal obligations through an exchange of the produce of their work with wealthy traders against the very barest minimum to stay alive. I tried to show that the exchange was deeply unequal and that prices paid to children had multiplied many times by the time the products reached centres of world demand. My conclusion was that children's exploitation should be understood as the outcome of complex interlocking patterns of local and supra-local forms of both reciprocal and unequal exchange. In other words, the embeddedness of reciprocal exchange in relations of domination is not neutral. Embeddedness makes for reciprocity to be conditional upon giving up wealth[2] that is siphoned-off to those who hold power both locally and globally over the children and their parents.

The issue is particularly important for global childhood studies both politically and theoretically. Politically, putting reciprocity in children's work at the centre of analysis carries the danger of sanctifying the most horrid forms of exploitation. Children who work in Thailand's sex industry are a case in point. The children themselves see in the practice: 'not an issue of morality versus immorality but of turning a socially unacceptable form of earning into a way of fulfilling their familial obligations' (Montgomery, 2002, p. 157).

The alternative that focuses on exploitation is likewise fraught with difficulties. The consequences of threats of US trade sanctions against products made with the labour of children have for instance brought to international attention that child labour abolition may push the children concerned into worse forms of abuse such as prostitution (Boyden et al., 1998, p. 294). Theoretically, separating reciprocity from inequality has led to maintaining a sharp contrast between what is judged morally adequate or even laudable (child work) and what is deemed unacceptable (child labour). What is lost in the analysis is that in a situation of domination such as the one under which most children have to work, reciprocal and unequal forms of exchange are inextricably tied together. In this chapter I suggest that focusing on the interconnection between these two forms of exchange could help overcome the political and theoretical double bind of the child labour debate.

The literature on how to address child labour touches on such topics as trade-related sanctions, poverty eradication, schooling, state and civil society, cultural practices and universal values and the right of children to speak out for themselves. The breadth of topics and diversity of opinions have brought new theoretical insights about the nature and significance of children's work to light (Boyden et al., 1998, pp. 127ff.). These insights are often highly critical of notions that have become part of the language employed by policy-makers and child advocates. Conceptions of *the child* and *labour* have been deconstructed as typical categories valid for the relatively limited areas of the world where there is a clear-cut separation between childhood and the labour market. In these areas, wage labour is the prevalent form of work. In vast areas of the south, non-wage labour is rather the rule and includes work in agriculture, fishing, hunting and gathering; domestic manufacture of goods paid at a piece rate; housework, including gardening, tending small game, drawing water and collecting firewood; childcare; work that is paid in kind (for instance domestic service) or in exchange for mutual services (such as helping during harvests, in childcare or home construction); vending and transporting goods. Assisting adults and performing a myriad of services and work obligations is part of the normal practice of childhood. The term *child labour* has therefore been problematized for its failure to address common practices of working children in the south.

Detailed studies of these practices have also evinced the importance of an approach that takes the sociological field in which they take shape as the focus of research (Robson, 2004; Hashim, 2004; Schildkrout, 2002; Invernizzi, 2001; Kenny, 1999; Nieuwenhuys, 1994; Reynolds, 1991). Isolating work from this field gives a distorted picture of complex patterns of reciprocity and long-term support that provide the wider context in which children exercise their agency and base the *practical reasons* (Bourdieu, 1994) for their choices and actions. Looking at work from today's working children's experiences and perspectives evidences the need for creative approaches that depart from earlier models of child labour eradication as devised in nineteenth-century Europe and the USA (Liebel, 2003; Hanson and Vandaele, 2003; Invernizzi and Milne, 2002). In devising these approaches children are now increasingly seen as active participants if not social agents in their own right. It may not surprise therefore that researchers working from this perspective propose to make a distinction between what children do (children's work) and the subjects of such actions (working children). The distinction helps overcome the idea that what children do is either not labour or reflects negatively on children's childhood. It is also the one I am adopting here.

Recognition that children are actively engaging in the economy – in its wider meaning of wealth creation in society – is now inspiring a newly emerging strand of economic and sociological thinking. Theorizing focuses on the interdependence between two areas of social life that both economists and social scientists have traditionally seen as mutually exclusive: childhood and the market. There are two distinct directions: one looks at children's engagement with the market (Zelizer, 2002; Lavalette, 2000; Song, 1999; Mizen et al., 1999) the other broadens the definition of the economic to include children's non-monetized roles and has taken issue against considering traditional areas of child work such as the household and the school as falling outside the economy (Cohen, 2001; Becker et al., 1998; Morrow, 1996; Qvortrup, 1995).

Both approaches seek to understand children's value to society outside the realm of market transactions. They provide clues as to how, both in late industrial societies and in the global south, children play a key role in constituting and maintaining forms of wealth that are passed down from generation to generation. Taking the case of twentieth-century US society, Zelizer's pioneering work on the 'priceless child' makes a seminal distinction between economic value realized by adults in the market and the value that children acquire precisely because they are excluded from it (Zelizer, 1985). The other approach dwells on the regional limits of market transactions and focuses on peasant societies that only very partially realize wealth through market exchange. Caldwell's work on demographic transition in Nigeria and South India stands out for his adoption of the anthropological notion of intergenerational flows of wealth to explain the value of children in contexts that are not market-dominated (Caldwell, 1982).

The two approaches show interesting analogies in their identification of children's economic value in non-market work: school and housework in the industrial north and, in the south, unremunerated work in agriculture, in the household or under parental supervision. The separation of children from the market entails in both models that children do not or cannot claim compensation for their work. They are valued for their fulfilling moral obligations, their economic roles remaining largely invisible. In short, both models recognize children's substantial contribution to wealth creation in society and premise it on principles of reciprocity that do not obtain under market conditions.

What appears to be missing in both is acknowledging that exchange between generations is rarely symmetrical. For those down the social ladder, the exchange is unequal, tending to favour those with greater wealth and power. This is particularly evident in the case of the exploitation of children working for wages or under conditions of slavery. But also children who perform non-waged work can be highly exploited, as when their produce is sold at below-subsistence prices or when employers do not pay adults enough to feed themselves let alone to feed their children or pay for child-care and education. Children may then be obliged to spend most of their time in cultivating the family's plot, in foraging for food and fuel wood, in helping parents make and sell goods or looking after younger siblings. Work that is primarily undertaken as part of reciprocal exchange between generations can then turn into a form of subsidy benefiting not only local entrepreneurs but also producers and consumers, including children, in wealthier areas of the world.

In the dynamics of intergenerational exchange there are then evident asymmetries between middle-class children both in the north and in urban areas in the south and those living in the countryside or in urban slums. The former are, ideally at least, conceived as being untroubled with material concerns and fully preoccupied with self-development. They are conceived as endowed with a wide range of rights which their parents and the state are put in charge of realizing. The latter, by contrast, are overwhelmingly embedded in local systems of reciprocal exchange, and are viewed primarily as having duties towards elders and society. To contrast the two, Hecht makes a useful distinction between *nurtured* and *nurturing* childhood, which I also adopt here (Hecht, 1998). I contend that middle-class, *nurtured* childhood should be seen as a very partial rendering of the social field of interaction where childhood is continually created and recreated. Foregrounding the more common *nurturing* childhood in the analysis is a condition for obtaining a full view of the dynamics of the field.

My argument begins with a critical discussion of the link between children's work and poverty (Section 2). In Section 3 I maintain that working children are *nurturing* children and therefore creators of wealth. I suggest shifting the focus of child labour research from preoccupations with poverty to the unequal distribution of intergenerational wealth. In Section 4 I explore a possible redefinition of exploitation as the unequal exchange to which working children must agree in order to create the wealth that is exchanged between generations. To illustrate my point I compare outsourcing with the nanny-chain and highlight the unequal exchange that in both cases conditions *nurturing* children's embeddedness in intergenerational reciprocity.

2. Children's poverty

Child labour is generally condemned on two grounds: first because children would be unable to negotiate fair wages and labour conditions in the market, and second because selling children's labour far beyond its future value if children were going to school instead of working would be a form of value destruction. Applied to economies in the south, as I discuss in the first part of this section, the line of reasoning has been used to both explain poverty and provide a recipe for economic growth. Abolishing child labour would protect children from poverty and exploitation while, by the same token, giving the economy the boost needed to engender growth. In the second part of the section I focus on children's unpaid work obligations that the line of reasoning takes for granted. I argue that in the absence of the crucial role of the state in providing free health and education and in protecting adult jobs from international competition, nurturing children's moral obligations become a form of mandatory unpaid work. In other words, if eradicating child labour can engender economic growth without a protective state, it is essentially because hundreds of millions of children work for free.

The ILO is the key international authority on the child labour issue whose authority few, if any, would dare to challenge. In a recent publication on child labour, the agency summarizes, under the section heading 'A better understanding of child labour', the issue in the following terms:

> Child labour is clearly detrimental to individual children, preventing them from enjoying their childhood, hampering their development and sometimes causing lifelong physical or psychological damage; it is also detrimental to families, to communities and to society as a whole. As both a result and cause of poverty, child labour perpetuates disadvantage and social exclusion. It undermines national development by keeping children out of school, preventing them from gaining the education and skills that would enable them as adults to contribute to economic growth and prosperity.
>
> (ILO, 2002a, p. 1)

The quote is a typical reflection of the ILO consensus on the matter and is interesting on three counts: first, for its assumptions about childhood, second, for its making national development and economic growth conditional upon its enjoyment and, third, for what it conceals in terms of the conditions that must be fulfilled for children to enjoy childhood.

To begin with the first point, the assumption of 'enjoyment' in childhood suggests that what is held out as an alternative to work is something good, something that has nothing to do with 'labour' (semantically: to suffer), since labour prevents this enjoyment. What children must enjoy is represented as more or less the same everywhere, since the term is used in the singular even if the subject of the sentence is in the plural (*their* childhood). References to 'development' and 'physical or psychological damage' are additional pointers to the ILO belief that the failure to enjoy childhood leads everywhere to the same damaging effects. Finally, childhood is represented as a separate, unique social arena that all children possess by right, but that some, nevertheless, cannot enjoy because they must labour.

Second, being forced to labour means not only that a child is prevented from enjoying what he or she rightfully owns, but has catastrophic consequences at the national level as well. If children cannot enjoy their childhood, so runs the argument, the result is poverty, both for them as individuals and for society at large. In other words, economic growth and prosperity can only blossom if children do not labour. The implication may seem paradoxical, for when children work, one would expect them to contribute in some form or another to economic value. But this is precisely what the argument wants to contradict: children who labour destroy both their individual and their collective social value. The exploitation of children differs, in this perspective, from that of adults because it represents the dual destruction of the enjoyment of childhood at the individual level and the potential for growth and prosperity of a society that this enjoyment offers on the collective level.

Finally, the quote does not mention the conditions that must be fulfilled to stop child labour. The ILO recurrently mentions parental choices, state policies and public action, but the share of each remains vague. Though policy-makers may not be in agreement about the role of the state as provider of free services to children, global trade policies, as laid down in WTO agreements, prescribe that these services should as far as possible be privatized and respond to the laws of supply and demand. In other words, even if the quote does not state it explicitly, the fact that it is uttered in a climate of trade liberalization, implies that the conditions for enjoying childhood are envisioned as depending on the provision of services and assets that only money – be it public or private – can buy.

The ILO approach to child labour is not only predicated upon the removal of children from the labour market but implies also that whatever work children do outside this market has no other value than a symbolic one: it is by definition a form of enjoyment. This brings me to the second part of this section, which is about why international development agencies' positions on child labour justify the imposition of unpaid work on children.

One of the major differences between today's neo-liberal recipe for economic growth in the south and the economic conditions prevailing during the periods of intensive growth in the north is the role of the state in protecting markets, labour and farmers against global competition (see Wertheim, 1997). Labour protection took not only the form of an extensive legal system that limited access and dictated conditions of employment, but included redistributive measures such as a family wage, free health and education and so on. None of this is deemed positive in helping the poor break out of poverty in today's south. State protection and redistributive measures would make the poor 'risk-averse' and thwart their entrepreneurial spirit (Bachman, 2000).Consequently, the structural adjustment policies (SAPs) that were put in place from the beginning of the 1980s to foster economic growth chiefly targeted social spending, severely hitting protective measures for children – food subsidies, free education and health provisions – that national governments had been putting in place. The effects on children in the south have been devastating and continue to be so (Bradshaw, 1993).

For the World Bank the problem is however not with austerity but with a failure on the part of poor households to react adequately to new opportunities. Child labour is in its view just one aspect of a situation 'of capital market failures: when households cannot afford education for their children and cannot borrow for this purpose, although the long-term benefits would be high' (Fallon and Tzannados, 1998, p. 5).

The link between child labour and money could not have been stated more clearly. The authoritative *World Development Report* confirms that child labour is essentially, in the Bank's perspective, the result of households' 'inadequate risk management':

> As households move closer to extreme poverty and destitution, they become very risk averse: any drop in income could push them below the survival point. The poorest households try to avoid this even if it means forgoing a large future gain in income . . . These are the situations that lead to child labour and malnourishment, with lasting damage to children and the breakdown of families.
>
> (World Bank, 2001, p. 145)

For the World Bank, households are caught in a circle of poverty which they themselves originate and from which they, with a little help from governments and development agencies, would be able to break out provided they learn to manage risks adequately. Adequate choices would be refraining from exposing children to work deemed damaging for both their health and personal development, keeping them safely in the childhood arena and accepting risks – mainly by borrowing money from the bank to invest in family-run undertakings.

Low-cost safety nets must help those who do not have *informal* safety nets to fall back on. Where complex patterns of subsistence farming, mutual help in childcare, the exchange of services and loans among neighbours and kin and so on are still intact, as is widely the case in the south, no external support is deemed necessary (Ruel et al., 1999; Haddad and Zeller, 1996). Children play a crucial role in these activities, and it is telling that the global institutions that link economic growth to the removal of children from the labour market fail to find them problematic. Quite to the contrary, the ILO definition of salutary child work comprises 'activities such as helping their parents care for the home and family, assisting in a family business or earning pocket money outside of school hours and during school holidays' (ILO, 2002b, p. 15). Similarly, the World Bank believes that 'Not all child labour is harmful. Many working children are within a stable and nurturing environment with their parents or under the protection of a guardian and can benefit in terms of socialisation and from informal education and training' (Fallon and Tzannatos, 1998, p. 5). Children being full participants in all non-wage activities on which most people in the south subsist, the irony is that what both organizations hint at as beneficial engages an estimated 90 per cent of working children.

The discussion on adequate risk management and informal safety nets implicitly admits to the importance of children's unpaid work not only for the subsistence of households but also for economic growth. But how can activities that are not sold in the market and do not enter in the computation of GNP engender economic growth? In other words, what is the economic value of what nurturing children do? An answer to these questions begs for a more encompassing understanding of the economy than the one proposed by the market model informing the child labour debate.

3. Children's wealth

What needs to be done to understand the value of children's non-monetized work is putting intergenerational exchange at the centre of analysis. The economy is not merely about the conventional paid employment and production in view of realizing profits on the market. It should be understood in a wider sense that includes caring and household activities geared towards the reproduction of life. Sahlins reminds us that profit-making (or, as he terms it, 'negative reciprocity') is but a special and marginal form of exchange in society. Another kind of transaction, informed by *generalized reciprocity*, is at work at the core of social life:

> The material side of the transaction is repressed by the social: reckoning of debts outstanding cannot be overt and is typically left out of account.

This is not to say that handing over things in such form, even to 'loved ones', generates no counter obligation. But the counter is not stipulated by time, quantity, or quality: the expectation of reciprocity is indefinite.
(Sahlins, 1972, pp. 193–4)

Generalized reciprocity generates a huge mass of obligations and outstanding debts, which are part of the wealth passed down from generation to generation. Sets of social rules and divisions of tasks ensure that ever new generations of children are taken care of and acquire assets, resources, knowledge and relationships that will enable them to repay, as adults, their debt to the older generation.

Figure 10.1, adapted from Meillassoux (1983), summarizes schematically how, in populations depending on subsistence agriculture, production and consumption guarantee long-term reproduction. The surplus produced by able-bodied people between the ages of about 12 and 60 contributes both to maintaining the elderly (>60) and children between 0–12 years. The surplus can be more or less adequate, so that in conditions of extreme destitution, work from both children and elders may be solicited. But if children must work because it is their duty, elders have no duties towards their children and grandchildren, for they have already contributed their part and are now entitled to enjoy in peace their last years. In this line, altruism entails giving precedence to the care of elders above children. Failing to repay the intergenerational debt is the worst thing that a person can do and is dangerous in so far that it undermines the generational flow of wealth. An elder can then no longer claim the right to be looked after in old age

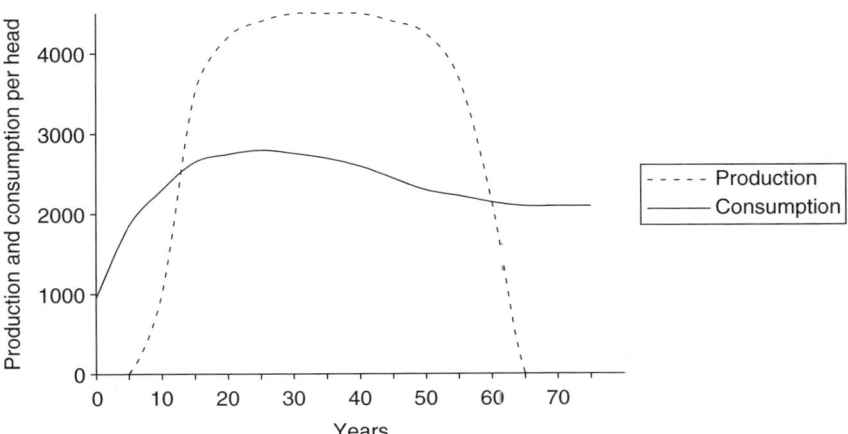

Figure 10.1: Production and consumption in subsistence agriculture (calories per day)
Source: Adapted from Meillassoux (1983).

and be surrounded with the love and respect due to a person who has discharged his or her duties to society. As the successful passage through the various stages of life ensures not only full embeddedness in local society but also a feeling of religious and personal fulfilment, the loss is not merely material but also social and spiritual. The failure to repay the intergenerational debt has long-term negative repercussions on the continuity of reproduction: if parents must be altruistic and children not (and vice versa), what is the point of having and caring for children?

Importantly, children have in themselves or by 'nature' no rights in intergenerational wealth. They must prove their worth and their ability to make what is invested in them profitable, acquiring thereby their place in the order of intergenerational reciprocal obligations. Anthropologists have explained that children acquire their place in this order by displaying such virtues as altruism, generosity, endurance and a capacity to postpone the satisfaction of immediate wants. For young children and girls, submission is the most evident way to be a 'good child'. This is also the case with teenagers, who can find a place in hereditary jobs, for example, inheriting their parents' farm or occupation (Nieuwenhuys, 2003). Lange observes for southern rural Togo, for example, that children sow about 50 per cent of the land of their family, but do so primarily because the land will be left to them in their father's will. The work done in childhood and adolescence is seen as an investment, the returns of which will accrue to them by the time they have families of their own (Lange, 2000, p. 271). The primacy of servicing the debt makes for even very young children to be engaged worldwide in subsistence activities such as collecting fruits, fodder and fuel wood, in fishing, hunting and looking after cattle, in making mats and baskets and so on, the proceeds of which are directly consumed or used by the household. Children start therefore as soon as they are able to repay the intergenerational debt by learning subsistence skills, as assistants of relatives and workers in their own right. In northern Ghana, for example, farming takes precedence over schooling, a good boy working many hours on the land of his father, a good girl taking charge of smaller children and the household. Schooling is something left for leisure time or as an alternative to farming for children too frail to work on the land (Hashim, 2004).

Numbers of researchers point out that systems of seniority predicated upon long-term reciprocity inform patronage relationships in which youngsters engage in unpaid work in the expectation of acquiring a position upon reaching adulthood (De Suremain, 2000; Levine, 1999; Morice, 2000; Robson, 2004; Hashim, 2004). In many cases, however, children must also seek to add to the family income by either selling some of their produce, selling services or engaging in paid work. What needs to be highlighted is that the governing rule is strengthening reciprocity rather than competition against adult workers in view of obtaining higher earnings. Children by and large therefore occupy economic niches where the proceeds are so low that they will not compete against adult workers who anyway will most often be their relatives. In my own study of rural Kerala, I brought out the strict rules of seniority applying in fishing, which left boys working fishing gear with insecure and very low catches or vending small-fry to poor neighbours, leaving the wealthier far-away markets to be serviced by adult vendors (Nieuwenhuys, 1994).

From children's perspectives what is problematic may then not be so much if and under what conditions they work as the work's relation to the future. Schlemmer puts it as follows:

> all children are working, but not under the same conditions. What makes the difference is not the fact whether or not an individual's activity deserves to be considered 'labour', but whether that work is to some extent exploited by another party or is an investment in his/her future good.
>
> (Schlemmer, 2000, p. 9)

Probably it is less often a question of choice between exploitation and investment than a case of trying to make the best of a situation in which the two are interwoven. Even when subjected to the worst forms of exploitation, as in the case of the Thai prostitutes mentioned in the introduction, a child may still be able to contribute to reciprocity. Thai child prostitutes take over sex work from an older sibling or mother as a way of being virtuous and earning the right to pass on the job to their own children in future. The case of prostitution suggests that when opportunities to contribute to generalized reciprocity are insufficient, children may have no choice other than to engage in what are undoubtedly severe forms of exploitation. If children submit to these forms, it is because they have other priorities in mind than their own, temporary, well-being. Hecht portrays the agony of Recife's street boys for failing to live up to their families' ideal of the 'good' son, an ideal that demands that a son be supportive and devoted to the well-being of his mother and younger siblings (Hecht, 1998). The ideal has little to do with a parental lack of altruism, as neoclassical economists may put it, or with parental poverty: at stake is children's embeddedness in generalized reciprocity, or to put it more precisely, their value to local society. If Recife's drug peddling and glue sniffing boys are homeless, it is because, as they repeatedly underline, they had failed to earn themselves the right to a place at home.

Children being positioned at the very core of the economy in this wider meaning, whenever relations of domination undermine people's ability to contribute and maintain intergenerational wealth, we have, to use Sahlins's term, a situation of negative reciprocity, or of wealth being siphoned off. It is with this notion, I suggest, that the notion of exploitation should engage. Seen through the lens of intergenerational reciprocity global development agencies' statements, discussed in Section 2, that economic growth is premised on children fulfilling their duties unpaid takes altogether an unexpected meaning. The statement underscores not only that no society can function without children contributing to intergenerational wealth exchange, but also, as I discuss next, that this wealth must remain invisible so as to conceal how it is drained off.

4. Devaluation and unequal exchange

As the 'poverty of children' argument underlines, families that value their children for their labour power are the most destitute, while those that make no economic demands on their children fare vastly better. As argued in Section 2, the major difference lies in the redistributive state policies that compensate families for forgoing the work contribution of *nurtured* children. Both in the south and the north, employers bear the costs of reproduction by paying adult workers family wages that allow them to maintain their children in school and keep them outside the labour market. But, as discussed, this situation is far from common and is not the whole story. If we accept that *nurturing* children are creators of wealth and that to contribute to intergenerational exchange they must consent to this wealth being partly siphoned off through negative reciprocity, we must ask the question to what extent *nurturing* children subsidize *nurtured* childhood. Here I want to suggest that *nurtured* and *nurturing* childhood may be seen as opposite poles of a global sociological field of childhood in which the positive pole (childhood as producer of wealth) transmits wealth to the negative one (childhood as a repository of wealth). I put forward the hypothesis that this wealth comes in the form of subsidies from the south to *nurtured* childhood in urban middle-class areas both in the north and in the south itself.

Some of these subsidies are evident, as in the case of the sport shoes made by women and children in South and Southeast Asia that are sold at very affordable prices to middle-class child consumers. The main part of the production of shoes sold under brands owned by multinational corporations is outsourced to factories in the south. The children and women who make the shoes can barely subsist on the wages they receive: in Lahore, for instance, workers earn about 50 per cent of the minimum wage and one-seventh of the estimated living wage for a single person (Clean Clothes Campaign, 2004, p. 2). Sub-subsistence wages can of course, as I have contended above, only be paid because workers have other sources of income on which to subsist. These sources are generally in kind, in the form of goods and services obtained from household members who do not engage in paid work. In this sense, unpaid work can be considered a form of subsidy that accrues unevenly to local entrepreneurs and consumers and multinational corporations and consumers in the north.

Crucially, this subsidy is instrumental in reducing the cost of labour below the subsistence minimum because it is not accounted for. When children perform unpaid work, treating it as enjoyment, socialization or training is evidently an expedient way of justifying that it is not attributed a market value. That this is pure fiction may become clear when one considers the price differential between the local production cost of a shoe and its final price. The local production cost of a US$100 sports shoe of an unnamed brand made in Lahore, is only US$5. The rest accrues mainly to the company in the form of profits (15.5 per cent) and brand name (33 per cent) and to the store where the shoe is sold (50 per cent) (Clean Clothes Campaign, 2004, p. 2).

But there are also more circuitous if not entirely invisible ways of wealth transmission that escape international attention for child labour. The example of the 'nanny chain' is significant. In rich countries such as the USA and Canada immigration policies simultaneously admit lone women workers, thus ensuring a continuous supply of cheap domestic labour including nannies and childminders from the south, and prevent their families from joining them (Katz, 2001, p. 713; Hochschild, 2000; Rose, 1993). For Katz, the difference between the cost of a nanny and the market income of a working mother should be considered a subsidy of employers and wealthier women by women of the south, whose children are left behind with relatives (Katz, 2001, p. 713).

But it would be too limited to think of the subsidy as being generated by the undeniably lowly remunerated immigrant women's work alone. In reality, every woman leaves a void behind which other caretakers have to fill. This generates a chain of increasingly low-valued care work. Selling her own care work allows the migrant nanny to earn cash which she will remit to the family at home to be used (in part) to hire a local nanny to look after her own children. The locally-hired nanny, in her turn, cannot buy care with her earnings and must leave her small children with elders and older siblings. When the elders of the local nanny are turned into free childminders, the intergenerational debt is cancelled: these elders not only no longer receive care but must provide care in exchange for food. The situation is mitigated by the presence of older children, who may provide care for younger siblings and support for the elderly. As their mother is likely to receive only a fraction of what the migrant nanny receives, their work contribution at home, as well as that of the elderly, goes largely unrecognized. In this way the devaluation of care work is passed down to the lower end of the chain. In Hochschild's words:

> If it is true that attention, solicitude, and love itself can be 'displaced' from one child (let's say Vicky Diaz's son Alfredo, back in the Philippines) onto another child (let's say Tommy, the son of her employers in Beverly Hills), then the important observation to make here is that this displacement is often upward in wealth and power. This, in turn, raises the question of the equitable distribution of care. It makes us wonder, is there

– in the realm of love – an analogue to what Marx calls 'surplus value,' something skimmed off from the poor for the benefit of the rich?

(Hochschild, 2000, p. 33)

The above examples suggest that intergenerational wealth resulting from children's unpaid work plays an under-researched role in the complex web of transfers from the global south towards the north. Why experts of global development institutions would belittle, ignore, naturalize or apologize for children's unpaid work – by far the most common type of activity that children undertake – while at the same time underscoring, as in the 'poverty of children' argument, its vital role in generating economic growth, is particularly intriguing. In view of my argument here, an explanation could be that the devaluation of nurturing children's contribution in the realization of intergenerational wealth is a crucial element of negative reciprocity not only locally but also globally. Generating a powerful political and popular rhetoric to stir up a global simulacrum of child uselessness while at the same time reserving the public and private means to effectuate the conditions of a *nurtured* childhood to a minority, seems a seminal ingredient of what is understood under economic growth. In other words, the canon of children's uselessness, apparently a protective measure against the abuse of little children in a globalizing world, may well turn out to be a wolf in sheep's clothing, cloaking the parasitic drainage of intergenerational flows of wealth on a global scale.

To conclude, I suggest that overcoming the political and theoretical deadlock of the child labour debate will critically depend on recognizing children as agents in the creation and transmission of intergenerational wealth. The analysis must take issue against the belief that *nurturing* children's unpaid work would be safe and even desirable and acknowledge that it can be highly exploitative when performed in the context of unequal power relationships. Children do what they do because they are active reproducers of social relationships and cannot partake in intergenerational reciprocity without also partaking in negative reciprocity which reproduces exploitative power relationships. The conclusion is however not that working children are caught in a vicious circle of self-exploitation, which they themselves reproduce in order to earn a place in the intergenerational order and guarantee their livelihood.[3] Children are not simply reproducers of a culture of domination to which they submit without questioning in order to find their place in society. Recognizing children's agency means understanding that to get what they need, children must be cunning and be able to manipulate even a highly oppressive situation to their own advantage and that this may involve trying to improve their situation by looking for opportunities outside the family or neighbourhood (see also Nieuwenhuys, 2003). Of course these children are particularly vulnerable to abuse and exploitation, but at the same time they are also strong, for they often show remarkable resilience and resourcefulness in facing unknown situations. So, it is not a matter of 'either . . . or', and Bourdieu's notion of *practical reason* could be helpful to grasp the dynamics by which children's practical experiences – however painful – add to their body of knowledge for everyday decision-making. Rather than seeing in them either broken lives or virtuous sons and daughters, working children who have experienced prostitution, drug trafficking, war and violence should be acknowledged for having precious real-life knowledge that will help them face whatever new difficulties come their way later in life.

Notes

1. For useful comments and suggestions I am grateful to Michel Bonnet, Erica Burman, Yvan Droz, Mohini Gulrajani, Karl Hanson, Allison James, Yuko Kitada, Marie-France Lange, Michael Lavalette, Deborah Levison, Claude Meillassoux, Per Miljeteg, Graciela Paillet, Jens Qvortrup, Pamela Reynolds, Gilbert Rist, Rosanne Rutten and Bernard Schlemmer. I also benefited from seminar presentations at the National Labour Institute, New Delhi; Institute of Social Studies, The Hague; Institut de Récherche sur le Développement, Paris; Advanced Study Center, International Institute, University of Michigan at Ann Arbor; Gustav Stresemann Institute Bonn; Norwegian Centre for Child Research, NTNU, Trondheim; TU Berlin; University Institute Kurt Bösch, Sion; DRC, University of Sussex; Dept of Anthropology, Johns Hopkins University at Baltimore; School of Social and Political Studies, University of Edinburgh. A French translation of parts of an earlier version of this paper has been published in Bonnet et al. (forthcoming).
2. Wealth includes the resources, assets, knowledge and relationships that guarantee a life experienced as fulfilled in a given social and historical context. The term includes the products of non-monetized subsistence and the services resulting from unpaid care work and seeks to avoid reductionist approaches that see well-being as merely resulting from the consumption of tangible objects or of goods and services bought from the market.
3. I am grateful to Yuko Kitada, Australian National University, for the inspiring discussions that helped me formulate these final thoughts.

References

Bachman, S.L. (2000) 'A New Economics of Child Labor: Searching for Answers behind the Headlines', *Journal of International Affairs*, 53 (2): 545–72.

Becker, S., J. Aldridge and C. Dearden (1998) *Young Carers and their Families*, Oxford: Blackwell.

Bonnet, M., K. Hanson, M.F. Lange, O. Nieuwenhuys, G. Paillet and B. Schlemmer (forthcoming) *Enfants travailleurs: Repenser l'Enfance*, Paris: Karthala.

Bourdieu, P. (1994) *Raisons Pratiques, Sur la théorie de l'action*, Paris: Seuil.

Boyden, J., B. Ling and W. Myers (1998) *What Works for Working Children*, Florence: UNICEF.

Bradshaw, Y.W. (1993) 'New Directions in International Development: a Focus on Children', *Childhood*, 1: 134–42.

Caldwell, J.C. (1982) 'Fertility and the Household Economy of Nigeria', in J.C. Caldwell, *Theory of Fertility Decline*, London: Academic Press, pp. 11–81.

Clean Clothes Campaign (2004) 'Stitched Up by the Big Brands', Euro 2000, www.cleanclothes.org/campaign/00–04-euro2000–2.htm.

Cohen, R. (2001) 'Children's Contribution to Household Labour in Three Sociocultural Contexts, a Southern Indian Village, a Norwegian Town and a Canadian City', *International Journal of Canadian Studies*, XLII (4): 353–67.

De Suremain, C.-E. (2000) 'Coffee Beans and the Seeds of Labour: Child Labour in Guatemalan Plantations', in B. Schlemmer (ed.), *The Exploited Child*, London and New York: ZED, pp. 231–8.

Fallon, P. and Z. Tzannatos (1998) *Child Labour, Issues and Directions for the World Bank*, Washington DC: The World Bank, Social Protection, Human Development Network.

Haddad, L. and M. Zeller (1996) 'How Can Safety Nets Do More With Less? General Issues With some Evidence from Southern Africa', FCND Discussion paper No. 16. Washington: International Food Policy Institute.

Hanson, K. and A. Vandaele (2003) 'Working Children and International Labour Law: a Critical Analysis', *International Journal of Children's Rights*, 11: 73–146.

Hashim, Iman, M. (2004) 'Working with Working Children. Child Labour and the Barriers to Education in Rural Northern Nigeria', Sussex: DPhil Development Studies, University of Sussex.

Hecht, T. (1998) *At Home in the Street, Street Children of Northeast Brazil*, Cambridge: Cambridge University Press.

Hochschild, A. (2000) 'The Nanny Chain', *American Prospect*, 11 (4): 32–6.

ILO (2002a) *A Future without Child Labour. Global Report under the Follow-up to the ILO Declaration on Fundamental Principles and Rights at Work*, Geneva: ILO.

ILO (2002b) *Eliminating the Worst Forms of Child Labour. A Practical Guide to ILO Conventions No 182*, Geneva: ILO and Interparliamentary Union.

Invernizzi, A. and B. Milne (2002) 'Are Children Entitled to Contribute to International Policy Making? A Critical View of Children's Participation in the International Campaign for the Elimination of Child Labour', *Journal of Children's Rights*, 10 (4): 403–31.

Invernizzi, A. (2001) *La vie quotidienne des enfants travailleurs, Stratégies de survie et socialisation dans les rues de Lima*, Paris: L'Harmattan.

Katz, C. (2001) 'Vagabond Capitalism and the Necessity of Social Reproduction', *Antipode*, 33: 709–28.

Kenny, M.L. (1999) 'No Visible Means of Support: Child Labor in Urban Northeast Brazil', *Human Organization*, 58 (4): 375–86.

Lange, M.F. (2000) 'The Demand for Labour within the Household: Child Labour in Togo', in B. Schlemmer (ed.), *The Exploited Child*, London and New York: ZED, pp. 268–77.

Lavalette, M. (2000) 'Child Employment in the Capitalist Labour Market', in B. Schlemmer (ed.), *The Exploited Child*, New York and London: ZED, pp. 214–31.

Levine, S. (1999) 'Bittersweet Harvest, Children, Work and the Global March against Child Labour in the Post-Apartheid State', *Critique of Anthropology*, 19 (2): 139–55.

Liebel, M. (2003) 'Working Children as Social Subjects: the Contribution of Working Children's Organisations to Social Transformations', *Childhood*, 10 (3): 265–85.

Meillassoux, C. (1983) 'The Economic Basis of Demographic Reproduction', *Journal of Peasant Studies*, 11 (1): 50–61.

Mizen, P., A. Bolton and C. Pole (1999) 'School Age Workers in Britain: the Paid Employment of Children in Britain', *Work, Employment and Society*, 13 (3): 423–38.

Montgomery, H. (2002) *Modern Babylon? Prostituting Children in Thailand*, New York: Berghahn Books.

Morice, A. (2000) 'Paternal Domination: the Typical Relationship Conditioning the Exploitation of Children', in B. Schlemmer (ed.), *The Exploited Child*, London and New York: ZED, pp. 195–213.

Morrow, V. (1996) 'Rethinking Childhood Dependency: Children's Contribution to the Domestic Economy', *Sociological Review*, 44: 58–77.

Nieuwenhuys, O. (1994) *Children's Lifeworlds, Gender, Welfare and Labour in the Developing World*, London: Routledge.

Nieuwenhuys, O. (1996) 'The Paradox of Child Labour and Anthropology', *Annual Review of Anthropology*, 25: 237–51.

Nieuwenhuys, O. (2000) 'The Household Economy and the Commercial Exploitation of Children's Work, the Case of Kerala', in B. Schlemmer (ed.), *The Exploited Child*, London and New York: ZED, pp. 278–91.

Nieuwenhuys, O. (2003) 'Growing Up between Places of Work and Non-places of Childhood: the Uneasy Relationship', in K. Fog Olwig and E. Gulløv (eds), *Children and Place*, London: Routledge, pp. 99–118.

Qvortrup, J. (1995) 'From Useful to Useful: the Historical Continuity of Children's Constructive Participation', *Sociological Studies of Children*, 7, pp. 49–76.

Reynolds, P. (1991) *Dance Civet Cat: Child Labour in the Zambezi Valley*, London: ZED.

Robson, E. (2004) 'Children at Work in Rural Northern Nigeria: Patterns of Age, Space and Gender', *Journal of Rural Studies*, 20: 193–210.

Rose, D. (1993) 'Local Childcare Strategies in Montréal, Québec: the Mediations of State Policies, Class and Ethnicity in the Life Course of Families with Young Children', in C. Katz and J. Monk (eds), *Full Circles: Geographies of Women over the Life Course*, London and New York: Routledge, pp. 188–207.

Ruel, M.T., L. Haddad and J.L. Garrett (1999) 'Some Urban Facts of Life: Implications for Research and Policy', *World Development*, 27 (11): 1917–38.

Sahlins, M. (1972) *Stone Age Economics*, New York: Aldine De Gruyter.

Schildkrout, E. (2002) 'Socio-economic Roles of Children in Urban Kano', *Childhood*, 9 (3): 344–68.

Schlemmer, B. (2000) 'General Introduction', in B. Schlemmer (ed.), *The Exploited Child*, London and New York: ZED.

Song, M. (1999) *Children's Labor in Ethnic Business*, Philadelphia: Temple University.

Wertheim, W.F. (1997) *Third World Whence and Whither? Protective State versus Aggressive Market*, Amsterdam: Spinhuis.

World Bank (2001) *World Development Report*, Washington: The World Bank.

Zelizer, V.A. (2002) 'Kids and Commerce', *Childhood*, 9 (4): 375–96.

Zelizer, V.A. (1985) *Pricing the Priceless Child: the Changing Social Value of Children*, New York: Basic Books.

11
The Priceless Child Revisited

Viviana A. Zelizer

Introduction

American novelist Frederic Tuten recalls scenes from his New York childhood during World War II:

> She was a thin woman without much fantasy. In her dress, I mean. Black from head to toe, in the Sicilian manner. She was a Sicilian, in fact, and she was my grandmother. She spoke little, and to my humiliation – I wanted to be like the other American kids in the Bronx – in Sicilian. And then, too, we were at the tail end of the war with Italy. So that in the street and other public places I answered her in English to distance myself.
>
> Not that my Sicilian was great. But at 8 or 9 I managed to tell her what she wanted to know about my world at school and to conduct her from butcher to grocer to order for her and to check the scales when she thought they were tipping high . . . I also, and more importantly, served as her translator for the American news on the radio, and for the American movies.

Tuten also remembers reading to his grandmother, Francesca LePare Scelfo. 'Not in the conventional way of translating word for word my childhood books' but instead, he says, 'by telling her – with my own editing and inventions – the stories in my reading' (Tuten, 2002). A half-century ago, a Bronx boy was contributing a crucial form of work to his Sicilian-origin family.

Move forward half a century. In Tucumán, Argentina, in 2002, twelve-year-old Manuel Cruz was engaged in a very different kind of work for his family. In the midst of the Argentine economic crisis, Manuel worked as a *cartonero*, literally a cardboard gatherer, but in fact also a collector and seller of paper, bottles, plastic, aluminium cans and a variety of other items for recycling. After returning from school, Manuel went out with Ana, his mother, and Maria, his grandmother. They trudged off to collect materials, working from 7 p.m. to 2 a.m. five days a week. On weekends, Manuel earned extra money watching cars and helping out in the Tucumán Lawn Tennis Club.

At the same time, Manuel was putting in one of the finest performances in his elementary school, recognized as the leading student as well as winning second place in the province's Mathematics Olympics. Interviewed by the national magazine *Gente*, this 'little hero', as the reporter called him, explained why he had not told his classmates about his work: 'I used to be embarrassed, but today I am proud. It's an honest job that allows me to feed my family . . . Although to tell the truth, I don't much like what I do . . . What everyone should understand here is that the only way to get out of poverty is studying. That is why I won't stop until I become an architect' (Quiroga, 2002). Meanwhile Manuel was helping to support his five younger siblings, Maria, Marcos, David, Pamela and Rodrigo, at a time of widespread unemployment, poverty and hunger.

The Bronx, New York in 1943 and Tucumán, Argentina in 2002: children of both places worked hard. But what they did, for whom, in whose company, and with what compensation they worked varied dramatically not only from place to place and time to time but also from family to family. Frederic Tuten gave his grandmother a distinctive sort of care – linguistic care – at home, just as he served as her intermediary with the anglophone world. Manuel Cruz split his great energy between schoolwork, gathering of refuse and weekend jobs for the present benefit of his large family and the future benefit of his own career.

Widely-held views about childhood mark an intense moral difference between the two experiences. Translating for a grandmother generally strikes observers as an appropriate and commendable childhood activity, but the *cartonero*'s night work looks like cruel exploitation. The young *cartonero* was indeed running risks: older *cartoneros* often attacked Manuel and stole his merchandise, while state authorities pursued his mother for allowing him to work. Still, the intense moral differentiation is puzzling. After all, both children are equally involved in virtuous activities, assisting their families while going to school. In fact, Manuel Cruz's efforts outshine Frederic Tuten's. Yet the two experiences look starkly different.

We cannot explain this differential evaluation if we only look at what a particular child – in this case Frederic or Manuel – is doing. Why not? Because the meaning and consequences of children's work depend on the social setting in which that work occurs. To understand what is going on, to explain puzzling variations, we need to look closely at the web of social relations in which these children's efforts take place.

Why is that so hard to do? What hinders understanding of the social processes occurring in these two cases? Analyses of children's work face two significant obstacles, both of them much more general misconceptions about intersections between the worlds of morality and economic activity. We might call the two misconceptions 'hostile worlds' and 'market work'.

The widespread, potent idea of *hostile worlds* imagines social existence as falling into two distinct spheres, one of rationality and self-interest, the other of sentiment and solidarity. Let them mix, goes the argument, and two forms of corruption result: the entry of sentiment and solidarity into the rational arena causes cronyism and inefficiency, while the entry of self-interest into the sentimental arena weakens solidarity, empathy and mutual respect. In a children's version, many observers fear that exposing tender youth to marketplace logic destroys virtuous childhood while introducing unreliable economic actors into the world of serious business. According to this logic, erecting a staunch boundary between childhood and adulthood defends against corruption in both directions.

But the hostile worlds theory fails to explain what actually happens in the course of economic activity. In fact, close studies of routine social life uniformly contradict the idea that the mingling of economic transactions with personal relations necessarily produces corruption in either direction (Zelizer, 2002a).

The *market work* doctrine holds that only work receiving monetary compensation qualifies as genuine. Housework, barter, volunteering, *pro bono* service, unpaid caring, family enterprises and most efforts by children fall into the zone of non-work. If this doctrine seems implausible to students of childhood, it nevertheless affects a wide range of thought and practice. Notice, for example, that national income accounting generally neglects such efforts and that western courts assessing damages for wrongful death or injury regularly value women's unpaid contributions at much less than similar efforts performed for wages. In this view, *cartonero* Manuel Cruz's midnight collecting may have qualified as work, but neither his stellar school performances nor Frederic Tuten's translations for his Sicilian grandmother meet the test.

Like the notion of hostile worlds, such an idea obscures more than it explains. Let us adopt a more generous and analytically useful conception of work: as any effort that produces transferable use value (Tilly and Tilly, 1998). The definition sacrifices the neatness of market value as the measure of all work, but gains instantly by identifying similar efforts that differ mainly by the social settings in which they occur. Thus we immediately recognize similarities and differences between maid service and housework, professional nursing and family healthcare, paid clerical work and the study of bookkeeping.

For further clarification, we should introduce a rough distinction between two sorts of work: first, effort that immediately produces transferable goods and services; second, effort that adds to existing capital, and thus contributes to future production of goods and services. Following Pierre Bourdieu (1990), we can pay attention to several different sorts of capital: the *physical* capital that serves production directly, the *financial* capital that provides fungible claims to means of production, the *human* capital that informs an individual's or a group's capacity to produce, the *social* capital that facilitates individuals' and groups' interpersonal connections to productive resources and the *cultural* capital that gives individuals or groups access to exclusive social settings. Obviously children play important parts both in immediate production of goods and services and in the accumulation of physical, financial, human, social and cultural capital.

To this insight, this chapter adds the observation that the meaning, organization, contribution and compensation of children's work in these regards varies systematically and dramatically from one social setting to another. Let us try to identify the principles of that variation. Here is how the overall argument runs:

- Children's work divides between immediate production of transferable use value and production of material, financial, human, social and cultural capital. For example, children often work directly in household economic enterprises, but in so doing they acquire skills and social connections that will later serve them in enterprises of their own.
- Some of the capital production remains with the child itself for later transfer, but some of it immediately increases the capital of social relations and groups in which children participate, notably that of their families and households. For example, a child's stellar school performance enhances not only the child's own future, but also the standing of his or her family.
- Permissible and forbidden forms of children's work vary strikingly with the social relations to which they are attached. For example, many parents require their children to weed the family flower garden, but any teacher who required his pupils to weed his own family's garden would risk losing his job.
- Within each social relation, more precisely, participants and third parties promote proper matching of meanings, monetary media and economic transactions, including the transactions we call work or production. For example, over a wide range of western households, parents can reasonably tie allowances to their children's household work, but could not possibly hire outside children to do the same work for the same rewards.
- Participants also mark the boundaries between different social relations with labels, symbolic representations and moral injunctions. For example, almost every household makes a sharp distinction between the rights and obligations of children that belong to their household and those of children who count as temporary visitors.
- Within those limits, however, children and other persons involved in their work incessantly negotiate the precise matching of meanings, media and transactions. For example, children across the world bargain with their parents about what clothing, toys or forms of entertainment they can and cannot buy.

For the sake of brevity, the chapter will not take up each of these points separately, but instead illustrate the main arguments, drawing from two main settings: household care work and immigrant enterprises. Both settings reveal an impressive variety of children's labour and illustrate the crucial contributions that children make to the maintenance of adult-run enterprises.

Care work

Does personal care – sustained attention that enhances individual welfare – qualify as work? In recent years, feminist critics, focusing exclusively on women's invisible caring labour – including housework, attending to children, the sick and the elderly in their families – have insisted that it does. In many cases, their arguments have changed legislation, establishing that in cases of lost personal attention, the loss deserved legally enforced compensation. Acknowledging children's care work, however, turns out to be even more challenging than recognizing their mother's efforts. Children, after all, are not supposed to be carers, but recipients of care.

Yet, as a number of researchers have recently shown us, children involve themselves in a great deal of caring work, ranging from babysitting their siblings to attending a sick grandparent. The kinds of caring work children engage in vary dramatically with social relations, for example children provide very different kinds of caring services to neighbours and to siblings. The various caring efforts vary also in their moral legitimacy. Like adults, children mark very strong boundaries between what they define as appropriate and inappropriate relations for care work. For instance, a child who regularly cooks for or takes an ailing grandparent to the bathroom would not ordinarily do the same for a neighbour. Both adults and children typically mark such boundaries with invocations of hostile worlds, noting the dangers of providing intimate services to the wrong people. Children, and adults, also distinguish care work from other types of child work, such as housework or wage work. What is more, children's paid care work, such as babysitting for other families, differs practically and symbolically from unpaid help around the house.

Children's care work matters. It extends to such crucial activities as making sure that ailing family members receive their medicine, and thus at times involve children in collabouration with healthcare professionals and social workers. In the course of such work, children not only produce goods and services directly, but also accumulate capital – for example the human capital gained by knowledge of medical treatment and the social capital gained with links to healthcare workers. In addition, children's individual accumulation of capital commonly enhances the store of capital available to the household as a whole. By connecting households with powerful outside institutions, children's mediation sometimes greatly affects the family's social position. Immigrant families, for example, often depend on their native-born children to establish a wide range of connections between the household's adults and the alien environment. Counter-intuitively, this means that a household lacking children will in certain circumstances accumulate less capital than those with children.

Children's caring efforts take a wide variety of forms, each corresponding to a different bundle of social relations. In her ethnographic account of pick-up time at an elementary school in a mixed-income, ethnically diverse area of Oakdale, California, Barrie Thorne (2001) reports:

> The pick-up scene offers glimpses of children actively constructing and negotiating everyday life, including divisions of labour within and extending beyond households. Kids take responsibility for locating younger siblings and getting them home; they organize themselves into groups to head for after-school destinations; they make phone calls to check up on adults who are late; they carry messages between school and home. In addition, kids sometimes help out on adult job sites – for example, by sorting dry cleaning at an uncle's store or by helping a mother clear tables in a restaurant. Children also contribute to housework.
>
> (Thorne, 2001, p. 364)

Ask the Children, Ellen Galinsky's national survey of a representative sample of more than 1000 US children in grades 3 through 12, offers some revealing glimpses into the variety of children's care work. The survey, supplemented with interviews, found children saying they 'take care' of their parents by findings strategies for reducing parents' stress and fatigue. One 12-year-old girl reported using humour to help out her mother: 'I try and make her feel better. My friend can make people laugh so easy. And so usually I'm like, "Chris, my mom feels kind of bad right now – you wanna come over and cheer her up?" and in just at least five minutes my mom is laughing so hard' (Galinsky, 1999, p. 240). Some of the children complained about their caring duties, feeling, says Galinsky, that 'their parents had become their children and that they were parenting them' (Galinsky, 1999, p. 240).

In a reversal of perspectives, Galinsky thus shows that children responded to their parents' work in interesting, unexpected ways. While most experts and parents worry that parents are not spending enough time with their children, children fretted less about the time deficit. They did worry a great deal about their parents, but mostly about the quality of their interchanges when parents were under a great deal of stress. Indeed, Galinsky points out, children often play detective, gathering 'mood clues' from their parents. One child told about calling her parents at work 'to get a reading on how they are feeling so she can determine whether she should clean up the house before they come home' (Galinsky, 1999, p. xvii). The scope, variety, intensity and value of children's caring labour clearly have not received the attention they deserve.

With precisely that deficit in mind, British advocates have coined the term 'young carers' to designate children who make crucial contributions to other people's welfare. Child carers attend to ill or disabled family members, typically their parents, but also siblings or grandparents. In the United Kingdom the 1995 Carers' (Recognition and Services) Act acknowledged these children's work, by adding children under age 18 to the category of private informal carers entitled to social services.[1] However, Richard Olsen (2000) points out that current definitions of child caring perpetuate dubious distinctions between qualifying and non-qualifying forms of children's care work. They single out caring in some relations to the exclusion of similar work in a wide range of others. For example, as Olsen points out:

> We see young carers defined not simply by the type and quantity of tasks that they do, but also by the fact that their activity is directed towards the 'care' of a 'dependent' disabled person. The eldest child in a large family, contributing significantly to the care of infant siblings, is typically excluded from the definition of a young carer, whilst a sibling of a disabled child, performing largely the same tasks (nappy changing, keeping an eye on, and so on), is included. Similarly a child of a disabled single parent who finds herself doing most of the housework, cooking, cleaning, and so on, is, typically, included in the definition of a young carer, whilst a child having significant housework duties in a so-called 'normal' family is excluded.
>
> (Olsen, 2000, p. 391)

As Olson says, such restrictive labels do not quite recognize how widespread children's caring labour is, and how much its acceptability or unacceptability depends not on the character of the child's effort but on the social context in which it occurs (on children's care work, see also Becker et al., 1998; Boulding, 1980; Robson and Ansell, 2000). Children actually provide a surprising range of services to their families.

Children as linguistic mediators

Consider the impact of children's linguistic skills for their immigrant parents. Even young children educated and brought up in the receiving country often have far greater skills in the new country's language than their parents (see, for example, Portes and Hao, 2002). In one crucial way, this reverses the usual skill distribution within the household. Studying Mexican immigrant households in Los Angeles, California, Abel Valenzuela (1999) recognized that these families typically faced urgent problems with respect to social and cultural capital. They knew little of how US institutions – schools, workplaces, churches, unions, courts and banks – functioned. Of more immediate importance, they often lacked the English language skills to negotiate with such institutions.

Children became their parents' indispensable allies. In 68 interviews, including 44 adult heads of immigrant households and 24 of their now-grown children, Valenzuela drew from their recollections of past inter-actions. He found that children occupied three key household roles. They served first as their parents and siblings' *tutors*, translating, interpreting and teaching. Besides straightforward translation of television news or govern-ment documents, the children mediated delicate transactions between their parents and physicians, teachers, bank officials and other authorities. Chil-dren's second role was as *advocate*, intervening on behalf of their parents in complex or controversial interactions; for instance, when a public official or salesperson misunderstood or became impatient with their parents or sib-lings. Finally, Valenzuela identified children's role as *surrogate parents*, per-forming household tasks, such as cooking, cleaning and caring for their younger siblings.

Valenzuela's interviews revealed a strong gender pattern; daughters assisted their parents with financial, employment, legal and political trans-actions more often than their brothers did. Regardless of gender, further-more, Valenzuela found that older children: 'often took the lead role in assisting younger siblings with what is usually done in the household by the mother, such as feeding and caring for younger siblings, getting the brothers and sisters dressed for school, transporting them to and from school, and baby-sitting' (Valenzuela, 1999, p. 728). Thus, second-generation Mexican children, especially girls, contributed serious work to their immigrant households. Although several forms of caring entered the mix, children's language skills made them essential within households and for households' links with outside institutions.

Following up the Valenzuela study, Marjorie Faulstich Orellana, Lisa Dorner and Lucila Pulido (Orellana et al., 2003a) went directly to observa-tion of young children (see also Orellana et al., 2003b). They studied bilingual 5th and 6th grade children of Mexican and Central American immigrants in four communities – one in central Los Angeles, California, two in Chicago, Illinois, and a fourth in Engleville, Illinois. Drawing on extensive interviews, participant observation in children's homes and classrooms and audiotaped data, Orellana and her collaborators closely documented the remarkable range of parental reliance on their children's linguistic skills. Children, they report, intervened as translators in seven different domains:

- *Educational*, for example, translate at parent–teacher conferences for themselves and/or siblings, cousins, friends; call schools to report their own or siblings' absences.
- *Medical/Health*, for example, translate at doctors' and dentists' offices during family visits; interpret instructions for medicine, vitamins, other healthcare products.
- *Commercial*, for example, shop for or with parents; complete refund transactions, settle disputes and check for mistakes in sales transactions.
- *Cultural/Entertainment*, for example, go to movies; translate plot and dialogue; read and translate stories, self-help guides, song lyrics, instructional manuals.
- *Legal/State*, for example, call an insurance company regarding car damage, car accidents; obtain welfare or social security by accompanying parents to office, answering questions.
- *Financial/Employment*, for example, cash or deposit cheques at the bank or currency exchange, help parents fill out applications for work or for unemployment benefits.
- *Housing/Residential*, for example, translate between parents and landlords; talk to managers regarding things broken in apartment (adapted from Orellana et al., 2003a, pp. 512–13, Table 1).

Children experienced most of these linguistic encounters as no more than daily routines of family life. Some of their interventions, however, not only demanded skill but also produced considerable stress. Skill and stress coincided most often when the children mediated between their parents and formidable outsiders. Take just two examples, one from the medical arena, another from the commercial:

> When I was about 8–9 years old we went to the doctor because my baby brother was 1 month or so. He had to go for a check up and a doctor told (asked) my mom if she was going to give my baby brother milk from he(r) breast, but I did not know what breast meant. So I told the doctor if she could explain what breast meant. She was nice and kind and said yes of course. She touched her breast and (I) told my mom what the doctor was saying. As far as I can remember this was the scariest translating thing I (had) ever done. I did not translate things that much this week but I did work long time ago translating stuff. Well, I felt so nervous to translate for the doctor because I thought I would not be able to understand the big words doctors use.
>
> (Jasmine, in Orellana et al., 2003a, p. 516)

> My mother has never gone to Jewels or Dominick's by herself. She has always gone with someone who can translate for her. I often and still order her cheese and ham from the deli. I recall a miscommunication sit-

uation that made my mother upset and made me feel very embarrassed. I was about 7 years old. My mother and I were at Jewels. My mother told me to stand in line while she shopped for other items and order a pound of American cheese from the deli. After about fifteen minutes of waiting my turn, the woman behind the counter asked for my order and I told her I wanted a pound of cheese. The woman then said, 'American, Italian, Swiss . . . ' I thought she was asking for my nationality. I responded saying 'Mexican.' In a frustrated tone of voice, she told me that they did not have any Mexican cheese.

(Beatríz in Orellana et al., 2003a, p. 519)

In these circumstances, children of immigrants assume serious responsibility for their parents' and their household's welfare. In the process, they are not only performing fundamental services but adding to their family's capital. Orellana et al. (2003a) note that children's knowledge of English and US cultural practices enhance their families' household reproduction. Nevertheless as Orellana and her collaborators warn, these children sometimes resist and negotiate their obligations, while parents sometimes impose them as family duties (see also Fernández-Kelly, 2002, p. 198; Menjívar, 2000, chapter 7). No one should therefore take the crucial contributions of children as mediators to be evidence of their untrammelled power.

Children in immigrant enterprises

As we saw with Valenzuela, linguistic services are by no means the only assistance that immigrant parents receive from their children. In a different study of Mexican and Central American immigrants in the Pico Union area of central Los Angeles, Orellana (2001) observed children involved in a variety of daily work, including 'running errands; caring for siblings; cleaning; doing the laundry; taking siblings to school, the library, and other appointments; helping siblings with homework . . . answering and making phone calls'. She also reports children's involvement in wage labour: 'selling food, clothes, or other merchandise alongside adult street vendors; helping their parents to clean houses, care for children, or mow lawns; cleaning tables in a *pupuseria* (a Salvadoran restaurant); sweeping the floors of a beauty salon' (Orellana, 2001, pp. 374–5; see also Orellana et al., 2001). Especially notable was the extent to which children served their families by caring for younger children.

Similarly, in immigrant family-run businesses, children often deploy not only their linguistic skills but their efforts in helping operate the family's shop or small business. Miri Song's (1999) study of Chinese take-away shops in Britain closely documents children's vital labour contributions (see also Sun-Hee Park, 2002). Interviewing 42 grown children (mostly in their early to mid-twenties) in 25 Chinese families inhabiting the southeast of England,

Song found – with some variation from family to family as well as by age and gender – that by age seven or eight most of them had begun helping out their parents. Young children started by assisting with simple kitchen tasks such as washing dishes, peeling prawns and potatoes. They gradually took up more public duties, dealing with customers' orders at the front counter, working evenings, after school, or during weekends.

Not that children simply complied with their parents' directions. Some children, Song reports, remember resisting the labour routines, while others reported collaboration among brothers and sisters, for example in setting up their own work schedules with the shop. Nevertheless, for the most part, children did not remember their business involvement as distinctive training, but rather as a 'natural' part of growing up in a family enterprise. For instance, when Song asked one of them; 'How did you start helping out in the shop? Did your parents ask you?' she responded: 'Well, we were just there. It wasn't even like "Come and help us." We were naturally there. We went there to eat' (Song, 1999, p. 53). In fact, they mark the boundary between what they did and regular wage employment by calling their own efforts 'helping out'. Accordingly, they treated the payments they received from their parents not as standard wages but as a perk, or a bonus, a symbol of appreciation for their labour. Some of the children, on the other hand, resented parents' payments as bribes for unwelcome work demands.

As we saw with Mexican and Central American immigrants in the USA, Song found her British-Chinese respondents involved not only with shop work, but also with domestic work, and caring labour. Linguistic services also figured prominently in these children's lives. Song reports how children served as translators and intermediaries for their Chinese parents who spoke, read, or wrote little or no English. One of her interviewees, Wong, explained how crucial language skills became in ordinary shop transactions, such as taking customer's orders:

> The moment you have, 'Can I have the chicken chow mein, but I don't want some bean sprouts, and I want extra onions,' then you know, that's exactly the scenario. I just want to show you how it [his parents' communication with customers] breaks down. To say 'chicken chow mein' that's fine, no problem, but as soon as you say more . . . That's the sort of thing they'll [his parents] have problems with.
>
> (Song, 1999, p. 54)

Immigrant enterprises frequently rely on children not only for productive labour and mediation with outside authorities, but also for linguistic mediation between their owners and clients.

Household caring work and immigrant enterprises amply illustrate the themes with which we began: the division between children's immediate production of goods or services and their contributions to individual or family capital; the distinction of acceptable and unacceptable forms of children's work, dependent less on the basis of that work's intrinsic quality than on the social relations within which it occurs; the variable matching of work and compensation to those social relations; the further negotiation of meanings, compensation and working conditions within the limits set by existing social relations; finally, the substantial contributions children make to household production and capital accumulation.

Children's work reconsidered

Obviously we could pursue the same themes through a wide range of other children's work, not all of it as desirable as the cases we have examined. Child soldiers, child prostitutes, child thieves, child entertainers, child athletes, child volunteers, child speculators, child merchants, child factory workers, homeless children and children in home production all deserve attention for the ways they and the adults around them organize their lives. So do schoolchildren's efforts both inside and outside of school.[2] Nor have we followed up the fascinating complexities of children's contributions to personal and family capital. But at least the variety of children's activities we have encountered in household caring and immigrant enterprises should alert us to the fine differentiation of children's work according to its social context, and to the sense in which it consists not of solitary effort but of energetic social interaction.

Recognition of children's work as varying systematically by social context produces a valuable clarification of debates over proper and improper efforts by children. The very same child effort, we have seen, qualifies as acceptable or unacceptable depending on whether it produces benefits for participants in the social interactions the effort involves, who it produces those benefits for, and with what consequences for the children themselves.[3] As a result, any moral or policy position that imposes wholesale classifications of effort alone on children's work misses crucial distinctions, for example between helping parents in a shop and doing similar work for outsiders.

To be sure, some forms of effort so uniformly damage children and others that we can condemn them from the start; we can no doubt forbid child military service, child prostitution, child involvement in the distribution of hard drugs, and children's mine labour without worrying much about the social relations that lead children into those activities. But beyond that extreme we cannot effectively weigh goods and evils of children's work without serious consideration of the social relations within which the work occurs. Whether the same sort of effort constitutes exploitation or valuable experience depends heavily on the social context. Moralists and policymakers will do well to take that insight from close studies of children's work into account.

The study of children's work thus brings out valuable parallels with economic sociology as it has been developing over the last few decades. Once a relatively sharp division of labour between economics and sociology developed during the twentieth century, sociologists who cared about economic processes generally left the close analysis of production, distribution, consumption and capital formation to economists while studying the prerequisites and consequences of economic change or variation. Starting in the 1970s, however, economic sociologists began to analyse economic processes more directly, either by extending economic models to sites economists themselves had not studied closely (for example schools, churches and voluntary associations) or by showing how social contexts affected economic processes (for example how interpersonal networks shape labour markets).

More recently, economic sociologists have dared increasingly to propose alternative explanations of economic processes: the formation of markets, the management of risky transactions, the interaction of firms and so on. In that alternative economic sociology, the analysis of differentiated interpersonal ties, their variable meanings, and their shaping of economic transactions has become a major preoccupation. Without fanfare, this chapter's treatment of children's work has drawn heavily on insights from economic sociology (Smelser and Swedberg, 1994; Swedberg and Granovetter, 2001; Swedberg, 2003; Zelizer, 2001).

Twenty years ago Basic Books published my *Pricing the Priceless Child*. That 1985 book documented a shift in American practices: during the nineteenth century, on the whole, American moralists and families alike valued children for their useful contributions, while by the century's end a shift occurred, toward a conception of children as priceless, with rejections of children's paid employment, increasing emphasis on children's unpaid work as moral training, adoption of insurance on children's lives as an educational investment rather than a practical necessity, growing awards for children's wrongful death, and proliferating restrictions on payments for adopted babies. Reading me now, some readers may think I am repudiating that earlier book. I am not. It is true that I have actually learned something during the last two decades (see Zelizer, 2002b). I have gone much farther in pursuit of questions that *The Priceless Child* barely sketched: how people manage the mingling of monetary transactions with morally charged social relations, how boundaries between proper and improper economic transactions arise, how people negotiate and enforce those boundaries, what happens when legislatures, lawyers, judges and juries get involved in setting prices for different sorts of social relations and transactions. Nevertheless, my 1985 book clearly distinguished between the powerful representations of children that affected social practices, on one side, and the fact that children continued to do a wide range of productive work, on the other.

The chief change in my perspective since then recognizes how representations and practices interact. The two sides do not simply struggle with each other as illusion and reality or ideology and praxis. Instead, their interaction illustrates an extremely general social process. In this process, representations and practices combine to establish social boundaries between different kinds of social relations. As people erect and enforce such boundaries, they generate three simultaneous effects: first, the boundaries separate social relations whose distinction matters greatly for routine social life. Second, they reinforce the proper matching of meanings, monetary media and economic transactions within each social relation thus distinguished. Finally, they define the rights and obligations of third parties with respect to each sort of social relation.

This view of children's work challenges the doctrines of hostile worlds and market work. It challenges all hostile worlds' notions by establishing that children's value-producing efforts repeatedly mingle economic transactions with intimate personal relations, yet the mingling does not corrupt. It causes neither the relaxation of means–end rationality that supposedly stems from the entry of personal relations into the economic sphere nor the crippling of interpersonal solidarity that supposedly follows from the entry of economic rationality into personal relations. My view of children's economic efforts challenges market work doctrines by emphasizing how much genuine adding of value occurs in efforts that take place outside of wage-mediated markets as conventionally defined. The dual challenge holds across a wide variety of economic activity: not just children's work, but also household production, the informal economy, and much more. In a wide variety of settings, we find economic actors drawing boundaries, establishing rights and obligations within those boundaries, and matching social relations with meanings, media and permissible economic transactions.

Children's work – widespread but camouflaged – conforms to these patterns. It takes place within differentiated social ties, acquiring different meanings and consequences depending on those ties. The productive child engages in social interactions that are every bit as complex as those pursued by adults.

Notes

For advice and information I am grateful to Nicole Esparza, Jens Qvortrup, Charles Tilly, Barrie Thorne and Marjorie Orellana.

1. See http://www.hmso.gov.uk/acts/acts1995/Ukpga_19950012_en_1.htm.
2. Examples of recent work on this subject are Alexander 1991; Bachman 2000; Blagbrough and Glynn 1999; Bock and Sellen 2002; Cohen 2001; Kruse and Mahoney 1998; Goodwin-Gill and Cohn 1994; Kenny 2002; Krueger 2002; Lee and Kramer 2002; Lewis 2001; Mayall 2002; Lavalette 1999; Levison 2000; Nieuwenhuys,1996; Qvortrup 1995; Sereny 1984, Solberg 1994; Strom 2003; Woodhead 1999; Wuthnow 1995.
3. For an intriguing variant on these themes notice that a considerable movement against doing school work at home after school arose in the United States between 1897 and 1941; see Gill and Schlossman 1996, 2000.

References

Alexander, S.J.G. (1991) 'A Fairer Hand: Why Courts Must Recognize the Value of a Child's Companionship', 8 *Thomas M. Cooley Law Review* 273.

Bachman, S.L. (2000) 'A New Economics of Child Labour: Searching for Answers Behind the Headlines', *Journal of International Affairs*, 53: 545–72.

Becker, S., J. Aldridge and C. Dearden (1998) *Young Carers and their Families*, Oxford: Blackwell Science.

Blagbrough, J. and E. Glynn (1999) 'Child Domestic Workers: Characteristics of the Modern Slave and Approaches to Ending such Exploitation', *Childhood*, 6: 51–6.

Bock, J. and D. W. Sellen (eds) (2002) 'Special Issue: Childhood and the Evolution of the Human Life Course', *Human Nature*, 13: 153–325.

Boulding, E. (1980) 'The Nurture of Adults by Children in Family Settings', in Helena Lopata (ed.), *Research in the Interweave of Social Roles: Women and Men*, Vol. 1, Greenwich, Connecticut: JAI, pp. 167–89.

Bourdieu, P. (1990) *The Logic of Practice*, Stanford: Stanford University Press.

Cohen, R. (2001) 'Children's Contribution to Household Labour in Three Sociocultural Contexts: a Southern Indian Village, a Norwegian Town and a Canadian City', *International Journal of Comparative Sociology*, 42: 353–67.

Fernández-Kelly, P. (2002) 'Ethnic Transitions: Nicaraguans in the United States', in B. Ostendorf (ed.), *Transnational America. The Fading of Borders in the Western Hemisphere*, Heidelberg: C. Winter, pp. 177–203.

Galinsky, E. (1999) *Ask the Children*, New York: Morrow.

Gill, B. and S. Schlossman (1996) ' "A Sin against Childhood": Progressive Education and the Crusade to Abolish Homework, 1897–1941', *American Journal of Education*, 105: 27–66.

Gill, B. and S. Schlossman (2000) 'The Lost Cause of Homework Reform', *American Journal of Education*, 109: 27–62.

Goodwin-Gill, G.S. and I. Cohn (1994) *Child Soldiers*, Oxford: Oxford University Press.

Kenny, M.L. (2002) 'Orators and Outcasts, Wanderers and Workers: Street Children in Brazil', in D.T. Cook (ed.), *Symbolic Childhood*, New York: Peter Lang, pp. 37–63.

Krueger, A.B. (2002) 'Putting Development Dollars to Use, South of the Border', *New York Times*, 2 May.

Kruse, D. and D. Mahony (1998) 'Illegal Child Labour in the United States: Prevalence and Characteristics', Working Paper 6479, National Bureau of Economic Research, Cambridge, MA.

Lavalette, M. (ed.) (1999) *A Thing of the Past? Child Labour in Britain in the Nineteenth and Twentieth Centuries*, London: Palgrave.

Lee, R. and K.L. Kramer (2002) 'Children's Economic Roles in the Maya Family Life Cycle: Cain, Caldwell, and Chayanov Revisited', *Population and Development Review*, 28: 475–99.

Levison, D. (2000) 'Children as Economic Agents', *Feminist Economics*, 6: 125–34.

Lewis, M. (2001) 'Jonathan Lebed's Extracurricular Activities', *New York Times Magazine*, 25 February: 26.

Mayall, B. (2002) *Towards a Sociology for Childhood*, Buckingham: Open University Press.

Menjívar, C. (2000) *Fragmented Ties. Salvadoran Immigrant Networks in America*, Berkeley: University of California Press.

Nieuwenhuys, O. (1996) 'The Paradox of Child Labour and Anthropology', *Annual Review of Anthropology*, 25: 237–51.

Olsen, R. (2000) 'Families under the Microscope: Parallels between the Young Carers Debate of the 1990s and the Transformation of Childhood in the Late Nineteenth Century', *Children & Society*, 14: 384–94.

Orellana, M.F. (2001) 'The Work Kids Do: Mexican and Central American Immigrant Children's Contributions to Households and Schools in California', *Harvard Educational Review*, 71: 366–89.

Orellana, M.F, J. Reynolds, L. Dorner and M. Meza (2003b) 'In Other Words: Translating or "Para-phrasing" as a Family Literacy Practice in Immigrant Households', *Reading Research Quarterly*, 38: 12–34.

Orellana, M.F., L. Dorner and L. Pulido (2003a) 'Accessing Assets: Immigrant Youth's Work as Family Translators or "Para-phrasers"', *Social Problems*, 50: 505–24.

Orellana, M.F., B. Thorne A. Chee and W.S.E. Lam (2001) 'Transnational Childhoods: the Participation of Children in Processes of Family Migration', *Social Problems*, 48: 572–91.

Portes, A. and L. Hao (2002) 'The Price of Uniformity: Language, Family and Personality Adjustment in the Immigrant Second Generation', *Ethnic and Racial Studies*, 25: 889–912.

Quiroga, C. (2002) 'Infancia Cartonera', *Gente*, 22 October: 1944.

Qvortrup, J. (1995) 'From Useful to Useful: the Historical Continuity of Children's Constructive Participation', *Sociological Studies of Children*, 7: 49–76.

Robson, E. and N. Ansell (2000) 'Young Carers in Southern Africa: Exploring Stories from Zimbabwean Secondary School Students', in S.L. Holloway and G. Valentine (eds), *Children's Geographies*, London: Routledge, pp. 174–93.

Sereny, G. (1984) *The Invisible Children: Child Prostitution in America, West Germany and Great Britain*, London: Andre Deutsch.

Smelser, N.J. and R. Swedberg (1994) 'The Sociological Perspective on the Economy', in N. Smelser and R. Swedberg (eds), *The Handbook of Economic Sociology*, New York: Russell Sage Foundation, Princeton, NJ: Princeton University Press, pp. 3–26.

Solberg, A. (1994) *Negotiating Childhood*, Stockholm: Nordplan.

Song, M. (1999) *Helping Out: Children's Labour in Ethnic Businesses*, Philadelphia: Temple University Press.

Strom, S. (2003) 'A Lesson Plan about Generosity', *New York Times*, 21 March.

Sun-Hee Park, L. (2002) 'Asian Immigrant Entrepreneurial Children', in L.T. Vo and R. Bonus (eds), *Contemporary Asian American Communities Intersections and Divergences*, Philadelphia: Temple University Press, pp. 161–74.

Swedberg, R. (2003) *Principles of Economic Sociology*, Princeton, NJ: Princeton University Press.

Swedberg, R. and M. Granovetter (eds) (2001) *The Sociology of Economic Life*, 2nd edition, Boulder, CO: Westview, 2001.

Thorne, B. (2001) 'Pick-up Time at Oakdale Elementary School: Work and Family from the Vantage Points of Children', in R. Hertz and N.L. Marshall (eds), *Working Families: the Transformation of the American Home*, Berkeley: University of California Press, pp. 354–76.

Tilly, C. and C. Tilly (1998) *Work under Capitalism*, Boulder, CO: Westview.

Tuten, F. (2002) 'Still Replying to Grandma's Persistent, "And Then"', *New York Times*, 21 October: E1–2.

Valenzuela, A. Jr (1999) 'Gender Roles and Settlement Activities among Children and their Immigrant Families', *American Behavioral Scientist*, 42: 720–42.

Woodhead, M. (1999) 'Combating Child Labour: Listen To What the Children Say', *Childhood*, 6: 27–49.

Wuthnow, R. (1995) *Learning to Care*, New York: Oxford University Press.

Zelizer, V.A. (1985) *Pricing the Priceless Child: the Changing Social Value of Children*, New York: Basic Books.

Zelizer, V.A. (2001) 'Economic Sociology', in N.J. Smelser and P.B. Baltes (eds), *International Encyclopedia of the Social & Behavioral Sciences*, 6, Amsterdam: Elsevier, pp. 4128–31.

Zelizer, V.A. (2002a) 'Intimate Transactions', in M.F. Guillén, R. Collins, P. England and M. Meyer (eds), *The New Economic Sociology: Developments in an Emerging Field*, New York: Russell Sage Foundation, pp. 274–300.

Zelizer, V.A. (2002b) 'Kids and Commerce', *Childhood*, 4 (November): 375–96.

12
Work, Welfare and Generational Order: Towards a Political Economy of Childhood

Helmut Wintersberger

Introduction

The perception of childhood in social, economic and political theory as well as practice is vague, unclear and ambiguous. While on one side children are seen as precious beings, on the other they are perceived as a burden to their parents and to society. This ambiguity is connected with two interdependent socioeconomic and sociopolitical shifts, concerning children's economic role and the generational division of labour on one hand and old age security, the generation contract and the welfare state on the other. In both realms this ambiguity is due to tendencies of increasing marginalization and exclusion of childhood.

In this chapter I will aim at a generational perspective of the division of labour and the welfare state; that is, the position of childhood and children in the two systems will be analysed and confronted with that of adults. In the first part I will be dealing with economic perspectives on childhood and the generational division of labour, in the second with the generational order of modern welfare states.

Economic perspectives on childhood and the transformation of the generational division of labour

No other transformation brought about such fundamental change for childhood in modern society as scholarization. Therefore, Hernandez (1993) is right when referring to this transition as the first childcare revolution. Everybody is aware of the beneficial consequences of this revolution for children; hardly anybody refers to the fact that along with scholarization we observe the phenomena of marginalization and exclusion of children with a view to the generational division of labour as well as to the distribution of resources. Below I will first elaborate on the evolution of economic modes of childhood by developing six stages with regard to children's economic role and by integrating the various stages in a model. Second, I will critically discuss this model by applying different standpoints, in particular child-centred perspectives.

The economic evolution of childhood: from pre- to post-industrial child labour

For any socio-historic analysis of modernization processes, the point of departure is traditional society. With a view to the evolution of the generational division of labour, the point of departure is therefore pre-industrial child labour in traditional society.

Traditional (pre-industrial) child labour

In the pre-modern age childhood was predominantly determined by agricultural and domestic labour. Children lived and worked together with adults in the domestic economy. Children's costs and benefits were balanced at the level of the family or domestic economy. Training was provided on the job. On the whole, children were not separated from adults, but integrated in the community. Economic production was determined by two main factors, namely land and labour, and an economic dilemma concerning children appeared for the first time in Malthusian writings: a vicious circle of increased fertility levels induced by the demand for additional labour which – in connection with a more or less constant area of agricultural land – would lead to overpopulation and recurrent famines. In the long run, Malthus' predictions were not borne out, because he considered human labour only in its quantitative, rather than its qualitative dimension, and some of the assumptions of his theory were overthrown by the process of modernization itself.

Early industrial child labour

The first major transformation came about with early industrialization when a growing number of children became involved in industrial child labour; that is, child labour not as directly applied in the domestic economy but as sold to a company. Using a Marxist concept, I refer to this transition as formal subsumption of child labour under capital. At this stage the unity of training and practice still existed; however, separated life worlds (work, family and so on) emerged. The generational division of labour was still synchronic; that is, both children and adults worked. Children's costs and benefits were partly balanced at the familial level; the surplus value of child labour was however taken by the capitalists. The predominantly negative outcomes of this transformation, such as child labour in sweatshops, were well described by Marx, and used by the Labour movement as clear examples of the inhumane, exploitative and finally unsustainable nature of capitalism itself. This period saw the first tensions emerge between the state – representing macroeconomic interests – and enterprises that represented microeconomic interests. Consequently, legal restrictions with regard to child labour were introduced.

Children as human capital

It was, however, not only the humanistic and socialist critique of early industrial child labour, but also the needs of maturing capitalism, that triggered off another transformation: real subsumption of child labour under capital, which is more often referred to in terms of human capital formation or scholarization of childhood. Based on technological progress the production process develops from generating absolute to generating relative surplus value; that is, the surplus value is not any longer derived from extending the working day and from premature exploitation of child labourers, but rather from more efficient use of better skilled adult (male) workers. At this stage the generational division of labour is characterized by the sequence of education, paid work and pension, that is, a diachronic division of labour. I argue that child labour was not only abolished because it was a hazard to children's health and development, but also because at a certain point of capitalist development, it became, on the whole, more profitable to 'exploit' children indirectly by sending them to school than to exploit them directly in sweatshops. School (instead of the factory) became a dominant life world and workplace for children (of school age). However, direct economic benefits disappeared with this transition, and the first tensions emerged between family and society concerning old age security and the generation contract.

Children as consumption durables

The process of sacralization or sentimentalization of childhood marks a further transformation of children from capital goods to consumption durables. As suggested by Becker (1976) in his early writings on fertility and family economics and, more recently, by Zelizer (1985), children are no longer materially useful to their parents and, therefore, the generation of benefits from children shifts from the material to the immaterial, the emotional or sentimental, dimension. At this stage, children are neither born as assets for their parents' old-age security nor for their own sake, but for the sake of their parents' self-realization. As the prevailing context for raising children at this stage, the bourgeois nuclear family, with its fixed distribution of gender roles, emerges as the dominant family form. The subsequent sexual revolution, in particular the progressive separation of sexuality and biological reproduction, reinforces the trend towards sacralizing and exalting children (as products of free decisions); at the same time, as consumption goods, children are in an increasingly competitive position with other consumption goods (television sets, cars, tourism, animal pets and so on), and hence fertility levels decline. However, at this stage parents' attitudes towards children are not necessarily only restricted by short-sighted egoistic

interests. Generally, parents are perfectly prepared for major economic, organizational and emotional investments in their children's *good* education,
because their self-realization depends not only on having a child or children
at all, but also on making a success of it, which includes participating indirectly in the child or children's successes. A combination of the present with
the previous stage (of human capital formation) provides a perfect precon-
dition for implementing a bourgeois adult-centred, developmental education and socialization project for children (Hengst, 1996), oriented towards
children's well-*becoming* rather than well-being.

Children as new consumers

The appearance of children as active and autonomous new consumers has
been the last shift so far. Besides the future-oriented adult-centred developmental education and socialization project *for* children, which was mentioned above, there emerges an alternative project of children as new
consumers – aiming at the generation and confirmation of pedagogically
diluted spaces for playing and learning. This project is focused on the
present and oriented towards children's well-being and autonomy. In this
connection Hengst (1996) refers to a revolutionary innovation of the children's market brought about by Mattel. This was the first company to deliberately ignore the bourgeois parental child culture concept by marketing
toys without any traditional pedagogical value directly to children, avoiding mediation by parents or child-professionals. Meanwhile the different
potentials of both child culture concepts, the bourgeois socialization project
for children and the alternative autonomy project *of* children 'are continuously monitored by the market and (for the sake of profit) the market
strengthens the dominant one, searches for new balances and transforms
them into different competing market segments' (Hengst, 1996, p. 118). The
mediation between children and a spaceless, but all-pervasive commercial
system through the media creates good conditions for strengthening the
project of children as autonomous consumers. However, from an economic
and cultural point of view it is an ambivalent project: while it may be interpreted as an enlightened progressive alternative to the socialization-oriented
project of adult bourgeois society, it may be observed more critically that
the penetration of the commercial system into the world of childhood also
constitutes a major risk.

Children as new (post-industrial) producers

Finally, with ever shorter cycles of technological, economic and social innovation processes, together with progressively more fluid concepts of work
and blurred boundaries between the spheres of production and consumption ('prosumption'), a new type of child labour may emerge; children
returning to the world of production as post-modern producers. However,
to grasp this development conceptually, we need to redefine work in order
to replace the strictly abolitionist ideology in relation to child labour (Liebel,

2000), which is inherent in the western model of the generational division of labour, with a more flexible approach and attitude towards children's part in the generational division of labour characterized by new mixtures of playing, learning and working (Hengst, 2000). This means that leisure activities, school, and both unpaid and paid work may be considered licit activities for children provided the mixture is balanced. The boundaries between the different types of activities may sometimes be unclear; and in the long run there may be convergence between patterns of time use by children and adults.

The various economic stages of childhood were introduced in a chronological sequence. In Table 12.1 this chronological order is indicated by the numbers added to each stage. While the first two stages (pre- and early industrial child labour) are located in the upper left cell, scholarization of childhood is represented by the passage from the upper to the lower left cell. Sentimentalization or sacralization of childhood lead from the lower left to the lower right cell, while the appearance of children as new consumers is schematically registered by the passage to the upper right cell. Finally, the transition of children from new consumers to new producers leads back to the point of departure, the upper left cell. However, the appearance of a circular development from traditional to post-industrial child labour is the result of a simplification. There are remarkable differences already evident between traditional and early-industrial child labour and this holds the more true with a view to post-industrial forms of child labour. If we introduce as a third dimension time (or history or development), evolution would not be circular but spiral. In addition, I take it for granted that in reality we have to allow for deviations from the ideal model as well as for the coexistence of different stages at the same place and/or time.

For integrating the different economic modes of childhood in the model, I introduce two dimensions: subjectivity/objectivity, and the predominant economic location of children in the spheres of production or consumption. By using these two dimensions I arrive at a circular or spiral evolution of children's economic role, in which child labour becomes a salient feature of childhood in the course of history. Although, seemingly, this does not hold true for contemporary childhood, it holds for the past and it will also deter-

Table 12.1: Economic evolution of childhood

Children in	Production	Consumption
Children as		
Subjects	(1) Pre- (2) early- and (6) post-industrial producers	(5) New consumers
Objects	(3) Human capital	(4) Consumption durables

Source: Wintersberger (2000).

mine the future of (post-modern) childhood. While we are on quite firm ground concerning the past, interpretations of contemporary phenomena depend to a large extent on standpoints or perspectives, and predictions for the future tend to be highly speculative.

A critical review: real subsumption of childhood under capital

In Table 12.1 I collected various available interpretations and theories from different sources and assembled them in a model. For explaining the transition from pre- to early-industrial child labour I use the Marxist concepts of absolute surplus value and formal subsumption of (child) labour under capital, and I assume that also among non-Marxist historians, economists and social scientists the use of these concepts would not arouse major opposition.

For interpreting the transition from early industrial child labour to human capital formation, I introduce the concepts of scholarization/human capital formation as well as of real subsumption of child labour under capital. While scholarization and human capital are widely used noncontroversial concepts, the concept of real subsumption of child labour might provoke resistance from both mainstream and Marxist social scientists. In addition, the terms not only describe one and the same transition in different languages, but offer different meanings for the transition itself, that is, they describe different transitions and outcomes. In the table the development is perceived in terms of adult-centred conventional wisdom, whereas the concept of real subsumption of child labour under capital shifts the perception of the transition towards a childhood perspective. Thus the outcome would not be human capital formation in the sense of transforming children as raw material and passive objects into human capital, but of children themselves as the producers of human capital. A similar argument may be found in Maria Montessori's writings, where she constructs an analogy between the worker at large as the creator of wealth in the Marxist sense and the child as the worker whose task is to generate the (adult) man or woman (Hedderich, 2001). These child- and actor-centred interpretations would, however, be in contrast with a view to the rationale underlying the model.

Nevertheless I prefer this concept, because it underlines the continuity of child labour as well as of the economic relevance of children under changing circumstances: under conditions of real subsumption of childhood under capital, child labour is performed in an entirely new context, namely school. In this way the euphemistic ideology of the concepts of scholarization and human capital is also revealed. I believe this to be a creative application of a Marxist concept, although I am aware that a majority of Marxist thinkers would be critical, particularly with a view to defining school attendance as work. However, in a sociocultural perspective, for children the factory was replaced by school, and children's working conditions (content and organization) changed (along with the working conditions of adults) from blue- to white-collar work (Hengst, 1981). On the whole it seems to be more correct and realistic to assert that children's economic productivity has shifted to the production of human capital, than that they have become economically useless. While from an adult-centred perspective it means transforming children from producing labourers to produced capital goods (human capital); in a paedo-centric one, children are the primary producers of human capital themselves. In a microeconomic perspective this appears as an exclusion of children from the productive system, at the macroeconomic level, it might be interpreted just as a more efficient integration of children in the generational division of labour.

Although school or human capital formation as outcomes of the transformation processes outlined above determine the everyday life of children of today, this was not the last step; others followed and/or still continue. With a view to the subsequent stages and the corresponding transitions, I refer mainly to existing literature. Zelizer (1985) describes the passage from stages (3) to (4) as sentimentalization or sacralization of childhood. Again the perspective is adult-centred, in this case familial or parental: children as passive objects being 'emotionally exploited' by their parents. The role of children themselves is not focused upon at all in this connection. Hengst (1996) instead elaborates on the emergence of a further paradigm of children as active consumers (5). Finally, the last stage of children as post-industrial producers (6) refers to ongoing discussions on reconceptualizing adults' work and on revising the western approach with a view to child labour, abolitionist attitudes in particular.

One could also interpret the evolution of childhood in the context of changing historical blocs, constellations and alliances that define the meaning of childhood itself, or – as Shamgar-Handelman (1994) phrased it – 'To Whom Does Childhood Belong?'. In this connection, the question of who benefits economically (and immaterially) from children is of major importance. In traditional society this was the domestic economy and the extended family. Along with the process of industrialization, new alliances emerged which did not follow exactly the same patterns in all countries (Cunningham and Viazzo, 1996). However, in many instances capital and parents may have had a common interest in exploiting child labour. The next stage, scholarization, was also introduced in different ways to different countries, but mostly it can be explained on the basis of a new alliance, relevant for most modern states and economies, between advanced capital and its demands for a better qualified labour force and the provision by the state of basic education and training. The shift to the next stage, of children as consumption durables, would mark an enlargement of the previous coalition of capital and state by parents in the context of the bourgeois socialization project for children. Only stage (5) of children as new consumers would bring a real revolution, because – in the frame of this alternative child culture project – for the first time children participate actively (together with capital) in a historic alliance concerning childhood. There remains however the problem of children's economic dependence, which has to be overcome in order to set free the liberating effects of this transformation. This could be solved possibly (not necessarily) in the next transition of childhood: children's return to production.

Table 12.1 was designed to facilitate the comprehension of the economic evolution of childhood; however it is still based on rather conservative adult-centred perspectives and does not fully reflect the complexity of the historical developments concerning children, child labour and the economic relevance of childhood. Therefore the question may be asked whether the economic evolution of childhood in western society was not a peculiar way of achieving a new balance of leisure, education, paid and unpaid work. If some productive involvement of children is both point of departure and final goal, why then should so much emphasis be put on the segregation of children from the productive system and the total abolition of child labour? We can structure the whole evolution in two parts: first, economic segregation of childhood finding its utmost level of realization in scholarization and the bourgeois socialization project, and second, economic reintegration of children in the productive system as post-industrial producers. While in the previous explanations the term 'real subsumption of child labour' was reserved for the mode of children's schoolwork, in this context the process of real subsumption would be completed only with children's return as post-industrial producers. Scholarization and the bourgeois socialization project would only mark a particular intermediate point in the process of real subsumption of childhood at which child labour reaches the highest level of alienation.

These considerations concerning a reinterpretation of different economic modes of childhood in western countries would also allow generalization to other parts of the world, in particular less affluent nations. It seems that the western development path from early to post-industrial childhood – passing through a period of child/adult apartheid with a view to the generational division of labour – has been long, complicated, expensive and inefficient. Less affluent countries might consider different – more flexible, direct and efficient – development paths allowing for softer transitions to new mixtures of playing, learning and working, thereby acknowledging not only the negative, but also the positive side of children's experience with labour, as suggested by the Colombian researcher Munoz Vila (1996):

> If we recognize that it is through work, thought and language that mankind has transformed the environment, for better or for worse, we have to conclude that work is an important component of the human identity. Why then should we prohibit children from working? . . . Perhaps it is time that we made an effort to change our negative perception of children's work, translating its unrecognized value, like that of women's work within the home, into positive values associated with

cooperation as well as into monetary value. If we do not, we are implying that their work is without worth.

(Munoz Vila, 1996, p. 104)

Welfare states and generational order

In the previous part – dedicated to children's changing economic role in the
wake of modernization – I have shown that children's role in the modern
economy is much more relevant than generally assumed. In the following
part – dealing with child welfare and children's position in the welfare state
– I assert that the gap between children's actual relevance for the economic
and productive system and the adult-centred perception of their role as marginal influences to a considerable degree their position in the welfare state.
While emphasizing, however, the economic and sociopolitical relevance
of children, I do not argue for an exclusively 'productivist' orientation of
welfare states. On the contrary, even if children were not as relevant and
productive as they are, they would nevertheless have needs, interests and
legitimate claims in regard to the welfare state and the generational distribution of societal resources as do other social groups.

I will first discuss the evolution of child welfare and generation contracts
in a historical perspective. Then I will focus on typologies of modern welfare
states. From there I will revert to a feminist critique of welfare state analysis, which is in general andro-centric or male-biased. This will be the point
of departure for underlining the necessity of overcoming the adult-centred
bias of both patriarchal and feminist approaches and elaborating on the prerequisites of a paedo-centric or child-centred analysis of the welfare state.

Child welfare and generation contracts: a historical perspective

'The history of childhood is a nightmare from which we have only recently
begun to awaken. The further back in history one goes, the lower the level
of child care, and the more likely children are to be killed, abandoned,
beaten, terrorised, and sexually abused' (deMause, 1992, p. 48). In his history
of childhood deMause identifies a number of modes of child welfare (or
rather of child abuse), starting with the infanticidal mode, passing through
the abandonment, the ambivalent, the intrusive and the socialization
modes, and finally, arriving at the helping mode.

On the one hand deMause offers an interesting and useful stage theory of
childcare and welfare, on the other hand he has to be criticized for some
limitations of this theory. First of all, I doubt whether the evolution of childcare and welfare may be described as a sequence of continuous improvements; this is in my view far too optimistic. Second, deMause restricts the
assessment of child welfare exclusively to the familial dimension of
parent–child relations. He may be right that, before modernization, there
had been little public interest in childcare and welfare, which therefore were

predominantly determined by parent–child relations. However, along with modernization, public interest in child matters has increased and – in spite of the fact that families and parents have remained of primary importance for the welfare of their children – we have to include child welfare policies in the assessment of child welfare.

While deMause concentrates predominantly on child welfare modes as determined by adult (chiefly parental) interventions, with a view to two-sided generational relations, we also have to ask the question of children's impact on the welfare of adults. This question was addressed by Qvortrup (1995) who supposes a kind of reciprocal generation contract between the different age groups or generations: children, adults of working age and the old. The point of departure is again traditional society, and scholarization (along with the establishment of old-age pension insurance) turns out to be crucial in the development of generational relations and welfare.

In traditional society the relevance of children for welfare was very visible; in particular children provided an insurance against the manifold risks of old age. There was direct intergenerational reciprocity of children's costs and benefits at the level of the household or domestic economy. Parents invested in their children for some years, and expected to benefit from them sooner in terms of traditional child labour and later through old age security. In modern society – due to both scholarization and the establishment of public pension insurance – this relation of simple reciprocity was terminated. The impression was created that old age security was no longer dependent on biological reproduction and the willingness of younger generations to care for the old. In particular in the post-World War II period, the prevailing perception has been that the rationale of national pension schemes was exclusively determined by legal regulations concerning contributions and entitlements.

Only recently, in connection with the ageing of advanced societies, the fiscal crisis of the welfare state and the financial problems of pension insurance, has the hidden generational contract underlying pension systems been rediscovered and again become part of public discourse. There is now an awareness that generational relations are still characterized by some reciprocity, albeit not by simple reciprocity at the level of the family, but a form of enlarged reciprocity at the level of society. While investments in children are still predominantly a responsibility of the parents, the benefits from children have to a large extent been nationalized or socialized.

Modes of western welfare states: three worlds of welfare capitalism

While the concept of welfare is, in principle, timeless and may be applied to all historical periods, the idea of the welfare state is tied to the modern age. I will, therefore, concentrate now on child welfare and generational contracts in modern society only, and leave the earlier ages to social historians. Thus it makes sense to discuss welfare state paradigms rather than individual child welfare at the level of the family. The European Social

Report (European Commission/Eurostat, 2000), covering the 15 countries of the EU, introduces a typology of four welfare state paradigms: the Nordic, the Anglo-Saxon, the Central and the South European. This geopolitical typology is to a large extent based on three welfare state paradigms developed by Esping-Andersen (1990, 2002). He identifies two major cycles in the development of welfare states internationally. The first is connected with the German conservative Chancellor Bismarck, who – confronted with the dual challenges of unbearable social problems among the working class and a growing Socialist movement – introduced social security legislation in Germany. This approach influenced quite a number of other countries, and traits of the German reform might be identified not only in central European countries, such as Austria, but probably in all developed welfare states. Due to wars and economic depressions considerable time was necessary to accomplish the project. In Austria, for instance, the act extending pension insurance to blue-collar workers had to wait until 1945.

By that time Roosevelt and Beveridge had already initiated the second great transformation, and the universalistic welfare state was on its way to gaining hegemony over other models. However, the most authentic implementation was achieved neither in the USA nor in Great Britain, but in the Nordic countries, in Sweden in particular. Again all European and also many non-European states integrated elements of the Swedish model into their systems to a greater or lesser extent, and it took decades before this process was accomplished. Italy might be considered an interesting case of a latecomer, which in its struggles for health and environmental reforms as well as abolition of closed psychiatric institutions during the period of an emerging 'historical compromise' did not only adopt Scandinavian elements, but adapted and modified them in a quite innovative way, strongly involving workers' and citizens' direct participation.

Today however, the second transformation is losing momentum and coming to an end; partly this may be due to the dominance of neo-liberalism, partly also to newly emerging problems, for example, those connected with financing generous pension systems in ageing societies. At the beginning of a new century there are indications of another transformation, which according to Esping-Andersen might lead towards a new type of European welfare state, an alternative to the American minimal welfare state. It is somehow premature to judge whether such optimism is justified. On the one hand most European countries try to imitate successful American economic policy, and modest welfare standards are an indispensable part of this approach. On the other hand there is considerable diversity, largely to be explained by different historical backgrounds, with regard to welfare systems among European countries themselves. It seems doubtful that this combination of inner divergences combined with external convergence towards the American model offers good grounds for the growth of an authentic European alternative.

According to Esping-Andersen (1990) three welfare state paradigms resulted from the two major transformations: the citizenship-based Nordic, the employment-centred Bismarckian, and the residual Anglo-Saxon welfare state. This typology addresses a political logic and order, and thus relates welfare states to the main ideologies of modern western societies, namely social democracy, conservatism and liberalism. Generally the reality of welfare states does not correspond to the ideal of one of the paradigms, but is rather reflected in a mix of different models and welfare policies, which is determined by similarities and/or differences in histories, cultures and traditions as well as varying socioeconomic and political constellations. A thorough analysis of welfare states would allow us to identify crucial choices concerning welfare state regulations in the respective socioeconomic, political and cultural contexts of different countries and times.

The three welfare state paradigms are to a large degree determined by different levels of commodification/decommodification of labour and consequently shaped by different balances between economic efficiency and social justice and equity. Only in the early period of industrialization did the relationship between economic efficiency and social justice seem to be an antagonistic one. After the Fordist revolution, at the latest, it became clear that there cannot be mass production without mass consumption; therefore, reasonable income levels and social justice are also prerequisites of an efficient and flourishing production system. However, there is still some room for choice between different welfare state models, and the nature of these choices reveals different beliefs about social justice and about what constitutes a fair balance between economic efficiency and social justice.

In the social democrat model, social justice means more or less social equity. In the conservative welfare state, integration in the labour market and social insurance are leading principles; benefits for persons not integrated in the labour market are predominantly derived from previous employment or from the employment status of relatives. The liberal residual model is the least interventionist one; social inequities are accepted as long as minimum standards are met; only when persons or households fall below these standards are they entitled to assistance from society. However, economic efficiency, too, is a common feature of all the three models, and the experience of the Nordic countries proves that it is possible to combine economic efficiency with high standards of social justice and equity.

A feminist critique: implications for childhood research and policies

Feminist theory revealed that there were a number of blind spots and missing links in traditional welfare state theory and practice. A particular limitation was due to an andro-centric bias, or the absence of gender distinctions and women in welfare state analysis. Feminists had pointed out that mainstream social thinking was basically andro-centric, oriented towards the male labourer or worker as the model. The discrimination against women on the labour market as well as in the domestic sphere was neglected or even accepted, partly in an open, partly in a hidden way. This was a focus of research and lively debates within and beyond the women's movement.

European welfare states are still characterized by a more or less patriarchal gender order, as reflected in the labour markets, in the social security and welfare systems as well as in the domestic spheres. In order to reveal this patriarchal order as well as to identify both similarities and differences between European countries, Schunter-Kleemann (1992, 1997) poses a number of questions:

> Do we find an open or secret intention to bring women home or is it the aim of a measure to promote an egalitarian division of labour between parents? To what extent do family benefits offset income losses and family maintenance costs? How can we characterise the gender profile of the family benefits and tax systems? Are they neutral, or either female or male centred? Is the child allowance dominated by the intention to stimulate the birth rate, or are the benefits birth-order related in particular? Are family benefits given only to matrimonial families or do they support also new patterns of living with a child, for instance single parents? To what extent do family policies contribute to the stabilisation of social stratification patterns? Which types of families are supported and which groups of families, for instance, migrant families are excluded from access to family benefits?
>
> (Schunter-Kleemann, 1997, p. 11)

Based on an analysis of these questions, Schunter-Kleemann (1992) identifies the following five paradigms.

Patriarchy with the beginnings of egalitarian working and social structures

Denmark would be a good example for this most advanced paradigm, but the other Nordic countries would also fit. Nordic women have greater economic independence and freedom to decide number and timing of their children; although part-time working women in particular are still dependent on their partner's income. In addition, some achievements of the Nordic welfare state, including services for women and children, have been threatened by budgetary cuts and/or privatization. Whether women will be politically strong enough to defend comparatively egalitarian social structures is still to be seen.

Family-centred patriarchy

France is the leading example of a social policy aiming at maintaining and stabilizing the family as a central focus. This idea dominates a number of other policy areas, such as taxation, labour market and pension legislation.

French women's and family policies are inspired by Catholic social doctrines rather than by socialist or feminist values. Therefore – from a feminist angle – France is less advanced than the Nordic countries, but French family benefits and services are definitely more focused to the needs of women and children than those in Germany and the remaining countries.

Marriage stabilizing patriarchy

Unlike France, in Germany family policy is dominated by the principle of subsidiarity. It is a marriage stabilizing regime, which is not women- or child-centred, but primarily structured around the interests of the male head of the family.

Market-oriented patriarchy

The United Kingdom is a paramount example of this paradigm, characterized generally by a social policy dominated by selectivity and means-testing, and in regard to families – women and children in particular – by very modest monetary family transfers and the lack of statutory regulations on local, regional or central authorities to provide childcare facilities for children under five years old.

Agrarian-ecclesiastical structures in transition to market-oriented patriarchy

The welfare regimes of Spain and other South European countries have retained a relatively strong agricultural basis, a rudimentary household or subsistence economy and an expanding underground economy; however, major social and family policy reforms have been implemented in the last years.

Although the feminist perspective is also in principle adult-centred and paternalistic in its view of children, it is still relevant whether an andro- or gyno-centric approach is being taken. Women's and men's different biological natures and social experience mean that children do count much more in the gyno- than in the andro-centric perspective. In addition, gender studies have been a major source of inspiration and enlightenment for childhood studies, which is underlined also by the presence of a number of feminist researchers in this relatively new research domain. Further, without the women's movement questioning the stronghold of patriarchy, innovations concerning childhood research and policies would most probably not have come about at all.

As Therborn states:

> The rise of women made two central contributions to the emergence of child politics. One was of *visibility*, the other of *conceptualisation*. Women's fights for and entry into participation in public life, in the labour market, in public debate, in places of power made children more visible to public discourse . . . The 'family' was *individualised*, comprising

individual members, who had but who should not have unequal rights and powers. This individualist egalitarianism (or egalitarian individualism) first and most explicitly asserted the individuality of the woman. But in so doing, it undermined the patriarchal collectivism of the family, and opened up a space for discussing the individuality and the rights of the child as well.

(Therborn, 1996, p. 384)

In conclusion, including women closed a gap in welfare state theory and practice, but there is still another blind spot to be focused on: childhood and children. However, while the growing stock of feminist research on gender relations and welfare states has prepared the ground for including children and the generational dimension, and generational welfare state analysis may derive positive momentum from the achievements of feminist research, it has simultaneously to overcome some feminists' resistance to including childhood in alternative welfare state discourses.

From gender to generational, from adult- to child-centred approaches

While feminist researchers introduced the dimension of sex for revealing the gender order of patriarchal welfare states, the generational dimension in childhood research is in principle about age. But as in the case of sex and gender, we should make a distinction between biological and social age as the generational order of society. While biological age can easily be defined by the day of birth, the social meaning of being, for instance, 17-years-old varies cross-nationally and culturally as well as for different periods in history. When reverting to the feminist research paradigm, we should also be aware of the differences between sex/gender and age/generation. While the range of age is the continuum (of time), the range of sex is that of a binary relation: the dichotomy of female and male. While the nature of gender relations is often conceived as a difficult balance between diversity and equity, behind generational relations is the concept of development. However, a generally valid and acceptable perception of human beings developing with age and establishing thereby shifting balances between autonomy and dependence was reduced under an adult-centred paternalistic perspective into another dichotomy, that of maturity and competence versus immaturity and incompetence. Therefore, although sex and age relations are of fundamentally different nature, both gender and generational relations use dichotomies, which are more open to discrimination, marginalization and exclusion.

With regard to the generational order, all welfare states are to a large extent adult-centred and paternalistic. First of all, welfare states are to a large degree child-blind in the sense that children are neglected both conceptually and practically. Second, when children are considered at all, this is mostly done in a paternalistic way, in the sense that parents and other adults decide on what is good for (or in the best interest of) children. Third, while in welfare state regulations adults are increasingly being considered and addressed as individuals, familialism still prevails in the attitude towards children. Fourth, social policies for children are in a number of respects visibly among the less important social policy baskets.

In addition, there are sometimes ideological resistances against including the generational dimension in welfare state analysis. In 2003, an Austrian leftist magazine, usually very dedicated to class and gender issues, argued that the generational dimension and childhood was part of a neo-liberal welfare state discourse. The article missed the point in mixing up a socio-structural dimension in general with its neo-liberal instrumentalization in a particular context. There may be abusive instrumentalizations of the generational dimension and childhood (as well as of other structural concepts and population groups!), however, the best remedy for reducing the risks of such abuse is developing and promoting discourses rather than avoiding or repressing them.

On the other hand, the type of welfare state regime realized in a country does matter for child welfare. The relative advantage of the social-democrat Nordic welfare state is clearly indicated by international comparison of child poverty rates. It is also much easier to combine the new rights of children enshrined in the UN Convention on the Rights of the Child (CRC) with the architecture of the Nordic model. In this case extending citizenship from adults to children would not be such a fundamental problem as in the Conservative welfare state in which citizenship is derived from the position on the labour market. Also the gender order of a welfare state is relevant for children: a women-friendly welfare state is more likely to be child-friendly, as a women-hostile one is more likely to be child-hostile. But from there it does not follow that women- and child-friendliness are equivalent concepts.

What could be the criteria for building a generational typology of welfare states? At a first glance, I would not hesitate to identify as one paradigm the 'enlightened paternalist welfare state' in the comparatively child-friendly Nordic countries. Consequently the question might be asked: Why is it that the Nordic countries are leading countries with a view to class, gender and generational integration? Obviously there have to be interdependencies between the three dimensions in the sense that a society committed to social justice is more likely to be both women- and child-friendly, and that a women-friendly society is also more likely to be child-centred. I could continue this exercise of reorienting Esping-Andersen's and Schunter-Kleemann's typologies in a paedo-centric perspective. A market-oriented, adult-centred, paternalistic welfare state could be another paradigm; and it would not be too difficult to identify criteria for identifying the relevance of the market for the provision of childcare, the dominance of working over family life for parents, the market dominance for children in education and socialization and so on. However, for elaborating a complete typology we require some conceptual work and empirical research covering questions still to be defined and answered.

For the conceptualization the CRC and its 3 Ps (the three principles of protection, provision and participation) might provide a useful point of departure. Protective versus participative welfare states may be defined on the basis of varying balances between child protection and participation (Lüscher, 1996). Compensating versus caring welfare states is another aspect to be considered: depending on levels of and balances between financial compensation (direct family transfers) and (public) social services for children and families (for example, childcare) different contours of welfare states may be distinguished. The distribution of responsibilities between parents and society might be another criterion: while the CRC reflects a broadly family-oriented culture, cultural changes towards a more society-oriented philosophy should not be excluded for the future. Does child welfare policy address children primarily as human becomings or beings (Ben-Arieh et al., 2001)? Olk (2004) raises a similar question when asking whether a productivist or distributive logic determines welfare states, that is, whether social policy expenditures are dependent on returning benefits to be expected or rather on needs to be met.

A generational view of children's well-being should also be included here, but there is not enough space to do so. In addition, there exist still major theoretical and methodological problems to be solved (for example, how to determine a 'fair' equivalence scale). With regard to child poverty I refer to existing literature, for example, Bradbury and Jäntti (1999), Bradshaw and Finch (2002) and UNICEF (2000).

Conclusion

This chapter consists of two parts, which consider the location of childhood in the economy and in the welfare state. There is at least one interdependence between the two parts which has been made explicit: the marginalization of children in the economy (and economics) leads to (or is at least instrumental in preserving) the marginalization of children in the welfare state (analysis), too. In addition to this interdependence, there are various other features common to both subjects; some of them will be addressed in this conclusion.

For both parts *proper visibility* of children is a leitmotiv. Children are partly invisible, partly the visions of children are adult-biased, distorted and crippled; therefore I use the term *proper visibility*. Increasing visibility out of invisibility may be an easier task than generating proper visions where public and scientific discourses are spoilt by distorted views of childhood. Before opening a new perspective, one has to struggle with the old ones, and that might provoke cognitive dissonances. The concept of the *cost of children* is a typical example relevant for both parts. In the mid-1990s an international seminar was held in Fiesole with the title 'The cost of being a mother, the cost of being a father.' I gave a paper for which I chose as title 'And what about the cost of being a child?' (Wintersberger, 1996). While the majority of the participants found it difficult to overcome the barriers of traditional family and gender discourses which treat children as objects, costs and burdens, there was a compact group of Italian feminists who considered the introduction of a childhood discourse rather as an enrichment than a threat with a view to their cause. *Who Pays for the Kids?* is the title of an excellent book by Nancy Folbre (1994), and while the title sticks to the old rhetoric the content is wider and on various occasions childhood perspectives are introduced in addition to gender.

Both parts of this chapter deal with *children's citizenship*: the extension of economic and social rights (as well as responsibilities) to children. It was mentioned in the first part that the explicit exclusion of children from the labour market was, under the given circumstances necessary, but the continued proclamation of this principle (in and for western countries) has also undermined children's economic citizenship today. In this respect the UNCRC is also conservative, just reiterating the traditional abolitionist positions. While in times of structural unemployment in advanced economies it is obvious that labour parties and unions claim the right to work for adults, hardly anybody raises the question of a child's right to adequate work and the value of children's work-like activities, such as school, which are not recognized as productive contributions to society. The description of the Conservative welfare state paradigm in the second part refers to the link between economic citizenship by employment and social protection through the welfare state. A different location of children with a view to the economy would provide better grounds for defining children's position with a view to the welfare state. Besides that, I argue that distribution in general and generational distributive justice in particular should not follow primarily a productivist, but rather a needs-oriented logic.

Similarly in regard to the dynamics of political discourses between the economy and the welfare state: a classical liberal position demands a Marxist-Socialist response; both of them provoke critique by feminists; and from there the demand for a generational extension eventually becomes obvious.

On the whole, this chapter is about *balances*: balances between the social and the economic, between rights and responsibilities; a balanced generational division of labour and a balanced mix of activities comprising education, work and leisure are itemised in the first part; a balanced mix of welfare providers and a balanced distribution of resources are considered in the second.

Both parts are work in progress; further studies will be needed. The introduction of children as post-industrial producers is still tentative and vague;

and the criteria for a child-centred welfare state typology are rather general and have to be specified and completed. In particular output indicators will have to be added to input indicators.

References

Becker, G.S. (1976) *The Economic Approach to Human Behavior*, Chicago: University of Chicago Press.

Ben-Arieh, A., Natalie Hevener Kaufman, Arlen Bowers Andrews, Robert M. Goerge, Bong Joo Lee and J. Lawrence Aber (2001) *Measuring and Monitoring Children's Well-being*, Dordrecht/Boston/London: Kluwer.

Bradbury, B. and M. Jäntti (1999) 'Child Poverty across Industrialized Nations', Innocenti Occasional Papers EPS 71, Florence: UNICEF.

Bradshaw, J. and N. Finch (2002) 'A Comparison of Child Benefit Packages in 22 Countries', DWP Research Report 174, Corporate Document Services, Leeds.

Cunningham, H. and P.P. Viazzo (eds) (1996) *Child Labour in Historical Perspective 1800–1995*, Florence: UNICEF ICDC.

deMause, L. (1992) 'The Evolution of Childhood', in C. Jenks (ed.), *The Sociology of Childhood: Essential Readings*, Milton Keynes: Open University, pp. 48–59.

Esping-Andersen, G. (1990) *Three Worlds of Welfare Capitalism*, Cambridge: Polity Press.

Esping-Andersen, G. (2002) *Why we Need a New Welfare State*, Oxford: Oxford University Press.

European Commission/Eurostat (2000) *The Social Situation in the European Union*, Luxembourg: European Communities.

Folbre, N. (1994) *Who Pays for the Kids? Gender and the Structures of Constraint*, London and New York: Routledge.

Hedderich, I. (2001) *Einführung in die Montessori-Pädagogik*, München: Ernst Reinhardt Verlag.

Hengst, H. (1981) 'Tendenzen der Liquidierung von Kindheit', in H. Hengst, Michael Köhler, Barbara Riedmüller and Manfred Max Wambach, *Kindheit als Fiktion*, Frankfurt am Main: Suhrkamp.

Hengst, H. (1996) 'Kinder an die Macht! Der Rückzug des Marktes aus dem Kindheitsprojekt der Moderne', in H. Zeiher, P. Büchner and J. Zinnecker (eds), *Kinder als Außenseiter?* Weinheim und München: Juventa, pp. 117–33.

Hengst, H. (2000) 'Die Arbeit der Kinder und der Umbau der Arbeitsgesellschaft', in H. Hengst and H. Zeiher (eds), *Die Arbeit der Kinder*, Weinheim and München: Juventa, pp. 71–97.

Hernandez, D.J. (1993) *America's Children. Resources from Family, Government and the Economy*, New York: Russell Sage Foundation.

Liebel, M. (2000) 'Ein Recht auf Arbeit und gesellschaftliche Anerkennung. Forderungen arbeitender Kinder aus der Dritten Welt', in H. Hengst and H. Zeiher (eds), *Die Arbeit der Kinder*, Weinheim and München: Juventa, pp. 241–54.

Lüscher, K. (1996) 'Politik für Kinder – Politik mit Kindern', paper at the Deutschen Jugendinstitut in München.

Munoz Vila, C. (1996) 'The Working Child in Colombia since 1800', in H. Cunningham and P.P. Viazzo (eds), *Child Labour in Historical Perspective 1800–1995*, Florence: UNICEF ICDC, pp. 91–105.

Olk, T. (2004) 'Kinder und Kindheit im Wohlfahrtsstaat – eine vernachlässigte Kategorie?' *Zeitschrift für Sozialreform*, 1–2: 81–101.

Qvortrup, J. (1995) 'From Useful to Useful: the Historical Continuity in Children's Constructive Participation', *Sociological Studies of Children*, 7: 49–76.

Schunter-Kleemann, S. (ed.) (1992) *Herrenhaus Europa – Geschlechterverhältnisse im Wohlfahrtsstaat*, Berlin: Edition Sigma.

Schunter-Kleemann, S. (1997) 'Monetary Union and Family Policies in the EU Countries', Discussion papers 1/WE-FF Universität Bremen.

Shamgar-Handelman, L. (1994) 'To Whom Does Childhood Belong?', in J. Qvortrup, M. Bardy, G.B. Sgritta and H. Wintersberger (eds) (1994) *Childhood Matters – Social Theory, Practice and Politics*, Aldershot: Avebury, pp. 249–65.

Therborn, G. (1996) 'Child Politics: Dimensions and Perspectives', in E. Verhellen (ed.), *Monitoring Children's Rights*, The Hague/Boston/London: Martinus Nijhoff Publishers, pp. 377–91.

UNICEF (2000) 'A League Table of Child Poverty in Rich Nations', Innocenti Report Card No. 1.

Wintersberger, H. (1996) 'E qual è il costo di essere un bambino?' [And what about the cost of being a child?], in F. Bimbi (ed.), *Costo dei figli e diseguaglianze del genere* [The cost of children and gender inequalities], *Inchiesta*, 111: 84–93.

Wintersberger, H. (2000) 'Kinder als ProduzentInnen und KonsumentInnen', in H. Hengst and H. Zeiher (eds), *Die Arbeit der Kinder*, Weinheim und München: Juventa, pp. 169–88.

Zelizer, V.A. (1985) *Pricing the Priceless Child: the Changing Social Value of Children*, New York: Basic Books.

13
Social Justice and the Rights of Children

Hilde Bojer

Introduction

Most of us feel that children have rights. We are revolted to hear that children are abused and exploited. There is nothing more pitiful on television than starving children, their mothers with empty breasts. Child poverty is rightly seen as a grave social problem. Families with children compete with old age pensioners for the attention of voters and politicians. In politics as well as in daily discourse, provision for children is seen as important.

And yet, very little on the position of children is to be found in contemporary theories of social and distributional justice. Since John Rawls's path-breaking book, *A Theory of Justice* (1971), there has been a flowering of publications discussing principles for the just society in general and just principles of economic distribution in particular. But justice to children is very rarely mentioned. Rawls (1997) explicitly writes that children are not parties to the social contract he proposes. In spite of this, I find that the logic of Rawlsian theory is well suited to discuss the rights of children. The main part of this chapter will discuss children's place in a Rawlsian theory.

In Bojer (2000) I argue that two much-cited classes of theories, namely welfarism and libertarianism, not only ignore children they simply do not apply to the situation of children. By welfarism, I mean utilitarianism and economic welfare theory. Amartya Sen explains welfarism in this way: 'Welfarism in general, and utilitarianism in particular, see value, ultimately, only in individual utility, which is defined in terms of some mental characteristic, such as pleasure, happiness or desire' (Sen, 1992, p. 6). Moreover, the tastes (preferences) that determine the individual's happiness are assumed to be unchanging over time and not subject to change or manipulation by the economic and social environment. This assumption can be defended as a useful simplification in the case of adults, but is manifestly absurd applied to children.

A basic tenet of libertarianism is that an individual is entitled only to what he himself produces, or what other producers freely choose to give her. Since children are not, and cannot be, producers, the entitlement theory cannot apply to them. Children are excluded from the framework of libertarian distributional justice; they have no economic rights or entitlements.

There are several reasons why children do not fit easily into any philosophy of social justice, whether systematic philosophical theories or intuitive tenets. One reason is the connection between justice and deserts, or merits. Children are essentially innocent: they have (not yet) merited either rewards or punishment from society. In particular, it is impossible to reward children according to effort or according their contribution to society, 'the fruit of their labours'. Another reason is that children are regarded as a part of the family and of a private life, outside the domain of public justice.

But children are also of the utmost importance to society. They are what in economic terminology is called a public good.[1] That is, the birth and upbringing of children have effects on all members of a society, the childless as well as parents. One reason is that human labour is the most important factor of production, of development and growth. This is the basis for the utilitarian argument for 'investing in children', and makes the production and education of children a public concern of the greatest importance. Furthermore, economic problems are caused both by too few and too many children being born. Natality is now so low in several industrialized countries that the size of the population will decline in the long run. One effect is that the welfare state is said to be threatened because there are too few youngsters growing up to feed the many elderly. Conversely, a large rate of growth in the population is considered a hindrance for development in the third world. Even though some of the problems created can be (and are) mitigated by migration, public policies are still needed that can regulate population growth, increase it in some countries, decrease it in others.

At the same time, the begetting of a child is an intensely intimate human experience. Thus, the most private of actions can have momentous public consequences. There is an intrinsic connection here between the private and the public interest which has had some extremely unpleasant consequences in governmental policies for reducing the birth rate. A well known example of government brutality in the 'public interest' is the forced sterilization of men carried out by Indira Gandhi's government in India. Another is the one-child policy of the present Chinese government. Fortunately, it has now become clear that the most efficient way of reducing the number of births to combat over-population is a more humanitarian and attractive policy, namely that of empowering women to control their own fertility. Being pregnant, giving birth, and then nurturing and caring for children is a painful, burdensome, time consuming and expensive project that the majority of women do not enter on lightly.

Public policies to encourage women to bear children are correspondingly easy to recommend. They consist in providing time and money to assist the parents, and the mothers in particular, in their task.

From the point of view of justice, however, it is not obvious that parenthood in itself creates rights. In modern society, having a child is a voluntary decision, and people should, it is claimed, take responsibility for their own actions. Eric Rakowski writes: 'If the cultivation of expensive tastes, or silly gambles, or any other intentional action, cannot give rise to distributional claims, how can procreation?' (Rakowski, 1993, p. 153). I have heard people ask why acquiring children should be regarded differently from acquiring any other expensive commodity, like cars. In one way, these views are simply silly. Still, since they are sometimes heard in public debate, let me spell out some differences between children on the one hand, cars and gambling debts on the other.

Children are human beings, not consumer goods. Procreation, acquiring children, is the same as acquiring moral, legal and economic long-term obligations different in nature from any others. A single gambler takes risks that concern himself only. A bad father risks the life and happiness of his child. A car can be resold, traded in, or left in the garage to rust if the buyer finds that it does not make him happy after all, or if he prefers another model. No such way out is possible if parenthood turns out not to give happiness, or if the acquired child is not up to standard. Becoming a parent is irreversible.

Becoming a parent also, always and in every society, entails responsibilities that no distributional policies or social arrangements can entirely remove. But both the extent and precise content of parental responsibilities are shaped by society, and vary considerably from one society to the other. The importance of social circumstances for the consequences of parenthood is most starkly seen in the hugely differing situation of unmarried mothers, and their children, in various societies at various times.

Therefore there is every reason to discuss the justice of parents' claims, apart from the fact that, as argued above, society has an interest in children being born, educated and socialized. I shall try to show that the Rawlsian social contract also covers parents' rights.

Children are in the first place the responsibility of their parents. I like the way John Locke put it:

> From Adam the world is peopled with his descendants who are all born infants, weak and helpless, without knowledge or understanding. But to supply the defects of this imperfect state, till the improvements of growth and age hath removed them, Adam and Eve, and after them, all parents were, by the law of nature, under an obligation to preserve, nourish and educate the children they had begotten, not as their own workmanship, but the workmanship of their own maker, the Almighty, to whom they were to be accountable for them.

. . .

> The power then, that parents have over their children, arises from that duty which is incumbent on them, to take care of their offspring during the imperfect state of childhood. To inform the mind, and govern the actions of their yet ignorant nonage, till reason shall take its place, and ease them of that trouble, is what the children want, and the parents are bound to.
>
> (Locke [1689] 1993, pp. 142–3)

Here, Locke makes it clear that parents do not have unlimited power over their children: they hold the children, as it were, in trust.

But the parents may not have adequate means to 'preserve, nourish and educate' the children they have begotten. On the other hand, parents sometimes have the means, but not the will, to fulfil their obligation. Moreover, nourishing and caring for children takes time, time that cannot be spent earning one's living. So we must ask the questions: do children have just claims on society as a whole as well as on their parents? And to what extent are parents accountable to society and the state as well as to the Almighty for the way they treat their children?

Distributional policy aimed at children raises three different questions of distributional justice. The first is that of distribution over the life cycle; distribution between children and adults. The second is that of distribution between children. The third is that of distribution between generations. Rawls himself discusses the just distribution between generations, but makes his analysis depend on the assumption that each generation cares for the well-being of the next; a type of assumption he does not use as a basis for the main part of his work.

The present chapter will discuss distribution over the life course, and, to some extent, the distribution between children. In the following sections, I shall discuss how these questions are answered within the Rawlsian framework for social justice.

Children and the Rawlsian social contract

Rawls deduces his social contract from a thought experiment. Imagine an *original position* where free and equal persons meet to decide on the basic structure, the social contract, of a just society. The agreement must be made behind a thick *veil of ignorance*: the parties to the contract do not know their sex, their talents, their political and religious persuasion, their economic and social position in society. They do, however, know everything else there is to know about humankind and society. They are also rational, in the sense that the agreement is made on the basis of enlightened self-interest.

In other words: the parties must choose a social contract for a society they could like to live in whatever kind of person they will turn out to be, and whichever ultimate good they will turn out to have for their lives. Their problem can be stated as a form of choice under uncertainty.

Rawls argues that the parties will unanimously choose a society based on two fundamental principles: a principle of freedom and a principle of social and economic equality. The principle of freedom implies all the basic political liberties as well as the freedom for every individual to pursue the life project she chooses, to the extent that the project does not infringe on the similar liberty of other persons. The principle of equality Rawls states in a form which he confusingly calls the *difference principle*: social and economic inequalities are permissible only to the extent that they are to the advantage of the least favoured group of society. The reason why a certain degree of inequality might be of advantage to the least favoured lies in the possibility of economic incentives contributing to make production more efficient: increasing the 'size of the pie'.

Several critics have argued that the difference principle does not follow logically from Rawls's premises. But we do not have to accept the difference principle in order to find out what follows for the situation of children and their parents in the just society. The parties in the original situation are not ignorant of the facts of life in general, just of their own position in the order of things. Therefore, they know *with certainty* that they will start life as helpless infants, and spend their formative years utterly dependent on adults for their shelter, nourishment and care. They also know that the overwhelming majority of humankind wants to have children if they command the necessary time and other economic resources.[2]

It would seem then, that the parties in the original position would first of all secure for themselves favourable conditions during childhood. It is impossible to believe that rational agents would choose to face the risk of spending their childhood without rights, and without a lawful claim on society for protection from abuse, neglect and starvation. In particular, they would not wish to be the unconditional property of their parents. This will hold, I feel, whatever conclusions one may reach about the difference principle, and whatever weight we give to economic equality among adults.

In order to say something stronger about conditions for children, we need an idea of what is 'the good of children'. I shall discuss this below.

For reasons explained in several papers, and especially in 'The Idea of Public Reason Revisited' (1997), Rawls deliberately limits his discussion of justice to the rights and duties of normal adults as free citizens. He does not want his theory to encroach on what he considers to be private life. I suspect this is because private life, understood as the position of women and children in the family, is a particularly touchy matter in a 'multicultural' society, and often connected to what are perceived as religious duties and tenets. However, if we look at Rawls's premises, they contain nothing that should make the parties exclude childhood from their deliberations. And, in spite of Rawls's liberal worries on this score, a society where the state protects the rights of children while otherwise based on the Rawlsian social contract, will be a liberal one for the adults. There is nothing illiberal in the nanny state for children: children *need* nannies. For adults, there will be every kind of freedom, except the freedom to neglect and abuse their children. There will, moreover, be a civil society and a private sphere free from government intervention. But the boundary between government and civil society, between public and private spheres, will be drawn differently from that envisaged by Rawls and traditional political liberalism.[3]

The Rawlsian social contract can be interpreted as a framework for social insurance: every member of society is insured from before birth against certain contingencies. The parties in the original position determine the terms of insurance, and which contingencies it covers. One near certainty it is reasonable to cover is that of becoming a parent. Therefore, in a society built on the Rawlsian social contract, parents as well as their children have a moral claim for support. Rakowski is wrong: procreation does give rise to claims even though gambling does not.

The good of children: primary goods and capabilities

Rawls defines a liberal society as a society which allows several conflicting and incommensurable ideas of the good. The good here means the good life: what we want to live for and strive for in life. The good may but need not be welfare, well-being, happiness. In a liberal society, these several goods cannot, by definition, be provided by the state, since the state cannot, indeed ought not, know the good of each separate citizen. Individual welfare, or well-being, in particular, neither can nor should be the goal of public policy. The individual is responsible for her own welfare; the business of the state is to provide each person with the means necessary for obtaining welfare – or whichever other good she strives for.

Therefore, Rawls does not accept welfare as the goal of distributional or any other policies. He postulates that there exist what he calls primary goods, goods that every rational human being has a use for, whatever her preferences. As examples of primary goods he gives 'rights, liberties, and opportunities, and income and wealth' as well as 'the social bases for self-respect'. The first edition of *A Theory of Justice* can be read as if the primary goods were rooted in basic human nature, genetically and biologically determined. In later papers, particularly in 'Social Unity and Primary Goods', Rawls (1982) stresses that primary goods are not based on a specific philosophical view of human nature. Primary goods are necessary to every person as a citizen in society, and to underline this Rawls calls them 'social primary goods'. Here again, he clearly does not have children in mind. In particular, the primary good, 'income and wealth', is not suitable as the distributary good directed at children.

Another way of defining the quality of life and human advantage, independently of the preferences of the individual, is the capability approach advocated by Martha Nussbaum and Amartya Sen.[4] The rationale of the capability approach is found in Sen's statement that the important thing is 'the alternative combinations of things a person is able to do and be – the various "functionings" he or she can achieve' (Sen, 1993, p. 30). The term *capabilities* denote what a person is capable of being and doing. The 'beings and doings' themselves are called *functionings*.

By the capability approach is meant that the good to be aimed at in distributional and other public policies should be a bundle of capabilities for each individual; capabilities to achieve valuable functionings. The qualifier, 'valuable', here is important, since there are, conceivably, a great many desirable functionings. Examples of valuable functionings are adequate nourishment and social participation. Sen (1993) uses the example of lack of nourishment to illustrate the difference between a capability and the corresponding functioning. A starving person lacks the capability to nourish herself. A person who fasts, does so voluntarily. She has the capability of nourishment, but has chosen not to achieve the functioning.

The just distribution of income in capability terms is therefore the distribution that secures a just distribution of capabilities. Equality of income does not secure equality of capabilities for a number of reasons; these are most clearly set out in chapters 3 and 4 of Sen's *Development as Freedom* (1999). One of them is that different people may need different amounts of economic goods to achieve the same capabilities. The obvious examples are people with chronic illnesses like diabetes who need medication in order to function normally and people with physical handicaps who need special equipment in order to be mobile.

Martha Nussbaum distinguishes between three kinds of capabilities. There are basic capabilities, like hearing and seeing and the newborn child's innate capability for developing speech and language. Then internal capabilities that are developed in the adult person, like the capability for sexual pleasure and for free speech. Finally, there are combined capabilities 'which may be defined as internal capabilities *combined with* suitable external conditions for the exercise of the function' (Nussbaum, 2000, pp. 84–5).

The concept of combined capabilities brings out the idea that capabilities depend both on the endowments of the individual and on the way society is organized. An external condition for free speech is, of course, a society which allows freedom of speech, while a necessary external condition for the capability of sexual pleasure is the absence of genital mutilation.

The last example may be used as another illustration of the difference between the capability of functioning and the functioning itself. Sexual pleasure is not necessarily a functioning that everyone chooses to achieve. We may choose to remain celibate for a variety of reasons, religious or practical. The point of the capability approach is that there should be a free choice. Genital mutilation deprives women of that choice. Whether some of them would have chosen to abstain from sexual pleasure in any case is not to the point. Claiming the capability of sexual pleasure for every human being is different from claiming that social welfare increases with the number of orgasms per capita achieved.

No government can secure that all capabilities are equal. The government cannot make us all healthy or supply us all with equal amounts of the hormones that determine sexuality. But the government can provide a public health service and forbid genital mutilation. The government can deliver *the social basis* of such capabilities.

Sen (1999, pp. 30–1) argues that the capabilities to be targeted by public policy in a given society should be decided on after and by means of open democratic deliberation. This attitude is very much in the spirit of John Rawls, who argues that the goods to be distributed according to the difference principle should be 'a practical and limited list of things (primary goods) which free and equal moral persons . . . can accept that they in general need as citizens in a free society' (Rawls, 1982, p. 183). Moreover, the concepts of capabilities and of social primary goods are closely related: 'The capabilities approach, as I have articulated it, is very close to Rawls's approach using the notion of primary goods. We can see the list of capabilities as like a long list of opportunities for functioning, such that it is always rational to want them whatever else one wants' (Nussbaum, 2000, p. 88).

It seems to me that children's present and future capabilities are admirably suited to be the targets of government policies. The capability approach is as yet just that: an approach. It may or may not be operationalized as a set of measurable goals for public policy. It may or may not be superseded by other approaches. For the time being, it seems to be the best available theory of the public good covering the whole life cycle within the framework of liberal egalitarianism.

Just policies toward children

The Rawlsian social contract, modified to make individual capabilities the target of public policies, gives us a framework for discussing both distribution over the life cycle (between children and adults) and distribution between children.

I claimed above that rational choice in the original position would secure favourable conditions for every person in childhood. These favourable conditions will first of all consist in securing for every child the right to protection from abuse, neglect and starvation. Second, they would consist in securing for every child the flowering of present and development of future capabilities. These principles would obtain independently of the degree of economic equality chosen for adults. We do not need a fully worked out operational set of goals in order to set out the broad features of public policy to secure a satisfactory social basis for children's present and future capabilities. We know that children need love, security, a reasonable amount of material comfort, education, healthcare and opportunities to grow and develop.

The state, however benevolent, cannot secure love and emotional attachments. These matters are, and must be, the responsibility of the parents, biological or social. In the just society, we have seen that children are not the property of their parents: children's rights take precedence over parents' rights when there is a conflict. It is in the children's best interest that there is a balance of power between parents and public authorities. This balance of power I imagine must be continually discussed and revised.

The bases for other capabilities are a public responsibility. Some policies can and should target the children's capabilities directly, independently of the parents: free education and healthcare of reasonable quality for all are the most important. I feel the capability approach is a useful framework also for discussing the contents of education, but this is outside my competence.[5] The capability approach does not imply equality in the economic resources spent on children; public resources should be distributed according to need in the sense of what is needed to develop valuable capabilities.

Conditions for physical security, opportunities for play and interaction with other children and with grown-ups cannot in modern urban societies be left to the parents; they must be part of the physical public planning of the environment. When children and parents live together, the necessary material comfort of children cannot be separated from that of the parents. Securing an adequate home to live in is of particular importance, and an area where parents tend to need some financial and practical assistance.

Since children live with their parents, there will be economic inequality among children as long as there is economic inequality among adults. Now, there is no possible moral justification for economic and social inequality between children except what may be needed to secure the just distribution of their present and future capabilities. But complete equality in external conditions during childhood can only be obtained by completely cutting them off from parents and family and letting them grow up in government-run institutions. Such a policy seems unduly brutal towards both parents and children.

A policy geared towards securing every child the necessary resources to develop her capabilities will, however, ensure that there will be considerably less inequality between children than between adults, and that the remaining inequalities will not seriously damage the future prospects of less favoured children.

The policies I have sketched above constitute, in one form or another, the family policy of the traditional welfare state. They are also encoded in the United Nations Convention on the Rights of the Child. Some of them are under attack in the present political climate. I have tried to show that the Rawlsian social contract gives a strong moral justification for resisting these attacks.

Notes

1. Economic theory distinguishes between individual goods and public goods. Individual goods can be divided up and distributed among individuals. Public goods cannot be so divided, and therefore affect all members of society. The environment is a public good in this sense, as pollution is a public bad. On children as a public good, see also Folbre (1994).
2. According to Øystein Kravdahl, Professor of Demography, about 95 per cent of the population (private communication).
3. For a more detailed discussion, see the lucid and convincing exposition of liberalism, women's rights and religion in Nussbaum (1999).
4. Good sources are Nussbaum (2000) and Sen (1992 and 1999). See also the discussion in Nussbaum and Sen (1993). The website www.fas.harvard.edu/freedom has copious references and posts papers on the subject.
5. Gutman (1980) is an interesting paper on the subject.

References

Bojer, H. (2000) 'Children and Distributional Justice', *Feminist Economics*, 6 (2): 23–39.

Folbre, N. (1994) 'Children as Public Goods', *American Economic Review*, 84 (2): 86–90.

Gutman, A. (1980) 'Children, Paternalism and Education: a Liberal Argument', *Philosophy and Public Affairs*, 9 (4): 338–58.

Locke, John ([1689] 1993) *Two Treatises of Government*, London: Everyman.

Nussbaum, M.C. (1999) 'Women and Cultural Universals', in M.C. Nussbaum, *Sex and Social Justice*, Oxford: Oxford University Press, pp. 29–54.

Nussbaum, M.C. (2000) *Women and Human Development. The Capabilities Approach*, Cambridge: Cambridge University Press.

Nussbaum, M.C. and A.K. Sen (eds) (1993) *The Quality of Life*, Oxford: Clarendon Press.

Rakowski, E. (1993) *Equal Justice*, Oxford: Oxford University Press.

Rawls, J. (1971) *A Theory of Justice*, Cambridge, MA: Harvard University Press.

Rawls, J. (1982) 'Social Unity and Primary Goods', in A.K. Sen and B.Williams (eds), *Utilitarianism and Beyond*, Cambridge: Cambridge University Press, pp. 159–85.

Rawls, J. (1997) 'The Idea of Public Reason Revisited', *University of Chicago Law Review*, 64: 765–807.

Sen, A.K. (1992) *Inequality Re-examined*, Oxford: Clarendon Press.

Sen, A.K. (1993) 'Capability and Well-being', in Martha C. Nussbaum and Amartya Sen, *The Quality of Life*, Oxford: Clarendon Press, pp. 30–53.

Sen, A.K. (1999) *Development as Freedom*, Oxford: Oxford University Press.

14
Collective Action and Agency in Young Children's Peer Cultures

William A. Corsaro

Introduction

The notion that children are active agents in their own development and socialization is now generally accepted in psychology, sociology and education. Although nativist or biological and behaviouristic views of individual development still draw attention, constructivist developmental psychology, as seen in the theoretical approaches of Piaget (1950) and Vygotsky (1978), has had great influence on our appreciation of children's agency. More problematic and enduring is the image of the agency of the individual child; that is a focus on individual human development and how the child internalizes adult skills and knowledge.

Consider, for example, the views of the developmental psychologist William Damon who argues that the level of analysis for the study of human development and children's life transitions must always be at the individual level because 'it is the individual who does the moving, bringing along the vestiges of those interactions and relations that *this individual's* knowledge, memory and other systems of psychological awareness will allow' (Damon, 1996, p. 471; emphasis in the original). Children do, of course, develop individually, but throughout this development the collective processes they are always part of are also changing. These processes are most accurately viewed as occurring in the interwoven local or micro-cultures making up children's worlds (Geertz, 1983). When we discuss these collective processes developmentally or longitudinally, we must consider the nature of children's *membership* in these local cultures and *the changes in their degree or intensity* of membership and participation over time. We also must consider how different structural and institutional features constrain and enable the collective processes of interest. From this view human development, or perhaps better phrased the development of humans, is always collective and transitions are always collectively produced and shared with significant others. Thus, in reaction to Damon (1996), I argue that the level of analysis for studying childhood and children's life transitions must always be collective, the individual in interaction with others within cultural context (see Corsaro et al., 2002).

231

Some have argued that a new sociology of childhood should rid itself of this deeply ingrained focus on individual development and agency by disengaging completely from psychological views (James et al., 1998). Such disengagement is, to my mind, a mistake on two counts. First, it draws attention away from the great strides in sociocultural psychology (Rogoff, 1995, 1996; Wertsch, 1998) and to some extent system-based theories of human development (Thelen and Smith, 1998) which have raised provocative questions about the limits of individual internalization of knowledge and skills for human development and life transitions. Second, ridding ourselves of individualistic psychological views does not solve the problem of the micro–macro debates within sociology and anthropology regarding human agency where individualistic views of human agency still hold a great deal of prominence.

In my view of interpretive reproduction (which I have offered as an alternative to the term socialization; Corsaro, 2005) I have tried to bridge the micro–macro gap by stressing children's agency in their production and participation in their own unique peer cultures. These peer cultures result from children's creative appropriation of information from the adult world to address their own peer concerns. On the other hand, in line with the notion of reproduction, I argue that children are not simply internalizing society and culture, but are also actively contributing to cultural production and change. This emphasis on reproduction also implies that children are, by their very participation in society, constrained by the existing social structure and by social reproduction.

The overall focus on the importance of children's collective actions in producing their own peer cultures while at the same time contributing to forces of reproduction which are both enabling and constraining owes much to the theoretical work of Giddens (1984), Bourdieu (1977) and Qvortrup (1991). All three of these theorists have offered views of social practice which, although giving primary focus to the constraining forces of social structure and social reproduction, allow for a certain degree of human agency. Of these theorists it is Qvortrup in his argument that childhood is a social form and children are active co-constructors of their social worlds that best brings children and childhood into the picture of social practice and agency. For Giddens and Bourdieu there is little reference to children or childhood in their views of human agency. Qvortrup (1991), on the other hand, points to the importance of children at the macro-historical level and how their agency and contributions to society have changed over time. For example, he notes the importance of children's active engagement in their schooling as crucial to forces of social production in modern societies and how children often contribute to family work in the household given changes in family structure and the nature of the work force. However, while children's agency is obviously inferred from their contributions to social institutions like the school and family, the actual examination of the nature of children's collective actions demands a more micro- and temporally-situated view of agency.

Human agency as a temporally embedded process of social engagement

In a recent paper the sociologists Emirbayer and Mische (1998) set out to reconceptualize human agency as a temporally embedded process of social engagement. Emirbayer and Mische define human agency as:

> *the temporally constructed engagement by actors of different structural environments – which, through the interplay of habit, imagination, and judgment, both reproduces and transforms those structures in interactive response to the problems posed by changing historical situations.*

> (1998, p. 970; emphasis as in original)

In line with this definition, Emirbayer and Mische present a 'triad of agency' which involves: (1) an *iterational* element in which actors routinely incorporate *past* patterns of thought and action in practical activity; (2) a *projective* element in which actors imaginatively generate possible future trajectories of action through the creative reconfiguration of present structures of thought and action in relation to their hopes, fears, and desires for the *future*; and (3) a *practical-evaluative* element in which actors make practical and normative judgements between possible trajectories of action in response to emerging demands, dilemmas and ambiguities in *presently* evolving situations (1998, p. 971). Although the authors bracket out these three different temporal elements of agency for purposes of explication, they note that all three dimensions are found to varying degrees within any concrete empirical instance of action.

There are clearly strong cognitive elements to Emirbayer and Mische's temporal approach to agency. However, their insistence on situating interpretive processes in time and space helps to break down the individualistic, overly cognitive, and goal-oriented approaches to agency we see in rational choice and other theories in sociology based on means–ends rationality or assumptions of underlying cognitive schemas which guide decision-making and action (Coleman, 1990; Elster, 1989; Sewell, 1992). I have found in applying Emirbayer and Mische's triad of agency to children's collective actions in early education settings that behavioural and emotional aspects of agency rise to equal, if not greater, importance than cognitive aspects. Furthermore, when the theory is applied to actual cases the relational and collective nature of agency tends to overwhelm a focus on the individual actor.

I now turn to several examples from my research on children's peer cultures, examining agency in children's peer relations in terms of Emirbayer and Mische's iterational, projective and practical evaluative dimensions.

The iterational element: fantasy and role play in children's peer culture

According to Emirbayer and Mische the iterational element of agency refers to '*the selective reactivation by actors of past patterns of thought and action, as routinely incorporated in practical activity, thereby giving stability and order to social universes and helping to sustain identities, interactions, and institutions over time*' (1998, p. 971, italic as in original). Here Emirbayer and Mische place Bourdieu's (1977) 'habitus' and Giddens's (1979) 'routinized practical consciousness' both of which they see as related to a type of routinization that allows for strategic mobilization in specific interactional situations (1998, p. 978).

In my own work I have also built on these theorists in defining routines in children's peer cultures as providing both familiarity and security and the power to embellish and display personal styles and identities. Furthermore, in extending Giddens I see routines as not only providing security, but also an emotional camaraderie of doing things together. A much researched, but greatly under appreciated, example of the iterational element of agency in children's peer cultures is fantasy play. Piaget (1952) saw such play as almost totally emotional and egocentric, while George Herbert Mead (1934) and Vygotsky (1978) saw it as an important in the internalization of society and the development of self. However, micro-ethnographic research has identified the creativity and improvisational character of young children's fantasy play in a wide range of subcultural and cultural groups (Corsaro, 1985, 2005; Goldman, 1998; Sawyer, 1997; Schwartzman, 1978).

Emirbayer and Mische have referred to improvisation in routinized behaviour as '*maneuver, the improvisational orientation toward habitual practices, largely tacit and unreflective, which takes place in ongoing dialogue with situational contingencies*' (1998, p. 979; italics in original). In fantasy play this type of improvised 'maneuver' involves the children's use of shared knowledge of underlying themes or plots (such as danger-rescue, lost-found, death-rebirth) which they have developed as shared knowledge from the media and their repeated fantasy play (Corsaro, 1985, 2003). The 'maneuver' involves the use of this shared knowledge established in the past to create highly improvised fantasy play in the present. Furthermore, such improvisation is often accomplished without explicit reference to the shared knowledge or specific plans of action. In short, children impressively create much of their spontaneous fantasy activities totally in frame through collective turn-by-turn talk and physical action.

In spontaneous fantasy children use a number of identifiable communicative strategies. Here I examine a sequence from a longer play event that has a general theme of danger-rescue produced by children in a Berkeley pre-school I studied in 1975.

> Example 1 Improvisation in fantasy play
>
> Rita, Leah, and Charles (all around four years old) were kneeling around a sandbox playing with toy animals. I began videotaping the play shortly after the children entered the area.
> 'Help! Help! I'm in the forest,' says Rita as she moves a toy horse up and down in a hopping fashion.
> Charles hops his rabbit near the center of the sandbox and says, 'After you madam, into this fence.'
> Leah then places a goat next to Rita's horse, and asks, 'Where's your home?'
> 'Into this sandpile,' says Charles as he moves his rabbit under the sand.
> 'In here!' shouts Leah, moving her goat to the top of the sandpile.
> Charles removes his rabbit from the sand and places it near Leah's goat, 'Into this . . .'
> 'Into this hole!' yells Rita cutting Charles off as she moves her horse near his rabbit. Then Leah and Rita put their animals in the sand and cover them up. Rita hums, 'Do-do-da' as they do this. Charles watches with rabbit in hand near the top of the sandpile.

Highly important in spontaneous fantasy is the children's use of paralinguistic cues like voice quality and pitch. In their talk they use high pitch, heavy stress at the end of utterances, and rising intonation to mark that *they are the animals they are manipulating.* The children begin to structure their play through their manipulation of the animals, calls for help, and identification of a home inside the sandpile.

However, the play is just beginning to emerge. There are no suggestions offered regarding a plan of action for exactly what the play might involve (for example, 'Let's pretend we are the animals, this is our house, and there is a big storm'). Instead the kids rely on the nature of their speech and actions and the responses of their playmates to signify that they are playing together and must fit into the fantasy play with appropriate responses when necessary. In this case, appropriateness is tied to the contingencies of the ongoing play and is spontaneous in that the kids improvise the play theme by plugging into and expanding upon the contributions of each other.

Example 1   Continued

The play continues as Charles moves his rabbit up and down on the top of the sandpile and says, 'This is our b-i-i-i-g home! And I – I'm a freezing squirrel.' He then buries his animal in the sandpile. Leah takes another animal and buries it in the sandpile.

Rita then takes her horse from the sand and says, 'And this got out. And I'm freezing! Whoop-whoop-whoop-whoop!' Rita moves her horse up and down with each whoop.

Leah is smoothing the sand so the pile is higher and says to Rita, 'Get in the house.'

Rita now puts her horse in the sand and covers it saying, 'Oh-wow-get in the house!'

Rita next picks up a handful of sand and sprinkles it onto the pile. As she does this she shouts, 'Oh look, it's raining. Gonna rain.'

Charles now takes his squirrel from the sand and says, 'Rain. It's gonna be a rainstorm!'

'Yeah,' replies Rita.

'And lightning. Help!' yells Charles.

Charles now moves his squirrel away from the sandpile to the other side of the sandbox and says, 'But I won't be hit, though – cause lightning only hits a bigger – bigger – will hit our house cause it's the biggest thing. Cause our house is made of –'

Leah interrupts Charles as she and Rita take their animals from the sand saying, 'Going-going-'

'But our house is made of steel,' continues Charles. 'So the lightning just falls to the ground.' Charles now returns his squirrel to the sandpile.

'Right,' says Rita. 'Won't get horsie.' Rita and Leah now place their animals back in the sandpile.

Charles introduces the idea that the sandpile can be a home for the animals, and that he (the rabbit he is holding) is a freezing squirrel. In his first turn of speech in this sequence Charles stresses the adjective 'b-i-i-i-g', elongating it to mark his transformation of the sandpile into a home for the animals. Rita then takes her horse from the sand and connects her activity to Charles's by repetition of the phrase, 'I'm freezing.' Here Rita is tying her action to Charles's earlier one by repeating his original idea (the animals are freezing when outside the house). Leah then takes a turn telling Rita to 'get in the house'. Here we have an expansion on Charles's original notion in that Leah is telling Rita that it will be warmer inside. Rita responds appropriately by putting her horse back in the sand.

The interesting thing about Rita's action is that her speech and physical manipulation of the toy horse are fused as she describes her action as she does it. I have found in spontaneous play that kids consistently provide verbal descriptions of their behaviour. When viewed from an adult perspective such descriptions might be labelled as 'egocentric' speech. Piaget characterized much of the language and thought of pre-school children as egocentric, arguing that it was basically emotional and self-directed rather than social. However, the description of ongoing activity in spontaneous fantasy is important in that it cues other participants to what is presently occurring and allows the kids to take up and expand upon the emerging social event. As we saw, that is what happened in this case as the kids respond to descriptions of actions to extend their play.

After Rita puts her horse in the sandpile home she does something which is an excellent example of the improvisational nature of spontaneous fantasy. As she covers her horse with sand she notices that the sand was falling on the pile like raindrops, and says, 'Oh, look it's raining. Gonna rain.' The emergence of the rain was spontaneous and unpredictable. It occurred because Rita happened to be sprinkling the sand from above rather than raking it onto the pile. In her utterance Rita calls attention to her spontaneous extension of the play and then states it. Thus, she provides for the organization of her behaviour and a semantic base and underlying plot (danger-rescue) on which the other children can build.

This is just what Charles does, first marking Rita's new addition and extending it to a 'rainstorm' and receiving confirmation from Rita. Charles then goes on to add 'lightning' to the rainstorm and suggests leaving the house to avoid a lightning strike because the house is the biggest thing. As Charles communicates this idea he takes his animal from the house as do the two girls. However, in this very process of cautioning about the possibility of lightning striking the house, Charles reverses his thinking. He decides that the house is made of steel, so 'the lightning just falls to the ground'. He is describing a sort of 'lightning rod' idea. He then puts his animal back in the sandpile, as do the two girls, with Rita noting that the lightning 'won't get horsie'.

An awful lot has happened in this sequence in just a few minutes of play. The children reach an agreement that they are the animals they animate, that the animals have a home, that it is cold outside the home and warm inside, that it begins to rain, that the rain becomes a storm with lightning, that the lightning might hit the house because it is a big target, and finally that the house is safe from a lightning strike because it is made of steel. The kids accomplish the collaborative fantasy play through subtle use of various features of language. In no case do they offer up a script or plan of action nor do they use stage directions which place them outside the action (for example, 'Let's pretend there's a rainstorm'). In short, the fantasy play is constituted totally in the social interaction itself. This complex improvised feat is accomplished by the use of paralinguistic cues (voice, pitch, intonation), orchestrated manipulation of play objects (the toy animals and sand), verbal descriptions of actions, repetition of speech and action, and semantic tying and expansion (for example, from rain, to a rainstorm, to lightning).

It is easy to overlook the improvisational nature of spontaneous fantasy play of this type because for most adults it is seen as 'just kids playing make believe'. However, I would challenge any adult to try to produce such make-believe play in this totally in-frame (that is, without 'out-of-frame' discussion of plans for action), implicit, improvised way. It seems easy until you analyse it very closely or try to do it. Adults are appreciative of the complexity of such improvisation, *if adults are doing it*. We pay to see improvised comedy shows like *Second City* and sing the praises of and lavishly reward comedians like Robin Williams. However, for pre-school children, it's just 'kids playing make believe around a sandbox'. We see what we look for.

One reason for this misconception of fantasy play is its routinized nature as something kids do all the time. The fact that it is iterational in Emirbayer and Mische's sense makes such play taken for granted by the children themselves. However, agency in involved in several ways. First, through the linkage of present ongoing activities to shared knowledge acquired in the past (that is, underlying plots or themes like danger-rescue, lost-found and death-rebirth) through play, in fairy tales told to the children, and from films they have seen. Second, the improvised nature of the production of the fantasy play takes the children beyond simply imitating or repeating shared knowledge from the past, to refining, extending, and transforming it in ways that emerge through coordinated activity in the present.

Therefore, we see that when we look at the fantasy play on its own terms it clearly displays young children's collective agency. I go further to claim that pre-school children are more adept at this type of creative activity than are older children (who abandon fantasy play for games with rules) and adults. In this sense, we not only overlook a key aspect of agency of young children, but as we were all children once, we lose, through a lack of practice, the very skills to produce such improvised activities in our routine activities.

The projective element: *discussione* and meta-narratives in role play

Emirbayer and Mische see imaginative engagement of the future (or projectivity) as a crucial component of agency. The locus of agency in projectivity is:

> *hypothesization* of experience, as actors attempt to reconfigure received schemas by generating alternative possible responses to the problematic

situations they confront in their lives. Immersed in a temporal flow, they move "beyond themselves" into the future and construct changing images of where they think they are going, where they want to go, and how they can get there from where they are at present.

(Emirbayer and Mische, 1998, p. 984; italics in original)

According to Emirbayer and Mische the projective element of agency often arises in a variety of interactive situations, two of which are conflict resolution and the reflective awareness that occurs in narrative construction. In this chapter for the purpose of space I will examine only the first of these, conflict resolution.

Until relatively recently conflict among children was seen in a negative light and the little research that existed focused on how children acquired skills and strategies to avoid or resolve conflict. However, recent research has shown that conflict is a natural element of children's peer relations. Furthermore, it contributes to the social organization of peer groups, the development and strengthening of friendship bonds, the reaffirmation of cultural values, and the individual development and display of self (Corsaro, 1994; Corsaro and Rizzo, 1988; Goodwin, 1990; Maynard, 1935; Shantz, 1987). In my research with Italian children I have found that they frequently participate in highly complex and stylized debates and discussions which Italians refer to as *discussione*.

Discussione is highly valued in Italian culture and children participate in such discussions and debates from an early age with peers, teachers and parents (Corsaro, 2005; Orsolini and Pontecorvo, 1992; Pontecorvo et al., 2001). Here I consider a debate among three boys (Dante, Mario and Enzo, all around six years old and in their last year at a pre-school in Bologna). The boys had just finished playing a board game and were now considering a new play alternative. Dante suggested playing with Clipo (a type of building material) that he was especially adept in using to build spaceships and other objects. Enzo and Mario immediately rejected this suggestion and a debate ensued that first centred around Dante's expertise in building things with Clipo. Enzo agreed that Dante does indeed construct beautiful things with Clipo, but he argued that this was because Dante has Clipo at home. Therefore, when he watched cartoons with spaceships he could practise building models of them. In his argument Enzo actually pretended to be Dante at home changing the channels on his television to find a particular programme 'Transformers' that changed from robots to spaceships. Enzo said after Dante watched the show he used Clipo to copy the spaceships in the programme. Dante rejected this interpretation of his expertise and the debate then turned to coming changes in peer culture that will occur when the children leave the preschool and move on to elementary school.

Example 2   Clipo

Enzo: Ma no, è lì il problema il clipo non è mica l'unica cosa al mondo che c'è. Ci sono tante altre cose, eh?
(But no, there is the problem, clipo is not the only thing that there is in the world. There are many other things, eh?)

Dante: Enzo, questo qua non è vero. Tu dici che – questo qua – queste cose qua non sono mica vere.
(Enzo, what you just said is not true. You said that – these here – these things are not true.)

. . .

E: Si ma poi dopo vedrai che tu ti ci annoi dopo un po' a giocare a clippo, capito Dante?
(Yes, but then you'll see that after a while you get bored playing with clipo, understood D?)

D: No, non è vero questa cosa.
(No, this is not true.)

E: Allora sta' a vedere che io ho ragione, perché quando tu avrai vent'anni e saprai già scrivere, clippo non l'avrai, non li avrai più i giocattolini.
(Now do you want to bet that I'm right, because when you're twenty and already know how to write, clipo you won't have it, you won't have them anymore these little toys.)

. . .

D: Perche veramente, ascolta, io ci gioco sempre per costruire le astronavi e per vedere se (mi vengono) se e possible farle. Io davvero da grande posso fare il lavoro che mi piace perche io –
(Because really, listen, I always play with it in order to build spaceships and see how they come out and to see if it is possible to make them. When I'm grown up, I'll really be able to do the work that I like because I –)

E: Si, ma prima tu ti devi allenare a fare quella roba li. Non e mica che tu ti scegli un lavoro quando non lo sai neanche fare.
(Yes, but first you have to practise doing that stuff. It's not that you choose for yourself a job when you don't even know how to do it.)

In the first part of the discussion there is a shift away from talk about expertise in making things with Clipo, to a more general evaluation of the activity as an important feature of peer culture. In a series of turns, Enzo skilfully dismisses the importance of Dante's expertise with Clipo by arguing that the activity is a childlike pursuit that will be left behind with the children's transition to elementary school.

We see that Enzo is looking to the future and arguing that activities and objects valued in the present will pale in comparison to future alternatives. Although Enzo is overestimating how long it will take to learn how to write, he is aware that instruction in writing begins in elementary school and that the acquisition of this and other skills will lead the children to look back on activities like playing with Clipo as silly and boring. In short, Enzo is telling Dante that to remain part of this friendship group it is necessary to look to the future and not cling to the childish activities of the present.

In the second part of the discussion, Dante makes a final attempt to hold his ground in the debate with Enzo and Mario. His argument is complex. First he gains the floor with the stylized phrase 'Because really, listen.' Attention markers of this type are frequently used in Italian adult and children's *discussione* to both secure a turn at talk and to signal a coming disagreement to the previous claims of others. Dante then goes on to note that he does indeed play with Clipo to build spaceships, but then he argues that he does so 'to see how they come out, to see if it is possible to make them'. This last phrase is striking in that Dante relates his building of spaceships in play to the possibility of the more serious activity of design engineering. In short, Dante is attempting to link the activities of the current peer culture to his perception of possible adult activities in his future. This attempted linkage is highly creative in that he is implicitly arguing that real engineers work first from models not all that different than the ones he creates with Clipo.

Enzo quickly interrupts Dante, however, and argues that it is not possible just to choose a profession so easily. He maintains that it takes training and practice. Again the boys' perception of the timing and nature of the socialization process is striking. Enzo seems to be saying that Dante's linkage of pre-school peer activities to adult professions involves too big a leap of faith and that occupational socialization is much more complex than he thinks it is. The projective element of agency is obvious in this debate as the boys build 'hypothetical resolutions' (Emirbayer and Mische, 1998, p. 990) which they evaluate and debate further. In the process they project themselves into their futures both near (when in elementary school) and far off (when they are in adult occupations).

Conflict, negotiation and peace: children's creative articulation of the past, present and future

Emirbayer and Mische argue that the problematization of experience in response to emergent situations calls for increasingly reflective and interpretive work for social actors. They refer to this reflective and interpretive work as the practical-evaluative dimension of agency (1998, p. 994). The primary locus of the practical-evaluative dimension of agency lies in what

Emirbayer and Mische refer to as the 'contextualization of social experience' (1998, p. 994). Here they borrow from the pragmatic philosophers Mead and Dewey and their views are very similar to the pragmatic approach of discourse analysts such as Gumperz (1982). In the contextualization of social experience actors arrive at shared definitions of the nature of ongoing interaction and 'gain in the capacity to make considered decisions that may challenge received patterns of action' (Emirbayer and Mische, 1998, p. 994). Thus, social actors go beyond the tacit manoeuvres and embellishments of the iterational and to some extent the projective dimension, to 'exercise agency in a *mediating* fashion, enabling them (at least potentially) to pursue projects in ways that may challenge and transform the situational contexts of action themselves' (Emirbayer and Mische, 1998, p. 994; emphasis in original).

Within the contextualization of social experience in the practical-evaluative dimension of agency, social actors recognizing that a concrete situation at hand is ambiguous or unresolved – what Emirbayer and Mische call ('problematization') – examine the ambiguity in terms of existing habitual activity, predispositions or schemas ('characterization'), evaluate possible courses of action against the backdrop of broader fields of possibilities and aspirations ('deliberation'), reach consensus on a provisional course or courses of action ('decision') and carry out such actions ('execution'). In this view agency is not the result of individual reflection or based on means–ends rational choice, but is instead deeply imbedded or situated in collective activities in concrete social settings. For example, 'decisions' are always somewhat ambiguous and provisional, argue Emirbayer and Mische, and they refer to Dewey (1940) who spoke of flexible 'ends-in-view' rather than of clear and fixed objectives (1998, p. 999).

Another example from children's collective actions in a pre-school setting can capture the practical-evaluative dimension of agency. In a pre-school I studied in Modena, Italy, the children were members of one of four groups: a three-year-old group, a four-year-old group, and two five-year-old groups. Because the children stayed together in the same group with the same teachers from their entry to the school at age three, the kids in the four- and five-year-old groups had already spent a considerable amount of time together and formed close bonds. A key object of my research was to investigate the school and peer culture of one of the five-year-old groups and then make the transition with them to elementary school. Shortly after I joined and was accepted into my group of five-year-olds in February 1996, the kids in my group made a point of telling the kids in the other five-year-old group that 'Bill is part of our class!'

This was just one indication of a mostly friendly (but at times serious) competition between the two five-year-old groups. The kids in the two groups mixed well together in activities which involved the whole school such as the party at *Carnevale* (Mardi Gras) and another party at the end of the school year. The boys from the two groups also joined together at times for games of soccer, and girls from the two groups occasionally visited and talked during free play in the outside yard. However, during such free play there was always some tension and, at times, conflict which had to be settled by teachers (something which seldom occurred within the groups where the children were almost always left alone to settle their own disputes).

The example we consider took place in mid-April a few weeks before children from both five-year-old groups would be visiting the nearby elementary school that most of them would attend in the autumn. The children now were aware of the fact that their time in pre-school was coming to an end, and that when they attended first grade they would become part of a new group of kids with new teachers. Let's consider the example which I recorded in field notes that involves the escalation and resolution of a dispute between the children in the two five-year-old groups.

Example 3   *La Guerra Del'Erba* ('The Grass War')

The outside yard had been freshly mowed with cut grass lying all around. Some of the girls (Elisa, Carlotta and Michela) begin gathering the grass and take it to an area under the climbing structure where they make a bed. At one point, Michela and then others lie down on the bed and say: 'Che morbido!' ('How soft it is!'). Several other girls enter the play, but Elisa, Carlotta and Michela control the activity. The new recruits are allowed to bring grass, but not place it on the bed.

Later Carlotta returns to say that one of the boys from the other five-year-old group hit her while she was gathering grass. The other girls become upset and decide to go get the boy. The girls march over carrying grass, come up behind the boy, and pummel him with the grass. The girls then run back to the climbing structure and celebrate their revenge – especially Carlotta who is all smiles. Eventually the boy gets a few of his friends and they come by and throw grass at the girls. The girls chase after the boys who are outnumbered and take the worst of it in another exchange of grass throwing.

The grass war now escalates with girls and boys on both sides becoming involved. In fact, all but a few of the five-year-old group I am part of are now in the grass war. The war continues for some time until Marina suggests to the kids in our group that they make peace. All of the other kids except for Carlotta agree. Carlotta argues against the proposal saying that the other group started the conflict. However, Marina with several kids behind her marches up to the boy who hit Carlotta and offers her hand in peace. The boy responds by throwing grass in

Continued

> Marina's face. Marina returns to the group, and Carlotta says: 'They don't want peace!' But Marina says she will try again. The second time she offers her hand the boy throws grass again, but over the objections of another boy who is in his group. Marina stands her ground after being hit with the grass. The second boy pulls his friend aside and suggests they make peace. The other boy is against the proposal, but eventually agrees and the two then shake hands with Marina. Marina then returns to the group and declares: 'We now have peace!' The two groups now meet for a formal round of handshaking and pats on the back. I also exchange handshakes with kids from the other five-year-old group who identify me as part of the opposing group.

It was clear to me as we went out into the yard on the day of this example that the kids would probably end up throwing grass. It was too tempting to merely leave the grass on the ground and not incorporate it into their play in some way. I was impressed by the girls' idea of making beds with the grass and also their division of labour in line with the general rule of 'who comes up with the play idea has ultimate control over it'. Here we see a common feature of peer culture, the kids appropriating adult actions and materials (the cutting of the grass and the grass itself) and creating a play activity.

I was with the girls at the climbing structure and did not actually see what happened between Carlotta and the boy from the other five-year-old group. I doubt he actually hit her, perhaps he pushed or shoved her for some reason. In any case, Carlotta's report is taken seriously by the other girls, and, in line with the ongoing tension between the two groups, the girls decide quickly to come to Carlotta's defence. It also gives them an opportunity and reason to 'throw grass' at the offending party.

To this point in the play the children's activities are much in line with Emirbayer and Mische's iterational element of agency in that conflicts between the two groups were quite common. What makes this particular conflict more interesting is that it is girls against boys (at least at the start) and the fact that there was grass to use as a weapon in a playful war. In this sense the dramatic and emotional elements of the activity are heightened and a normal conflict is embellished. Given the playful nature of the grass war and the fact that no child went to the teachers to complain, the teachers did not intervene. Like me I think they expected that there was bound to be some grass throwing and probably would have intervened if things got out of hand.

Marina's suggestion that the children in our group make peace with the other group is what defines the situation as problematic and different from past conflicts. The idea of trying to gain peace during disputes was quite common, but I only saw it occur within the group I studied and not between my group and other groups in the school. There is some question as to why Marina suggested peace in this instance. It cannot be known for sure, but the fact that both of the five-year-old groups were nearing the end of their time in the school may have been important. The children were aware that most of them (in both groups of five year olds) would be attending the same nearby elementary school. Furthermore, there had already been talk of visits to the school that both groups would make in a few weeks. In fact, at least some of the children from both groups may have realized that they may be in the same class in elementary school.

Although my interpretation of factors that motivated Marina are some-what speculative, the fact that she does propose peace takes the activity beyond the ordinary and makes it recognizable as something '*ambiguous, unsettled, or unresolved*' (Emirbayer and Mische, 1998, p. 998; italics in origi-nal). Marina's proposal sets in motion a deliberation and a decision in her group to seek peace. Not everyone agrees. Carlotta argues against the idea and several other children are silent. However, when Marina walks over to the boy who started the conflict all of the children (including Carlotta) follow behind her, implicitly endorsing the decision and its execution (that being Marina's offering of her hand in peace). The result is negative as the boy throws grass in Marina's face in response to her offer. However, instead of resuming the conflict Marina reconvenes her group, and over the objections of Carlotta (who says, 'They do not want peace!'), Marina says she will try again. In Marina's second attempt the boy still throws grass, but over the objections of another boy in his group. At this point the episode has become highly dramatic as the two boys from the five-year-old group huddle together to discuss a response while Marina awaits their decision. Now there is in Dewey's (1940) terms an 'ends-in-view' as the boy who set off the conflict with Carlotta is still resistant to peace. However, in the end he agrees and the boys decide to make peace and shake hands with Marina. Marina then returns to our group and announces peace. The announcement is followed by a round of handshaking among all the members of the two groups.

The decision to try to establish peace and its execution and accomplish-ment is highly symbolic given the tension that has existed between the two groups throughout the year. Now near the end of their time together in the school they reach a highly public resolution to a major conflict. They have acted rightly and effectively and their action is nicely characterized by Aristotle who notes that to respond 'at the right times, with reference to the right objects, toward the right people, with the right aim, and in the right way, is what is appropriate and best and this [is what] is characteristic of excellence' (Aristotle, 1985, p. 44 as quoted in Emirbayer and Mische, 1998, p. 1000).

Conclusion

I have argued that full examination of children's agency must be grounded both in the careful examination of theoretical traditions and approaches to the concept and in the application of these theoretical approaches to the actual practice of agency in children's peer cultures. I selected the temporal pragmatic approach to agency of Emirbayer and Mische (1998) as the most fruitful among various perspectives. In doing so I provided examples and analyses of Emirbayer and Mische's iterational, projective and practical-evaluative elements of agency as produced in various activities in children's peer cultures. I argue that these examples take us from general claims that children are active agents to evidence of their agency situated in concrete activities and in the theoretical perspectives on agency in sociology more generally. In this way, we see that the study of children and childhood is important in its own right, while it can also contribute to important theoretical debates in sociological theory.

References

Aristotle (1985) *Nicomachean Ethics*, translated by T. Irwin, Indianapolis, IN: Hackett.

Bourdieu, P. (1977) *Outline of a Theory of Practice*, New York: Cambridge University Press.

Coleman, J. (1990) *Foundations of Social Theory*, Cambridge, MA: Harvard University Press.

Corsaro, W.A. (1979) 'Young Children's Conception of Status and Role', *Sociology of Education*, 52: 46–59.

Corsaro, W.A. (1985) *Friendship and Peer Culture in the Early Years*, Norwood, NJ Ablex.

Corsaro, W.A. (1994) 'Discussion, Debate, and Friendship: Peer Discourse in Nursery Schools in the United States and Italy', *Sociology of Education*, 67: 1–26.

Corsaro, W.A. (2003) *'We're Friends, Right?': Inside Kids' Cultures*, Washington DC: Joseph Henry Press.

Corsaro, W.A. (2005) *The Sociology of Childhood* (2nd edition), Thousand Oaks, CA: Pine Forge Press.

Corsaro, W.A., L. Molinari and K.B. Rosier (2002) 'Zena and Carlotta: Transition Narratives and Early Education in the United States and Italy', *Human Development*, 45: 323–48.

Corsaro, W.A. and T.A. Rizzo (1988) *'Discussione* and Friendship: Socialization Processes in the Peer Culture of Italian Nursery School Children', *American Sociological Review*, 53: 879–94.

Damon, W. (1996) 'Nature, Second Nature, and Individual Development: an Ethnographic Opportunity', in R. Jessor, A. Colby and R. Shweder (eds), *Ethnography and Human Development: Context and Meaning in Social Inquiry*, Chicago: University of Chicago Press, pp. 459–78.

Dewey, J. (1940) 'Creative Democracy: the Task before Us', in S. Ratner (ed.), *The Philosophy of the Common Man: Essays in Honor of John Dewey to Celebrate his Eightieth Birthday*, New York: Greenwood, pp. 220–8.

Elster, J. (1989) *The Cement of Society: a Study of Social Order*, Cambridge: Cambridge University Press.

Emirbayer, M. and A. Mische (1998) 'What is Agency', *American Journal of Sociology*, 103: 962–1023.

Geertz, C. (1983) *Local Knowledge: Further Essays in Interpretive Anthropology*, New York: Basic Books.

Giddens, A. (1979) *Central Problems in Social Theory*, Berkeley, CA: University of California Press.

Giddens, A. (1984) *The Constitution of Society*, Oxford: Polity Press.

Goldman, L.R. (1998) *Child's Play: Myth, Mimesis and Make-believe*, New York: Oxford.

Goodwin, M.H. (1990) *He-said-she-said: Talk as Social Organization among Black Children*, Bloomington, IN: Indiana University Press.

Gumperz, J.J. (1982) *Discourse Strategies*, New York: Cambridge University Press.

James, A., C. Jenks and A. Prout (1998) *Theorizing Childhood*, New York: Teachers College Press.

Maynard, D. (1985) 'On the Functions of Social Conflict among Children', *American Sociological Review*, 50: 207–23.

Mead, G.H. (1934) *Mind, Self, and Society*, Chicago: University of Chicago Press.

Orsolini, M. and C. Pontecorvo (1992) 'Children's Talk in Classroom Discussion', *Cognition and Instruction*, 9: 113–36.

Piaget, J. (1950) *The Psychology of Intelligence*, London: Routledge & Kegan Paul.

Piaget, J. (1952) *The Language and Thought of the Child*, London: Routledge & Kegan Paul.

Pontecorvo, C., A. Fasulo and L. Sterponi (2001) 'Mutual Apprentices: the Making of Parenthood and Childhood in Family Dinner Conversations', *Human Development*, 44: 340–61.

Qvortrup, J. (1991) 'Childhood as a Social Phenomenon: an Introduction to a Series of National Reports', in *Eurosocial Report No. 36*, Vienna: European Centre for Social Welfare Policy and Research.

Rogoff, B. (1995) 'Observing Sociocultural Activity on Three Planes: Participatory Appropriation, Guided Participation, and Apprenticeship', in J.V. Wertsch, P. Del Río and A. Alvarez (eds), *Sociocultural Studies of Mind*, New York: Cambridge University Press, pp. 139–64.

Rogoff, B. (1996) 'Developmental Transitions in Children's Participation in Sociocultural Activities', in A. Sameroff and M. Haith (eds), *The Five to Seven Year Shift*, Chicago: University of Chicago Press, pp. 273–94.

Sawyer, R.K. (1997) *Pretend Play as Improvisation*, Mahwah, NJ: Lawrence Erlbaum.

Schwartzman, H. (1987) *Transformations: the Anthropology of Children's Play*, New York: Plenum.

Sewell, W.H. Jr (1992) 'A Theory of Structure: Duality, Agency, and Transformations', *American Journal of Sociology*, 98: 1–29.

Shantz, C.U. (1987) 'Conflicts between Children', *Child Development*, 58: 283–305.

Thelen, E. and L. Smith (1998) 'Dynamic Systems Theories', in R. Lerner (ed.), *Handbook of Child Psychology*, New York: Wiley, pp. 563–634.

Vygotsky, L.S. (1978) *Mind in Society*, Cambridge, MA: Harvard University Press.

Wertsch, J.V. (1998) *Mind as Action*, New York: Oxford University Press.

15
Life Times: Children's Perspectives on Age, Agency and Memory across the Life Course

Allison James

Introduction

There is – or at least there used to be – an English saying that 'your school days are the best days of your life' and as such, this phrase forms part of the contemporary mythologizing of childhood in England. This widely portrays childhood as a time of happiness, as a time for being carefree and innocent, a time when the world's woes are held at bay (Gittens, 1998). In this chapter, however, I use the term mythology more deliberately, recalling Roland Barthes's (1976) usage to describe the stories or 'myths' that are told about life events and which, in time, become motifs around which particular complexes of ideas are strung or through which particular personae emerge. These cultural myths, which we tell ourselves or which are told to us, he suggests, provide schemas for our thinking and a charter for our actions.

In this chapter I explore time passing across the life course as a key feature of the mythologizing of childhood through examining the narratives of ageing through which childhood is conceived. First I show how the concept of 'age', as a life-course marker, is used by adults to structure individual children's life-course careers in particular ways to produce particular kinds of childhood identities. I then move on to ask whether children themselves similarly use ideas of age and ageing across the life course as mythologies for the self and, if so, in what ways do they use them? To what extent, for example, do children use memories of past events and the anticipation of events yet to come as age-based schemas for the self, as ways in which particular subjectivities can be narrated and brought into being? And, to what extent therefore, do these temporalized identities work as myths that provide children with charters for the self and for individual action?

In exploring these issues I want to achieve three things: first, to reclaim for children their subjectivity, an ability to be reflexive about their lives and their identities and to articulate this to themselves as well as to others. That children are still rarely credited with this kind of agency, despite the growth in more child-centred perspectives both within and outside the academy, leads to my second reason for examining children's ideas of age and the life course: to argue that, although the concepts of autobiography or of life history have been most often used by social scientists with respect to adults, they are also pertinent to the discussion of children's lives, despite the relative shortness of the time children have lived. Finally, I want to consider the extent to which framing children's thinking and being in this reflexive way, rather than seeing children simply as 'becomings' (Lee, 2001), might enable us to question the 'ageism' with which children are saddled and which often, for individual children, poses problems for their everyday lives and social relations (see James and James, 2004).

Age and ageism in childhood

It was the French historian Philippe Ariès (1962) who was one of the first to suggest that modern definitions of childhood are bedevilled by concepts of numerical age when he indicated the extent to which being able to know one's age is a fundamental necessity of modern life, a bureaucratic demand that comes with every form that has to be filled in. By contrast, in premodern times, as Gillis (1996) has more recently argued, the accounting of numerical age played an insignificant role in people's everyday lives. Schooling, for example, was not simply something which took place in childhood. Instead, those who had access to it – for not all social classes did – might dip in and out of education over a long period of time, as and when it could be fitted in with the demands of family life and making a living. It was only after 1870 that the acute age-consciousness, with which we are now so familiar, emerged. From then on, Gillis notes, 'so as not to appear unnatural, everyone did their utmost to "act their age" from birth to death' (Gillis, 1996, p. 84). Thus, as Hockey and James (2002) argue, the precise chronologization of ageing, regarded as a 'natural' and unremarkable feature of contemporary representations of the life course, is in fact a relatively recent social phenomenon, a by-product of the rationalization of all aspects of life which industrialization brought with it.

But what did this rigid chronologization of the life course achieve? As Hockey and James (2002) argue, the marrying of biological processes to sequential units of time imposed an orderliness over the changing and transitory *physical* body, by overlaying the bodily experience of 'getting older' with a variety of *social* meanings and obligations. Thus, for example, it is not simply as a result of the physical ageing process per se, that children leave childhood and become adults. Though their bodies change and mature willy-nilly, the status of 'adulthood' has to be socially achieved – in the UK, currently, by reaching the age of 18, the age of legal majority when children can assume 'adult' rights and their associated responsibilities. Elsewhere (and despite the United Nation Convention on the Rights of the Child

(CRC) making 18 the universal age of adulthood) the assumption of adult status may, however, be marked more through the practical taking on of domestic or social responsibilities than through the symbolic achievement of an age per se.

'Adulthood' thus represents primarily a particular *social* category in the chronologized life course that is highly characteristic of modernity, which may – but need not – reflect processes of bodily maturation (Hockey and James, 2002). In this sense, therefore, the categorical stage of 'adulthood' (and therefore correspondingly of 'childhood'; Jenks, 1996) can be regarded largely as arbitrary, fixed as it is by custom and practices of law. Thus, as Lee (2001) has recently argued, the idea of a 'standard adulthood' as completeness is a fiction from the Fordist era, something which potentially is now becoming destabilized by changes in both the economic and intimate lives of adults. It follows then that the social category of childhood is also in many ways arbitrary and not necessarily determined by the age and biology of children's bodies, despite the increasing push towards standardizing childhood embedded within the discourses of developmental psychology and child health promotion (James, 2005, forthcoming).

Notwithstanding such observations, the social and cultural fixing of a chronologized and numerical identity for children (and adults) within the life course has consequences for our understanding of lives as lived and for the kinds of myths people live by. In the case of children, for example, it is their *lack* of age which sets them apart and which sequesters them within special child-spaces such as schools and playgrounds while simultaneously denying them access to adult spaces, such as the factory and the pub. Indeed, it is precisely such everyday separatist policies that have lead Mayall to conclude that the 'study of children's lives . . . is essentially the study of child–adult relations' and thus in order to understand childhood, the concept of 'generation' must be regarded as key (2002, p. 21). And Mayall goes on to argue for a new concept of generationing, defined by her as 'the relational processes whereby people come to be known as children, and whereby children and childhood acquire certain characteristics, linked to local contexts, and changing as the factors brought to bear change' (Mayall, 2002, p. 27).

As noted elsewhere (James and James, 2004), a key driver of this wedge between children and adults has been the discipline of developmental psychology and its assertion of a common developmental and *age-based* path for *all* children. Its normalizing remit plots for children a steady progression, over time, of the acquisition of skills and abilities, and while clearly there is some utility in identifying stages of developmental progress, in order to identify any problems a child might be encountering, tying this to a rigid age scheme creates anomalies. Those who fail to make the mark in good time risk being identified as 'abnormal'. In English this is rendered colloquially in developmental terms as being 'backward' or, 'developmentally delayed', that is, as being literally behind times (James, 2005, forthcoming). And when this practice is translated into more 'social' contexts – used in the UK for example in the target-setting of children's educational achievements or for judging the 'age' at which children can be allowed some agency and participation in their own affairs – its value is even less certain.[1]

The findings of a recent study of practitioners who work as advocates for children in the courts in Britain illustrates the powerful role that the developmental model has in filtering understandings of children's competencies and abilities to express their views.[2] Practitioners argued, for example, that they would not bother consulting very young children about their wishes and feelings and at only around middle childhood, say nine, ten or eleven years old, did they assume this to be worthwhile and practicable. Younger children, they felt, simply could not be trusted to express a (reliable? truthful?) opinion:

> 'I think the child at four is almost at the lower age range really to be doing individual work [with them]' (Guardian Ad Litem)
> 'at the age of twelve you take into consideration what that child is saying' (Guardian Ad Litem)
> 'you've really got to go ... by ... what that fourteen year old is saying because, in this day and age, they'll vote with their feet' (Family Court Welfare Officer)

Summing up his feelings on the matter, one Family Court Welfare Officer remarked:

> 'I like to think of it as a sliding scale in terms of the older the child the more emphasis is placed on a child's wishes and feelings' (Family Court Welfare Officer)

However, notwithstanding the usefulness of this rule of thumb as a guide for their professional practice, these officers of the court were also well aware that, in everyday life, the ideally snug fit between chronological age and competence was conditioned by a variety of other factors. It was readily acknowledged by them, for example, that the experiences of some individual children might make them more socially mature and thus more able to reflect on their lives than other children; that boys may often be less mature than girls so that gender has always to be taken into account when judging children's competence in relation to age; and that older children are not immune from manipulation by adults and that therefore their testimonies might not be a reliable or true expression of their wishes and feelings. For these practitioners, then, there was in their everyday work with children always a tension between what childhood 'is' and what childhood 'should be' as portrayed in a developmentally inscribed life-course trajectory (see James et al., 2004).

Such mythologizing of the age basis of childhood and the determining role which numerical age plays in children's lives is a constant tension with which children themselves have to live and, as Bytheway (1995) has suggested, children might be regarded as victims of a kind of 'ageism', just as elderly people are. Thus, for example, in a recent study of children's time use,[3] 10-year-old children were asked, using a series of age-based vignettes, to consider at what age they thought their parents would let them travel on the bus into town. Most 10 year olds said that this would happen when they were 12, but, even then, they would only be allowed to travel with friends and not by themselves. To travel alone they would have to be even older.[4] They recalled the time when, as younger children of 7 or 8 years old, they had been allowed to walk to school by themselves but, now that they were 10, they had to negotiate further with their parents in order to be allowed to stay out playing a little longer in the evenings, to stray a little further from their homes or to go to bed a little later. Decisions about all such activities were made by their parents through reference to 'age' and so the children eagerly looked forward to being 16 or 18, the age at which they thought that their mums would no longer be able to tell them what to do. This suggests that a staged developmental and chronologized life course for children is as pervasive in parenting practices as it is in the work of welfare practitioners.

And, as a consequence, it also informs to some degree the ways in which children themselves think about 'age', as time passing, across their own life courses. The children's responses to our questions about age-related activities were, on the whole, fairly similar, albeit there were some gender differences with regard to concepts of maturity. Some girls expressed the view, for example, that girls were more sensible and that therefore they could be trusted to travel alone at 11 years of age, whereas boys were likely to meet other boys and start a fight. Some boys, by contrast, argued that, because boys are stronger, they could be allowed to travel alone at an earlier age than girls. Boys, they reasoned, would be able to get themselves out of trouble more easily than girls. However, many of the children thought that girls and boys ought to be treated the same and, as they talked about these issues, the children revealed their own mythologizing of the sliding life-course developmental scale, mirroring the use made of it by practitioners, as described above:

> Martin: 'Cos you can . . . go to the shops now [at 10] for your mum but before, when you was younger, then you never, they never used to send you.'
> Charles: 'My mam always says: "When you're sixteen, you can do what you want".'

Thus, for children, as well as adults, a developmentally-based, chronological schema works to mythologize childhood change by providing a charter for action and a cultural framework to think with and through. This is mapped out as the accrual of a series of age-based stages, each of which will move the child inexorably, step by step, towards the greater freedoms, responsibilities and self-determination of adulthood.

Narrative and the life course

However, although children's generalized views of age and change across the life course would therefore appear simply to replicate those of adults, such a model cannot fully account for the rather more ragged truth of children's own individual and subjective experiences of times passed, and indeed their views of time future. Thus, if we are to fully appreciate what 'ageing' means for children we have to explore, with a little more precision, the ways in which children as individuals come to understand, and learn to live with, the chronologized life course through which their lives are culturally narrated. As Rapport has argued: 'a social milieu can be barely comprehended apart from the individuals who compose it at any one time, nor a cultural symbology appreciated apart from the individuals who continue to find it meaningful' (Rapport, 2003, p. 26).

It is, then, to children's more individual perceptions of the chronologized life course that this chapter now turns in order to explore children's perceptions of ageing. In the sections that follow I shall show the ways in which collective expressions about ageing become 'imbued with subjective meanings and are made to serve the interests of [children's] individual perceptions' (Rapport, 2003, p. 26). The stories of the future and the past which children tell about themselves can be seen, therefore as narratives of the life course, narratives through which children construct their own world view or sense of place in the world. As Christensen (1999) has argued, 'childhood' unfolds, empirically, through 'children's experiences, understandings and practices . . . [and the] multiple, different forces . . . that influence their lives' (Christensen, 1999, p. 30). Thus, the potential age-based commonality of childhood, which structures children's experiences chronologically according to the ideas of development and of generation, is open to fracturing by other structural issues, such as class or ethnicity, and by the very diversity of children's own subjective, everyday experiences of the social world.

Adopting such a children's standpoint (Mayall, 2002), therefore, enables an understanding of children's social and psychological 'development' as rather less a matter of the effect of increasing age – of time passing – and rather more as a situated and context-specific experience, along the lines argued by Woodhead (1996) in his radical critique of developmental psychology. And by focusing on the narratives children tell about themselves it becomes possible to see how children, as individuals, interpret and make sense of their ageing selves, for as Rapport argues:

Narrative entails sequence: the placing of data, of details of perception and cognition, in a particular order such that connections are seen between them and an accumulative momentum is gained . . . There are numerous forms that these stories can take and limitless informational details that they can concern themselves with; what is common to them is the sequential narrational form, and the particular understanding that this form gives rise to. (Rapport, 2003, p. 29)

Children's chronological narratives of the life course

i. The future

I shall consider first the question of how children respond to the process of numerical chronologization through which the life course is often represented and through which, as children, their futures are popularly held to be developmentally determined. To do this I draw on the evidence contained in the time-lines constructed by twenty-two 10-year-old working-class children and consider this alongside other conversations held with children about the ageing process. The children were given two paper charts, entitled respectively 'My Life' and 'My Next Year' and were simply asked to plot out their lives (see Christensen and James, 2000); in later conversations they revealed other ideas they had about ageing and the life course.[5] These data fragments were collected while carrying out the research into children's understanding and perceptions of time[6] and, although children's ideas about the life course were not the main focus of the research, that this data is both rich and evocative is, in itself, indicative of the extent to which children *do* reflect on their life course and *do* have a sense of their own active part in shaping it.

A first observation to make is that children's narratives attest to the importance of chronological thinking about the passing of time in the modern life course for the ways in which ageing is depicted. Although revealing some differences in detail between children, nonetheless, collectively, this can be said to represent a child's standpoint on the life course (see Mayall, 2002). Thus on the majority of time-lines, although not all, numerical ages are indeed marked out. This suggests that 10-year-old children have begun to envision their lives in terms of the acquisition of numbers of years. On most charts the children inscribed 0 at one end, to represent birth, and 70 or 80 at the other, to represent old age and, for some children, death was indicated by a cross or a picture of a coffin. However, besides these numbers, upon which there appears to be some measure of agreement among the children, there is little other commonality in the numerical reckoning of age other than a tendency to signify the future as the relentless passing of the decades until death – 20, 30 40, 50, 60, 70.

That the future is only imaginable as the dull thud of years to be lived through indicates already the importance, for children, of 'age' as an experiential, rather than simply chronological status! Interestingly, even 18 – the official end of childhood according to the UNCRC – remains unremarked by children, with the assumption of adult status noted instead as occurring at the age of 20, the first of many future adult decades to live through. One girl writes:

I think in the future I will go to college and live a happy life age: 20

However, for most of these 10-year-old children, the life which lies ahead of them seems not only to be unknown and unplanned but also, in many cases, unimaginable. While some children note that the stages of adulthood and old age are what lie ahead of them, what these periods in the life course might entail is rather unclear. Most children left the future entirely blank, except for marking the inevitably of death in old age. That experience at least is a certainty.

However, some children did visualize the future in terms of chronological age and saw old age beginning at 50 or even earlier. For example, Alan said 'my grandma's fifty and she's old', while Kim revealed that, in her view, old age begins at 40.

Nora: 'My dad's forty.'
Kim: 'Ooh!'
Allison: 'You think that's old do you?'
Nora: 'No.'
Kim: 'Yeah, forty is the old, forty's coming into old.'

However, although the future is of course unknowable (and for most apparently unthinkable!) those children who did reflect on the lives that lie ahead of them did so subjectively, from their standpoint as children. That is to say, their visions of the future draw on their own embodied experiences as children in the world.

Allison: 'What do you think you'll be doing when you're ninety?'
Carl: 'Sitting in my bungalow.'
Alan: 'Sitting in a bungalow, reading the paper, like get your walking stick and take vitamins.'
Allison: 'What do you think it will feel like to be that old?'
Alan: 'Horrible.'

Kim and Nora agreed that to be 80 would represent being really old and that this would also be a time of physical incapacity:

Allison: 'Can you imagine being eighty?'
Kim: 'Might not even be alive.'
Allison: 'You might not be, but say you were alive, what do you think it

would be like to be eighty?'
Kim: 'You would live in a bungalow.'
Nora: 'Have a set of walking sticks.'
Kim: 'You can't get to the loo.'

And, at this point, the girls dissolved into gales of laughter.

What do these conversational snippets tell us about children's subjective understanding of the life course? First, it is clear that old age, like childhood, has its own mythical status, represented here through a set of shared cultural symbols – walking sticks, the need for vitamins, the necessity of living in a house without stairs, and the possibility of becoming incontinent. However, for children, an additional key concern, which reflects their own subjectivities and experience of the ageing process, centres on the changing body: to be so bodily incapacitated, as old people can become, is simply unimaginable and fantastical to children whose own bodies, although also changing, are in the peak of fitness. Being old, you wouldn't be able to do anything, or more correctly, any of the things, such as sport, that children can do:

> Martin: 'A lot of people when they get to ninety they start to get arthritis and things like that, so they wouldn't be able . . . to do much sports or anything then, so it would start to get a bit boring.'

Drawing on their own knowledge and bodily experiences as children, the future looks very bleak indeed. However, as noted, for most children the future is in some senses a blank slate, so that when the future *is* imagined it is depicted either through traditional rites of passage in the life course – getting married, getting a job, having children or retiring – or in terms of fantasies such as winning the lottery. Such transforming events often, though not exclusively, share a similar sequencing, but are not necessarily age-related. It is for instance common that, on the time-lines, jobs appear before marriage and getting a car but there are no common ages attached to these events. However, despite the mythical quality of these narratives – in the sense that they are shared cultural representations of future life transitions – this does not mean that some children do not think about their own futures in more concrete terms. Cora and Amy, for example, have reflected rather extensively on the nature of marriage:

> Allison: 'Do you think you'll both get married and have children?'
> Cora: 'Yeah, definitely.'
> Amy: 'Yes.'
> Allison: 'And how old do you think you would be?'
> Cora: 'About in my twenties. No younger than that 'cos . . . you need to get ready for it and be prepared and when you're seventeen you like want to go out and stuff but when you've got children you can't go . . .'

Amy: '[children] stop you from doing a lot of things until they're a certain age.'
Allison: 'About what sort of age, do you think?'
Amy: ''Til they're about ten or eleven.'
Cora: 'Ten or eleven.'

Another girl, Lorna, is less sanguine about having children. Having at first said that she didn't want to get married and have any children she continued to reflect on these matters:

Lorna: 'I might have a kid when I'm older, but not when I'm younger, 'cos they ruin your life.'

Her friend Susan agrees. Susan's mother has been married three times, the first time when she was eighteen which, she told Susan, was 'a bit too young'. The girls continue to talk:

Lorna: 'You don't have to get married to be together and love each other do you?'
Allison: 'No, you don't.'
Susan: 'But I most probably will get married, when I'm about in my thirties . . . once I've got my life sorted out.'
Lorna: 'You've done something with your life.'

And not only have the girls reflected on the prospect of having children and the effect this might have on their lives as grown women, but they have also thought about the nature of marital relations themselves. In the following conversation the importance of children's, albeit second-hand, knowledge and experience as the basis for their thinking becomes clear. Continuing to discuss the restrictions which having children and being married place on women, Amy said:

Amy: '. . . Because men, they just get to go out and do what they like, they don't care.'
But Cora disagrees: 'They don't though, do they? They go to work and stuff, it's not as if they're not working . . . It depends who you get married to, don't it?'
Amy: 'Yeah . . . Laura's just had a baby and her boyfriend he goes to work and he's real helpful, he lets Laura go out on a night . . . And she lets him go out as well, but he let's her go out, do you know, when she wants to.'

Amy's opening pronouncement of a familiar cultural stereotype – men's (bad?) behaviour in marriage – is challenged by Cora's more temperate and everyday observations. She disagrees with Amy, arguing that men, in fact, don't just do what they like and that they have to work. Moreover, she argues, all men are not the same: although there is a collective cultural category of men, individual men will differ so that, whether a husband cares or not will depend on whom one marries. Amy is persuaded. Indeed, she confirms Cora's judgement, thinking about someone she herself knows – Laura's boyfriend appears to be very much the antithesis of that common male stereotype.

Lorna, Susan and Maria had also reflected on such matters, drawing on the diversity of the lives and experiences of those adults they knew, to envisage different futures for themselves. Susan told me:

> Susan: 'I'm going to try and stay with one person, but I don't know [if that will happen] . . . and if you have children when you're young then you can't do anything, 'cos you'll have to look after them.'
> Lorna: 'And you can't get a job 'cos they'll be too young.'
> Susan: 'But I really want children though, 'cos I love children . . . some time like in my thirties.'

Maria, on the other hand, was most definitely set against both marriage and children:

> Maria: 'I don't like kids and I don't want to get married . . . I don't wanna be like a little housewife who's got to cook, iron and wash and all that lot. I don't mind washing my own clothes . . . but I don't think I can be bothered to like wash someone else's clothes.'

Conversations with 10-year-old boys, by contrast, revealed few insights into how they, as boys, conceived of such matters. When I asked Carl and Alan what they might be doing when they were eighteen Carl replied:

> Carl: 'Having a job, a car, a girlfriend, a house.'

This short blunt list of future possessions to be acquired was not, however, framed within any context of marriage or relationships. Indeed, both Carl and Alan told me that they didn't want to get married but, when pressed, admitted that they had not really ever thought about it. Other boys were equally vague and noncommittal.

As noted above, a second common feature of the children's depicted futures is getting a job and, once more, girls seem to have reflected far more than boys on what this might entail. Sara, for example, wants to be an actress and intends, when she goes to secondary school to work really hard:

> Sara: 'I want lots of homework . . . cos, do you know, my big brother, well he hasn't made much of his life. He like sits in and . . . I don't think he's

got a job still . . . I wanna be an actress. I've always wanted to be one since I was a little girl.'

Boys too sometimes expressed views about what kind of job they may have when they become adult, such as becoming a policeman, but, as in their conversations about marriage, they appear to have reflected in less detail about what this might entail or the steps which might need to be taken in order to achieve such ends. These differences suggest, therefore, that girls are more oriented towards the future than are boys. This confirms findings of earlier studies (James, 1993)[7] and recalls Steedman's (1982) analysis of little girls' knowledge of their lives as adults, knowledge drawn from the observed experiences of their own mothers' lives.

The relative blankness of the future, depicted in the 'My Life' time-lines and discussed above, contrasts strongly, however, with the near future depicted on the charts for 'My Next Year'. These time-lines reveal that children not only have quite a detailed knowledge of events which are going to take place during the next year – family birthdays, starting secondary school and going on holiday – but that they also have a sense of purpose and planning, combined with a reflexive and anticipatory view of what is likely to happen to them or things that they wish to do. For example, ongoing regular activities such as going swimming or playing football are marked out alongside wished-for events, such as 'get my ears pierced', 'win some more trophies' and 'get bored of high school'. Thus, although the near future is in one sense more knowable, and therefore easier to think about than the distant future, in terms of children's subjectivities both sets of charts depict children as active agents of change. The children present a narrative account of themselves as people, if not in charge of their own lives, at least with opportunities to take decisions. Thus, in contrast to the passivity of the chronologized, developmental life course through which childhood is often depicted, children's narratives of the self offer us a rather different standpoint: events do not just happen to them, children can also make things happen. But, what then about the past? How do children make sense of this part of their lives? The next section turns its attention to this.

ii. The past

Even though children have lived only a comparatively short quantity of time it is important to consider children as having life histories, and to see them as capable reflexive autobiographers, for what children narrate about their lives can provide insight into not only their individual life experiences, but also into the nature of 'childhood' within the life course *as children themselves see it*. The significance of this lies in its potential to demythologize 'childhood'; that is, to understand what children, rather than adults, consider as important in their pasts and about the process of 'growing up'.

Recent work on the life course (Hockey and James, 2002) has suggested that the social structuring and chronologization of age is insufficient as an account of how the individual – whether child or adult – identifies themself as aged or ageing. To simply work at the level of categorical identities, as so often happens, for example, when models of child development are used to locate children in the life course (James and James, 2004) is to fail to get to grips with the *process of* identification itself – that is, the way it is that the social *and* individual identities of children are inhabited and come into being (Jenkins, 1996). Instead, the process of reflexive embodiment, already illustrated in the examples above, has to be taken into account, for as Hockey and James (2002) argue it is this which facilitates the links between social and individual identities. It is through remembered experiences of times past and the envisioning of the future that people – be they adults or children – come to know that they are ageing. However, though in this sense it can be argued that 'memory serves as both a phenomenological ground of identity . . . and the means for explicit identity construction' (Antze and Lambeck, 1996, p. xvi), the role of memory in identity construction is nonetheless ambiguous. Unconscious processes of selectivity, besides those of simple memory loss, work to shape particular 'truths' about ourselves, truths devised to fit or, indeed, to contrast with who we now think we are (Radstone, 2000; Chamberlayne et al., 2000). Antze and Lambeck (1996, p. xvi), for example, ask: 'If I am constituted by what I remember, what about all that I do not remember but that I know, because of other sources including my common sense tell me, must have been mine? Or what about that which I remember but would prefer to forget?'

Central to the argument put forward by Antze and Lambeck (1996), then, is that memory is a discourse of identity, serving to construct and reconstruct notions of the ageing self. In this sense, then, memory is more than a way of accessing the past. It is also fundamental to the present, and by implication to the future.

In relation to understanding children and ageing this is a critical insight. It helps to free ourselves from the tight hold which the mythology of the developmental model, and its static and staged ageing categories, has over our thinking about childhood. It makes us focus, instead, on the particular embodied experiences of children in particular social and cultural contexts (James and James, 2004). If children's present knowledge of their 'selves' as aged beings is, in part, a function of their memories of previous ages then it matters a great deal both *how* and *what* they remember about those lifecourse moments. As children tell us their memories and make comparisons between themselves then and now, they use their present knowledge and standpoint to make sense of and to interpret past events.

Turning first to the 'My Life' time-line, in contrast to depictions of the future, the past features on all of the children's charts and it is depicted in a rather different way. While chronology emerges as significant, gone is the emphasis on decennial reckoning. Instead, a variety of different and specific ages are identified and, again in contrast to the uniformity of imagined futures, children's pasts are infinitely more varied and revealed through many different kinds of narratives.

The specific ages identified by the children represent the ages at which significant life-course events, *as understood by children*, occurred. In this sense the past is recalled not simply as an individual experience but as an individual experience of 'childhood', one which is historically and culturally located and therefore collectively shared by children. Thus, for example, five out of the 22 charts identify the start of school; six children record the age at which they got a bike; six children identify accidents and illnesses they have had in the past and six children mention the death of a pet. These suggest a commonality of childhood experiences which can be set alongside more individualized accounts – one child mentions the birth of a sibling, another notes when the family moved house.

However, we also have to ask about absences in these life-course representations. Clearly memory does have a part to play. Some events may simply have been forgotten. But, in addition to this, it may be that some events are not able to be recalled by children as fixed points or moments in time in quite the way demanded by the artificial constraints of the time-line.

For example, the absence on the time-lines of what adults might regard as a key life-course event in a child's life – parental divorce – suggests that children's memory of this family event may be rather particular. As an embodied experience, the family split may not have been an event in time, but rather experienced as a process, a process of gradually accumulating knowledge and awareness over time.[8] Thus, Lucy, whose parents' divorce does not feature on her time-line, nonetheless does remember the time before and after her parent's separation. But for her it is the changes in the kinds of birthday parties she had which symbolizes these contrasting times:

> When I was little every year I used to have like a party in the back garden where I used to live. I used to have a real big back garden and there was like all my friends from school, like about half of the street went and everything, 'cos we was like real close to our neighbours. When I was seven, like ... my mam and dad had split up and my dad was still living in the old house and I was living with my nana and we just went out ... we had like a dinner out ... in a restaurant.

In this example, Lucy reflects on how her parents' divorce changed her life. It clearly had some very practical, experiential consequences – mentioned here, for example, are the loss of a big garden and the loss of friends close by and that sense of a familiar neighbourhood which, as a child, were important to her. However, for Lucy now, at 10 years old, the divorce was also an integral part of her growing up, and she contrasts the dinner in the restaurant favourably with the more childish birthday parties that she used to have in the garden of the old family home. It may be, then, that the absence on the time-lines of what adults would regard as such a major turning point in a child's life is because of the ways in which children experience them. That is to say, children do not, as such, remember or experience their parents' separation. What they experience instead are its practical consequences, embodied experiences and knowledges through which they, as children, construct a narrative for and about the self.

Just so, with other recalled experiences. The time-lines often highlight highly personal events, rather than those more structured life-course transitions. Thus, although starting school does represent a chronologized life course transition, it is also, for children, a highly personal, sometimes highly traumatic, event in their lives, to be placed alongside other events such as accidents and illness, the death of pets and special birthdays. For children, these are the keys to narrating the child-self. Thus one boy records on his time line the following story:

> When I was little I had a big garden and two chickens and I went in the garden. I got bit on my toe. That was when I was two.

A girl similarly records an equally personal and embodied experience:

> I remember when I was only about 5 I was on my uncle's shoulders and I fell off and I had to go in an ambulance.

The extent to which these *are* actually memories is not the issue. Rather such events in the past, just as future events, are the markers in time through which children locate their present selves. They are stories which children tell themselves, about themselves. Sarah has such a story to tell:

> When I was three years old I fell out of the bedroom window. Oh, I was in hospital, but I've still got the newspaper from when I actually fell out the bedroom window . . . I was in a wheelchair . . . I went to the fair but I wasn't allowed to go on any rides. I can't remember falling out, but I can remember like [being in hospital]. Oh it was real funny. My dad came to stay one night and he slept in the same bed and I fell out 'cos he took up all the space, so he had to put me in this cot and it was a massive cot . . . I was only in hospital for five days, but I got like a fractured skull. I didn't even have a bruise on me. I was scratched . . . but I fell on concrete . . . I can't remember me falling out, but I can remember 'cos my brothers and that was like messing about and mam told us to go upstairs, so they started fighting on the bed, but not real fighting. And I got real hot so I said 'Can I open the window?' And they said: 'No.' So I asked them again and they said: 'Okay'. Then I opened the window and I sat on the

window ledge like that and . . . I don't know, I can't remember what happened or anything after that.

Striking about Sarah's story is the absence of a logical chronology in its telling, as she weaves in and around the event itself. But as the narrative develops so Sarah carves out a space and identity for her self as a little girl of three living in a family with older brothers who fight. Whilst admitting throughout her narrative that she cannot actually *remember* what happened, nonetheless she still feels able to narrate the event in graphic detail. And, as she does, so she places herself at the centre of the action, as a person with agency – she feels hot, she asks twice for the window to be opened and she climbs out onto the window ledge.

Such rememberings of things done 'when they were little' are, then, one of the ways in which children come to an understanding of the life course as, through the past, they are able to locate their present selves. That is to say, as children reflect back on such events they simultaneously distance their older selves from them. As Leanne said:

'Cos you're older and like you see, you look back and you think: 'Oh, that's babyish that.'
I used to like be clinging to my mum's legs: 'Oh, no, please don't leave me.'

This distance between the 'me' then and the 'me' now is quite clear in Charles's memory of getting lost.

I was looking round at the toys and my mam was coming and I went somewhere else to see if I could get me mam and I couldn't find her. I looked everywhere, I couldn't find her. I went to one of the people and asked and I said: 'I'm lost. Can you help me find my mam?' And they said, and they put it on one of them speaker things . . . It's like in this real big shop . . . and I was looking at all the sports gear and stuff and then me mam just went out. Me mam went somewhere, outside the shop, to see if I was there. But I couldn't find my mam, so I just sat down in a corner and started crying.

Charles says that he remembers something that happened when he was three years old. But that the event took place in exactly the way Charles narrates it seems unlikely. A three-year-old would not, for example, be able to hold the conversation with the shop keepers as Charles relates it. Moreover, as Charles elaborates on the story he tells us specifically that he was looking at sports gear. This is again something unlikely for a three-year-old to be doing. What does this story tell us then about the past or, more precisely, about the importance of the past to Charles's present life?

First, whether Charles actually remembers this event or not is immaterial. It may be, for example, that this is a family narrative, told and retold, again and again, as a story about the time Charles got lost. Alternatively, it may be that this event happened to Charles at a point in time much nearer to the present in his own life history, say at eight years old. The picture of the child sitting crying in the corner may be much nearer the 'truth' than the portrayal of the cool and responsible child interlocutor of the shop-keeper. It matters not which explanation we choose for what Charles's story reveals is precisely the process which memory plays in identity construction that Antze and Lambeck (1996) have described. In his narrative 10-year-old Charles uses a story from the past to distance his grown-up self from the little child he once was, be that only a couple of years ago. In this way Charles comes to understand the ageing process, and the ways in which his own development and maturing have taken place. Looking back, just over the space of one year, 10-year-old Lucy achieves a similar and more grown-up sense of her self:

> My mum was a bit overprotective when I was about nine, and the shop like across the road, she wouldn't even let me go. It was only across the road.

Conclusion

These brief fragments of data are, I suggest, indicative of the value to be gained by adopting a life-course and biographical approach in work with children, an approach that can enable us to understand how it is that children experience time passing as ageing across the life course. Despite the brevity of their lives, children have much to say not only about their pasts but also about the plans and ideas they have for the future. In these accounts children position themselves as active agents in the making of their own histories, histories which are both varied and highly contrastive and histories which are the outcome of their participation in the unique settings of their own everyday lives. Such work offers, then, a counterpoise to the determinism of the developmental project which for many, if not all, children works as a strong structuring factor on the ways adults – teachers, practitioners and parents – understand and subsequently endeavour to order their lives for them. This data suggests, therefore, that were we to listen more carefully to the (hi)stories children are able to construct about their life course, we would, as adults, be better placed to assist children in the shaping and determining of their own lives.

Notes

1. It is interesting to note that the latest proposals for educational reform in the UK have suggested an abandonment of the chronology of achievement. The proposed new diploma would be a four-stage qualification that can be taken at any time in the life course.

2. The study, entitled 'Constructing Children's Welfare: a Comparative Study of Professional Practice', was funded by the Economic and Social Science Research Council (2001–3). The project researchers were Adrian James, Allison James and Sally McNamee.
3. ESRC funded project (1997–2000) 'Changing Times: Children's Perception and Understanding of the Social Organisation of Time'. The project researchers were Allison James, Pia Christensen and Chris Jenks and the study was undertaken in four schools (two primary and two secondary schools) in urban and rural areas in northern England.
4. This may also be a function of increased parental concern about 'stranger danger'. It would be interesting, therefore, to compare these 'age-based' parental permissions with those of earlier generations.
5. The concept of a time-line is familiar to English schoolchildren, featuring as it does in discussions of history and historical events. In this sense, then, although these methodological devices did of course impose an in-built linearity on children's conceptualization of the life course, since this *is* a feature of the way in which time passing is chronologized in the modern life course, this was not perceived as problematic either by us, as researchers, or by the children themselves. The children were able to complete the task easily.
6. See note 2.
7. This may perhaps explain the differential gap that currently exists in the educational achievements of girls and boys in England. Throughout primary schooling and increasingly during their secondary schooling girls now outperform boys. Perhaps it is in these rather different temporal orientations that one explanation may lie: girls look to their futures, while boys concentrate on their present lives.
8. Adults may well shield children from this knowledge so that this, in itself, will contribute to the piecemeal way in which children may actually have to get to know about changes in family circumstances.

References

Antze, P. and M. Lambeck (eds) (1996) *Tense Past: Cultural Essays in Trauma and Memory*, London: Routledge.
Ariès, P. (1962) *Centuries of Childhood*, London: Jonathan Cape.
Barthes, R. (1976) *Mythologies*, London: Paladin.
Bytheway, B. (1995) *Ageism*, Buckingham: Open University Press.
Chamberlayne, P., J. Bornat and T. Wengraf (eds) (2000) *The Turn to Biographical Methods in the Social Sciences*, London: Routledge.
Christensen, P. (1999) *Towards an Anthropology of Childhood Sickness: an Ethnographic Study of Danish School Children*, unpublished PhD thesis, University of Hull.
Christensen, P. and A. James (2000) *Research with Children*, London: Falmer.
Gillis, J.R. (1996) *A World of their Own Making*, Oxford: Oxford University Press.
Gittens, D. (1998) *The Child in Question*, Basingstoke: Macmillan.
Hockey, J. and A. James (2002) *Social Identities across the Life Course*, London: Palgrave.
James, A. (1993) *Childhood Identities*, Edinburgh: Edinburgh University Press.
James, A. (2005, forthcoming) 'The Standardized Child: Issues of Openness, Objectivity and Agency in Promoting Child Health', *Anthropological Journal on European Cultures*.
James, A. and A.L. James (2004) *Constructing Childhood: Theory, Policy and Social Practice*, London: Palgrave.

James, A.L., A. James and S. McNamee (2004) 'Turn Down the Volume? – Not Hearing Children in Family Proceedings', *Child and Family Law Quarterly*, 16 (2): 189–203.

Jenkins, R. (1996) *Social Identity*, London: Routledge.

Jenks, C. (1996) *Childhood*, London: Routledge.

Lee, N. (2001) *Childhood and Society*, Buckingham: Open University Press.

Mayall, B. (2002) *Towards a Sociology of Childhood*, Buckingham: Open University Press.

Radstone, S. (ed.) (2000) *Memory and Methodology*, Oxford: Berg.

Rapport, N. (2003) *I am Dynamite: an Alternative Anthropology of Power*, London: Routledge.

Steedman, C. (1982) *The Tidy House*, London: Virago.

Woodhead, M. (1996) 'In Search of the Rainbow: Pathways to Quality in Large-scale Programmes for Young Disadvantaged Children', *Early Childhood Development: Practice and Reflections*, 10, The Hague: Bernard van Leer Foundation.

16
Structuration of Childhood: an Essay on the Structuring of Childhood and Anticipatory Socialization

Ivar Frønes

Perspectives on childhood

Traditional sociology has subsumed childhood under a concept of social-ization as a process of integration, where cultural patterns were transformed into inner motivation (Parsons, 1951; Jenks, 1993). Psychology, on the other hand, often pictured a developing child without childhood, in the sense that the social and cultural framework constituting the life and conditions of children was not part of the developmental analysis. Ariès (1962) brought a historical and structural perspective to childhood; childhood became a cultural and social realm, influencing the life of its historically-constituted inhabitants. In the later sociology of childhood, the perspective pursued was how a variety of structures and mechanisms frame childhood as the cultural, economic and social conditions for children and as the images and narra-tives of childhood. From this perspective, children can be seen as members of a social class, as a minority group, as a marginalized category or as a group waiting to enter society (Qvortrup et al., 1994; James et al., 1998). All per-spectives on childhood illustrate an important heritage from Ariès: child-hood as the role of the child, assigning a set of characteristics to all children. Childhood constitutes a framework structuring the factual life of children, a cultural realm with rights and entitlements, and the role and image dis-tinguishing children from adults. The realm of childhood is a blessing for children historically speaking. Without childhood, there would not be any rights of the child or right to a childhood, implying a right to play and leisure. Children's position as being under development entails the right to education and growth; their vulnerability implies the right to protection. Childhood, as a social category, underlines the role and societal position of children, not the gradual transition towards maturity and adulthood pre-sented by developmental psychology.

Sociology chooses various angles for studying childhood. Analysis of the discourses constituting the role and images of the child across historical periods and political regimes aims at understanding both history and the present modernity. The distribution of resources in relation to childhood and other age groups is inspired analytically as well as politically by the perspective of theories of class and gender. This structural and historical perspective brought children into the foreground as a category. Nevertheless, this framework also entails analytical, political and cultural challenges. The analytical problem is not only rooted in a possible implicit interpretation of the factual lives of children as deriving from the idea of childhood. The challenge is that the category of childhood may confuse the formation of the cultural category and ideology of childhood with the processes of being a child, and thereby not providing a theoretical framework that can inform empirical studies at the level of children's lives. As the life of children, childhood is a developmental, cultural and social process: as a cultural and social realm, childhood is the framework through which children pass.

One childhood or many?

The main character in *The Children of Sánchez* (Lewis, 1961) states that he had no childhood, a situation he shares with many children globally in the sense that their childhood is filled with the burden of work and not with play and leisure. The argument for a plurality of childhoods has often been related to the global disparity between affluent and poor countries and regions, as well as to class divisions, variation between cultures and differences between cohorts. Childhood has also been traditionally gender divided; boys often had a period of youth and a certain autonomy in later childhood that girls seldom achieved. Girls were moved from their father's household to their husband's household (as they still often are), sometimes at a very young age. The (relative) gender equality between children in modern societies is a new historical phenomenon. That ethnic differences observed between children's lives today are often gendered is not surprising. Children and young people are exposed to the varying economic, cultural and social capital of their parents and to the diverse consequences of their parents' religious and cultural profiles. The more variations there are in tradition and normative patterns, the more visible are those patterns as cultural and social constructions, as is illustrated by modern gender patterns, in the family as well as the schoolyard. The family illustrates the construction of gender along ethnic and class lines; the schoolyard illustrates gender patterns as constructed by the children's resources, values and the local peer dynamics (Thorne, 1993).

In rapidly changing societies, children from relatively close birth cohorts may experience different childhoods, related to living conditions, media exposure, level of education, type of toys and activities as well as to social patterns of families and peers. Relations between cohorts also vary with historical periods, both between cohorts as age groups with divergent historical moorings, and as relations between biological generations within the family.

The plurality of childhoods refers not only to differences between regions, cohorts, cultural enclaves, nations or classes, but to processes of differentiation within territories and categories. The analytical challenge is to grasp not only the variety of childhoods but also the variety of children's lives as social practice.

Homogenization and differentiation of childhoods

Cultural modernization is traditionally understood as entailing homogenization, an assumption often applied to childhood. The construction of the cultural sphere of childhood inherently contributed to homogenizing childhood, socialization and upbringing, by the idea of the role of the child, and the common social and cultural characteristic of all children. The integration of children into the expanding educational systems, from pre-schools to higher education, illustrates the homogenization of children's life-worlds. But locating all children in the same institutional framework and opening an identical panorama of educational choices for all, also illustrate that homogenization may bring differentiation. The homogeneous educational system does not provide children with identical personal or cultural capacities for making choices in the common opportunity structure. The educational institutionalization of children interacts with their social and economic background and personal capacity. The consequence is that children move through the years of childhood along very different paths; differences are produced not despite, but because of the institutional integration. The expansion of educational institutions provided the basis for the educational childhood of the middle classes, but also contributed to the constitution of the working-class 'lad' constructing his identity partly by fighting the school system (Willis, 1977). The educational society underlines educational attainment, and produces high achievers and educational careers as well as functional illiteracy and the cultural category of dropout.

Young people's integration into the world of mass media produces the same dynamics of integration and differentiation. Modern screens present children worldwide with exposure to increasingly global popular cultures, as well as with access to electronic communication. But this semiotic integration also produces differentiation, as illustrated by the panorama of lifestyles, the variety of groups chatting on the internet and the youthful subcultures and counter-cultures. The creolization of popular cultures and the panorama of 'narrowcasts', global magazines and internet sites addressing special groups, all demonstrate the ability of the globalized media to produce cultural diversity. The ethnic groups watching the television of their homeland in the ethnoscapes of Europe demonstrate that modern media also may act as a factor working against social integration.

Modern differentiation is partly rooted in the institutionalization and structural homogenization of childhood. Mass media integrate homogenization and a potential variety of choices and identities. The educational system is identical for everyone in most countries up to 15–16 years of age, and for most young people until 18–19 years, but produces differentiation in interaction with other structural, cultural and individual factors. Families vary in resources and in profiles of culture and values; peer relations are shaped by local communities, school environments and general cultural factors. The paradox of parallel integration and differentiation, homogenization and variety, is rooted in the differentiation produced in the interaction between social and cultural structures at different levels, and between the active subject and contextual and structural conditions.

The social subject and childhood as a process

The explanatory and descriptive power of theories of modern differentiation depends not only on their capacity to conceptualize children as part of social, economic and cultural structures, but also on their ability to establish childhood as a process and children as active subjects. Research that does not conceptualize children as actors will not only construct theories that are too structurally inclined but will also lack the capacity to grasp the dynamics of social change and the mechanisms of differentiation. The role of the child defines childhood as something to which one belongs. As the process of moving through the framework of childhood, childhood is something children *do*.

Whereas the active subject in rational choice theory optimizes utility, phenomenology seeks to sort out the actor's construction of meaning, which is also necessary for identifying utility. This does not imply that the native's viewpoint identifies the actor's intention or motivation; meaning and motivation are embedded in context. But the subjective constitution of meaning is necessary for theorizing on the dynamics of agency and structure.

Psychological theories on development point towards becoming or the 'outcome' of a developmental process; the consequences of the conditions of the child are interpreted as related to the developmental process. But the causal mechanisms of psychology tend to underline the importance of the *past*, as family resources, as biographical structures and special experiences, or as the unconscious shadows of parents and the early biographical history. The causal explanations of sociology put emphasis on the past as social background, as cultural and economic capital. The correlations between the past and the present exist, but the causal mechanisms indicated by the contingency tables are shallow.

The active reflexive subject is oriented towards the *future*. Traditions govern through the idea that the future will be like the past. The future becomes visible and influential when the horizon becomes heterogeneous and complex, as does the subject. The idea of an open future, where the future life course is something one achieves, requires the strategic subject, navigating towards the complex future, moving through the framework of childhood. Childhood as a process is not an invention of developmental psychology; it is childhood as seen from within. Children are not only unavoidably 'growing'; a basic characteristic of childhood from children's viewpoint is development and process: soon you will be bigger and older.

Phases, structures and paths: the diachronic and synchronic structuring of childhood

Childhood is seen as a framework defining the age group belonging to the category, and laying certain premises for children's passage through the period defined as childhood, through the structuring of this processes. Childhood as a process is not understood as a developmental process in which certain cognitive or psychosexual stages can be identified; children's development is staged in interaction with complex social and cultural structures. While psychology identifies stages of development, a sociological analysis of childhood as a process seeks to identify the social structuring of the process of growing up, by institutional and cultural arrangement in interaction with the various dimensions of development. Age in modern society is in itself a cultural grading of maturity; a child's definition of him or herself as, for example, 'older' or 'younger' than someone else, is based on cultural interpretation of age-related positions. Age is important as a general indication of social maturity, and the institutional arrangement for children is strictly differentiated according to this principle; coming of age implies transitions and the changing of cultural and social positions. The cultural and institutional structures, interacting with the developmental processes, shape a structure characterized by sets of phases of various characteristics and contents. This is not only an external structure provided by institutions and culture; it is an important part of childhood as seen from within. Growing up is expected to be a process with a specific structure of positions and phases, with corresponding norms and expectations. The expectations of the coming age-phases play an important part in childhood as the process of growing.

As this model is designed, a *phase* is understood as a period of a certain structural stability, *transitions* refers to postulated more fluid periods of moving from one phase to the next. This opens for the conceptualization of *synchronic* and *diachronic* structures: the *diachronic* structures refer to the set of transitions and phases, the *synchronic* structures to the structure and dynamics within the more stable phases. The synchronic phases are obviously stable only relatively speaking, but they are identified as phases with certain structural and symbolic characteristics by the general culture and the institutions of childhood as well as by the children; one characteristic of the framework of modern childhood is an increasing differentiation of phases. Analytically, conceptualizing childhood as a set of differentiated diachronic structures implies that the analysis of the synchronic structures can be partly separated from the analysis of transitions.

The point of departure of a life-course perspective on childhood (Elder, 1974) would encompass the structure organizing the moving through childhood and the structure of the various phases, as well as the structuring of children's ways of moving through the period of childhood. The life-course perspective seeks to conceptualize childhood as a set of social and cultural structures – as the variety of paths of moving through childhood; and as the process of moving as experienced subjectively – as a series of social acts. A *life-course path* represents the structuring of the individual movements through the structured framework of childhood. This structuring of childhood as a process may vary with class and ethnicity, and children of divergent backgrounds move along divergent paths. Patterns of paths may vary with cohorts, as may the structure of childhood, since childhood as a framework is always gradually changing. In certain historical periods the whole framework or part of it may undergo rapid changes, producing tensions in socialization practices, and watersheds between some of the cohorts of that historical period.

Institutional structures are transformed into social and cultural structures through the interaction between children's culture and the institutional structure. This implies that the framework can only be fully identified from within, from the children's perspective. Some phases and transitions that are important to children may be invisible to adults who are removed from children's life-worlds. To be a first grader is not only an institutional characteristic; it is a phase in the structure of childhood. To this phase belongs a symbolic vocabulary, such as 'school bag', signifying social age. Approaching new phases entails new symbols on children's walls and new clothes, demonstrating the transitional character of symbolic vocabularies.

Each phase in the diachronic structure takes the form of a field of action in Bourdieu's (1984) sense, a framework of cultural patterns, possible positions, identities and competencies. Whether a phase is understood as one field, or as a set of fields, depends on the angle of the factual empirical analysis. The structure and content of phases shape tensions and positions within each phase, and influence the possible paths of transition between phases. Moving from one phase to another opens up new repertoires of lifestyles and social identities. Positions at various levels are correlated but also discontinuous, such as when reaching a new phase changes the status hierarchies among children.

Within the general structural arrangements of childhood, social groups will be constituted not primarily as divergent positions but as divergent structures of the moving through childhood. *Paths* refer to the individual ways of moving through childhood and *tracks* to sets of correlated paths, related to such factors as class, gender, ethnicity, region or other social categories. Tracks refer to the life-course structure of social categories. Tracks may be defined statistically as correlated paths, or the dominating paths of a defined group. Some social tracks are also strong signifiers of who you are and where you are heading; social categories and positions are constructed and visualized as tracks. A track is used in two different meanings: as the factual correlation between paths of a specific category, and as the narrative or cultural idea of tracks associated with specific social categories. Often the factual tracks change before the cultural expectations. This cultural lag is illustrated by the educational gender revolution, which had been under way long before the gendered cultural expectations started to change.

As a set of transitions and levels, the educational system represents an age-graded hierarchy, transformed into significant phases of childhood through the interaction with the cultures and social systems of children and young people. High schools in the United States have juniors and seniors and so on; moving to junior high is a marker of leaving childhood in many cultures, and the overall educational structure creates transitions such as entering primary school. The grade system of the school is in itself interpreted as a set of levels of maturity.

Phases are complex multidimensional entities, not structured identically along all dimensions, and the structure of a phase looks different from different positions and angles. In the kindergarten or pre-school, children and the schools operate with phases, whereas the mass media for a long period seemed to define children under about five years of age as one category. In Norway, television for pre-school children was relatively constant from 1970 to 1990, illustrated by the same series being broadcast over and over again. Television for 'tweens' (about 9–12 years old) changed enormously during this period (Haldar, 1994), indicating a change in the cultural perception of this period of childhood. In recent years, new television series have indicated that the pre-school group is increasingly being differentiated into cultural age groups.

Institutional changes influence the structuration of childhood. Sports clubs recruit children at younger ages than before and contribute to a further differentiation of levels; new media structures, contents and devices such as videogames contribute to new images and vocabularies for young age phases. Institutional changes also influence the *metastructure* of childhood: that is, the way in which the transitions to adulthood are organized. In the industrial society, the role of an adult manifested itself as mature and settled men and women in their early twenties, an age level at which sexuality, family and occupational position merged as the natural age for the transition into adulthood, and at which the period of teenage youth was left behind. The educational society dissolved this simple transition to adulthood. The long educational period brought a new life phase, a period of being a young and 'single' adult, moving the peak of the period of youth from the late teens to the middle twenties (Frønes, 2001). At the same time, the emphasis on the need for competence and autonomy in the modern educational knowledge society contributed to early social maturity; independence and autonomy were listed as the most important aims of upbringing in Norway, well ahead of obedience (Lindseth, 1998). The common age level for the transition to adulthood diversifies into a series of levels and dimensions of maturity. Phases may change in different ways along different dimensions, as when teenagers of the educational society become more socially mature and less economically autonomous. Children from different social backgrounds may move at a different pace along different dimensions.

Cohorts move through structural frameworks that are changing over time. People defined as being children simultaneously because of being younger than 15 years old, such as being 5 years and 12 years, may be moving through different childhoods.

From waiting to navigation

In the industrial life course, children looking into the future saw early marriages, relatively well-paid jobs for men and housewifery for women. Not surprisingly, youth was categorized as a period of waiting. When the goal of the future for young girls was to find a husband and provider in their early twenties or late teens, education was not a strategic option for girls (or for their parents); hence, most girls in the industrial society lost the focus on schooling in their early teens. Gradually, becoming an adult woman was transformed from moving from adolescence into the 'women's room' (brilliantly described by Marilyn French as the world of suburban mothers) to moving into a future dominated by education and being single, with self-realization, experiences and especially friends at the centre of life. The educational society changed the dominant structure of the life period from 20 to 30 years of age, thus also transforming the whole period of childhood by changing the expected future.

Anticipatory socialization refers to how the future influences socialization through what one expects the future to bring. The visible role of an adult waiting in the early twenties implied that anticipation took place through a default position of the inner gyroscope, which is a characteristic of societies categorized as being governed by traditions. Traditions govern through the idea that the future will be like the past. The affluent educational society, with its emphasis on self-realization, choices and risks and the expectations of a complex future, transforms socialization from being guided by traditions and waiting to being guided by the principle of navigation. The future becomes visible and influential when the horizon becomes heterogeneous and complex. Reflexivity is a structurally rooted property: that is, an individual capacity required by the structural framework.

In the life course of modern childhood, anticipation refers to the reflexive navigating towards a distant future of opportunities and uncertainty, but also to the navigation related to the next transitional phase in a complex and changing landscape. Children must choose which positions in the new phase of life they will try to acquire or choose; the synchronic structure of the coming phase has to be anticipated. Climbing the diachronic ladder of childhood entails the cultural construction of not only social identity, but of individuality. The demand for reflexive navigation is not delimited to the capacity for planning careers and directions in the distant adult future; the demand for navigational competence is forced on children through the complex vocabulary of the coming phases and the complex diachronic steps between them.

In a society in which social class does not operate as traditional cultural divisions, the life course seems to be more open to individual choices, which to some degree is the implicit message of the concept of individualization. Statistics reveal, however, that individual life courses vary according to social background and resources, there are tracks corresponding to social class. The educational systems are illustrative; they are open to anyone in principle, but children's success or failure is correlated with the social and cultural capital of the parents.

Divergent paths: class, ethnicity and gender

The synchronic patterns allow a variety of positions at each phase, a variety that is increasing with the differentiation of modern societies, producing a correspondingly larger number of possible diachronic tracks and paths. The structural framework of modern childhood permits a diversity of ways of moving through childhood. These diachronic patterns of passing through childhood operate both as social patterns and as individual biographies, changing with historical periods and cohorts. Social heritage in a traditional class society could typically take the form of prescribed economic, cultural and social transfers between positions, illustrated by sons following fathers to the mines and the pub and women their mothers into housewifery. These mechanisms are weakened in the opportunity structures of the educational society. In modern knowledge societies, the mechanisms of reproduction are rooted in the interaction between social background and the educational system and can be identified as divergent tracks through childhood. Positions in the paths of childhood are more strongly correlated than are social background and the future adult positions; children who are marginalized in the educational system in an early phase of childhood are relatively likely to be on the same track later on. The formal educational opportunity structure means that social reproduction, the relationship between the position of parents and children, is created in dynamics involving such factors as the child's personal capacity, the parents' aspirations and involvement, the qualities of the community and the qualities of the school system.

The post-industrial society brought a gender revolution in educational achievement that is related to the dynamics of childhood more than to parental or societal planning (Frønes, 2001). In Norway, about 60 per cent of the students in higher education were women in 2001, against 47 per cent in 1980 (Statistics Norway, 2004). Boys seem to be more polarized than girls: they are often represented among both the most successful and the most marginalized in the educational system. The complex dynamics of childhood as a process is illustrated in the interplay of social class, gender and ethnicity; children from similar socioeconomic positions end up moving along divergent tracks. In the UK, the gap between boys and girls in compulsory schooling is widest among those with ethnic backgrounds in Bangladesh, Pakistan and the Caribbean (*Social Trends*, 2002). African-American youth have a similar gendered educational structure in the United States. The social backgrounds of boys and girls are identical in socio-economic terms, but cultural conditions and mechanisms differ. The situation of groups of boys indicates that some constructions of masculinity produce marginalization related to the educational system. In Great Britain, 66 per cent of girls with ethnic backgrounds in India achieved five or more GCSEs graded A to C when finishing compulsory schooling, whereas 22 per cent of boys with ethnic backgrounds in Bangladesh and Pakistan reach this level (England and Wales; GCSE is General Certificate in Secondary Education, the national school examination in the UK).

Studies in the United Kingdom (Williamson, 1997) indicated that people outside both the educational system and the labour market when they were in their mid-teens had a higher probability than the average of still being marginalized in their mid-twenties. In the structure of the industrial society, the teenage phase was a risk period that ended when young men and women were integrated into the expected adult role patterns through work and the establishing of a family. This easy integration was made possible by the conditions of the industrial society, with reasonably well-paid jobs available for young men with low education, and the corresponding cultural norms of transitions to adulthood as transition into family life. Postponing marriage because of education was correspondingly categorized as 'deferral of gratification' (Ramsøy, 1978). In the educational or knowledge society, to reach full status as an adult is harder to achieve, in the sense that integration into a reasonable position in the labour market requires educational attainment, and the cultural transitions are more complex. In this childhood of navigation, the various indicators of adulthood are not designated to the same age level, the result being that the line between youth and adulthood is blurred. When the full adult position has to be achieved along a set of dimensions, and is no longer served by heavily scripted transitions at a certain age, risk as well as success is related to the capacity to organize and plan one's own life course (Clausen, 1993). Some phases seem to represent a particular risk and vulnerability, such as the early teens, but risk is fundamentally related to the dynamics of the socialization process, indicated by the structuring of paths.

The dynamics of institutional integration and differentiation mean that, even if the institutional framework is identical for most children, the individual life-course paths are often structured in accordance with tracks related to class, ethnicity and gender, even when influenced by individual capacities.

Agency and structural patterns

The age differentiation of modern life-worlds is more influential in childhood than in other life phases. Age is a highly differentiated structure with normative expectations and distinctive vocabularies related to each phase, and seen from the inside, the next phase is high on the horizon of the navigating children. The interpretation of acts and attitudes changes rapidly with age: certain activities that are socially permitted at six years of age are no longer permitted at nine years. Being accused of being childish is a constant threat throughout childhood. Acting older or younger than your age is a powerful social signifier. For adults, age is only an aspect of what style signifies; for children, style strongly signifies age as social maturity.

This implies that choices of style reflect choices of age and maturity. Some choose in certain phases (like the early teens) to look mature and perhaps wear signs indicating aspirations towards a specific subculture associated with youngsters somewhat older; others choose less visible and 'younger' positions. Some positions are regarded as 'safe' to occupy while postponing certain lifestyles and challenges, such as being a 'horse girl', or staying with football or computer games for boys, in the early teens. The prolonged childhood may function as a safe haven for a certain period until the demands of the phase make this position deviant and risky. Other choices imply the testing of limits or playing with (hopefully simulated) fire. Styles seem to be divided into a set of basic social categories, being the visible markers that make navigation through complex transitions more easy, and also being the signifiers that may transform series of individual choices into tracks signifying social categories. Being this or that kind of person, as illustrated in films about teens and tweens, means belonging to a (sub)cultural category. Or the other way around, belonging to a specific category signifies a certain lifestyle and personality. The position as member of a category may also indicate your life-course track: what social category you belong to signifies your positions in the future.

Actions and styles can only be interpreted in contexts; in childhood, age as a life phase comprises an important contextual factor. What is risky at 13 is normal at 15, and not participating in this at 17 may be considered weird. Some phases constitute risk through special characteristics. The playful or simulative mode of modern social puberty implies that actions and symbols are interpreted within an ambiguous framework of role play that blurs the lines between play and reality (Frønes, 1995). The symbolic vocabulary of this phase signals a situation of play in the classical sense of Gregory Bateson (1972). The playing dogs signal that the bite is not a bite, this is real but not real, it is simulated. Play in this sense opens the way for social experimentation and 'playing' with social identities and signifiers. Devotion and identification may be intense: the social situations are real for the actors, but seen from the outside it is play. Puppy love is intense but not real in a mature sense. This type of play is real and not real, certain signifiers signal the 'playful' framework of action (Frønes, 1995). This field of simulation implies that social and communicative competence can be learned by doing: for example, by using this field of action for the testing roles and styles. But learning by doing involves risk if the simulative mode is transformed into reality, by the play and/or by intruders. Young girls being seduced or abused by adult men they met on the internet illustrates this crossing of lines; the simulation becomes real. The most mature positions of the early teens involve styles that signify both belonging to a social category and personal uniqueness. Among this age group, the sublime and the extreme may easily be mixed, thus increasing the risk if the child moves outside the fences of the social playground.

The individual paths through childhood are structured in interplay between the reflexive subjects and structural and contextual characteristics. The position in one phase is influenced by the path constructed by earlier phases, and the position in a phase influences the future individual path. Individual paths construct biographies, as patterns of individual paths constitute the tracks and narratives of gender, class and ethnicity.

The dynamics of fields and transitions

The model presented here pictures childhood as a process of passing through sets of phases, being confronted both with the dynamics and values of specific phases and the transitions between them. The model does not imply that the frameworks that young people are facing are to be understood as identical for all groups, even if the institutions produce common structural conditions. Social groups face divergent expected tracks through the common framework, as well as variations of the frameworks of childhood itself. Variations exist in time as well as space; some phases and transitions acquire hegemonic positions for a period, other periods are characterized by variations. Changes over time may produce new conditions for varying social groups. There is an interaction between social factors and cohorts, illustrated by the educational revolution among women.

The theory sketched implies that phases can be understood as social fields, and the movements between phases as transitions. Some transitions represent dramatic changes of symbolic vocabulary, possible lifestyles and identities, as well as a leap in expected social and cultural maturity; others are more smoothly regulated transitions. The characteristics of transitions are not only intrinsic qualities of the phases and the relations between them, but develop in interaction with groups and individuals. A phase may be a smooth transition for some, and a social upheaval for others.

Phases represent a certain social structure, cultural and normative patterns, and specific social and cultural dynamics. Transitions represent movement from one structural and normative field to another and from one social dynamic to another. This may imply changes in the mechanisms of status patterns: the behaviour that gave social status in the field you leave may no longer apply in the field you approach. Phases are assumed to become increasingly complex with age, requiring a corresponding capacity from the children. The capacity to cope with complexity may influence the position in the new approaching field.

Transitions presuppose that the competencies required are immature when children face the new phase. The characteristics of the phase imply that development takes place within phases, not only in the transitions, but even with this flexibility the transitions and the coming new phase may for many children seem threatening. The transition presents no formal 'instructions' on how to develop in the new social context, but development and competence is intensively required by the demands of the new field. There is a dynamics of identity formation in the movement from the position in one phase to the position in the next. What I am leaving and where I am going indicates social identity; who I was and who I hope to be. For the child the new context is about social survival and existential matters, securing high motivation for mastering the coming next phase. There is no going back or jumping off the process for anyone other than Peter Pan.

Some transitions' existential dimensions are especially intense when it comes to the phases signifying the moving out of the 'child-phases' of childhood, and into the lower teens. Transition as social leap entails that choices are made on the basis of expectations and ideas about the new context, which is more fully understood only after the transitions. This requires a certain sensibility and strategic capacity. Transitions entail the risk of pursuing wrong positions in the phase one approaches. When the map is vague, caution is required.

Simple normative transitions can be illustrated by the child that suddenly lets her mother leave the pre-school in the morning without expressing the usual sad look. The child explained to the observer that she had now graduated from being an 'infant' (a special branch or ward in the school building, and age phase in the pre-school system) to becoming a medium-level child. Although infants (according to this child) were supposed to at least look sad when parents left them in the morning, this was not the case for a medium-level child subject to a different normative regime.

School start is one of the most ritualized transitions, but may imply very different experiences and consequences for different children and categories of children. More complex are changing norms restructuring the transitions between phases of 'child' and 'youth', where competencies and qualities bringing status to younger children are suspended while new ones are required. The development among the tweens and young teens illustrates the dynamics of the changing diachronic structures and new social and cultural patterns at the synchronic level. The tweens evolved into an early teenage phase, called *fourteeners* in Norway, referring to a specific modern teeny-bopper phase ranging from about 12 to 15 years of age. This is defined as a phase in which experimentation with styles, identities and cultural codes is the prime concern, through an intense focus on peers and social categorization, and a certain licence for immaturity and excess. This social puberty is related to the biological puberty described by Anna Freud (1946) but biology is in the background.

This transition requires a new critical awareness about the choices of style and cultural markers, of which children are well aware. The marking of transitions as institutional breaks, makes transitions something children relate to before they take place. Interviews indicate that children are reflective and strategic concerning lifestyle choices (Wærdahl, 2003). For example, a 12-year-old girl informs a researcher that she will buy Levi jeans when she enters junior high. She plans to spend her first months in the new school in an outfit signifying that she is not childish but not extreme either, she plans to reflect on her future choices of styles and tracks from this reasonably invisible mainstream position. The Levis are regarded as a safe symbol in this transition that some kids characterized as moving from 'playing' to 'talking'. Roles and outfits signalling that you want to stay outside the turmoil a while (like being a 'horse girl') offer another strategic option, the leap in symbolic vocabulary meant to signify social maturity or/and subculture is another (Wærdahl, 2003). In these 'semiotic dialogues', silence is impossible, and children know this. You always belong to a category; even mainstream is a choice.

Symbols function not only as indicators of age and identity but also as markers of future achievements in significant areas of life. Some styles indicate that a child is on the fast track in the school system and others that a child is likely to drop out. (Drop out does not represent leaving the 'system'; it is rather a special track partly produced by the system.) Risk factors such as early maturity may be pushed by biological maturity but are signified by style. Being too late may also be risky, but is related to a different set of dynamics and is often not registered as a risk position.

Childhood as a structure, process and reflexive action

This chapter argues that modern childhood has to be conceptualized as the framework of diachronic and synchronic structures, that is, as a set of phases with their social structures and vocabulary of lifestyles, as a set of transitions between the phases, and as the process of moving through the framework. As the conditions for children in a historical period, childhood is a social realm and a structural framework. As growing up, childhood is a process, something children do. As a process modern childhood operates a series of choices confronting subjects defined as autonomous but equipped with uneven resources and divergent cultural profiles for the choices and strategies required. The structure of individual ways of passing through childhood is identified as paths, different social positions as life-course tracks, ways of moving through childhood characterizing social categories. Rapid social change implies that cohorts relatively close in age may be moving through divergent frameworks of childhood.

Being a child is defined as belonging within the framework of childhood. The lives of children as *social practice* are represented by the processes of moving through childhood. Children move along a variety of paths and tracks through the structure of childhood, influencing this structure while moving through it.

Modern transitions are only to a modest degree ritualized by structures and forces outside the child or youth culture, increasing the likelihood of tensions and risk. The possible dramatic transitions existing in the modern framework of childhood cannot be avoided, but they can be approached through various strategies. Transitional problems can be modified by the choice of paths and positions. The transition that most vividly illustrates this strategic structuring of dramatic transitions by the actors is the moving from 'tweenage' to social puberty.

Childhood is a process, something children do. Children are social subjects, and they are in a process of developing. Childhood is also the economic, social and cultural framework constituting children's lives and positions. The ambitious aim of childhood research must be to include all these perspectives, as well as the interaction between them.

References

Ariès, P. (1962) *Centuries of Childhood: a Social History of Family Life*, New York: Vintage Books.

Bateson, G. (1972) *Steps to an Ecology of Mind: Collected Essays in Anthropology, Psychiatry, Evolution, and Epistemology*, London: Intertext Books.

Bourdieu, P. (1984) *Distinction: a Social Critique of the Judgement of Taste*, London: Routledge & Kegan Paul.

Clausen, J. (1993) *American Lives: Looking Back at the Children of the Great Depression*, New York: Free Press.

Elder, G.H. Jr (1974) *Children of the Great Depression: Social Change in Life Experience*, Chicago/London: University of Chicago Press.

Freud, A. (1946) *The Ego and the Mechanisms of Defence*, New York: International Universities Press.

Frønes, I. (1995) *Among Peers*, Oslo: Scandinavian University Press.

Frønes, I. (2001) 'Revolution without Rebels: Gender, Generation, and Social Change. An Essay on Gender, Socialization and Change', in *Transitions of Youth Citizenship in Europe: Culture, Subculture and Identity*, Strasbourg: Council of Europe Publishing, pp. 217–34.

Haldar, M. (1994) 'Barndom på boks' [Childhood on tape], Oslo: Department of Sociology, University of Oslo.

James, A., C. Jenks and A. Prout (1998) *Theorizing Childhood*, Cambridge: Polity Press.

Jenks, C. (1993) *Culture*, London: Routledge.

Lewis, O. (1961) *The Children of Sánchez: Autobiography of a Mexican Family*, New York: Random House.

Lindseth, O.H. (1998) 'Norsk barneoppdragelse i 1990-årene', *Samfunnsspeilet*, 1: 10–16.

Parsons, Talcott (1951) *The Social System*, London: Routledge and Kegan Paul.

Qvortrup, J., M. Bardy, G.B. Sgritta and H. Wintersberger (eds) (1994) *Childhood Matters: Social Theory, Practice and Policies*, Aldershot: Avebury.

Ramsøy, N.R. (1978) 'Do the Well-educated still Defer Gratifications?' Oslo, INAS memoranda from the Occupational History Study, 17.

Social Trends (2002) National Statistics No. 32, London.

Statistics Norway (2004) 'Arbeidsmarkedet mot 2030: Flere høyt utdannede kvinner' [The labour market towards 2030: more highly educated women], Kongsvinger: Statistics Norway, at http://www.ssb.no/vis/magasinet/-2004-02-11-01.html.

Thorne, B. (1993) *Gender Play. Boys and Girls in School*, New Brunswick, NJ: Rutgers University Press.

Wærdahl, R. (2003) 'Learning by Consuming: Consumer Culture as a Condition for Socialization and Everyday Life at the Age of 12', Oslo: Department of Sociology and Human Geography, University of Oslo, 4.

Williamson, H. (1997) *Youth and Policy: Contexts and Consequences. Young Men, Transition, and Social Exclusion*, Aldershot: Ashgate.

Willis, P.E. (1977) *Learning to Labour: how Working Class Kids get Working Class Jobs*, Farnborough: Saxon House.

Index

283